FUNDAMENTAL TRIAL ADVOCACY

By

Charles H. Rose III

Assistant Professor of Law
Associate Director, Center for Excellence in Advocacy
Stetson University College of Law

AMERICAN CASEBOOK SERIES®

THOMSON
™
WEST

Mat # 40553016

American Casebook Series and West Group are trademarks
registered in the U.S. Patent and Trademark Office.

© 2007 Thomson/West
  610 Opperman Drive
  P.O. Box 64526
  St. Paul, MN 55164–0526
  1–800–328–9352

Printed in the United States of America

ISBN–13: 978–0–314–17708–7
ISBN–10: 0–314–17708–6

 *TEXT IS PRINTED ON 10% POST CONSUMER RECYCLED PAPER*

Dedication:

"For my wife, Pamela. Where ever she has been, there has been my Eden."

"In seeking wisdom, the first step is silence, the second listening, the third remembering, the fourth practicing, the fifth—teaching others."

Ibn Gabirol, poet and philosopher (1022–1058)[1]

---

[1] The Painter's Keys, http://www.painterskeys.com/auth_search.asp?name=Ibn+Gabirol.

Summary of Contents

Acknowledgments

Writing a book is a herculean task, and one that is frankly impossible without the assistance of more people than can possibly be mentioned, but I must take a moment to express my gratitude to those that truly made this text possible. First, last and always is my wife Pamela. She rescued me many years ago and stands beside me now, making possible the time and focus necessary to accomplish all that I have done. My late father-in-law Patsy James Richards taught me the worth of each person, regardless of their status, and shared with me his passion for a good argument. His memory is captured in the faces of my children and the chapter of this book addressing closing arguments.

Everyone with whom I have ever taught trial advocacy or studied trial advocacy under is also responsible for the generation of the thoughts captured here. It would be impossible to thank you all, but from Notre Dame to Fort TJAGSA, and on to NITA; and from Jim Seckinger to Joshua Karton; let me try - thanks. Each of you has touched my craft in ways I continue to discover.

The students, staff, and faculty of Stetson University College of Law made this book possible. I work at the premier law school for advocacy, and teaching at an institution that supports your life's passion is a true pleasure. I wish to express my particular thanks to my research assistants Michael Bagge and Pamela Buha. Their work and editing has been invaluable.

Finally I must thank Ms. Jennifer Simpson-Oliver, my teaching and research assistant for the past year. Ms. Simpson-Oliver has been the voice of the student in this book, and there is not one page that has not passed through her capable hands. The text speaks to students in a new way, and her involvement is in no small part the reason for its quality. Without her dedication this book would still be a thought halfway to completion. She is a credit to Stetson and to the profession of law and I humbly thank her for her contributions to this work. The mistake within, and I am sure that there are many, are of course my own. Enjoy!

Charles H. Rose III
Fall 2006

PREFACE
WHY ANOTHER ADVOCACY BOOK?

"All the world's a stage,
And all the men and women merely players:
They have their exits and their entrances;
And one man in his time plays many parts,
His acts being seven ages."[1]

Advocates are the heroes of every century. They stand tirelessly between their clients and the unknown—with courage, skill, and determination. In courtrooms across the United States and around the world, advocates work tirelessly on behalf of those who have entrusted their property, their liberty, and sometimes their very life to another. They survive in that moment as best they are able, drawing upon their legal education, personal

> **Core Organizational Concepts of This Book:**
> The Law -
> The Skill -
> The Art -
> of Advocacy.

commitment, and practical training, representing those who trust them to do what is best and what is right. This book is designed to empower advocates everywhere to more effectively represent clients. It does so by focusing on the law, the skill, and the art of advocacy, combining these three portions of the advocacy process to ensure that the final product outweighs the sum of its parts. If you are holding this book in your hands then you are preparing to embark upon a hero's quest. Welcome. There is no better way to spend your life than in service to another, and all advocates serve those whom they represent.

---

[1] WILLIAM SHAKESPEARE, AS YOU LIKE IT, act 2, sc. 7.

The title of this book is FUNDAMENTAL TRIAL ADVOCACY. My goal is to expose you to a particular methodology of learning and applying advocacy skills that help you to become an attorney competent in the basic fundamental skills necessary to effectively advocate for your client. This book takes the common sense approaches of the National Institute for Trial Advocacy (NITA)[2] and Professor Mauet's work at the University of Arizona, combining the best of their methodologies with a superior structure for case analysis and an attention to the art of advocacy that is not normally discussed. I am fortunate enough to teach trial advocacy at Stetson University College of Law, a law school that is routinely ranked as one of the top advocacy schools in the nation by U.S. News & World Report.[3] This book, in no small part, reflects the lessons learned within the courtrooms and classrooms at Stetson, as well as in every location where attorneys gather, struggling for a way to communicate the ethos, pathos, and logos of their clients' position.

By the end of this book you will have the ability to successfully apply advocacy skills in a coherent, effective, and persuasive manner. The famous golf instructor Harvey Penick once noted that "An old pro told me that originality does not consist of saying what has never been said before; it consists of saying what you have to say that you know to be the truth."[4] Trial advocacy instruction is definitely an area of the law where this applies. My thoughts on what advocacy truly is and how to teach it have been formed in the crucible of my own experiences, and I am to a certain extent defined by them. I have learned at the feet of many different masters, and the thoughts within this book are as much theirs as mine. To the extent possible, I have noted within this text the genus of

---

[2] *See* the National Institute for Trial Advocacy at www.nita.org.

[3] *See* U.S. News & World Report at http://www.usnews.com/usnews/edu/grad/rankings/law/ brief/lawsp07_brief.php (ranked first in trial advocacy in 2006); http://www.usnews.com/usnews/ edu/articles/950320/archive_011049_2.htm (ranked first in trial advocacy in 2005); http://www. usnews.com/usnews/edu/articles/010409/archive_001774_3.htm (ranked second in trial advocacy in 2001); http://www.usnews.com/usnews/edu/articles/000410/archive_018201_3.htm (ranked second in trial advocacy in 2000); http://www.usnews.com/usnews/edu/articles/980302/ archive_004544_3.htm (ranked first in trial advocacy in 1998); *and also* Thirteenth Annual Willem C. Vis International Commercial Arbitration Moot 2005–2006 at http://www.cisg.law.pace. edu/cisg/moot/awards13.html (second place); *and* Twelfth Annual Willem C. Vis International Commercial Arbitration Moot at http://www.cisg.law.pace.edu/cisg/moot/awards12.htm (first place).

[4] HARVEY PENICK, HARVEY PENICK'S LITTLE RED BOOK: LESSONS & TEACHINGS FROM A LIFETIME OF GOLF 21 (Simon & Schuster 1992).

my thoughts. Where I have failed to do so the mistake is mine, but I acknowledge full-well that without the instruction of those who have taught me I would have nothing of great import to say. The Bible tells us that there is "nothing new under the sun."[5] When it come to the art of advocacy, truer words have rarely been spoken. I have merely attempted to uncover the treasures of this ancient art and then arrange them in a fashion I find to be both pleasing and useful. I share the roots of my knowledge with you so that you have some sense of where I come from and why I have chosen to address instruction in the art of advocacy in this fashion, as well as to honor those who have helped me to grow and develop as an advocate and teacher.

The roots of my advocacy methodology stretch back to the National Institute for Trial Advocacy in Notre Dame, Indiana and the Notre Dame Law School Barristers Trial Team. My experiences there form the bedrock of how I approach advocacy skills training. I believe wholeheartedly in the development of certain fundamental skills and in learning by doing, the core concept of the NITA methodology. It is ineffective to teach a person about the entire process and not provide them with the fundamental knowledge and ability to perform the discrete tasks that create the whole. If you buy into no other thought presented in this book it will still serve you well as a resource for developing and honing fundamental advocacy and presentation skills, the foundation upon which all other effective employments of the art of advocacy must rest.

Judges Jean Jordan and Sandy Brook, along with Professors Jim Seckinger and Tom Singer, initially introduced me to the art of trial advocacy. Their competent and caring hands shielded me as I began to find my own voice as an advocate, and later as an advocacy professor. My initial organizational constructs and methods of teaching grew out of my experiences in the courtroom as a Judge Advocate in the United States Army where I served as both Senior Trial Counsel and Senior Defense Counsel. Colonels Craig Schwender and Keith Hodges created multiple opportunities for me to learn in the crucible of military justice practice. As judges they were without compare. They embodied the concept of "soldier first, lawyer always," and remain embedded in my psyche as examples of all that Judge Advocates can and should be.

---

[5] THE NEW DICTIONARY OF CULTURAL LITERARY, THIRD EDITION (E.D. Hirsch, Jr., Joseph F. Kett & James Trefil, eds., Houghton Mifflin Company 2002) (adapted from Ecclesiastes 1:9) (available at http://www.bartleby.com/59/1/nothingnewun.html).

I later taught Trial Advocacy for three years at the Judge Advocate General's School in Charlottesville, Virginia.[6] During that time I was certified as a NITA instructor and now teach trial advocacy for NITA in a variety of programs, including their annual Harvard "Train the Trainers" course. While in Charlottesville, I met Joshua Karton, a giant in the field of theater skills and courtroom presentations.[7] While teaching there I came to the realization that the way I organize and apply trial advocacy skills was useful to a number of my students as they took the next step in their own personal journey as developing advocates. Together, through the pages of this book, we will take the next steps in your development as an attorney and advocate.

Now is the time in your legal career when the law becomes personal, immediate and powerful. After studying this book you will understand and feel comfortable in combining your legal acumen with the trial advocacy skills this text is designed to develop. Developing the ability to combine the practical communications skills each of us possess in various degrees with the intricacies of the law is a crucial step in becoming a superior advocate. We will accomplish this by learning concrete, specific advocacy skills and by identifying in the context of those developing skills the underlying values, judgments, and societal pressures that influence the use and application of each skill. To that end, we will discuss specific physical exercises and techniques that you can use to immediately increase your persuasive power.

> "Law school begins a lobotomizing process that is complete when upon graduation a human being has been turned into a lawyer."
>
> Joshua Karton

Law school teaches you how to think critically. You learn how to deconstruct cases and sift through the rubble of appellate opinions for nuggets of precedence or principles of law to apply in other instances. Most classes utilize some

---

[6] The Judge Advocate General's Legal Center and School, Charlottesville, Virginia.

[7] Joshua's ideas about the use of theater skills for the legal professional are revolutionary. We taught together in the Advanced Trial Advocacy Program in Charlottesville, and Joshua has taught at Gerry Spence's Trial Lawyers College in Dubois, Wyoming for years. He brings a freshness to the art of advocacy that is so necessary in today's overanalyzed and overdeveloped world of advocacy instruction. He opened-up several new vistas that I hope to share with you throughout the course of this book.

form of the Socratic Method to accomplish this task. The Socratic Method is many things, but efficient it is not. It is designed to teach you to analyze and approach issues in a different way, and does an excellent job of developing the analytical skills and thought processes so necessary for the practicing attorney or legal academician. The Socratic Method does not, however, lend itself well to the development of trial advocacy skills.

This book is designed to help you transition from the traditional Socratic Methodology to a skills-based learning experience. My goal is to assist you in combining your hard-won legal way of thinking with your personal history, common sense, and intrinsic knowledge of human nature. In order to accomplish

> Superior legal knowledge is not the end of advocacy skills development, but rather its beginning. It serves as the foundation for the house of persuasion each advocate builds.

this we will learn skills that apply your intellect to concrete moments in the trial experience. This approach encompasses the NITA "learning by doing" methodology, but goes beyond that basic approach to address the larger questions of case analysis and persuasion.

The process of learning how to try cases will require you to rediscover the human being lurking underneath your lawyerly exterior, while developing the fundamental advocacy skills that will allow you to *actually* practice law. You should not abandon the ability to think like a lawyer that you have learned through the Socratic Method. You must merely combine it with the ability to again think like a human being. Hopefully, when you are done with this book you will be able to do both. To lose your humanity in a search for academic or professional excellence is both short-sighted and foolish. Many of the skills and techniques offered in this book are predicated on the belief that the type of person that you are at your core matters in your development as a trial advocate. This book provides a way for you to develop trial advocacy skills while remembering and honoring the humanity of everyone involved. In the process it will also help to make you a superior trial advocate.

Most of us would agree that learning to think like a lawyer changes a person. Anyone who has been chastised by their children for a rigorous cross examination, or by a loved one who has watched you pick apart an issue as simple as what type of tile should be placed in the kitchen, would agree with the proposition that lawyers just think differently. We have been trained to analyze, deconstruct, and question every fact and every rule.[8] That would be fine if you spent your day surrounded by other lawyers and never had to deal with clients, witnesses, or juries. Most trial advocacy situations require lawyers to communicate with the lay community, a skill that has sometimes atrophied from lack of use by the time a law student or attorney makes it to a trial advocacy class.

All of us share in the human condition. It defines us. We bring to our endeavors our experiences, prejudices, beliefs, and values. Research has shown that when confronted with facts or events we rewrite them to fit into our understanding of life in order to give a contextual whole to what we are witnessing so that it is coherent to us.[9] Clients, defendants, judges, and juries are no different. Each of us learn from the stories that surround us in our daily lives. It is how we communicate. As an advocate you can use your understanding of man as a storyteller to prepare persuasive and interesting ways to present your case. When you reach beneath the surface certain themes flow throughout humanity. This may include myths, pop culture, fears, etc. This book will provide you with some concepts and methods to tap into the ways in which we as people communicate and relate to one another.

To effectively communicate, you must also understand yourself: what you believe, what you stand for, and what is important to you. The ethical framework of how you intend to practice law is important. Your understanding of the professional responsibility rules, how you will apply them, what your state Bar requires, and the rules of court all become relevant to your advocacy presentation. Where appropriate, this book will raise common ethical issues faced by attorneys practicing the art of advocacy. Many ethical issues will be raised here. I will propose possible solutions for the identified issues, but ethics are a lot like religion; each of us believes we are right and most of us see the world somewhat differently from others. The degree to which you personally choose to walk the paths identified in this book will determine its relevance and impact on your ability to empower your own advocacy skills. With that in mind, let us begin.

---

[8] *See* THOMAS MAUET, TRIAL TECHNIQUES, (Aspen Publishers, Inc. 6th ed. 2002).

[9] *See* STEVEN LUBET, MODERN TRIAL ADVOCACY: LAW SCHOOL EDITION, (NITA 2d ed. 2004).

Points To Ponder . . .

1. What kind of advocate do you want to be? What are three things you will do to achieve that goal?

2. Should ethical concerns impact on your practice of the art of advocacy? If so, how? If not, why?

3. What do you believe are your three strongest personality characteristics that will help your advocacy? Why are they your strongest? What will you do to nurture them?

CHAPTER ONE
THE TRIAL PROCESS

"Though justice be thy plea, consider this,
That in the course of justice none of us
Should see salvation; we do pray for mercy,
And that same prayer doth teach us all to render
The deeds of mercy."[1]

A. INTRODUCTION.

You hold in your hands a book designed to combine the skill, law and art of trial advocacy into a collective whole that empowers you to represent clients to the best of your ability through the trial process. It is predicated on the idea that effective trial advocacy must encompass the fundamental development of your legal acumen, presentation skills and personal style. This book is a practical text that tells you what a skill is, where the law impact the skill, and how you perform the skill. It also serves as an excellent introduction to the ethical, legal and policy issues present whenever humans create a system to choose the party that prevails in a dispute.

> **The Rule of Threes:**
>
> - Tell them what you are going to tell them.
> - Tell them.
> - Tell them what you told them (and what it means).

Upon completion of your study you will be able to combine the discreet portions of this text into a body of

---

[1] WILLIAM SHAKESPEARE, THE MERCHANT OF VENICE, act 4, sc. 1.

knowledge that assists you in effectively trying cases. To that end it uses a building block approach so that each lesson is presented at the moment in time when it will best assist you in developing as an advocate. Just as you learned to balance, crawl and then walk as a child, it helps to learn certain trial advocacy skills in order. Doing so will ensure that you have the requisite ability to later handle the most complex advocacy issues with certitude and aplomb.

Certain fundamental concepts are reiterated throughout the text of this book, to include the Rule of Threes, Case Analysis & Preparation, and the proper use of Basic Questioning Techniques. These three skill sets are the necessary foundation for everything else presented in this text and are the core trilogy upon which this book is based. They constitute the next three chapters of the book, and regardless of your prior trial experience, a review of these concepts is necessary before proceeding with the rest of the book.

> ### The Three Primary Steps in Case Analysis:
>
> - Identify and analyze the legal issues.
> - Identify and analyze the factual issues.
> - Develop a moral theme, legal theory, and factual theory.

Many of you reading this may have some degree of experience in a courtroom. Hopefully for most of you that experience has not involved status as a party to litigation but rather as an observer or participating advocate. This chapter reviews the primary elements of the trial process, considering each through the lens of trial advocacy as defined, organized, and presented in this book. As we discuss each of the separate and complementary portions of the trial process we will point out where the skills you will develop through the study of this text are applicable. This chapter will address the trial process sequentially, but you will actually prepare for trial in a non-sequential fashion.

Since this book revolves around the trial process you need to take the time now to understand the various portions of a trial. The actual pieces of a trial and its investigative stages are heavily influenced by local rules of court, rules of procedure and the attitudes of the judiciary in your

> ### Three Basic Questioning Techniques
>
> - Headlines
> - Open or Non-Leading
> - Closed or Leading

jurisdiction. Certain elements of the process should be relatively similar regardless of where you practice or intend to practice. This book uses a notional idea of how most trials proceed based upon both federal state systems. For our purposes you can divide the trial process into the following steps: (1) Your client or the entity you represent becomes involved in a situation that will lead to litigation; (2) You begin case analysis, preparation, and investigation of the issues before you; (3) You file motions based upon that case analysis; (4) The court rules on your motions and you either settle, plead or set a trial date; (5) Jury selection occurs if appropriate; (6) Opening Statements are made; (7) Direct and Cross Examinations are conducted; (8) Closing Arguments are made and jury instructions are given by the court; (9) The jury deliberates and a verdict is rendered.

B. CASE ANALYSIS AND PREPARATION.

While case analysis, preparation and investigation, occurs throughout the trial, the first time you are introduced to a case is important for a number of reasons. It is at this point that certain decisions that have long term impact on the case must be made. Those decisions include an analysis of which facts exist and will the law allows me to admit those facts. These decisions are important because they will drive the steps you take throughout the rest of the trial. Case analysis forces you to identify your factual theory - what you believe happened, your legal theory - how the law impacts the facts, and your moral theme - why your side should win. You will learn the mechanics of how to analyze a case and prepare for trial during chapter 3. For now it is sufficient that you understand it is a continuing process that requires a lot of front- loaded work.

During case analysis and preparation you will routinely review evidence, investigate issues, interview witnesses, prepare exhibits, and then compare the results of your work to see if you are on the right track. You then

> **SEVEN STEPS TO SUPERIOR CASE ANALYSIS & PREPARATION:**
>
> - Organize the Case File
> - Identify Legal Issues
> - Identify Factual Issues
> - Connect Facts to Law
> - Identify your Moral Theme
> - Backwards Plan your Presentation
> - Verify Evidence

redo this process until the case is complete, modifying as required based upon the portion of the trial in which you find yourself. The goal is to develop a cohesive presentation that is supported by the facts you can present and allowable under the current legal standards. It is also important that your position have a moral theme that identifies an injustice that the jury can rectify. These three elements of case analysis lead you to prepare the case based upon the targets you have identified that give you the best chance at a successful outcome. Case analysis is ongoing, and it is particularly important when you begin to develop directs, crosses, and use exhibits during witness testimony. It is also a crucial component that drives the jury selection process. We will discuss this topic at length in chapter 3, but you should internalize now that case analysis is the structure that drives every trial advocacy decision. Successful advocates proceed during each distinct portion of the trial in a specific fashion based upon their case analysis - you should too.

C. MOTIONS.

Seven Fundmental Tasks of Successful Motions Practice:

- Know the local rules
- Draft sound legal motions
- Identify the source of your evidence
- Do not forget to balance your law, facts and moral theme
- Know your audience
- Argue to the judge, not with opposing counsel
- Understand the effect of the

Motions practice is the vehicle that trial advocates use to get a sense of how the judge will rule on the specific legal issues present in the case. You will learn that one part of case analysis involves choosing a legal theory of the case that is best for your advocacy position. The legal theory you choose must be supported by the law in your jurisdiction. That means that your legal theory should bear itself out when the judge rules on the admissibility of evidence, which instructions will be given to the jury, and what the controlling law will be on substantive issues. Trial lawyers use motions practice to further refine their legal theories to develop the greatest degree of determinacy when dealing with the unknown of trial.

Superior motions practice will either turn cases into summary judgements, limit evidence that will be admissible against your client, or establish precedents that will shape the entire trial process in your favor. Motions allow you to set the stage from a factual perspective through the application of law. While many facts may be logically relevant, they are not necessarily legally relevant and therefore admissible. The extent to which you effectively learn how to use motions will impact on your success at trial. In addition to pre-trial motions, you also have the ability to respond to issues at trial by making motions before the court when they occur. Those motions may be as simple as to request an advance ruling on evidentiary issues, or as complex as determining the admissibility of key evidence that may very well be case dispositive. You also have the opportunity to re-address motions filed prior to the start of the actual trial. That is a decision that must be made in light of the court's earlier ruling and the predicted impact of addressing that issue in the presence of the jury. Rulings on motions impact the fact presented. The superior advocate will use motions to shape the courtroom battlefield.

D. THE THREE FUNDAMENTAL SECTIONS OF THE TRIAL.

1. Jury Selection and Opening Statements.

WHY VOIR DIRE?

Identify jurors to challenge for cause.

Identify jurors to peremptorily challenge.

Educate potential jurors about facts in the case.

Educate potential jurors about the legal issues.

Eliminate shocks and surprises.

Obtain promises of fairness.

Develop rapport with the jury pool.

The process of selecting a jury is called voir dire in most jurisdictions and encompasses pre-trial questionnaires, initial questions posed by the judge, and questioning by advocates in those jurisdictions that allow advocates to question jurors. Some jurisdictions, most notably federal courts, no longer allow advocates to conduct voir dire and require instead that all questions are provided in writing to the judge who poses them to the potential jury pool. Regardless of the format, jury selection is one of the first things that you do during the trial, but it, along with closing argument, is one of the last portions of the trial for which you prepare. Jury selection involves identifying those members of the prospective jury that you believe you will be unable to persuade to consider your evidence. It is not about picking those that like you, but rather about identifying those who don't like you and won't change their mind – those are the jurors you must remove. You will be best situated to perform this complex task only after you are fully prepared for trial. You must identify those jurors with a bias based upon your legal theory, factual theory or moral theme. If they oppose you fundamentally in any of these three areas they should go.

After the jury is selected you next tell them what you expect the case to be about. We call this phase of the trial opening statements. It is a storytelling opportunity that creates drama, forecast issues and previews solutions. They are a statement of your version of the facts; they are not an argument about what those facts mean. You cannot argue to the jury that facts have certain significance when they have not yet received those facts into evidence. Opening statement is the time to tell the jury what you expect the facts will be, and tease them with the promise of how

> **SEVEN BASIC LEGAL PRINCIPLES OF OPENING STATEMENTS:**
> * The judge sets the guidelines
> * Argument is not permitted, tell the story
> * No vouching for witnesses
> * No personal opinions
> * Don't mention excluded evidence
> * Only discuss evidence you have a good faith basis will be admitted
> * Never violate the "golden rule"

you will explain what those facts mean in closing argument. It is also a time to establish your moral theme -- that sense of injustice that they can repair, the wrong that human nature calls upon them to right. We'll discuss how to do that and more in the chapter on opening statements.

2. The Case-in-Chief.

During the case-in-chief evidence is received by the jury through the actions of counsel during the testimony of witnesses. This normally occurs during direct examination and cross examination. The party bearing the burden of proof presents evidence first. In a criminal case that is the prosecution, in civil cases, it is the plaintiff. Every question that is asked on direct or cross examination is designed to admit evidence, exclude evidence or explain the

---

**SEVEN STEPS TO A
SUPERIOR DIRECT
EXAMINATION:**

- Prepare based on Case Analysis
- Organize logically
- Use simple language
- Use exhibits
- Vary the pace
- Set the scene
- Listen to your witness

---

amount of weight that should be given to a particular piece of evidence. A lot happens during the case-in-chief, and advocates make their living by their ability to conduct directs, cross examine, object to evidence and ensure rulings from the judge that support their factual theory, legal theory and moral theme.

Advocates use direct examination to place the facts of their case before the jury. They are required to use open ended questions unless laying a foundation or dealing with a witness that allows to advocate to lead because of an infirmity. Direct examination showcases the witness. The goal is to present a clear and logical progression of witness observations and activities in a way that persuades the jury. Advocates us checklists for each witness to identify the facts and exhibits needed to make an effective closing argument that bookends the opening statement. The bones of that checklist are of course found in the case analysis and are developed further by the advocate when preparing and conducting direct examinations.

Cross examinations occur when examining an opposing counsel's witness. They usually happen after the opposing counsel has completed direct, but may occur during the direct examination when dealing with expert witnesses. During cross an advocate wants to control the witness, establish facts that build to a theme and theory, and establish facts that build up the credibility of their own witnesses while diminishing the credibility of your opponent's witnesses. These goals require the advocate to know more than

---

**SEVEN STEPS TO A
SUPERIOR CROSS
EXAMINATION:**

- Prepare based on Case Analysis
- Every cross is tied to theme, theory or credibility
- CONTROL THE WITNESS!
- Organize the cross to accomplish your goals
- Details give control
- Impeach by the probabilities
- Use the witness' own words

---

the witness does in order to be effective - case analysis will accomplish this. When preparing crosses, advocates identify and list the legal issues in the case and adapt their theme and theories to support them. During the chapter on cross examination we will develop those skills.

You should be noticing an advocacy theme at this point. Case analysis and preparation drive the entire trial process. Direct examinations and cross examinations are focused inquiries designed to highlight those facts and support the legal issues that you identified when you began to put your case together. Directs and crosses that are not focused on the ultimate goals of case analysis waste time, confuse issues and are opportunities lost. Using case analysis as the organizational template for your preparation will engender success.

3. *Closing Arguments and Jury Instructions.*

Once you have completed the case-in-chief portion of the trial it is time for the Perry Mason, Atticus Finch, Matlock moment of the trial – closing arguments. Closing arguments are given by the advocates to the jury after the defense has rested. The party with the burden of proof argues first and last. In between the party defending the case presents their closing argument. This is when the advocates argue about what the admitted evidence means. Now is the time when comments on evidence, the believability of witnesses and calls to common sense prevail. It is the advocates' moment to sway the jury, through logic, emotion and morality, to decide the case in their favor. Closing argument is the final destination. If you have done your case analysis properly you've arrived at the point where the jury can be lead to make the decision that favors your client – if not, well there will always be another case.

Once closing arguments are completed the judge charges the jury by instructing them on the law. The evidence is collected and the jury retires to deliberate. After deliberations are completed the jury returns to court and the verdict is announced. Next begins the post-trial advocacy process, including appeals, settlements, new trials and finality. But that portion of the advocacy process is a subject for another book. Now that you have some sense of the various portions of trial, let us begin to create within you the skills required to successfully join in as a participant in the trial process.

Points To Ponder . . .

1. Is our common law system of dispute resolution superior to the civil system prevalent in Europe? Why or why not?

2. If you were designing a system of dispute resolution in what fundamental ways would it differ from the trial process? Why would you adopt your system instead of the current one?

3. To what extent does our system of dispute resolution point towards the discovery of the truth? If it does not, why should we continue to use it?

CHAPTER TWO
ASKING QUESTIONS

"The man that hath no music in himself,
Nor is not moved with concord of sweet sounds,
Is fit for treasons, stratagems, and spoils . . ."[1]

Advocates do not build anything. We will never create a building, manufacture goods, or place items in the stream of commerce. We strive instead, as best we are able, to string together a few paltry words in the hope that somehow those words might persuade the jury to decide for our client. Sometimes we even find something approximating truth. If we are lucky and things come out right, our words create images, our questions define witnesses, and our silence speaks across the courtroom. The words that we use, the form of questioning that we choose, our physical presence in the courtroom, are the music of our profession. Before you can begin to recognize and make that music, you must first master the use of language with witnesses. Witnesses are our dance partner in the courtroom. If they cannot follow your lead, you have lost the competition before it has begun. In this chapter we will learn the fundamental skill upon which all other advocacy rests—how to ask questions that help us get out information and empower our witnesses to both understand what we are asking and to answer it completely. The most basic and universal skill that an advocate must master is the ability to ask cogent, relevant, and applicable questions while listening to the answers given by the witness.

A thorough knowledge and understanding of Basic Questioning Techniques[2] is an <u>absolutely essential skill</u> for any competent advocate in an adjudicative proceeding—at trial, during arbitration, or otherwise. Consider for a moment the fact that all relevant information received by the finder-of-fact

---

[1] WILLIAM SHAKESPEARE, THE MERCHANT OF VENICE, act 5, sc. 1.

[2] I owe my understanding of these **Basic Questioning Techniques** and the pedagogy involved in teaching them effectively to Professor Jim Seckinger at the University of Notre Dame Law School. Jim's materials on this subject are excellent and I commend them to you.

begins with a question posed by an advocate.[3] The substantive evidence introduced at trial is birthed from the art of asking questions. You must master all of the basic questioning techniques available to an attorney if you wish to maximize your effectiveness. Questioning is the primary means of presenting information to the fact-finder, and the ability to properly formulate and ask questions is a fundamental skill that all advocates must continually develop and practice.

> **Three Basic Questioning Techniques**
>
> **Headlines**
> - Basic Introductory Phrases
> - Transitional Phrases
> - Looping or Coupling Phrases
>
> **Open or Non-Leading Questions**
> - Wide Open Questions
> - Directive Open Questions
> - Probing or Testing Questions
> - Coupling Questions
>
> **Closed or Leading Questions**

There are three basic questioning techniques for examining a witness that you will learn: (1) Headlines, (2) Open or Non-Leading Questions and (3) Closed or Leading Questions. They apply at various times in every adversarial proceeding and must be mastered. You must not only know when you are allowed to use each type of question, you must also know why one type of question is superior to another in a given situation. Once you learn these Basic Questioning Techniques you will be able to use them to effectively achieve your purpose or goal in any situation. These Basic Witness Questioning Techniques should be a pervasive element in your planning and execution whenever questioning a witness.

An advocate uses these techniques in several different situations. Some are controlled by procedural rules, some by case law, and others by local practice rules. As we discuss the various portions of a trial where these techniques may be used, we will identify which techniques you should employ and why. Before doing that we must first fully identify each type of technique and discuss ways to employ them. Let us begin with how we introduce questions, through headlines.

A. HEADLINES.

---

[3] While the Federal Rules of Evidence give the judge the power to control the means of questioning, they also provide guidance on how questioning should occur. *See* Fed. R. Evid. 611 in Appendix III of this text.

A *Headline* is a statement consisting of two parts: an introductory phrase and a topic. There are three main types of Headlines: (1) basic introductory phrases, (2) transitional introductory phrases, and (3) looping or coupling introductory phrases. It is important to remember that Headlines are statements, not questions. The primary purpose of a Headline is to orient both the witness and the fact-finder to the area of the witness' testimony you wish to discuss. It also creates a feeling of flow and ease to the examination, showcasing witnesses on direct and limiting witnesses on cross. Effective Headlines are succinct and to the point. Advocates create ineffective Headlines when they construct long or complex introductory phrases. Long and complex Headlines defeat the primary purpose of orienting the witness and the fact-finder to the specific area or issue. Witnesses being cross examined will use these long and complex Headlines to misconstrue the question and respond in a non-responsive fashion or give an out right destructive answer.

> **Basic Introductory Phrases:**
>
> - *Let's talk about . . .*
> - *We will now discuss . . .*
> - *Please direct your attention to . . .*
>
> These are just a sampling of possible introductory phrases. You are limited by your knowledge of the English language, common sense, and ability to walk, talk, and chew gum at the same time.

Headlines can and should be used in all the various types of witness examination: direct examination, cross examination, redirect examination, impeachment on cross, rehabilitation on redirect, laying foundation for and using exhibits, expert testimony, taking depositions, and even when speaking to the judge, jury, or arbitrator on jury selection, opening statements, and closing arguments. When using Headlines in these situations you should always combine the use of the Headline with the other types of basic questioning techniques discussed in this chapter. Those include WideOpen Questions, Directive Open Questions, Probing or Testing Questions, Coupling Questions, and Closed or Leading

> **Transitional Introductory Phrases:**
>
> *Let's now talk about . . .*
> *Let's now move to . . .*
> *Now, I want to discuss . . .*
> *We will now turn to . . .*
>
> You are limited only by your imagination and grasp of the English language.

Questions. The Headline by itself does not provide substantive evidence to the witness. Headlines are signposts along the highway of your presentation. You want the finder-of-fact to travel along with you, and Headlines tell them where to go and sometimes why it is necessary to make the trip. Headlines will always signal where you are going, and keep you focused and on track, a rare skill for most trial advocates. Because of this, Headlines are useful during both direct and cross examination.

When examining your own witness, usually during direct or redirect at trial, Headlines help the witness understand the questions and the issue(s) that the advocate wants to discuss. This creates a degree of comfort on the part of the witness, allowing them to focus on telling the truth as they remember it. For the witness, court is usually not an everyday experience. They are nervous, worried, and sometimes frightened. When preparing your witness tell them that the two of you are going to have a conversation in the courtroom. All they have to do is listen to your questions and then truthfully answer them. Headlines will allow you to make certain that the witness understands where you want to go and will then help them take you and the fact-finder to that location. They assist the witness in testifying comfortably and persuasively, enhancing the witness' credibility. They also allow you to keep the witness on the topic you wish to discuss and provide a ready means to bring them back to the issues at hand if they begin to stray or wander while testifying.

In addition to assisting the witness in understanding the specific question asked, Headlines allow an advocate to create an organized, easy to follow and understandable direct examination. An organized direct examination is more compelling and persuasive for the fact-finder because it is easy to follow. This assists the finder-of-fact in taking notes or otherwise recording and understanding a witness' testimony. Some advocates use the technique of referring to different portions of their direct examinations by number. This technique can be effective when you have jurors who are taking notes. If you can get them to write down topic 1, 2, 3, or first, second, third, etc. you are providing them with a template that both of you can refer back to during closing argument when connecting the testimony of a particular witness to your theme or theory.[4] You can further refine this technique by using the same Headlines in the opening, witness examination and closing argument. By utilizing the Rule of Threes you greatly increase the chance that the fact-finder will remember both the Headlines and the response.

---

[4] Thomas H. Singer, a respected NITA faculty member, teaches this technique.

When examining an adverse witness, on cross examination or when taking a deposition, Headlines help the examining lawyer control the witness. Headlines keep the witness on the examining lawyer's topic, requiring the witness to answer the examining lawyer's question, regardless of the witness' desires. This allows you to establish control and limit the scope of a witness' testimony during cross examination. The caveat here is that Headlines also orient the witness being cross examined as to the subject you wish to discuss. In certain instances, depending upon the purpose of the cross examination, you may choose to forgo Headlines in order to ensure the witness does not have time to formulate a "coached" or "untrue" answer to your questions.

Headlines serve as road signs for anyone listening to the examination, focusing the inquiry. Using Headlines helps the judge and jury take notes, better understand the witness' testimony, and examine the advocate's case theme and theory. Focused Headlines also assist the judge in ruling on disputed evidentiary issues, creating jury instructions, and writing the judgment when the case is a trial to the bench. Finally, Headlines assist the appellate court to better understand the transcript and trial record on appeal.

B. OPEN OR NON-LEADING QUESTIONS.

An Open or Non-Leading Question is one that showcases the witness and not the advocate. It invites a complete answer from the witness on a topic chosen by the advocate. It does not, however, suggest an answer to the witness. Instead, Open Questions identify a topic with varying degrees of specificity, allowing the witness to testify fully regarding that topic. You can always tell an Open Question and corresponding answer because the witness will talk for a longer period of time than the advocate. There are also certain words that are used by advocates when posing Open Questions. There are a variety of Open Questions normally used when examining witnesses. The type of Open Questions chosen depends upon the demeanor and knowledge of the witness as well as the specificity of the issue the questioner wishes to discuss. Examples of Open Questions include: (1) Wide Open Questions, (2) Directive Open Questions, (3) Probing or Testing Questions, and (4) Coupling Questions.

Advocates use Wide Open Questions on direct examination to identify a particular topic they want the witness to address. Most effective Wide Open Questions are used immediately following a Headline that has oriented the witness to the topic the advocate

Wide Open Questions:
  Describe for us . . .
  Explain . . .
  Tell us about . . .

wishes to discuss. Wide Open Questions normally direct the witness to a specific **time**, **place**, **person,** or **event** identified in an earlier question or Headline.

After identifying the area you want to discuss with Wide Open Questions, you can use Directive Open Questions to narrowly focus the topic the witness should address. Directive Open Questions are normally coupled with a Headline so that the witness and fact-finder understand the scope and direction of the advocate's inquiry. Directive Open Questions, when coupled with a Headline, are an effective and capable means of orienting your witness to a very specific issue you wish to discuss, while also ensuring that the fact-finder and the judge understand exactly what it is you are discussing. Directive Open Questions normally appear after Wide Open Questions in an examination. They are often followed by Open Questions that allow the witness to further explain the specific issue you have identified through your Directive Open Questions.

Examples of Directive Open Questions Used With a *Headline*:

I'd like to draw your attention to the letter you received that day—what did you do with the letter?

Please direct your attention to the store on the corner of Fifth and Madison—did you or didn't you go into the store?

Let's now talk about the window of the store—could you see inside the store through the window?

A Follow-Up Wide Open Question Would Be:

What did you see?

Open Questions are designed to get out relevant information about a specific **time**, **place**, **person,** or **event** that the advocate wishes to discuss in greater detail by allowing the witness to answer with more details. The structure of Open Questions allows for the possibility of maximum explanation by the witness. Open Questions free the witness to answer with greater specificity by throwing open the door for them to answer completely based upon their own knowledge and experience.

Open Questions:
Who . . . ?
What . . . ?
When . . . ?
Where . . . ?

After you have gotten most, if not all, of the relevant facts from a witness you may need to employ a more specific type of Open Question to elicit those last few bits of relevant information. These types of Open Questions are usually referred to as Probing or Testing Questions. While they are narrowly construed, they are still Open Questions. They lead the witness to the specific fact you wish to discuss, but do not suggest the appropriate answer to the witness. These are focused questions that normally begin with a verb or have other elements that either clarify or explain an issue or point in the case. You are leading the witness to a particular issue when you use these types of questions, but you still are not suggesting answers. The test for an appropriate Probing or Testing Question is whether or not it is focused on a specific item about which further inquiry is necessary in order to explain a relevant point for your case.

Once you have wrung every last bit of relevant information from the witness on a specific item, you can then use Coupling Questions to emphasize the testimony of the witness that you wish the jury to remember. Coupling Questions can also be used to give a

> **Probing or Testing Questions:**
> *Did you . . . ?*
> *What about . . . ?*
> *How about . . . ?*

flow and continuity to the examination. They allow both the witness and the fact-finder to understand where the examination is going. It also mimics normal speech patterns, creating a sense of believability and credibility concerning the examination. A Coupling Question takes a word or words from the witness' answer and then uses it to connect or couple the answer from the last question to the current question.

Open Questions may be used during all portions of the trial, but must be used by advocates when performing a direct examination of their own witness.

> **Coupling Questions:**
>
> *Q: Mr. Witness, I draw your attention to what happened immediately after the gun went off—what did you see the defendant do next?*
>
> **A: I saw the defendant drop the gun to the floor and walk quickly towards the exit of the restaurant.**
>
> *Q: After the defendant let his gun drop to the floor and began to quickly walk towards the restaurant door, what did you do?*

We will discuss how you can use this requirement to develop a schematic for direct examination in Chapter 5. For now, accept on faith that whenever you call a witness that has not been declared adverse by the judge you must examine that witness with Open Questions. You will not be allowed to ask Closed or Leading Questions of your own witnesses on issues that are in dispute.

This fundamental premise regarding the questioning of witnesses is grounded in the idea that the witness is the person who was involved in the disputed events and knows the facts, not the advocate. Because the witness is the fount of factual knowledge at trial, the focus is on their ability to relate the facts without assistance from his/her own side. The desire of the fact-finder to hear directly from the witness created a system where advocates are not allowed to ask Closed or Leading Questions of their own witnesses whenever relating factual information that is disputed in the case. Most jurisdictions will allow Closed or Leading Questions to lay foundations for exhibits or to take care of background information. Don't worry about the particulars of this rule now. We will discuss it in much greater detail in Chapter 5 when we learn how to organize and present the direct examinations in a case.

While procedural law generally requires the use of Open Questions during direct examination of your own witnesses,[5] it does not prohibit you from using Open Questions during other portions of the trial. There is a difference however, between being *allowed* to do something and it being *a good idea* to do it. New advocates should concentrate on using Open Questions during direct examination and rarely, if ever, use them during cross examination. There are sound tactical reasons for adopting this strategy as a general rule. We will discuss these reasons in the Chapters 5 and 6.

C. CLOSED OR LEADING QUESTIONS.[6]

A Closed Question is designed to identify the witness' knowledge of the facts or to challenge the credibility of the witness. The structure of the Closed Question ensures that the witness can only respond with one possible truthful answer which is already known by the advocate posing the question. A variety of techniques are available to formulate Closed or Leading Questions. Some of

---

[5] *See* Fed. R. Evid. 611 in Appendix III of this text.

[6] Most authors of trial advocacy use the terms "closed questioning" or "leading questioning" interchangeably. Advocates should understand that regardless of the terminology used these questions focus the witness and suggest an answer. The attention of the jury should be on the advocate, not the witness, when asking these types of questions.

them include: (1) telling the witness instead of asking, (2) using taglines to force agreement by the witness, and (3) asking one-fact questions.

> **Telling the Witness Instead of Asking:**
> *"You got out of your car."*
> *"You closed the car door."*

These statements require agreement or disagreement from the witness, nothing more. In Chapter 6 we will discuss how you can use this technique to great effect during cross examination.

Using taglines to force agreement by the witness also requires agreement or disagreement by the witness. It can become an annoying habit and may invite some witnesses to argue. It may also lead to jury members keeping score of how many times you say the word "correct" in a cross examination. Every moment that juries spend focused on non-substantive issues is an opportunity lost. You do not want them to focus on various "quirks" in your presentation. An overwhelming use of taglines is distracting. While the choice of using taglines is one of style and demeanor, as well as local practice, I recommend losing them. They tend to become crutches and distract from your power during cross examination. We will discuss this further in Chapter 6.

> **Using Taglines To Force Agreement By the Witness:**
>
> *"You got out of the car, didn't you?"*
> *"You closed the car door, correct?"*
> *"We can agree that you walked across the sidewalk?*

The third tool that ensures your questions will be Closed or Leading Questions is to only ask one fact per question. Think of one-fact questions as the building blocks that allow you to make your ultimate conclusion to the jury during closing argument when the witness is not there to argue about it. Advocates use one-fact questions to control witnesses. It becomes very difficult for a witness to prevaricate when only one factual issue is posed in the question. Closed or Leading Questions are normally used during cross examination of adverse witnesses, when laying a foundation for the admissibility of evidence through any witness, or when the witness' demeanor or nature requires Closed or Leading Questions in order to assist the finder-of-fact in getting to the testimony of the witness. This usually occurs when the witness' ability to communicate is diminished due to their age or status as a victim of a violent crime.

> ### One-Fact Questions:
>
> *"You opened the front door?"*
> *"The front door of your house?"*
> *"You walked through the open door?"*
> *"You closed the door?"*
> *"You locked the door?"*
> *"You left your house?"*

Always keep in mind that these Closed or Leading Questions are used to control witnesses, to showcase the advocate, and to lay foundations for the admissibility of evidence. The focus for Closed or Leading Questions is on the advocate, not the witness. Closed or Leading Questions allow the advocate to probe for logical weaknesses or fallacies in the witness' testimony, while also providing a vehicle to test the credibility of the witness through the crucible of cross examination. We will discuss in great detail in Chapter 6 how to utilize these basic Closed or Leading Questioning techniques. When used in conjunction with case theme and theory, they create very effective and applicable cross examinations.

We have discussed several important concepts in this chapter on asking questions and have begun to develop a deeper understanding of the decision making process and case preparation that goes into asking questions. However, study of these three basic questioning techniques will never produce mastery. You must practice constructing these types of questions until they become second nature. The courtroom is a crucible of emotion and ego. The struggle between advocate and witness during cross examination is sometimes so frustrating that even seasoned advocates lose their way and ask the wrong question, in the wrong fashion, at the wrong time. This can also occur during direct examination when you have not asked focused questions and your witness has not provided helpful answers. You can minimize that possibility by inculcating within yourself these basic questioning techniques, allowing you to immediately adapt your question to the situation and the goal. We will apply these skills in direct and cross examination in Chapters 5 and 6.

Points To Ponder . . .

1. Should our procedural rules limit the type of questions we ask in different portions of the trial? Why or why not?

2. What benefits might come from allowing all types of questions in all types of circumstances during a trial? What costs?

3. Can you think of situations where your professional ethical obligations might impact what questions you can or cannot ask at trial? Should they? Why or why not?

CHAPTER THREE
CASE ANALYSIS

"When shall we three meet again
In thunder, lightning, or in rain?
When the hurlyburly's done,
When the battle's lost and won."[1]

A. INTRODUCTION.

In this chapter we will learn how to (1) perform case analysis, (2) understand a case file, and (3) conduct case preparation. To accomplish these tasks you must choose an organizational construct that processes information, prioritizes the value of that information and then identifies crucial legal and factual issues applicable to the case. Advocates have relied upon many different types of organizational techniques to get a handle on this process. The way in which you conduct case analysis has long-term consequences for the clarity and persuasiveness of your position at trial. A superior case analysis (1) assists jurors in understanding the relevant legal and factual issues, (2) brings clarity and focus to the issues the advocate wishes to emphasize, and (3) provides a moral theme that empowers the jury to decide the case in the client's favor. The Rule of Threes[2] provides a superior template to handle case analysis, organize case files, and prepare for trial in a way that allows an advocate to start on the right foot and be immediately successful. Every attorney must develop the ability to properly perform these tasks. While this skill is not normally taught in a law school environment, it can be learned. The use of logical constructs such as the Rule of Threes,[3] in conjunction with an attorney's heightened ability to logically reason,

---

[1] WILLIAM SHAKESPEARE, MACBETH, act 1, sc. 1.

[2] Michael Eck has created the most complete internet portal on this subject. *See The Book of Threes: A Subject Reference Tricyclopedia*, http://threes.com.

[3] Mark Twain referenced trilogies in his own inimical way in *The Autobiography of Mark Twain, see* http://www.twainquotes.com/Statistics.html, stating "Figures often beguile me, particularly when I have the arranging of them myself; in which case the remark attributed to

will assist advocates in creating persuasive trial presentations through a synergistic combination of the practical and the theoretical.

B. CASE ANALYSIS.

1. Introduction.

Case analysis is the process of organizing information, applying specialized knowledge to that information, and then viewing the results of that process in light of the advocate's personal understanding of the moral values existing within the community where the case is tried. This is the point in the practice of law where an attorney melds her legal knowledge with her common sense and world experience. At times this process overwhelms a new attorney. She is not quite sure where to start, or how in-depth her initial effort should be. The advocate often wanders aimlessly through the case file, attempting to generate sufficient activity to feel as though she is accomplishing something. This is rarely, if ever, successful, and even when it is, it is not efficient.

The more successful and practical approach addresses each case by applying an overarching structure. An old chestnut often attributed to Benjamin Franklin is "to fail to plan is to plan to fail."[4] This adage definitely applies to case analysis. The only way to overcome what appears to be an overwhelming project is to begin. It is a lot like eating an elephant—you do it one spoonful at a time. The Rule of Threes provides a common sense template to assist you in "eating the elephant"[5] of case analysis. This text uses the Rule of Threes as an overarching structure for case analysis, suggests a series of common sense checklists applicable in most situations, and provides an analytical tool that explains how the three main portions of any trial are connected when analyzing a case. Before applying the Rule of Threes to case analysis it is necessary to first provide an overview of how the Rule of Threes works.

Disraeli would often apply with justice and force: There are three kinds of lies: lies, damned lies and statistics."

[4] Often Attributed to Benjamin Franklin, see JOHN MARKS TEMPLETON, DISCOVERING THE LAWS OF LIFE. (The Continuum Publishing Company, 1995).

[5] BILL HOGAN, HOW DO YOU EAT AN ELEPHANT? ONE BITE AT A TIME! (Llumina Press 2004).

Seven Steps to Superior Case Analysis & Preparation:

- Organize the case file: use chronologies, time lines and topics
- Identify the procedural and substantive legal issues
- Identify the factual issues: separate facts into the good, the bad and the downright ugly
- Connect the facts to the law
- Identify the moral theme:the sense of injustice, or "the most appalling thing"
- Plan your presentation in reverse: from closing argument through the case-in-chief to opening statement (consider your opponent's case as well)
- Verify the evidence: ensure that you have the witnesses to admit sufficient evidence to support your legal theory, factual theory, and moral theme

---

2. The Rule of Threes.

The Rule of Threes is an organizational construct used to communicate ideas through the written or spoken word. It posits that when information is organized in triplets human beings are more likely to accept and internalize the messages contained within those three pronged packages. This three part harmony view of communication is a powerful tool if you accept its basic premise.

When deciding whether or not to use the Rule of Threes you should consider examples of communications recognized and accepted as instances of superior communication. Both western civilization[6] and Asian Heritage[7] provide

---

[6] Examples from western civilization include Greek philosophy, Judaism, and early Christianity.

[7] Classical Hinduism dates back to at least 500 B.C. with roots extending to 2000 B.C. The Hindu doctrine of divine trinity is called Trimurti(from Sanskrit "three forms") consisting of Brahma, Vishnu, and Shiva. Brahma is the Father or Supreme God, Vishnu is the incarnate Word and Creator, while Shiva is the Spirit of God. Hindus view them as an inseparable unity and worship them as one deity. See "trimurti," Encyclopedia Britannica, 2006, Britannica Concise.

many opportunities from which to choose when looking for effective examples of the Rule of Threes. The history of the United States contains many such instances where the use of the Rule of Threes delivered a message that resonated in the hearts and minds of the American people. Consider the words of Dr. Martin Luther King, Jr. Note his use of both the Rule of Threes and parallelism[8] in the organization of two complementary triplets dealing with the twin themes of hatred and love. The message he delivered is powerful, controlled, and ultimately uplifting. Dr. King touched the emotional core of his audience by using the Rule of Threes to arrange his message in a manner that ensured acceptance by the audience. He spoke to us in a way that we could understand. The strength of his message resounded from the depths of a jail cell in Birmingham, Alabama to the steps of the

"Hatred paralyzes life;
     Love releases it.
Hatred confuses life;
     Love harmonizes it.
Hatred darkens life;
     Love illumines it."

Dr. Martin Luther King, Jr.

Lincoln Memorial in Washington, D.C. Advocates who use the Rule of Threes to conduct case analysis will begin to develop skills that ultimately will increase their persuasive ability at trial.

The Rule of Threes has been used to create belief systems and memorable phrases that are part and parcel of the tapestry that forms our daily lives. The philosophy of the ancient world focused on *logos, pathos*, and *ethos* as a way of living, with an intrinsic understanding that who an advocate was mattered nearly as much as what they did[9] Trilogies teaching others how to live as a member of society exist within many great written works, including The Bible, where messages such as "When I was a child, I spake as a child, I understood as a child, I thought as a child: but when I became a man, I put away childish things" are easily found.[10] As noted previously, Hinduism believes in

---

[8] The Catholic Encyclopedia defines parallelism to mean "The balance of verse with verse, an essential and characteristic feature in Hebrew poetry. Either by repetition or by antithesis or by some other device, thought is set over against thought, form balances form, in such wise as to bring the meaning home to one strikingly and agreeably. In the hymns of the Assyrians and Babylonians parallelism is fundamental and essential." *See* http://www.newadvent.org/cathen/11473a.htm.

[9] *See* ARISTOTLE, THE ART OF RHETORIC, (H.C. Lawson-Tancred trans., Penguin Books 1991).

[10] 1 *Corinthians*, 13:11.

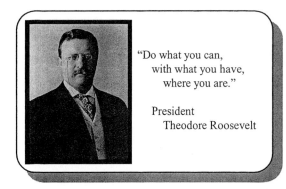

"Do what you can,
with what you have,
where you are."

President
Theodore Roosevelt

the Trimurti form of the divine trinity reflected in the gods Brahma, Vishnu and Shiva. The existence and use of the Rule of Threes in cultures separated by not only beliefs but time is striking from an organizational perspective and supports the argument that the Rule of Threes works because it is intrinsic to the human condition.

This connection exists across cultures and evidence of it can be found in Judea-Christian traditions, the mythology of ancient Greece[11], and the tenets of Hinduism. Beyond issues of faith however, the Rule of Threes is also grounded in our physical ability to perceive the world around us. It is part and parcel of how we think and communicate. Consider for a moment the world surrounding you. Your senses view the world from a three dimensional perspective. These three dimensions form the boundaries of your physical world. When our world does not accurately reflect all three dimensions our physical comfort is compromised. In the same way, words and thoughts that do not reflect a Rule of Threes organizational construct ring less than true in our minds, impinging on our ability to accept as true the message being presented.

Applying the Rule of Threes creates an internal sense of believability and acceptance on the part of the jury. Noted trial advocates have lectured on the use of this rule, including Terrence McCarthy, a successful and famous Chicago defense attorney and Thomas Singer, a respected member of the National Institute for Trial Advocacy and the Notre Dame Trial Advocacy faculty. When properly applied, this rule serves as a template for organizing, analyzing, and presenting a case.

The doctrine of primacy and recency is an excellent common sense example of an application of the Rule of Threes. Advocates use the doctrine of primacy and recency to (1) tell the jury what they are going to tell them (opening statement), (2) tell them (case-in-chief), and (3) then tell them what they told them (closing argument). Primacy and recency is also used to make

---

[11] Apollodorus, *Library and Epitome (ed. Sir James George Frazer)*. "[F]rom the drops of the flowing blood were born Furies, to wit, Alecto, Tisiphone, and Megaera."

certain that advocates start and finish strong. They are taught to put their best facts first and last, with a filling in the middle of their weaknesses. There is persuasive power in this type of organizational structure, but advocates should be careful to not focus on "hiding" bad facts and instead work on how to either neutralize them or turn them to their advantage.

"... [W]e can not dedicate—we can not consecrate—we can not hallow—this ground. ...The world will little note, nor long remember what we say here, but it can never forget what they did here. ...[T]hat government of the people, by the people, for the people, shall not perish from the earth.

Excerpts from the Gettysburg Address
President Abraham Lincoln

You will use these tools throughout the advocacy process, including in opening statements, direct examinations, cross examinations, and closing arguments. Before taking those next steps in your development as a successful advocate you must first learn how to understand and organize a case file. The Rule of Threes will serve as an excellent tool for breaking the case file down into its component parts, with the goal of fully answering three primary series of questions.

C. UNDERSTAND AND ORGANIZE THE CASE FILE

A case file can appear in your hands in a variety of ways, depending upon the firm or government entity where you work. Regardless of the source of the file, it is important to take the time to understand the filing procedures and reporting requirements for your office and the agencies they work with before you begin to delve into the depths of a particular case file. Have someone who normally works with these reports break it down for you and explain the different parts. Once you know how a proper file is supposed to look you will be better prepared to determine when one is incomplete, poorly developed, or improperly addresses the information it is supposed to contain. This is a common sense approach to understanding documents that is crucial to your later analytical process. If you do not know how a case file is supposed to be prepared, how can you make an initial credibility determination regarding the information presented in the file? In today's legal arena much of the business of case preparation will involve documents. You must begin to develop expertise in handling them from the outset of your legal career. Assuming that you have developed the necessary practical knowledge concerning a particular case file, what should you do when you actually get one?

> **Organizing a Case File:**
>
> Gather together all relevant documents and evidence, and organize the information. Use:
>
> 1. Chronological time lines.
> 2. Systems- examples of effective systems include:
>   a. Trial notebooks.
>   b. Witness folders.
>   c. Computer case management software.
>
> List all available information (evidence) without regard to its admissibility or whose argument it supports.
>
> Identify the relevant legal issues. Be sure to address:
>
> 1. Procedural issues (evidence and procedure).
> 2. Substantive issues (applicable statutes and the common law).
> 3. Constitutional issues (both state and federal).

Start by reading through the entire file. Take a moment after this first reading and jot down your initial impressions of the information you have just received. *What questions are in your mind? Is there something else you need to know? Have you made some initial judgments about the people involved?* These are the same types of questions that jurors will be asking when the case is presented at trial. It is at this point in the process that you are as close as you will ever be to thinking about the case the way a juror would. Once you've done this, set those observations aside in a safe place where you can later come back to them.

Your goal at this point is not to write the perfect brief or motion, but rather to get a handle on what you have before you. It is only after you gather together all of the relevant documents, legal pleadings, and other information and organize it in a systematic way, that you can see the "conceptual whole" of the case. This big picture understanding will allow you to identify strengths and weaknesses and potential moral themes and legal theories. The ability to correctly identify the underlying moral themes is crucial. Morality, right and wrong, black and white, good guys and bad guys—this is the language of the jury. It comes from our shared culture and is reflected in the societal vehicles that teach us about the law. Think in terms of the many television shows, movies, and books dealing with legal situations. The public is fascinated with the process of assigning moral blame and imposing legal judgment. If your client's story falls into an archetype that the jury understands you will benefit immensely from an advocacy perspective when you harness that archetype and make it part of your moral theme.

The initial step in deconstructing the case file uses the Rule of Threes to organize the information so that you can identify factual and legal issues and how they relate to one another. ***Organization in a systematic fashion is the key to successfully understanding a case file***. Once you have organized the information contained in the case file you can begin to analyze the contents using the three main steps of case analysis.

The Three Primary Steps in Case Analysis:

- Identify and analyze the legal issues.
- Identify and analyze the factual issues.
- Develop a moral theme and legal theory.

The three primary steps in case analysis are used for trials to a judge, a jury, an arbitration panel, or any adversarial dispute resolution proceeding. You should apply these three steps independently to each of the component parts of a trial or adjudicative proceeding to ensure that your case analysis is complete. Examples of where to do that include identifying closing argument topics, preparing direct, cross and redirect examinations, conducting discovery, deposing witnesses, creating juror profiles, choosing jurors, and selecting opening statement topics. This list is not exhaustive, but does provide a sense of the various portions of a trial to which you can and should apply the three main steps of case analysis.

As you perform these tasks consider the moral theme and legal theory of your case. Your theme and theory provide coherence and continuity to the facts presented at trial and connect those facts to the legal issues you choose in a way that demands victory for your side. If dissonance exists between the theme and theory and the facts or law of your case, you must adapt. Discover additional

> **Identify & Analyze Legal Issues:**
>
> 1. List the legal elements for the claims and defenses.
>
> 2. Analyze the legal principles and questions of law.
>
> 3. Develop a legal theory for each persuasive question of fact.

facts or law that support your position, modify your theme and theory, or settle the case. Whenever the theme and theory changes you must go back and reevaluate your case analysis in light of those changes. We will discuss applying the three main steps of case analysis to your moral theme and theory later in Chapter 13.

A systematic approach is necessary to ensure that you cover all of the possible legal issues. To identify the appropriate legal issues you must understand not only the law, but the specific area of the law that applies to your particular case. Procedurally you should identify admissibility issues while substantively looking for strengths and weaknesses where the law intersects with the facts. Always look for both substantive and procedural legal issues because either can be case dispositive.

The next step after identifying the important legal theories is to convince the judge that your interpretation of the law should apply in this particular instance. That discussion normally occurs in a pretrial motion or in a motion in limine. These arguments about which law applies are normally madeby counsel before the judge and outside the presence of the jury. When the issue is solely a question of law, it may be possible to argue motions without the need for evidence, but that is rarely the case. You should always remember that whenever a court is talking about evidence they are really talking about facts placed before the court through the testimony of a witness. The first thing that a good judge will ask counsel for when

> **Identify & Analyze the Factual Issues:**
>
> 1. List the contested claims and defenses, with the burden of proof for each.
> 2. For each contested claim or defense identify:
>   a. The contested legal elements.
>   b. The deciding questions of facts.
>   c. The persuasive legal theory for each deciding question of fact.
> 3. Develop a plan or identifying and managing the source of facts, including:????
>   a. Creating chronological time lines.
>   b. Arranging documents systemically.
>   c. Listing and cataloging all available exhibits.
>   d. Listing all potential witnesses.

arguments about the law are being made is what facts support their position and what evidence will be offered for the judge's consideration. Counsel can make a proffer of what the evidence will be, but that proffer is only counsel's opinion and not substantive evidence that the judge may rely upon when ruling. Evidence may be actual testimony, previous stipulations, or previously admitted evidence. Trial judges are not bound by the normal hearsay rules when determining most motions, and can rely upon written documents or other out of court statements for the limited purpose of ruling on a motion.

It is imperative that you develop the skill of identifying and analyzing those facts that are case dispositive. Dispositive facts are much more easily identifiable after you have developed the appropriate legal issues presented in the case. The facts of the case will determine whether the law applied by the judge assists or hurts your theme and theory. You must fully develop the relationship between the facts and the law. *Your ability to identify the ruling legal precedent, develop case dispositive facts, and then explain their relationship to the jury using an appropriate moral theme and legal theory is the essence of trial advocacy*.

We have identified three primary areas of case analyis that continuously shift in importance depending upon who you represent and the issues at hand. You must develop the ability to "sense" which is most important for a particular case. Some of that ability to find the best path will develop through experience, 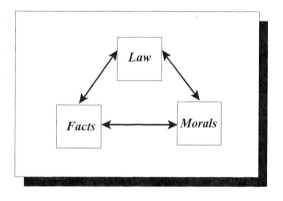 but a great deal of it is centered in the the type of person you are and in the way you personally prefer to view the world. You may have a preference for factual analysis, legal analysis, or moral issues. If you lean towards one of these areas then begin your case analysis from that perspective, taking care to ensure that you do not allow your personal predilictions to prevent you from seeing issues in areas that may not be your strongest suite. Others have refered to this technique as "mind mapping," and have presented it as a conceptual tool for case analysis.[11] There is a good deal of common sense and practical wisdom in this concept.

---

[11] Hugh Selby & Graeme Blank, Winning Advocacy pages (Oxford Press 2d ed. 2004).

At a minimum, starting from a perspective that ensures you are engaged in the process and can see relationships between categories is important. In order to find your best starting point some degree of personal introspection is helpful. Excellent tools exist to assist advocates in this process, including the Myers-Briggs test[12] and the Kiersey Temperament Sorter.[13] The methodology you choose is not important, taking the time to know yourself before you represent others, on the other hand, is not only important but vital to a developing trial advocate, from both a competency and ethical perspective. Once you have identified your starting point and analyzed the case you will have identified certain facts you want in or out at trial and legal rulings that will either strengthen or weaken your case. To accomplish this, advocates normally file motions with the court to identify which facts will be admissible and which law is applicable.

Motions practice at trial is an attempt by both sides to limit the admissible facts supporting the legal positions of opposing counsel while expanding the available admissible facts that support their own legal position. Once you have identified the legal issues and facts available to you it is time to take the next step—creating a vehicle that allows you to combine the law and the facts into one persuasive whole that will convince the jury to decide in your favor. A proper case analysis assists the advocate in choosing the correct moral theme and legal theory in light of the available facts. Failure to accomplish this results in a cognitive dissonance in the minds of the fact-finder. What comes out of your mouth does not match the facts as they see them. They will conclude that you are either incompetent or lying. Either way you lose.

The theory is the application of the relevant law to the specific facts of your case. It forms the basis for the legal or procedural reasons that you should win. The theory is how the jury goes about deciding the case your way and is derived from a complete case analysis discussed above. Considering each legal element of offenses and potential defenses will quickly identify possible legal theories. A case based solely on legal theories can be difficult from a persuasive standpoint. The shipwrecked crew adrift in a rubber raft that kills and eats the weakest member of their group and is then later rescued is a classic example of the difficulties with a purely legal defense. A murder occurred, but a potential

---

[12] NAOMI L. QUENK, ESSENTIALS OF MYERS-BRIGGS TYPE INDICATOR ASSESSMENT pages (John Wiley & Sons, Inc. 2000).

[13] DAVID KIERSEY & MARILYN BATES, PLEASE UNDERSTAND ME: CHARACTER & TEMPERAMENT TYPES pages (Prometheus Nemisis 1984); DAVID KIERSEY, PLEASE UNDERSTAND ME II: TEMPERAMENT, CHARACTER, INTELLIGENCE pages (Prometheus Nemisis 1992).

defense of necessity exists. That legal defense however, may not have a moral theme that supports it. In the shipwreck case a good argument could be made that the strongest members of the party had a duty to protect the weaker ones, not a duty to eat them. Conversely, it could be argued that the weakest member was going to die anyway, and killing him saved the lives of the others. It is often possible for valid legal theories to run into a lack of credibility when they require the jury to adopt an unpopular moral theme or to reject a cherished community belief. In either instance you may find yourself with an excellent legal theory that will never carry the persuasive burden. Jurors are not lawyers and most advocates would do well to remember that fact. *Legal theories must be combined with a solid moral theme to succeed.*

The theme is the moral reason that you should win. It is why the jury wants to decide the case your way. A good moral theme identifies an injustice that is being committed against your client and empowers the jury to right that wrong. Themes are as varied as the people, places, and situations they are designed to capture and represent. The theme provides the moral force that brings the case to life. A good theme not only gets the jury on your side, it creates a feeling of comfort within them about deciding things your way.

If you cannot find a theme within your case that will resonate with the jury, try to determine what sense of injustice exists in the case. Is there a wrong that has been committed against your client that you can use to energize the jury to decide for you? Perhaps the government rushed to judgment because your client is a minority. Or the man who committed the crime is walking around free while your client's exemplary life has been destroyed through the incompetence, stupidity, carelessness, or malfeasance of the opposing side. Other examples include the destruction of a way of life or the health of an individual through the greed of a soulless corporation. The storylines are as varied and complex as the tales of humanity that surround us each day. They exist in your shared experiences as a member of the collective society that is represented by the fact finder. Stay in touch with these perennial themes of life. They are the vehicle through which you can persuasively explain your case to others.

D. CASE PREPARATION.

Now that you have thoroughly analyzed the case you are ready to prepare for trial. Go back and review the initial impressions you wrote down after you read through the case file for the first time. Does the theme and theory you have chosen answer the questions you first wrote down? Do the facts that you will rely upon at trial reflect your earlier understanding of the case? If so, you are ready to proceed with case preparation. If not, you should take a long, hard look at the choices you made during your case analysis. It may be that you have done the best that you could as not all sides are equally arrayed in an adversarial proceeding. While it is your ethical duty to try as best you can to represent your client based upon the facts and the law available, bad facts rarely make for good cases, but they sometimes create excellent advocacy opportunities. Regardless of the strenght of your case, once you are convinced that you have fully and completely addressed all legal, factual and thematic issues, it is time to put it all together. We will use the Rule of Threes to accomplish this task. The trial is broken down into three primary sections: closing argument, case-in-chief, and opening statement. These are not listed chronologically because cases are not prepared chronologically, but rather in a logical fashion based upon the desired endpoint.

1. Closing Argument.

 When taking a trip, the first thing you do is pick your destination. You then plan backwards from that point, all the way back to the time of departure. Your closing argument is your destination. The case-in-chief is the route you will take and the opening statement is your departure point. The closing argument contains the words that empower the jury to decide the case in your favor. It melds the facts and the law of the case, casting them in a moral light. A good closing argument demands, sometimes loudly, sometimes quietly, sometimes reluctantly, but demands nonetheless, that the jury do nothing other than what you ask. How can you take a jury to that place if you yourself do not know where it is that you are going? It is imperative that you begin with your closing argument—from that destination all other decisions must flow.

If you have properly identified the legal and factual issues and have chosen the right theme and theory, the closing argument will come to you as an organic expression of what your hard work has shown you to be true. If you have not properly analyzed the case, you will struggle to find a closing argument that makes sense and fits the facts and the law of the case. There is great danger in choosing a closing argument that does not organically spring from the facts and the law. You may sound wonderful delivering it, but the jury will be left cold in the end, and will turn to the side whose argument makes the most sense, both rationally and emotionally. We will discuss formulating superior closing arguments in Chapter 13, but for now understand and internalize the belief that you start at the endwith your closing argument. If you cannot see yourself standing before the jury in that moment, with those words, then you have not done your job during case analysis and you are not yet ready to prepare the case for trial.

2. Case-in-Chief.

Once you have decided your final destination, you must choose your route. The testimony of witnesses is the primary means available to introduce evidence at trial. For every fact that you intend to argue in your closing argument, you must have a witness to introduce that fact. What you need to support your legal theory and  moral theme determines which witnesses you will call to testify. Each witness is a piece of the puzzle that you are building for the jury. This includes not only your witnesses, but your opponent's, and you should plan for both. By connecting expected testimony to the closing argument, you increase not only your persuasive ability, but more importantly, the believability of your theme and theory.

This process is double edged. Not only should you identify those issues that your witnesses will testify about, but you should also identify the issues that you can either introduce or buttress through the cross examination of opposing counsel's witnesses. By taking the time to do this, you are testing the validity of your theme and theory and also identifying the crucial testimony that you must plan to get out of witnesses on direct and cross. When properly done, this type of case analysis will produce a template that guides you in your selection of witnesses, your questioning of witnesses and your selection of topics for cross examination. The jury does not realize you have done this and instead merely hears the witnesses saying those things that support your legal theory and moral theme.

The use of this process is not limited to factual issues for the case-in-chief. The judge will rule upon motions and objections during the trial. Your ability to produce questions that support the admissibility or suppression of testimony or physical evidence is critical. Knowing that you want certain instructions from the judge before jury deliberations empowers you to make certain that your witnesses testify in a manner that supports the instructions on the law and the facts that you will request from the judge. If you can properly develop this, you can foreshadow the judge's instructions during your closing argument. The jury hears you say that the law is a certain way, and then the judge confirms your prediction and increases your credibility in the eyes of the jury by instructing the jury on the law in accordance with your argument during closing. As a consequence, you appear fair, impartial, and correct. This makes you trustworthy in the eyes of the jury. A famous Florida trial lawyer[14] is known to say "I'll give the other side the judge, if you give me the jury." Using instructions in this fashion can help you get both.

3. Opening Statements.

Opening statements are the first thing you do once the trial starts, but the last thing you plan for. This is the beginning point in your journey. Think of yourself as a tour guide telling your fellow passengers, the jury, where you are taking them. You will identify the final destination and explain the route that all of you must travel on to reach that destination. This allows you to tell the story of what happened, a technique we will discuss in Chapter 4, and then forecast the relevant law in light of where the case will be when it arrives at the final destination. If you analyze your case properly, the opening statement will be persuasive, but not argumentative. Few advocates reach this level, and most descend into argument during their opening because they have not connected the three main sections of trial together as described here.

4. Bringing It All Together

The following series of diagrams explain how to cohesively prepare your case, regardless of its relative complexity or simplicity. The concept is deceptively easy, allowing for additional layers of complexity as needed. This type of analysis can be done with nothing more than a piece of paper and a pencil by drawing three columns and labeling them as follows:

Opening Statement	Case-in-Chief	Closing Argument

Now think about your final destination. What do you need to bring the jury to the conclusions that require them to find in your favor? List those items in the Closing Argument column:

---

[14] Lee Coppock, J.D., Stetson University College of Law, National Trial Team Champion and current coach of the Stetson University College of Law Trial Team, is a legal legend in Florida. This quote is one of his favorites and captures a great degree of practical wisdom.

Opening Statement	Case-in-Chief	Closing Argument
		Moral Theme Factual Theory (evidence) facts 1, 2, & 3 Legal Theory (law) facts 4, 5, & 6

Now that you know where you are going, you have to choose the route to reach your destination. You will need a witness for every issue you will argue in closing. In our diagram you could lay that out as follows:

Opening Statement	Case-in-Chief	Closing Argument
	Direct Witness (DW) DW 1: facts (1) & (6) DW 2: facts (2) & (5) Cross Witness (CW) CW 1: supporting fact CW 1: credibility CW 2: facts (3) & (4)	Moral Theme Factual Theory (evidence) facts 1, 2, & 3 Legal Theory (law) facts 4, 5, & 6

The connection between your moral theme, factual theory, and legal theory becomes obvious when you use this tool. If you want to talk about a fact or get a legal instruction from the judge in closing, you have to produce that fact through a either your own witness or opposing counsel's. The same holds true for most persuasive facts and necessary legal rulings. If you lay out your case preparation in this manner, you will identify substantive weaknesses in your case based upon a lack of legal precedent, a dearth of facts, or a moral theme that simply does not comport with the facts and the law. This is a warning bell to perform additional investigation until you resolve these dichotomies. If you can not do so, it is time to settle this particular case if it is a civil matter, or plead it out if a criminal one. The last step in using this diagram is to list what you need in your opening statement in the diagram:

Opening Statement	Case-in-Chief	Closing Argument
Moral Theme (hook)	Direct Witness (DW)	Moral Theme
		Factual Theory (evidence)
Tell the story (facts) facts 1, 2, 3	DW 1: facts (1) & (6) DW 2: facts (2) & (5)	facts 1, 2, & 3
Foreshadow the law (instructions) facts 4, 5, 6	Cross Witness (CW)	Legal Theory (law) facts 4, 5, & 6
	CW1: supporting fact CW 1: credibility CW 2: facts (3) & (4)	

Consider the relationships between the three basic portions of a trial created above. By viewing them in a connected way, you create a coherent message for the jury. Although you planned it in reverse by beginning at the end, it plays forward when presented. The jury hears you tell them where they are going and how they will get there in the opening statement. You then transport them to the final destination through the testimony and remind them of where they are and what that means in closing argument. To the juror, you have told them what you are going to do, done it, and then reminded them you did it and explained what it all means. You have credibility now. The jury will view you as an ethical, straight-shooter who they can trust. More importantly, you will actually be an ethical advocate that has done the ground work to ensure success. Let us move on now to the actual skills supported by a superior case analysis and preparation.

Points To Ponder . . .

---

1. Why should you trust the jury? What impact does trusting the jury have on the way in which you persuasively organize your presentations at trial?

2. Is it really necessary to believe in what you are advocating for? How do you effectively represent a client whose goals you find personally repugnant? Should you?

3. What is the true purpose of the instructions on the law given by the judge to the jury? How can you use those instructions to your advantage? Do juries follow the instructions of the judge? If they don't, how do you deal with that fact?

CHAPTER FOUR
OPENING STATEMENTS

"Pause awhile,
And let my counsel sway you in this case."[1]

A. THE SKILL OF OPENING STATEMENT.

A young attorney stands before the jury, armed with nothing but a few facts that help, some facts that hurt, and the law. From those paltry tools, she is expected to fashion an introduction to her case that rings with truth, brings the jury to her side, and provides a roadmap to justice. A roadmap that not only helps the jury understand what happened, but why justice demands that the

---

Seven Steps to a Superior Opening Statement:

- Start with your theme. End with your theme.
- Structure your opening. Include the factual theory, legal theory, and moral theme.
- Use descriptive language. Limit passive voice and speak in the present tense when possible.
- Communicate directly with the jury. Establish rapport through body language and eye contact.
- Set the tone and pace for trial. Outline your case with confidence, but do not over reach.
- Tell the jury what you want and what the evidence demands.
- Tell the story of what happened and why it matters, but do not over promise.

---

[1] WILLIAM SHAKESPEARE, MUCH ADO ABOUT NOTHING, act 4, sc. 1

attorney's client prevails. This chapter will empower you to face that moment with confidence and a plan—a plan that highlights your facts, foreshadows the law, and establishes the sense of injustice that feeds your moral theme. As you work your way through this chapter, keep in mind the seven steps to a superior opening statement. Language is the tool of your craft. Use it.

The opening statement is the jury's first opportunity to hear your version of the case and you must make it count. Jurors are concerned with what happened, how it happened, and why it happened. Provide them with that information during your opening statement so they can begin to look for the solution to the issues that confront them. Your opening statement to the jury is a promise about the case, and can establish credibility as a viable guide

> The first, last, and best witness for the client is the attorney. Effective advocates build integrity and credibility in the eyes of the jury throughout the trial. Losing either destroys their ability to persuade. Jurors do not listen to lawyers that they do not trust.

during the trial. Promise is a powerful word, but appropriate in this instance. Jurors take your comments about the case as promises to them. You fail to keep them at your own peril. You chose the jury during voir dire, but during opening statement is when they begin to pick an attorney. When appearing before jurors, it is a good idea to adopt an old adage passed down through the enlisted ranks of most militaries: "Look good when they are looking at you, and never forget—they are looking at you all the time." You are the first, last, and best witness for your case. Your credibility, fairness, and trustworthiness are always being weighed and measured by the jury. Aristotle referred to this as the "character" portion of the art of rhetoric.[2] You can increase their belief in you by being what they are looking for—someone they can rely upon to help them in their charged task. If you lose your integrity, in their eyes, you are done. This selfish incentive should be sufficient to help you follow those ethical standards espoused by the bar and hoped for by the rest of the nation.

> Remember: you only get one chance to make a first impression.

The opening statement is your first and best opportunity to influence the jury's decision making process. Except for in those jurisdictions that allow attorneys to conduct voir dire, this is your first chance to

---

[2] ARISTOTLE, THE ART OF RHETORIC, pages (H.C. Lawson-Tancred trans., Penguin Books 1991).

be in charge. You should use the theme and theory identified in your case analysis to choose the most persuasive story of the facts that gives the jury a framework on which they can organize the evidence as it is received during the case-in-chief. It is much easier to persuade someone to adopt a particular position than to persuade them to change their mind after they have already adopted another way of thinking about things. Use the opening statement as an opportunity to prevent jurors from deciding to view the case in a way that is unfavorable for your client. Given these factors and the way jurors operate, counsel for the plaintiff or prosecution should *never* waive the opening statement, and a defense counsel should *rarely*, if ever, reserve the opening statement to the beginning of the defense's case. Possibly in instances where the criminal defense attorney is basing her entire case on the manner in which the prosecution proceeds, reserving opening may be appropriate. In those rare instances the defense is essentially choosing to allow the theme and theory of the case to develop based upon prosecution witnesses and mistakes. This happens in reasonable doubt cases, but it is dangerous territory for the new advocate and is best entered into only after careful consultation with more experiences trial advocates. Like most rules, exceptions exist, but they are rare.

Your objectives during the opening statement must include planting and cultivating the seeds of your theme and theory. The opening statement explains the factual and legal theory of your case in light of the selected theme that creates a sense of moral injustice for your client. Moral injustice is that wrong that the jury can only right by deciding in your favor. To accomplish these objectives a good opening statement will include a moral theme consisting of a "one-liner" of what the case is about. The theme grabs the emotions of the jury and relies upon their past human experiences and the shared humanity of the group. In order to be truly effective it must be coupled with a logical theory of the facts that is consistent with the legal theory of the case. The opening statement explains the relationship between the facts, the legal theory and the moral theme with an overview of potential admissible evidence. The best vehicle to accomplish these tasks in the opening

> **Examples of One-Liners that Grab the Jury's Attention:**
>
> If it doesn't fit, you must acquit.
>
> Where's the beef?
>
> Wrong place, wrong time, wrong attitude.
>
> The line between love and hate is thin, and the defendant crossed over that line.
>
> Trapped by circumstances.

statement is the grand storytelling tradition of humanity. Centuries ago we crouched around fires and told tales of how we caught the bison. Now we sit around the flame of the television set and watch stories from all over the world.

The methodologies found in the old oral traditions coupled with the organizational and thematic constructs of current entertainment vehicles such as TV and movies create a synergy that maximizes persuasiveness. Let us now identify the substantive pieces and procedural steps required when creating a superior opening statement.

B. THE LAW OF OPENING STATEMENT.

1. Rules of Evidence & Procedure.

Unlike many other portions of a trial, the opening statement is not governed by the rules of evidence. Instead the actual law that applies varies greatly from state to state, as well as within the federal court system. A review of the case law in those jurisdictions establishes certain fundamental concepts that advocates should rely upon when creating effective, passionate, and persuasive openings. Those techniques of persuasion, reaching back to Aristotle as well as those developed in the present day, are all fair game when formulating

---

Seven Basic Legal Principles of Opening Statements:

1. The judge sets the guidelines.
2. No arguing —tell the story.
3. No vouching for the credibility of witnesses.
4. No personal opinions—lawyers are advocates, not witnesses.
5. No mentioning evidence that was excluded during pretrial proceedings.
6. No referring to evidence in opening if there is not a good faith basis to believe it will be admitted.
7. Never violate the "golden rule" by asking the jurors to place themselves in a party's shoes.

---

the manner of your presentation. What is important is that it communicates your legal theory, factual theory, and moral theme to the jury in a fashion that brings them to your side. You have an ethical duty to your client to summon sufficient moral courage to make the opening that must be made. As long as you know where the land mines are in your particular jurisdiction that you should not step on, you are free to be creative. You should identify the local rules of court and review the relevant case law in the jurisdiction in which you practice. The seven basic legal principles for opening statements should keep you out of trouble. They apply in most, if not all,

> "To see sad sights move more than to hear them told."
>
> WILLIAM SHAKESPEARE,
> The Rape of Lucrece

jurisdictions. Most courts expect advocates to make powerful and persuasive opening statements that relay the facts, establish moral themes, and forecast legal issues. Beyond that there is relatively little uniformity between the various jurisdictions. Most will let you use exhibits—both tangible objects and documents—during opening if they have been either pre-admitted or there is a good faith basis to believe you will be able to admit them at trial.

Not only do judges have discretion in controlling the manner and substance of opening statements, they also instruct the jury about opening statements by letting them know what they mean and how to weigh them. You must review the standard jury instructions in your jurisdiction so that you know what the judge will tell the jury about openings. You should then use that as you fashion the most persuasive presentation you can summon.

Most new attorneys, and some senior ones, have difficulty with telling the story of what happened instead of arguing about what meaning can be found in what happened. While argument is easily identifiable once you have been practicing for a period of time, new advocates consistently identify this issue as problematic when creating opening statements. The inability to identify argument creates a tentativeness that has destroyed the effectiveness of more than one opening statement.

More experienced advocates know that they will be able to "sense" the wrongness of argument within an opening statement. To them something just does not sound or feel right about the presentation and the argumentative objection is made almost before opposing counsel has worked out why it was argument. New counsel can follow these rules of thumb with some degree of confidence: (1) Most opposing counsel will allow you to state your theme and theory in your initial opening and end your opening with the same. (2) One sentence of argument in opening gets opposing counsel's attention, two sentences will cause their body to tense and three sentences strung together will have them on their feet.[3] (3) How much argument is allowed within the opening can vary greatly from one jurisdiciton to another. Think of it this way: if you are telling what happened in the present tense from a point of view of someone who was either there or who would have seen the storyline being described, then it is not argument, although it may be extremely persuasive. If, on the other hand, you are interpreting what the evidence means, assigning relative worth, or discussing how the law will apply to a particular set of facts, then you are arguing, not explaining. Consider this first example:

> *On the ninth of October, Mary Lou gets off the elementary school bus just like she does every day. She did not know the new bus driver, but she was excited about getting home and playing with her new baby sister. Mary Lou leaves the bus and walks across the road, just like she did every day. But today was different because the bus was on the wrong street. Mary Lou looks around, unsure what to do when she sees six lanes of traffic. She walks to the median, making it safely across the three lanes of traffic stopped by the bus. When she steps into the fourth lane, her world ends. A black SUV slams into Mary Lou, taking her life.*

Example 1: Opening Statement; Telling a Story

In a relatively short period of time, Example 1 tells the story of what happened that day. It uses the present tense and has the jury there at the time of Mary Lou's death. Now consider this Example 2:

> *Members of the jury, you will learn that on the ninth of October the county school board negligently cared for Mary Lou because they placed an incompetent driver behind the wheel of a school bus and then gave him improper bus route information. These actions violated county regulations and are clear circumstantial evidence of their negligence in the wrongful death of this young lady. The decision made by the bus driver to park the bus and open the door is the "but for" causation factor that establishes their legal responsibility for Mary Lou's death. Don't let them get away with it.*

Example 2: Opening Argument

---

[3] Many thanks to Judge Jean Jordan for her effective description of this process.

The presence of legal terms such as "negligently," "clear circumstantial evidence," and "causation" are red flags indicating that counsel is arguing. Other red flags that counsel should be on the look out for include hyperbole that exaggerates, extrapolates, or speculates. Argument is not effective in opening statement because structurally the jury does not yet know the facts of the case. What practical sense does it make to argue facts they are not aware of? When doing so, you assume that they will view the facts the way you do, that the facts will come out as you envision, and that the jury will remember them. This wastes your opportunity to implant in the jury your version of what happened. More importantly, the lack of context for the jury when they hear sustained argument during opening statement renders it ineffective.

2. Jury Instructions.

The standard instructions on the law in most jurisdictions require the judge to instruct the jury to not make any decisions about the case until it is time

---

Sample Judicial Instructions to the Jury by the Trial Judge:

. . . [I]t is appropriate that I give you some preliminary instructions. My duty as the . . . judge is to ensure this trial is conducted in a fair, orderly and impartial manner according to the law. I preside over open sessions, rule upon objections, and instruct you on the law applicable to this case. You are required to follow my instructions on the law and may not consult any other source as to the law pertaining to this case unless it is admitted into evidence. This rule applies throughout the trial including closed sessions and periods of recess and adjournment. Any questions you have of me should be asked in open court.

. . . .

. . . You must determine whether the accused is guilty or not guilty based solely upon the evidence presented here in court and upon the instructions I will give you. Because you cannot properly make that determination until you have heard all the evidence and received the instructions, it is of vital importance that you keep an open mind until all the evidence has been presented and the instructions have been given. I will instruct you fully before you begin your deliberations. . . .

Example 3: Excerpts from author, MILITARY JUDGE'S BENCHBOOK, Preliminary Instructions page, (Department of the Army, Pamphlet 27-9 2002).

to do so during deliberations. This instruction is designed to ensure that jurors maintain an open mind until all of the evidence has been heard and each sides has been provided an opportunity to present their case. The ideas behind such instructions are noble, but whether or not the jury can actually follow them is an open question. Human nature makes it almost impossible for jurors to listen to a story without beginning to place the information they are receiving in context. Once people begin to receive information about a subject, they start to draw conclusions based upon what they have learned up to that point, filling in the

---

1.01 General: Nature of Case; Burden of Proof; Duty of Jury; Cautionary

Ladies and gentlemen: I will take a few moments now to give you some initial instructions about this case and about your duties as jurors. At the end of the trial I will give you further instructions. I may also give you instructions during the trial. Unless I specifically tell you otherwise, all such instructions - both those I give you now and those I give you later - are equally binding on you and must be followed.

. . . .

. . . You are the sole judges of the facts; but you must follow the law as stated in my instructions, whether you agree with it or not.

In deciding what the facts are, you may have to decide what testimony you believe and what testimony you do not believe. You may believe all of what a witness says, or only part of it, or none of it.

In deciding what testimony to believe, consider the witnesses' intelligence, their opportunity to have seen or heard the things they testify about, their memories, any motives they may have for testifying a certain way, their manner while testifying, whether they said something different at an earlier time, the general reasonableness of their testimony and the extent to which their testimony is consistent with other evidence that you believe.

Do not allow sympathy or prejudice to influence you. The law demands of you a just verdict, unaffected by anything except the evidence, your common sense, and the law as I give it to you.

Example 4: 8TH Cir. Civil Jury Instr. 4.51 (2001).

gaps with their versions of what they expect should happen next.[4] This is not a conscious attempt to modify the information, but a cognitive step human beings use when learning. Information received out of context with our expectations is dismissed, ignored, or modified to fit the perceptions of the listener. Juries do exactly the same thing throughout a trial, even when instructed not to do so. This process takes place beneath the surface and is not a conscious one, but it is very real and advocates ignore it at their peril. If you accept as rational this idea then it makes little to no sense to begin an opening statement by reminding the jury to keep an open mind and by telling them that what you are about to say is not evidence. That is the judge's job. Let her do her job. and you do yours. You are there to persuade within the limits of the law; do just that.

When you stop to think about this dynamic, it makes sense. As human beings, each of us weighs, measures, and categorizes our observations as they occur, and then reflect upon them afterwards. We are hardwired to take incomplete information and apply our paradigms to that information to create a cohesive and understandable whole. Jurors do the same thing when called to judge their peers. It would be hard to imagine them being unable to do otherwise. If this is so, it becomes imperative that you provide for the jury, as early in the process as possible, a logical and consistent framework that allows them to consider the evidence from your perspective.

C. THE ART OF OPENING STATEMENT.

1. Structuring the Opening Statement.

As we begin to discuss how to structure an opening statement, we would do well to consider the words of Associate Supreme Court Justice Joseph Story:

> *Be brief, be pointed; let your matter stand*
> *Lucid in order, solid, and at hand;*
> *Spend not your words on trifles, but condense;*
> *Strike with the mass of thought, not drops of sense;*
> *Press to the close with vigor, once begun,*
> *And leave, (how hard the task!) leave off, when done. . . .*
> *Victory in law is gain'd as battles fought,*
> *Not by the numbers, but the forces brought.*[5]

---

[4] *See* STEVEN LUBET, MODERN TRIAL ADVOCACY:LAW SCHOOL EDITION pages (NITA 2d ed., 2004). In the most recent edition of this book Professor Lubet does an admirable job of laying out the current state of psychological research into cognitive theory.

[5] JOSEPH STORY, ADVICE TO A YOUNG LAWYER (1831) in THE LAWYER'S ALCOVE: POEMS BY THE LAWYER, FOR THE LAWYER & ABOUT THE LAWYER 101–103 (Ina Russelle Warren ed., Doubleday, Page & Company 1900).

This advice, poetic as it may seem by today's standards, is nonetheless as appropriate today as it was in 1831.

A superior opening statement contains cohesive and complementary legal and factual theories as well as morally appropriate themes. While legal or factual theories do not win cases by themselves, their absence can undermine an otherwise powerful moral theme. The theme provides the moral force behind the decision making process of the jury. It is the moral imperative that empowers the jury to emotionally accept and apply the facts and law, ultimately giving one side victory.

 The opening statement begins with a thematic statement setting the stage for the story about to be told. These are often referred to as "hooks" by trial attorneys. Thematic statements are a sophisticated clue to the jury that connects them to the timeless human themes of this particular trial. Instead of beginning with "Once upon a time, in a kingdom by the sea, lived a sad and lonely princess . . ." opening statements might start instead with "Abandoned and abused by a family that did not love her, Jessica took the only steps she could towards freedom—steps that placed her in direct confrontation with the state. The state arrayed its overwhelming might against this young woman, and wonder of wonders—she fought back." A superior opening statement has a tagline that captures the essence of your theme and ties it to your legal and factual theory.

People remember better what they hear first and last. Placing a thematic statement at the beginning and end of your opening statement is an organizational construct often referred to as "bookending." This provides structure to the opening. Bookend the beginning and ending of your opening statement so that you can quickly capture and present your theme and theory of the case to the jury. The story that you tell between those bookends forecasts the evidence that supports your position and will have persuasive power. As the jury listens, your story is tied directly to the wrong that you are asking the jury to make right. The moral force of your position will complement and buttress your evidence, creating acceptance by the jury, or at least a willingness to potentially accept your version of the facts. This technique also relies upon communication theories of primacy and recency. Consider carefully the first words out of your mouth. You will never have more undivided attention from a jury than when you first approach them during opening statement and stand silently before them. Take advantage of that moment in time to ring the bell of truth through an appropriately crafted beginning. A proper theme and theory will resonate through the opening, be supported by the testimony of witnesses during the case-in-chief, and be expounded upon in closing argument. People remember the first thing and the last thing you say. Make yours count.

Though they should never be read, an opening statement must be well planned while still appearing to be extemporaneous. Outline your thoughts before you begin to practice your opening. By the time you prepare your opening you should have already identified the substance of your closing, interviewed witnesses, and ordered their testimony based upon the relative strength of their facts for your side and for your theme and theory. The opening statement is the preview of your case that makes the jury want to watch the rest of your movie and root for your hero or heroine. Do not make the mistake that many poor movies make of promising more than they can deliver. Audiences know when the best part of the movie is found in the previews. If that is happening in your case you are guaranteeing that the jury will think the lawyer who gave the opening statement is a great orator. You are also ensuring that they will not like the rest of the movie. While jurors cannot walk out in the middle of the trial, they do get to vote. Remember this, and only promise a portion of what you think you will be able to deliver during trial. While less is more, make certain that the less you deliver is coherent, both thematically and theoretically.

Paint an active picture for the jury through the use of words, pictures, and exhibits. Tell them the story of what happened without ever using the word "story." Ensure that your presentation has a clear beginning, middle, and end. When possible, use the narrative style in the present tense to ensure believability, simplicity, and movement towards persuasion. Some structures include using a chronological story line, flashbacks, and parallelism. Strive for that sense of transparency that removes the storyteller from the process, allowing the tale to stand upon its own merits. When you have identified the right theme in accordance with your legal and factual theory, it will strike a chord with those whom hear it. Making a connection with a jury member during opening statement is the beginning process in creating in that juror an advocate for your client in the deliberation room where the true final arguments are made.

2. Delivering the Opening Statement.

A lawyer and an actor are akin. It is true I have no mask, I have no set lines, I have no black cloth and I have no floodlights to bring illusion; but out of the miseries and the joys and the strivings and experiences of men, I must create an atmosphere of living reality so that it may be felt and understood by others, for that is advocacy.[6]

You set the stage for communication between yourself and the jury every moment that you are in the courtroom. The opening statement is a golden opportunity—you will never have the same degree of focus from the jury as you do in those first few precious moments when words have not yet been spoken. The canvas is blank. The colors with which you choose to paint are yours. The palette from which you may select includes eye contact, body movement, word choice, and delivery. It is that first opportunity in the trial where the preliminaries have been dispensed with and it is time to get down to business. You must feel enthusiasm for your case. That does not mean cheerleading or table pounding, but it does mean caring—and believing—strongly about the case and the position you are advocating. This care and belief is reflected throughout the opening statement and the trial by the words you choose and the manner in which you deliver them. You will achieve this degree of care and belief only when you are truly comfortable in your place in the process. Preparation, preparation, and more preparation will bring comfort. Gerry Spence says "Prepare, prepare, prepare, and win."[7] Truer words have rarely been spoken about trial practice. Command of the trial arena comes from developing the ability to communicate through the spoken word as viewed through your knowledge of, and comfort with, the factual and legal issues present in your case, and that comfort is the child of hard work.

All eyes in the courtroom should be on you when your opening statement begins. Getting the jurors engaged and keeping them that way is a necessary skill you must develop. There are several things you can do to increase dramatic tension and focus the jury on your message. The first is to truly connect with your audience. You may create those connections with words, movements, and eye contact. It begins with the judge looking at you and asking if you are prepared to proceed. Stand up, look the judge in the eye, and say something like, "Yes Your Honor, the state/defense/plaintiff/defendant is prepared to make an opening statement." The judge will then give you leave to proceed. Take a

---

[6] Sir Edward Marshall Hall, Famous English Barrister.

[7] GERRY SPENCE, HOW TO ARGUE & WIN EVERY TIME, page (St. Martin's Griffin 1996).

breath. Acknowledge the presence of the judge and opposing counsel in the courtroom, and then walk comfortably to a spot centered on the jury, but far enough away from them that you are not intruding into their personal space.

Stop. Plant both of your feet firmly on the ground and then look at your jurors. Eye contact is extremely important if you can manage it. It creates a connection between you and the jurors, opening a channel for communication that cannot be completely duplicated through alternative means. Nonetheless, some very successful communication specialists recommend looking at the forehead of the jurors, focusing on their nose or picking a spot above them and focusing on that spot when you speak to them to avoid the dangers of direct contact. This idea comes from public speaking courses in school that teach students who are afraid to make eye contact to compensate with such techniques. Some of you are unable to make direct eye contact, and this technique is a sufficiently successful option for those of you who become paralyzed by the fear of looking jurors in the eye. However, think about the thought process behind this type of advice. While it may work fine for public speaking situations with a large audience, in front of jury it is a poorer choice because it reflects fear—fear of connecting with others. It is a crutch designed to allow you to "get through" the opening statement, but it sends the wrong message to the jury and is an admission to yourself that you are not completely comfortable with the process.

More importantly, why should you be afraid to look the people who will decide the case in the eye? By the time openings begin, these people are not strangers. If you are not hiding facts or law from the jury then you have no external reason to fear them. The fear that you are feeling must come from within you and that is why you are afraid or uncomfortable with making eye contact. Give yourself permission to connect with this jury. If you stop and think, you should realize that you already know a great deal about the people you are facing. You have read their questionnaires, asked them questions in open court, and chosen who will remain. Now is not the time to be afraid to extend to them the gift of trust. Truthfully, you have to do it anyway. Regardless of how afraid you may be, the jurors are still going to decide this case. Overcome that fear and meet them eye to eye during your opening. Allow yourself this small gift of trust. Your eyes are the easiest and most accepted way of connecting with another person—do it. If you are not ready, then do not take this step, but a some point you should step off into this area of trust. Doing so can transform your attitudes about advocacy.

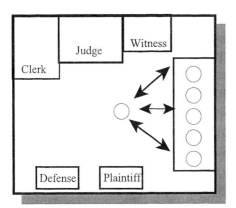

Figure 1: Possible advocate positions during opening statement.

The longer you are silent at the beginning of an opening, the greater the tension within the room. It will seem like forever to you, but not to others. Note our common courtroom diagram depicted in Figure 1. Center yourself on the jury, but not so close that you invade their personal space. Most advise you to never touch the railing in front of the jury. Many jurisdictions specifically prevent you from coming too close to the jury, but some do allow it. In those jurisdictions you should be careful to experiment in practice before attempting this technique. In any event, at all times during the opening statement you should be mindful of your size and the subordinate position of the jury by their being seated and therefore smaller than you. Find a comfortable position from which you can survey and connect with the entire jury. Make eye contact and include them all in your opening statement. If you are too close you not only make them uncomfortable, but you lose the ability to connect with those that may not be completely on your side. Frankly, you want this set of people as comfortable with you as possible, and you need to take the time to find what works for you in the moments of opening statement.

Once you have taken your position and used that moment of silence to draw the jury's attention to you, allow your hands to drop to your sides, exposing your body to the members of the jury. By letting your hands drop you are sending a message to the jury that you are not defensive and that you trust them not to hurt you. This position will make you feel exposed, but in actuality it is a position of power because there is no impediment between you and the jury. Try this exercise: Take a podium and place it between yourself and your audience. You feel safe behind that podium—protected and invulnerable. You are also cut off from those that you are speaking to by that object. Now step out from the behind the podium and face your audience with nothing between but open space and your words. Feel the difference? That feeling is what is accomplished by standing in front of a jury with your hands at your sides; you are both vulnerable and powerful at the same time. In that situation all you have is your case, your voice, and your body. Use all three to make the best impression possible.

The issue of what to do with the podium in the courtroom is one of the eternal conundrums that advocacy professors continually quibble over. Some have a personal preference for its removal, often citing to rationale similar to that mentioned in the proceeding paragraph. Others are devoted to its use and suggest that it serves as an anchor to which the advocate can tie themselves, creating security in an insecure situation. Still others suggest that perhaps it would be best to experiment with it, without it, and somewhere around it. The best advice is to use it as a tool when it increases your persuasive power and ignore it when it does not.

After you have acknowledged the presence of the jury through your body language and eye contact, you can begin to speak. Hit them immediately with a statement that captures your theme and theory. It can be something as simple as a one word like "Accountability," "Credibility," "Gold digger," "Rage," or "Greed." Find short pithy statements that capture the essence of what you want to say without adopting some cliché. The classic example of the last decade has been "If it doesn't fit, you must acquit." Be creative. You know your case better than anyone else at this point and make sure that knowledge and preparation is reflected in the theme found in the beginning of the opening statement. After you have begun you should allow your hands to move in concert with your words. Avoid haphazard movement, but use it when necessary to make a point. Every movement should be choreographed to bring a point home. Like your words, movement in the courtroom has persuasive power. Understand this and use it. Do not allow your nervous energy to leak out through various bodily tics and random movements that create the perception that you might be one or two tacos short of a combo platter.

There are several generally accepted verbal keys that you should have in your kit bag. One is tone of voice. Make certain that your tone matches the case you are trying. Outrage is good, but save it for the lying witness. The jury should be relatively neutral at this point so do not scare them over to the other side. Be persuasive without arguing through word choice, body movement, or voice inflection. Your language should be clear, concise, dynamic, and positive with a definite preference for the present tense as you tell the story of what you believe happened. Overly emotional presentations or theatrics should be avoided. They will not persuade anyone at this point and call into question your believability as well as expose your bias for your client. Strive for a conversational tone that accurately reflects the subject you are discussing. Talk *with* the jury instead of *at* them.

Jurors will summon mental images of people, places, facts, objects, and locations from the words you speak. Choose your words carefully, with a full and complete understanding of the possible connotations they may hold for the jury. While the terms "billiards parlor" and "pool hall" both describe a place where a game is played, they create very different images about that place. The billiards parlor is filled with well-heeled individuals who drink expensive whiskey and talk about their stock investments. The guys in the pool hall are crouched under a cheap, stained-glass, florescent lamp, counting the beer stain circles on the pool table railing. Gripping and persuasive language does not have to be flamboyant, but it should capture an image for the listener. Don't strain to be a poet or a troubadour. Capture the truth simply, using language that the jurors will accept, understand, and interpret in a way you can influence and predict. Avoid legal jargon and cop-speak. You do not want to remind the jury that you are professional doing your job. You want them to see you as a fellow human being helping them to discover the truth.

Little is gained by attempting to "stretch the envelope" of opening statement into the realm of argument as it is normally defined.[8] To a certain extent the entire opening is argument in that it is designed to lead the jury and prepare them to make conclusions. It is not, however, argument in the classic sense; you do not provide the jury with conclusions during the opening statement. Instead, save the conclusions for closing argument after you have prepared the jury through your case-in-chief to accept them. From a common sense perspective that makes sense. You cannot expect jurors to accept your conclusions during opening statement when they have not yet been exposed to the facts and the law. You have spent a great deal of time immersed in the facts and the law during your case preparation and analysis. Do not attempt to drown your jurors with a fire hose of conclusions based upon your preparation. Give them time to accept your facts and the law, and they will conclude on their own that you are right.

A well-prepared and well-delivered opening is persuasive in and of itself. When the statements made during opening cannot be tied to a fact that a witness will disclose through testimony, you are not making an opening statement—you are arguing. Comments on the credibility, believability, or reliability of the expected evidence are not a forecasting of what the evidence will be, but a comment on its validity. Once you start sliding down the slippery slope towards argument you lose the jury. This reminds them that you are doing a job for someone you represent, when you should be helping them sort through a complex issue to ascertain the truth. You become a lawyer and someone who

---

[8] For an alternative view on this subject see HERBERT J. STERN, TRYING CASES TO WIN: VOIR DIRE & OPENING ARGUMENT, (Wiley, John & Sons, Inc. 1991). While I agree with much that Judge Stern espouses concerning credibility in the courtroom and the methods of persuasion, we part ways in our view of the purpose of opening statement. Still, his excellent work is a must read for the true connoisseur of advocacy instruction.

cannot be trusted. Why sacrifice your credibility for a few glorious moments of argumentative prose? Save it for the closing when being argumentative is what you are supposed to do. In opening, only discuss what the evidence will show. There is no swifter way to lose credibility—and to play into the hands of an alert opponent—than to promise something in an opening and not deliver. This invites your opponent to flog you with not delivering on your promise during their closing. A good advocate watches for this mistake and makes the opponent pay, and pay, and pay.

By the same token, you should not waste this precious opportunity. Do not talk about the function of an opening statement, how it is not evidence, etc. It sounds defensive, juries don't care, and it invites them to ignore you. This is the judge's job—why should you do it for him? Worry about doing yours and let him do his. You are the advocate, so advocate. By beginning with a civics lesson during the opening statement, you are simply throat clearing and buying time because you are not prepared to deliver a cogent theme and theory. It is wasted time and space. This does not mean you should not mention legal concepts when appropriate, but you should do so in a manner that makes sense, advances the theme and theory of your case, and does not waste the time of the jury.

> **The Nine Modes of Impeachment:**
>
> 1. Oath
> 2. Perception
> 3. Memory
> 4. Narrative Ability
> 5. Bias: Corruption, Hostility, Interest, Motive & Prejudice (CHIMP)
> 6. Prior Criminal Convictions
> 7. Prior Bad Acts
> 8. Prior Inconsistent Statements
> 9. Witness' Character

The other side will hammer at your weaknesses. When you have a particularly strong part to your case, for example an extremely sympathetic victim or an informant with a checkered past, it is difficult to over-sell those positions of strength. Remember the nine modes of impeachment, and if you have one planned during the case that will be particularly persuasive, forecast that impeachment in your opening. Give the jury a taste of what is to come, much like a good movie trailer. On the other hand, do not forget to compensate for your weaknesses when appropriate. Volunteer and account for some, but not all, of those significant weaknesses. Address the obvious weaknesses in your case, such as compromises made by the victim, errors in lab results, admissions by the opposing party or "bad witnesses" that are impeachable under Federal Rules of Evidence 404(b), 405(a), 608, 609, 613, or

801(b). Expose these weaknesses when your theme and theory require it, but do so with a plan. This will establish candor and show a sense of balance while furthering your goal of getting the jury to pick you as the voice of reason. Where possible and practicable, couple admissions of weakness with a compensating fact that diminishes the damage and gives the jury a better context in which to place the weakness, hopefully in a fashion that supports your case theme and theory.

When considering what to do with exhibits during opening, remember these words: "To see sad sights moves more than to hear them told."[9] If you are going to take the jury's time to admit evidence during the course of the trial, refer to it and use it during the opening statement. Giving notice of your intent to use exhibits to opposing counsel and providing them an opportunity to object during a pretrial hearing are hurdles you should easily overcome if the evidence is to be admitted at trial. You can also handle those issues through pretrial admissibility. If it is important enough to admit the exhibits, it is important enough to use them. From your opponent's perspective, the best exhibits are those that are admitted but never used. Begin in the opening statement using those exhibits and continue to do so throughout the trial. If you do, the jury will see them at opening, anticipate them during direct and cross examinations, and listen to what you think about them during your closing argument. Finally, in the deliberation room, the jurors will hold those exhibits in their hands, and remember and adopt your words when discussing their impact on the case.

A proper voir dire will have identified certain jurors that you believe will be receptive to the factual theory, legal theory, or moral theme of your case. When you are discussing the issues, give that information to a particular juror through body language, eye contact, and inflection. When done correctly, the juror will take ownership of those facts and run with them, making your arguments for you during deliberations. The jury is there to do a job—to ascertain the truth. They are judging you to try and determine if they can rely on you and the evidence you produce to assist them in finding out what happened. The verbal and nonverbal clues you send to them go a long way toward helping the jury make that decision. In Chapter 5 we will look at direct examination, which provides the building blocks from which you form your factual theory, legal theory, and moral theme.

---

[9] WILLIAM SHAKESPEARE, THE RAPE OF LUCRECE. *See* http://www.bartleby.com/70/49.html

3. Examples of Actual Opening Statements.

Excerpts from the opening statements from the defense in the Lizzie Borden trial and the prosecution in the Zacarias Moussaoui trial follow. These two cases occurred more than one hundred years apart, but they are strikingly similar in fundamental ways. As you read through them, think about the elements of a superior opening statement. Consider carefully where these opening statements follow the advice found in this chapter and where they do not. Ask yourself why the advocate chose to organize and present their case in this fashion. When answering that question consider the issues at trial, the social environment, and the goals of the advocate. When you can see the decision points made by these counsel, you will be prepared to apply the final step in developing superior opening statements—your own individuality.

- Defense Opening Statement by A. J. Jennings -
- Lizzie Borden Trial, June 15, 1893[10] -

May it please your Honors, Mr. Foreman and Gentlemen of the Jury: I want to make a personal allusion before referring directly to the case. One of the victims of the murder charged in this indictment was for many years my client and my personal friend. I had known him since my boyhood. I had known his oldest daughter for the same length of time, and I want to say right here and now, if I manifest more feeling than perhaps you think necessary in making an opening statement for the defense in this case, you will ascribe it to that cause. The counsel, Mr. Foreman and gentlemen, does not cease to be a man when he becomes a lawyer.

Fact and fiction have furnished many extraordinary examples of crime that have shocked the feelings and staggered the reason of men, but I think no one of them has ever surpassed in its mystery the case that you are now considering. The brutal character of the wounds is only equaled by the audacity, by the time and the place chosen, and, Mr. Foreman and gentlemen, it needed but the accusation of the youngest daughter of one of the victims to make this the act, as it would seem to most men, of an insane person or a fiend.

A young woman, thirty-two years of age, up to that time of spotless character and reputation, who had spent her life nearly in that immediate neighborhood, who had moved in and out of that old house for twenty or twenty-one years, living there with her father and with her stepmother and with her sister - this crime that shocked the whole civilized world, Mr. Foreman and gentlemen, seemed from the very first to be laid at her door by those who

---

[10] http://www.law.umkc.edu/faculty/projects/ftrials/LizzieBorden/jenningsstatement.html

represented the Government in the investigation of the case.

We shall show you that this young woman, as I have said, had apparently led an honorable, spotless life; she was a member of the church; she was interested in church matters; she was connected with various organizations for charitable work; she was ever ready to help in any good thing, in any good deed; and yet for some reason or other the Government in its investigation seemed to fasten the crime upon her.

Perhaps some of you have read the drama of Richelieu, perhaps some of you have seen it played, and you remember that most dramatic scene, one of the most dramatic in all literature, where, when the king, in the exercise of absolute authority, without right or justice, sends to drag the pure and virtuous ward of Richelieu from his arms, how the old Cardinal draws that circle about her, and no man dares to cross it.

Just so, Mr. Foreman and gentlemen, the law of Massachusetts today draws about every person accused of this crime, or any other, the circle of the presumption of his or her innocence, and allows no juryman or jury to cross it until they have fulfilled the conditions required; until they show that it has been proved beyond a reasonable doubt that he or she is the guilty party, they are not allowed to cross the line and take the life of the party who is accused.

Now, Mr. Foreman and gentlemen, I want to say a word about the kinds of evidence. There are two kinds of evidence, direct evidence and circumstantial evidence. Direct evidence is the testimony of persons who have seen, heard or felt the thing or things about which they are testifying. They are telling you something, which they have observed or perceived by their senses. For instance, if this was a case of murder by stabbing, and a man should come before you and testify that he saw the prisoner strike the murdered person with a knife, that is direct evidence; that tends directly to connect the prisoner with the crime itself.

Circumstantial evidence is entirely different, and I want to say right here, Mr. Foreman and gentlemen - I call your attention to it now, and I do not think that the Commonwealth will question the statement when I make it - that there is not one particle of direct evidence in this case, from beginning to end, against Lizzie Andrew Borden. There is not a spot of blood, there is not a weapon that they have connected with her in any way, shape or fashion. They have not had her hand touch it or her eye see it or her ear hear of it. There is not, I say, a particle of direct testimony in the case connecting her with this crime. It is wholly and absolutely circumstantial.

Now in certain cases circumstantial evidence may be as sure and certain as direct evidence, in some cases more so because the eye and ear deceive as well as circumstances and events; but, Mr. Foreman and gentlemen, there is no class of evidence known that under certain circumstances is so dangerous and misleading as circumstantial evidence. Our books are filled with cases where the accused has evidently been proven by circumstantial evidence to have committed the crime, and subsequent investigations or confessions have shown that he did not.

Circumstantial evidence has often been likened to a chain. These facts, which have to be proven in order to allow you to draw the inference as to her guilt or innocence, have been called links in the chain, and every essential fact, Mr. Foreman and gentlemen, every essential fact in that chain must be proved beyond a reasonable doubt - everyone of them. You cannot have it tied together by weak links and strong links. You cannot have certain facts in there, which you believe and tie them to some other facts of which you have a reasonable doubt. You cannot put them together. You must throw aside every fact about which you have any reasonable doubt, and unless with the links, which you have left, you can tie this defendant to the body of Andrew J. Borden and Abby Durfee Borden, you must acquit her. That is the law, and that is the law you have sworn to apply to the evidence.

Now these facts might be classed, perhaps, under the four heads of motive, weapon, exclusive opportunity, and conduct and appearance of the defendant.

Now, Mr. Foreman, we contend that, with the evidence that has already appeared in this case, and what will be shown to you, there is absolutely no motive whatever for the commission of this crime by this defendant. They have not a scrap of evidence in the case but that, which was given by Mrs. Gifford, and you have heard also the evidence of Bridget Sullivan.

But it may be said that it is not necessary to prove the motive. Somebody killed them; what motive did somebody else have? We cannot tell, Mr. Foreman and gentlemen. One of these persons that is killed is this girl's own father. And while in direct evidence, where the person was seen to kill, where they have been directly connected with the killing, it is of little or no importance whether a motive is shown or not, yet where, Mr. Foreman and gentlemen, you want the motive in order to have it as one of the links of the chain which connects the crime with this defendant, it becomes of tremendous importance. And we shall show you, if not already shown, that this defendant lived there quietly with her father; that the relations between them were the relations that ordinarily exist between parent and daughter. We shall show you by various little things, perhaps, that there was nothing whatever between this father and this daughter that should cause her to do such a wicked, wicked act as this.

And I want to say right here, Mr. Foreman and gentlemen, that the Government's testimony and claim, so far as I have been able to understand it, is that whoever killed Abby Durfee Borden killed Andrew J. Borden; and even if they furnish you with a motive on her part to kill the stepmother they have shown you absolutely none to kill the father. Absolutely none; unless they advance what seems to me the ridiculous proposition that she, instead of leaving the house after killing the mother, waits there an hour or an hour and a half for the express purpose of killing her own father, between whom and herself there is shown not the slightest trouble or disagreement whatsoever. In measuring the question of motive you have got to measure it in this case as applied between the defendant and her father, because, as I understand it, the Government claim that whoever killed one killed both.

Now as to the weapon, Mr. Foreman and gentlemen, I do not know as it is necessary for me to say much about that. The blood that was shown upon the axes, which were guarded so carefully at first in this case, as shown by the evidence, has disappeared like mist in the morning sun. The claw-headed hatchet that Dr Dolan was so sure committed this deed at the Fall River hearing, so sure that he could even see the print, which the claw head of the hatchet made in the head of Mr. Borden, has disappeared from the case.

And, Mr. Foreman and gentlemen, I contend that as to the weapon, they have either got to produce the weapon which did the deed, and, having produced it, connect it in some way directly with the prisoner, or else they have got to account in some reasonable way for its disappearance.

Now as to the exclusive opportunity I do not propose to spend very much time farther, Mr. Foreman and gentlemen, in regard to the opening of this case. The attempt has been made here to surround this house, completely close it in. You have seen it; you have seen how it is shut in; you have seen the opportunities that anyone would have to escape through it. And, Mr. Foreman and gentlemen, I want to call to your attention right here that there has not been a living soul, in all this search and investigation that has been made about the whereabouts and the doings of Mr. Andrew J. Borden upon that morning, there has not been a living soul put on the stand here to testify that they saw Andrew J. Borden come down street from his house. From his house to the Union Savings Bank he has been absolutely invisible. Was it any easier for him to be [unseen] than it would be for somebody escaping from this house if they walked quietly away? But we shall show you, in addition to that, that there were other strange people about that house; people who have not been located or identified. We shall show you that the Government's claim about Miss Lizzie's not having been out to the barn is false and that this - well, if it was not for the tremendous importance, I should be tempted to call it cakewalk of Officer Medley in the barn, exists in his imagination alone.

As to the burning of this dress, we shall show you that it did have paint upon it, according to the statement which was made by Miss Lizzie in the testimony of Alice Russell; that it was made sometime in May; that soon after it was made this was got upon it; that the dress was soiled and useless, and that it was burned there right in the broad light of day in the presence of witnesses, with windows open, with the inside door open, with officers on every side of that house.

And so, Mr. Foreman and gentlemen, without spending further time, we shall ask you to say whether the Government have satisfied you beyond a reasonable doubt that she did kill not only her stepmother, Abby Durfee Borden, but her loved and loving father, Andrew Jackson Borden on the fourth day of August last.

- Prosecution Opening Statement by Robert Spencer -

- Sentencing Phase of U.S. v. Moussaoui, March 6, 2006[11] -

September 11th, 2001 dawned clear, crisp and blue in the northeast United States. In lower Manhattan in the Twin Towers of the World Trade Center, workers sat down at their desks tending to e-mail and phone messages from the previous days.

In the Pentagon in Arlington, Virginia, military and civilian personnel sat in briefings, were focused on their paperwork.

In those clear blue skies over New York, over Virginia, and over Pennsylvania, in two American Airlines jets and in two United Airlines jets, weary travelers sipped their coffee and read their morning papers as flight attendants made their first rounds.

And in fire and police stations all over New York City, the bravest among us reported for work. It started as an utterly normal day, but a day that started so normally and with such promise, soon became a day of abject horror. By morning's end, 2,972 people were slaughtered in cold blood.

And that clear, blue sky became clouded with dark smoke that rose from the Trade Towers of New York, from the Pentagon in Virginia, and from a field in rural Pennsylvania. And within a few hours out of that clear, blue sky came terror, pain, misery, and death, and those 2,972 never again saw their loved ones, never again gave their kids a goodnight kiss. That day, September 11th, 2001, became a defining moment, not just for 2,972 families, but for a generation.

Killers were among us that day and for more than just that day. Those killers had lived among us for months, planned for years to cut our throats, hijack our planes, and crash them into buildings to burn us alive.

On that day, September 11, 2001, a group of cold-blooded killers from distant lands capped their plan, their conspiracy, to kill as many innocent Americans as possible. Those killers, part of the terrorist group al Qaeda, came up with their plan, trained for it, practiced it, worked on it, kept it secret, and then carried it out, hijacking four commercial planes on September 11 and crashing them on purpose to kill as many Americans as they could.

---

[11] http://www.law.umkc.edu/faculty/projects/ftrials/moussaoui/zmspencer.html

One of the people in that plan, one of the conspirators is among us still, right here in this courtroom today. That man is the defendant, Zacarias Moussaoui. He is a loyal al Qaeda soldier, as were the other al Qaeda murderers. He trained to kill, as did the other murderers. He did his part, as did the other murderers, and he succeeded, as did the other murderers, including their leader, Usama Bin Laden.

Moussaoui's part in the end was to lie to allow his al Qaeda brothers to go forward with a plot to kill Americans. He lied so that the plot could proceed unimpeded, and that's exactly what he did. He lied and nearly 3,000 people perished. Moussaoui stands before you today, an admitted terrorist, a convicted terrorist, a proud and unrepentant terrorist. He pled guilty, as the Court has already told you, on April 22nd, 2005 to all charges against him in this case.

He is guilty. This trial is to decide what his punishment shall be.

On that day, September 11th, 2001, Moussaoui was a member of al Qaeda. On that day Moussaoui was part of the plot to hijack planes and crash them into U.S. buildings to kill as many U.S. Americans as possible. Moussaoui trained with al Qaeda as part of the plot. Moussaoui traveled to the U.S. as part of the plot. Moussaoui took flight training as part of the plot. Moussaoui purchased short-bladed knives, all part of the plot, all financed by al Qaeda as part of the plot. He was in the thick of it.

And then he got arrested. He was arrested on August 16th, 2001 in Minnesota where he was training on a Boeing 747 simulator as part of the plot. But even though he was in jail on September 11th, 2001, Moussaoui did his part. He did his part as a good, loyal al Qaeda soldier, he lied so that his brothers could go forward with their plan.

When he was arrested and questioned by federal agents, Moussaoui lied to them. And with that lie, his part, he caused the deaths of nearly 3,000 people, the destruction of the Trade Towers in New York, part of the Pentagon in Arlington, Virginia, and four commercial aircraft.

And he rejoiced in the death and destruction, because he knew he had done his part to kill Americans, and that the plot had succeeded. Now, he caused the deaths by lying to federal agents about what he was doing in the U.S., and his lies permitted his al Qaeda brothers to go forward, and that's what they did. That's exactly what happened.

Had Moussaoui just told the truth on August 16th and 17th, 2001, it would all have been different, and those 2,972 people, or at least some of them, would be alive today.

Now, this trial has been divided into two parts. In the first part of this trial you will be asked to decide whether Moussaoui is eligible for the death penalty, whether he intended to cause and caused deaths on September 11th.

If you decide that he is eligible for the death penalty, then we will have a second part of this trial, and in that second part, you will hear about what happened on September 11th and what the effect has been on the victims. And then you will decide whether the defendant, Moussaoui, should be executed.

In the first part of the trial we will prove to you why Moussaoui lied and what effect those lies had. We will prove that he lied intentionally so his co-conspirators, his al Qaeda brothers, could go forward with their murderous plot. And, ladies and gentlemen, you will see there is really no dispute about that. He has admitted that. He has told us that's why he did it, and the other evidence will bear it out.

Second, I will show you that Moussaoui lied, his lies had their intended effect, that he succeeded and that his lies caused nearly 3,000 deaths, because had he not lied to the agents in August of 2001, had he told us then what he told us in April of 2005, the U.S. government would have stopped those deaths, or at least some of them, and those people would be alive today.

When he was arrested on August 16th and 17th, 2001, this man knew that there was a ticking bomb in the United States. He knew there was a plot about to unfold where jets would be hijacked and flown into buildings. He knew it because he was part of the plot.

And he lied to allow the plot to go forward. His lies provided the operational security to allow his brothers to go forward and kill on that horrific September morning.

The arrest and the lies. In August 2001 Moussaoui was arrested in Minnesota by federal agents. He attracted the attention of agents because he was at the Pan Am International Flight Academy, training on a Boeing 747 simulator, and he stood out because he barely knew how to fly a single engine airplane, and the other students learning how to fly a 747 were all experienced, with long aviation backgrounds.

He didn't have that. The agents suspected that he was a foreign terrorist here up to no good, and they confronted him with that. And he lied. He said no, it is a dream of mine to fly a Boeing 747 simulator. I'm just a tourist here in the United States. I'm not a terrorist. Those are lies.

They asked him about the source of his money that he used to pay for the expensive simulator training. He said: Oh, that money came from a business in England called NOP. Again, false. That money came from al Qaeda.

He told these lies instead of telling the truth, saying that he was from al Qaeda, that he was here to kill by hijacking planes, and that there were others in the United States in a plot about to unfold.

Now, what Moussaoui really knew. What he said in August 2001 was a lie. We know it is a lie and even he has now admitted it is a lie. Years after he lied, he admitted in this very courtroom that he is a terrorist. On April 22nd, 2005, he pled guilty to every one of the six charges against him in this case. Three of those charges, as the Court has told you, carry a potential sentence of death.

When he stood before this Court and admitted his guilt, he signed a written Statement of Facts. That is an extremely important document in this case. In that Statement of Facts he told us some of what he knew about the plot, the plot to hijack planes and kill Americans.

If you look at the screen I am going to read you some of the most important parts of those admissions and they will also come up on the screen for you to follow along. Paragraph 4: Moussaoui became a member of al Qaeda and pledged loyalty, a term known as bayat, to Bin Laden, whom he called his father in Jihad.

Paragraph 7: Al Qaeda members conceived of an operation in which civilian commercial airliners would be hijacked and flown into prominent buildings, including government buildings, in the United States. To effect this attack, al Qaeda associates entered the U.S., received funding from abroad, engaged in physical fitness training, and obtained knives and other weapons with which to take over airliners. Some al Qaeda associates obtained pilot training, including training on commercial jet simulators, so they would be able to fly hijacked aircraft into their targets.

Paragraph 9: Moussaoui knew of al Qaeda's plan to fly airplanes into prominent buildings in the U.S., and he agreed to travel to the U.S. to participate in the plan. Bin Laden personally selected Moussaoui to participate in the operation to fly planes into American buildings and approved Moussaoui attacking the White House. Bin Laden told Moussaoui, "Sahrawi, remember your dream." "Sahrawi," Ladies and Gentlemen, is a war name that Moussaoui used in al Qaeda.

An al Qaeda associate provided Moussaoui with information about flight schools in the United States.

Paragraph 12: On February 23rd, 2001 Moussaoui traveled to Norman, Oklahoma where he attended the Airman Flight School and received training as a pilot of smaller planes. In summer 2001 an al Qaeda associate directed Moussaoui to attend training for larger jet planes.

Paragraph 13: While in Oklahoma, Moussaoui joined a gym and bought knives. Moussaoui selected certain knives because they had blades short enough to get past airport security.

Paragraph 14: In early August 2001, an al Qaeda conspirator using the alias Ahad Sabet, wire transferred money from Germany to Moussaoui in Oklahoma so Moussaoui could receive additional flight training.

In August 2001 -- this is paragraph 15 now -- Moussaoui trained on a Boeing 747-400 simulator at the Pan Am International Flight Academy in Eagan, Minnesota. Moussaoui told an al Qaeda associate that he would complete training before September 2001.

And paragraph 16: After his arrest, Moussaoui lied to federal agents to allow his al Qaeda brothers to go forward with the operation to fly planes into American buildings.

The Statement of Facts is a startling document. It tells us what Moussaoui knew. It tells us what Moussaoui did. And it is all the government needed to know to stop 9/11. And we will show you how.

But Moussaoui didn't give this information in August 2001. Instead, he lied, even after he was arrested, to allow his al Qaeda brothers to go forward. He lied, he told the agents none of this vital information, he told the agents none of what he later told the Court, and he and his terrorist conspirators killed people.

Thus, the Statement of Facts is the focus of the first part of this trial. The information shows that Moussaoui's lies killed the 9/11 victims as surely as if he had been at the controls of one of the four planes on that day.

The part of the 19 hijackers who died on September 11th, who killed innocent Americans, their part was to hijack the planes and fly them and kill Americans. Moussaoui's part, as it turned out, was to lie so they could go forward. With the information in Moussaoui's Statement of Facts from April 2005, the United States Government would have stopped the September 11th attacks, or at least saved some lives, in two ways.

One, offensively. The FBI and other government agencies would have unraveled and discovered the plot. Two, the FAA, the Federal Aviation Administration, if they had that information, would have tightened airport security and stopped the hijackers from getting on the planes that day.

Now, because Moussaoui's lies are the focus of the first part of this case, we will not be concentrating our proof and our efforts on what role Moussaoui would have had had he not been arrested on August 16th. In other words, you are not going to learn what plane he would have been on if he hadn't been arrested, but make no mistake, the evidence will show you that Moussaoui was training to hijack a commercial jet and fly it into the White House as part of the plot, and he has admitted that much. And the rush to get him to jet simulator school and finished with his training before September 2001 tells you all you need to know, that he was supposed to be in that plot.

And that was a plot, after all, that was still in flux as of that time he was arrested. After all, none of the 12 hijackers on September 11th had yet reserved or purchased their tickets for September 11th on August 16th, the date Moussaoui was arrested.

What is important for this part of this trial is the role Moussaoui played after he was arrested, whether he disclosed the unfolding plot, the ticking bomb, or whether he lied to cover it up. And he chose the latter, and the murders flowed from that.

Here is some of what you will hear in the evidence in this case.

You will hear some brief background about al Qaeda, what the organization is, how it operates, and that it is dedicated to killing Americans. You will hear from an FBI special agent named Michael Anticev from New York. He has devoted his professional career to battling al Qaeda.

He will tell you that al Qaeda is headed by Usama Bin Laden and that Bin Laden, by the mid-1990s, had devoted his followers to killing Americans in the greatest number they could find, anywhere in the world they could be found.

Next, you will hear about the 9/11 plot. You will hear about this plot from FBI Special Agent Jim Fitzgerald. He will summarize for you what the FBI has learned from the largest criminal investigation in its history.

You will hear how the hijackers came to the U.S. and lived among us while they plotted the hijackings and the killings. You will hear how they lived under their real names, entered the U.S., took flight lessons, worked out in gyms and fitness training facilities, trained in the martial arts, bought small knives and box cutters.

You will hear how they were funded from al Qaeda from abroad, how they trained in jet simulators. You will learn that the 9/11 plot was complex, requiring years of training and practice, and requiring strict operational security. And, remember, it was Moussaoui's lies that provided that operational security.

You will also hear, of course, about Moussaoui during this trial. Moussaoui was born in France. He is of Moroccan descent. He is 37 years old. He joined al Qaeda, pledged loyalty to Bin Laden, used several war names in al Qaeda, and trained at the al Qaeda terrorist training camps in Afghanistan.

On al Qaeda business he traveled to Pakistan and Malaysia, and in the fall of 2000 he sent e-mails asking about pilot training to the Airman Flight School in Norman, Oklahoma. In February 2001 Moussaoui entered the U.S., flying from London to Chicago to Oklahoma City. When he came into the United States he brought with him over $30,000 in cash.

He enrolled at the Airman Flight School in Oklahoma in late February, 2001. He was an interested and good student in ground school, but once he got in the air, he didn't have much of a knack for flying an airplane. He also told people there various stories about what he was doing in flight school and what he was going to do afterwards.

None of them, not surprisingly, was true. He told nobody that he was an al Qaeda operative, he was part of a plot to hijack planes and fly big jets into buildings to kill Americans. By May 2001 Moussaoui had dropped out of Airman Flight School, out of single engine plane training, and was looking around to get himself into jet simulator school as soon as possible. He was also interested in global positioning systems and small knives.

By July 2001 Moussaoui had secured for himself a spot at the Pan Am International Flight Academy in Eagan, Minnesota. He obtained, on July 31st, his training schedule from that simulator school, and the training schedule had him finished with his training on August 20th.

On August 2nd and 4th, Moussaoui received from Germany via Western Union wire transfer a total of about $14,000. It was sent to him by an al Qaeda conspirator using the fake name, the alias, Ahad Sabet. The sender of the money was really Ramzi Bin al-Shibh, an al Qaeda operative who had tried to get into the United States to become a hijacker, but whose visas to enter the United States were repeatedly rejected.

Once Moussaoui received the money from al Qaeda from Germany by wire transfer, he bought several small-bladed knives and he told his Oklahoma roommate, Hussein al-Attas, that the knives would be easy to hide. Moussaoui then drove from Oklahoma to Eagan, Minnesota, home of the Pan Am Flight School, where he paid $6,800 in cash for the 747 simulator training.

Once there, Moussaoui attracted the attention of the flight instructors. The other students learning on a Boeing 747 simulator were either commercial aircraft pilots looking to move to larger aircraft or military jet pilots looking to get an airline job. Moussaoui had no such background. He could barely fly a single engine propeller plane, having just over 50 hours in the air in that kind of plane.

The school called the local FBI, and Special Agent Harry Samit of the Minneapolis FBI, himself a pilot, knew something was wrong. Agent Samit, and an INS agent named John Weess, arrested Moussaoui when they noticed that he had overstayed his visa. They arrested him as an illegal alien, and he has been in jail ever since.

On August 16th and 17th those agents interviewed Moussaoui. And we will talk about that a little bit later.

The information that Moussaoui knew, that he admitted to knowing when he pled guilty here, is shocking and it is also credible and specific. Had he not lied and revealed the basic facts of why he was actually taking 747 simulator training, the FBI and other government agencies would have put out an all out press, every agent available on the case to find out about the existing and pending al Qaeda plot to hijack planes inside the United States, to find the ticking bomb somewhere hidden in the country.

The response from the U.S. government, as I said, would be both offense, the FBI looking for the hijackers, and defense, the FAA changing airline security to not let people on planes with small knives or box cutters.

Now, in this case you will hear a lot about the terrorist threat situation in the summer of 2001. What you need to know about that summer as it unfolded was that there was a high terrorist threat or a high threat environment. The U.S. intelligence agencies knew that al Qaeda would like to strike America, but the intelligence suggested that the threat would come outside the United States, not inside, and it didn't indicate a specific strike against American aviation.

You will also learn more generally that for intelligence to be useful or valuable, it should be credible, specific, and timely, and Moussaoui's information, what he finally told us in April 2005, was all that and would have been more in August 2001. It was specific, a suicide hijacking plan by al Qaeda using short-bladed knives. It was credible, he was a Muslim fundamentalist who admitted he had been to Pakistan, who was right then in jet simulator school, inexplicably. And it was timely, as the judge has already told you, it was about three weeks before that morning of September 11th.

Put simply, Moussaoui's information would have put the threat environment through the roof. And every available resource would have been put to finding that ticking bomb, and perhaps, more important, it would have focused the search. You will see that intense efforts have been undertaken before to discover and stop the plot.

This has happened before. For instance, in late 1999 the FBI and other intelligence agencies stumbled on to a plot and were warned of a plot to bomb Los Angeles International Airport and elsewhere.

Intense, specific efforts prevented these things. Without Moussaoui's specific information in August 2001, the FBI and the U.S. government was left with generally high threats but nothing specific enough to direct the investigation. No one knew there was going to be an attack inside the U.S. No one knew it was going to be taking over airplanes, commercial airplanes with primitive weapons like box cutters and short-bladed knives.

And no one knew why Moussaoui was training on a 747 simulator, and perhaps most important, no one knew that there were others doing exactly the same thing, preparing to kill people on September 11th.

You will hear Minnesota FBI Agent Harry Samit. He tried hard and in vain to get more information from Moussaoui and about Moussaoui in August 2001. He could not get a search warrant to search Moussaoui's belongings, neither a criminal search warrant nor a search warrant under the Foreign Intelligence Surveillance Act or FISA. But Agent Samit had a hunch about Moussaoui, and unfortunately that hunch turned out to be correct.

Agent Samit interviewed Moussaoui for about three and a half hours over two days, August 16th and 17th, 2001. He did not, however, get the information that we got in April 2005 during Moussaoui's guilty plea. He got instead a series of lies.

What Agent Samit did get was sent dutifully to FBI headquarters in Washington, and on to the CIA and the FAA. And had Moussaoui told the truth, the FBI would have put every available agent on the case and found the plot.

You will hear in the case from former FBI official Mike Rolince, who in August 2001 was the head of the FBI's International Terrorism Section. Mike Rolince was also there during the Millennium threat in 1999, and there in the summer of 2001 when the threat environment was generally high but not specific.

Like the discovery of the Millennium plot, Moussaoui's information would have led to an all-out effort by the FBI. One of the primary agents involved in terrorism investigations for the FBI and in the investigation of 9/11 is former FBI Special Agent Aaron Zebley. Mr. Zebley will describe the investigation into the 9/11 attacks. He will also take you through in some detail how the 9/11 plot could have been discovered had the FBI received Moussaoui's true information.

Using leads from the Statement of Facts, from that information, Agent Zebley will take you to 11 of the 19 hijackers. And Zebley will show you how those 11 hijackers could have been found using three paths, using standard law enforcement techniques, like financial information records and phone records.

First, when the agents arrested Moussaoui in August 2001, they knew he had paid in cash for the expensive jet simulator training, so they asked him about the source of his funding. He lied. He said he got his funding from associates in England and from a business called NOP.

This, of course, was false. It really came from an al Qaeda conspirator using an alias who sent it via Western Union. The English information sent the agents off on a false trail toward England. When Moussaoui did admit the truth in April 2005, it was obvious he had gotten it by Western Union.

If you look at the screen you will see Western Union records that show a transfer from Germany to Moussaoui in Oklahoma. If we look at the next slide, please, Gerard, we will look at the corresponding transfer -- can you switch the document order on that, Gerard -- corresponding transfer from the United Arab Emirates, UAE, to the man using the false name Ahad Sabet in Germany. Contained within the records from that transfer from the United Arab Emirates to Germany, which later went from Germany to Moussaoui, is the contact cell phone number of the caller. That number, 050-520-9905, comes back to a UAE cell phone. The sender of that money from the UAE, again, gave that as a contact number.

Using standard law enforcement techniques, specifically, finding phone records, the FBI can tell what numbers in the United States called that UAE cell phone number that funded Moussaoui for the jet simulator training.

Mr. Zebley will explain how the FBI got this information after 9/11 and how the FBI could have gotten this information in August 2001 had Moussaoui not lied. There are nine U.S. numbers that called that UAE cell phone, it turns out. They all come back to prepaid calling cards.

The next logical step is to see whether those calling cards were used to call any numbers within the United States. When you trace that back, you come to nine U.S. numbers total that were called. Eight of those numbers come back to hijackers. And if you look at that chart on the bottom you will see even just on the initial round, that three of those come back to some of the 9/11 hijackers.

From those eight numbers the FBI can continue on and get the name and location and address of five hijackers, including addresses where some of the hijackers were staying until August 30th, 2001, and from tracing this even further up the path of investigation, you can readily get to six more hijackers.

Second, the second avenue that Mr. Zebley will describe relates to flight schools. In August 2001 Moussaoui lied to the agents. They asked him about his associates. He named a gentleman named Atif Ahmed in England. When Moussaoui told the truth during his guilty plea in April 2005, he admitted that his al Qaeda associates gave him something besides money, they gave him information about flight schools in the United States.

In Moussaoui's belongings that he left in Oklahoma is a two-page list from a German aviation magazine listing United States flight schools. Agents finally were able to get this after September 11th with a search warrant. They would have gotten it early, mid-August, had Moussaoui not lied.

The two-page list has U.S. flight schools. It is a simple manner for the FBI to send an agent to each of these flight schools and ask whether any of the students stand out. Four of these flight schools are in Florida, where the phone records show there were hijackers. Two of these flight schools have Arabic notation written by hand in the margin.

If you go to those flight schools and you ask if any students, any foreign students stand out, and you will hear this from employees of those flight schools and you will see it in the flight schools' records, two of these flight schools, Huffman Aviation and Florida Flight Training Center, there are students who would stand out, Mohamed Atta, Marwan al-Shehhi, and Ziad Jarrah; three of the four pilot hijackers from September 11th.

Florida Flight Training Center even has the records for a hijacker who couldn't get into the United States, Ramzi Bin al-Shibh, who applied several times for a U.S. visa and was rejected, went so far as to apply to Florida Flight Training Center.

He would have come and been a pilot hijacker, except he couldn't get into the United States. Bin al-Shibh even lists his contact number on that application, in Germany, 49-40-718-99042. That information is written somewhere else. That is written in the notebook that Moussaoui had with him in Minnesota.

An employee from FFTC, Florida Flight Training Center, will even tell you that she knew that Bin al-Shibh was related, was connected with Ziad Jarrah, one of the hijackers, because Jarrah went so far as to come and try to get Bin al-Shibh's deposit back to FFTC after Bin al-Shibh's visa was denied.

Next, there is another list of flight schools in Moussaoui's belongings. It is a list of Pan Am facilities. Remember that Moussaoui was training at the Pan Am International Flight Academy in Eagan, Minnesota. This is a list found in his duffel bag that he left behind in Oklahoma that agents were finally able to get to after September 11th, and they would have gotten there before had Moussaoui told the truth, not lied.

The 13 schools on this, eight of them feature jet simulators. The FBI canvassed these schools after 9/11, could have done it before 9/11, if Moussaoui hadn't lied. One of these schools, Arizona Aviation, an employee from that school will come in, Peggy Chevrette, she will tell you in her experience, one student stood out, one student stood out because he didn't have the requisite aviation background to be taking simulator training on a Boeing 747. That student, Hani Hanjour, the fourth pilot hijacker.

Thus, had Moussaoui told the truth and not lied, the FBI quickly would have been on to all four pilot hijackers who hijacked planes and crashed them to kill Americans on September 11th.

The final avenue that Mr. Zebley will describe involves another item recovered from Moussaoui's belongings after September 11th, again would have been discovered before September 11th had he not lied. This is a letter, a false cover letter stating that Moussaoui is the marketing representative for a Malaysian company called Infocus Tech, owned by someone named Yazid Sufaat. This letter is signed by someone named Yazid Sufaat.

Had Moussaoui not lied, FBI agents would have had this letter and investigated Yazid Sufaat. A rudimentary investigation of Yazid Sufaat connects him not only to Moussaoui, but also to another one of the 9/11 hijackers named Khalid al-Midhar. Now, Midhar was a name that had already been given to the CIA and the FBI in that summer, and a little bit before, in 2001. The FBI got the name al-Midhar and another 9/11 hijacker named Nawaf al-Hazmi in August of 2001.

But nothing connected those two gentlemen to an aviation plot. Had the FBI had this letter and the corresponding information, it would have connected al-Midhar and al-Hazmi to the 9/11 hijackers, to Moussaoui, and Sufaat, and thus to an aviation plot by al Qaeda.

Those are the avenues of investigation that Mr. Zebley will describe to you. Had the FBI pursued them using standard law enforcement techniques, in mid-August, they would have gotten to the hijackers. What you are left with if you follow these paths is 11 of the 19 hijackers and two of their addresses.

That's a summary sheet of where that investigation leads you. It includes all four pilot hijackers: Atta, al-Shehhi, Hanjour, and Ziad Jarrah. But finding and arresting some of the hijackers is only half the battle. The other half is not letting named hijackers on to airplanes and not letting anyone on a plane with a short knife or a box cutter.

The FAA is responsible for commercial airline security in the United States. Where the FBI would be the offense looking for the plot, had Moussaoui not lied, the FAA would be the defense. The FAA routinely sends out security information to U.S. airlines and airports. They do it all the time and they did it in the summer of 2001.

In the summer of 2001 there was an elevated threat environment, as they say, but you will see that the threats were directed toward threats outside the United States, aviation outside the United States, and the FAA security at that point was focusing on its traditional fears, one, people smuggling bombs onboard airplanes and, two, a traditional hijacking where hijackers take over an aircraft and negotiate the return of the airplane and the passengers and crew in exchange for some demands.

Had Moussaoui told the truth instead of lying, the FAA would have known about the plot to hijack airplanes using primitive weapons, short-bladed knives and box cutters. The FAA would have done three definite things in response. One, the FAA would have received from the FBI that list of 11 hijackers, put them on a no-fly list, they are not on a plane, and that includes all four of the hijackers trained to fly commercial jets with some aviation training on 9/11.

But even if the FBI didn't get the name and didn't get to the FAA, there is a simple solution, and that is had the FAA known of the plot, they would not have let anyone on a plane with a short-bladed knife or a box cutter. If Moussaoui had not lied and said what he was doing and what we knew he knew, because he told us in April 2005, the FAA would have changed the gate security.

That would have kept the hijackers from getting on the planes with the weapons you will learn that they used to hijack the planes and kill Americans.

Also, had Moussaoui not lied, the FAA would have changed the focus of its gate security in another important respect. The FAA had in September 2001 and still has today a program called CAPPS, and that acronym stands for Computer Assisted Passenger Preselection System. It is a computer program to select potentially dangerous passengers and select them for additional security before boarding a commercial flight.

Before 9/11, anyone selected by the CAAPS system couldn't check their bag on to a plane until they themselves boarded the plane. Why? Because the FAA before 9/11 was concerned about people smuggling explosives in checked luggage onto planes.

They weren't concerned at that point about people taking over a plane with a primitive weapon. Traditionally the thinking, in addition, was that someone smuggling a bomb on a plane wouldn't get on the same flight. Even so, on the morning of 9/11, ten of the 19 9/11 hijackers were selected by the CAAPS system, but because many of them didn't have checked luggage and because that wasn't the method they used to destroy aircraft, made little difference.

If you look at this next slide here, that shows some of the hijackers going through gate security, the hijackers of American Airlines 77 at Dulles Airport. The next slide shows you Nawaf and Salem al-Hamzi, brothers, hijackers, they had been selected for CAAPS screening and they were getting their carry-on bag swabbed for explosive residue as part of the secondary screening there.

Had Moussaoui not lied and admitted the basics of the plot, the CAAPS security screening would have been changed to look not for explosives but for small knives and box cutters, and that would have prevented the terrorists from getting on the plane and getting on the plane with the weapons they used to turn those aircraft into weapons to kill Americans.

There are specific and definite examples of when the FAA has responded to terrorist threats to prevent harm from those threats. An example is from 1995, the FAA took specific defensive measures known as the Bojinka plot, which was intended to blow up U.S. airliners flying over the Pacific. In the end, had Moussaoui admitted in August 2001, instead of lying, what he told us in April 2005, it would have been a very straightforward effort for the FAA to keep those hijackers and to keep anyone with a knife or a box cutter off a plane.

Now, what Moussaoui admitted in April 2005 is shocking. It is shocking for all of us to have somebody come into a courtroom like this one, stand up, proudly admit that he is a terrorist, and say that he has devoted his life to killing Americans. It is shocking to hear someone embrace evil.

But it is also shocking because it lays out the information that necessarily would have saved lives on September 11th. But it did not. And the reason it did not is because a loyal al Qaeda soldier did his part. He did his part because when he could not pilot a plane to kill Americans, he made sure by lying that his al Qaeda brothers did.

This man, the terrorist Moussaoui, did his part. He did his part and he came in here later and told us all why, so that his al Qaeda brothers could go forward and kill Americans. Moussaoui lied so that murders could follow. He intended to kill Americans and he did.

Moussaoui acted by lying, and 2,972 people died. They were brutally murdered. He lied so his al Qaeda brothers could commit those murders and those people were killed. They were because of Moussaoui's actions.

Hold him accountable for causing those horrible deaths. Thank you.

D. RELEVANT EVIDENTIARY & PROFESSIONAL RESPONSIBILITY RULES.

1. Evidentiary Rule Matrix.

Table 1 serves as a starting point for additional inquiry into the relationships between specific tasks on direct examination and the rules of evidence. Your case analysis should assist you in identifying when these particular issues will arise. You should use the table to review your knowledge of the evidentiary rule so that you can include that in your legal theory of the case. Your understanding of these rules and their impact on the admissibility of evidence will assist you

Issue Arising During Opening Statements	Applicable Federal Rule of Evidence
Character of a witness for truthfulness	608
Out of court statements offered for the truth of the matter asserted therein (hearsay)	801–807
Offering evidence of other crimes, wrongs and acts (FTA chapter 10).	404(b)
Prior convictions of a witness. (FTA chapter 10).	609
Legal relevancy: Is the probative value substantially outweighed by the danger of unfair prejudice.	403
Are the questions logically relevant?	401 & 402
Competency of a witness	610
Personal knowledge of the witness	602

Table 1 - Potential Evidentiary Rules Applicable During Opening Statements

in determining which facts you can rely upon with confidence during your opening statement. This knowledge is crucial if you wish to prevent over promising during opening statements. A faulty understanding of these rules will cause you to promise jurors facts the judge will not allow your witnesses to deliver.

2. Professional Responsibility Rule Matrix.

Issue Arising During Opening Statement - Rule Section & Summary	Applicable Rule of Professional Responsibility*
(a)(1)–(3): A lawyer must not offer false evidence.	**RULE 3.3: Candor Toward the Tribunal**
(e): A lawyer must not "allude to any matter that [she] does not reasonably believe is relevant or that will not be supported by admissible evidence . . ." She must not "assert personal knowledge of facts in issue . . . or "state a personal opinion as to the justness of a cause, the credibility of a witness, the culpability of a civil litigant or the guilt or innocence of an accused."	**RULE 3.4: Fairness to Opposing Party & Counsel**
(a): A lawyer must not illegally "seek to influence a judge, juror, prospective juror or other official." (d): A lawyer must not intentionally disrupt the court and must conduct herself with respect for the court.	**RULE 3.5: Impartiality & Decorum of the Tribunal**

Table 2: The Most Prevalent Professional Conduct Rules During Opening Statement

      Table 2 serves as a starting point for additional inquiry into the potential professional responsibility issues that are implicated during opening statements. These rules for the most part reflect goals of civility and integrity. Counsel must ensure that they do not cross certain lines delivering opening statements. You should pay particular attention to rule 3.5, impartiality and decorum of the tribunal. If you internalize now the normative practices embodied in these rules you will be taking the first steps towards not only being an effective advocate, but an excellent colleague and credit to our profession.

* Unless otherwise specifically indicated, all professional conduct rules referenced are taken from the Delaware Supreme Court's professional responsibility rules. Those rules are almost identical to the model rules promulgated by the American Bar Association and are public domain documents.

Points To Ponder . . .

1. How far should advocates be allowed to blur the lines between argument and statements of fact through storytelling during opening statement?

2. When should you object to an improper opening statement? Might there be sound tactical decisions in allowing opposing counsel to argue during opening? What could they be? Do you find them persuasive?

3. What are your greatest fears about giving an opening statement? How will you use your own unique qualities to empower your opening statements? How can you leverage that fear? Should you?

CHAPTER FIVE
DIRECT EXAMINATIONS

"To-morrow, and to-morrow, and to-morrow,
Creeps in this petty pace from day to day
To the last syllable of recorded time,
And all our yesterdays have lighted fools
The way to dusty death. Out, out, brief candle!
Life's but a walking shadow; a poor player
That struts and frets his hour upon the stage
And then is heard no more. It is a tale
Told by an idiot, full of sound and fury,
Signifying nothing."[1]

A. THE SKILL OF DIRECT EXAMINATION.

1. Understanding Direct Examination.

Each of us have seen trial movies where a witness is called and enters the courtroom, walking slowly to the witness stand.   All eyes in the courtroom are drawn to the witness as they are sworn in by the bailiff and take their seat in the witness chair. The witness looks to the advocate and the direct examination begins. In that moment the witness is the focus of the entire courtroom.   The manner in which the advocate conducts the direct examination will determine whether the witness remains the focus of everyone's attention. One of the primary jobs of the direct examination is to ensure that the attention of the jury remains

> Open ended questions may be used during all portions of the trial, but ***must*** be used by attorneys when performing a direct examination of their own witness. Attorneys are ***not allowed*** to ask leading or closed questions of their own witnesses on issues that are in dispute.

---

[1] WILLIAM SHAKESPEARE, MACBETH act 5, sc. 5.

upon the witness and does not wander away. This is the moment in the trial where the focus of the jury should be on the witness, not the lawyer. You are merely the tool empowering the witness to tell their story in a way that is understandable and believable.

Advocates use direct examination to place the facts of their case before the jury using primarily open ended questions. This forces your approach to direct examination on the idea that direct examination showcases the witness, not the attorney. The effectiveness of the information delivered to, and accepted by the jury is much greater when it comes from the witness and not the advocate. A deft touch is required to manage the flow of information from the witness to the jury without impeding its believability. Your goal should be to elicit from

---

Seven Steps to a Superior Direct Examination:

- Start and end direct preparation with case analysis.
- Organize logically. Be as brief as possible, but take all the time you need.
- Use simple language.
- Use exhibits.
- Vary the pace through voice tone, body position, and the use of Headlines, orientations, transitions, and coupling questions.
- Set the scene though descriptive words, action words, and witness background.
- Listen to your witness, and build your next question on their response. Remember to ask the questions you planted in the juror's mind during voir dire and opening statement.

---

your witnesses, in a clear and logical progression, their observations and activities so that the jury understands, accepts, and remembers the testimony. Direct lays the foundation for the admission of physical or demonstrative evidence and begins the preparation for your closing argument. As part of this process you should make a checklist for each witness that identifies the facts and exhibits needed to make an effective closing argument that bookends the opening statement. The bones of that checklist are found in the case analysis.

Your opening statement lays the foundation for the relevancy of the witnesses' testimony. Direct examination provides the jury the information it must have in order to decide the case. How should you take the facts from the witness and package them for presentation in a way that the jury will accept? Experienced attorneys consistently advise that the key to success in the courtroom is preparation, preparation, and more preparation – of both the trial lawyer and the witness. Hopefully the attorney has been in court before, the witness probably has not.   It is critical for the witness to be comfortable and confident enough to tell the facts as they occurred, without becoming overly nervous and unsettled to the point where serious mistakes occur. In order to properly and effectively prepare the witness for testimony you must first prepare yourself. That preparation begins with applying the rule of threes to case analysis and then applying that same paradigm to each witness.

Perform a thorough case analysis for each witness, determining which factual and legal theories are supported by their testimony. After identifying facts to witnesses, schedule a witness preparation session with each witness individually. The goal for each witness preparation session is to make the witness more comfortable and to clarify which facts each witness can, or cannot, testify about. This is an excellent time to determine potential conflicts between witnesses and to begin to identify potential areas of possible cross examination. While we will discuss the impeachment of witnesses in a later chapter, rely upon the following general areas of potential impeachment when interviewing witnesses: (1) ability to take an oath or make an affirmation, (2) perceptions, (3) memory, (4) narrative ability, (5) bias, (6) corruption, (7) hostility, (8) interest, (9) motive, (10) prejudice, (11) prior criminal convictions, (12) prior bad acts, (13) prior inconsistent statements, and (14) bad character.

2. Structuring Direct Examination.

Direct examination is an educational opportunity. You are teaching the members of the jury a set of facts. Determining which facts and how to present them is the crux of matter. Your initial case analysis drives the structure and substance of each direct examination, including the subsequent witness case analysis you must perform for each witness called. You build your directs upon the bones of those facts and issues already identified. Before you begin to create a direct, take the time to sit down and review your earlier case analysis. What facts does your theme and theory require you to get out of

> **Three Steps to Identify Topics on Direct:**
>
> 1. List all factual theories for the witness with supporting facts for each one.
> 2. Decide whether to avoid any factual theories for the witness based upon your case analysis, and then create a final list of topics (factual theories) that address the best and worst facts for each witness.
> 3. Organize the presentation order for each topic in direct examination.

this witness? What weaknesses did you identify?

To accomplish this task, prepare an outline of all topics relevant to your theme, legal theory, and factual theory of the case and use that overarching outline to determine which portions the testimony of the witness will support. This outline must address the in-court oral testimony on direct examination, the anticipated cross-examination of the witness, and possible redirect examination based upon the anticipated cross. Part of this process includes a review of all documentary evidence relating to each witness, including depositions or prior statements, and a personal interview of each witness that forms the basis for initial witness preparation. Only prepare a witness after you know where you intend to go with that witness.

The initial witness interview may well focus you on issues that you otherwise would ave missed. You must now perform a specific case analysis for the direct of that witness. This case analysis is a subset of the overall case analysis, and identifies those disputed and undisputed facts from the witness that supports the overall theme and theory of the case. Now that you know what the witness can and should relate, decide then when and how they will testify. The tool that maximizes your success in determining what will be said, when it will be said, and how it will said is an outline of topics, key facts and sources for the facts for each witness.

> ### Step 1: List All Factual Theories:
>
> * Documents authored by the witness
> * Documents associated with the witness
> * Other exhibits associated with the witness
> * Other witnesses
> * The witness

Meet with your witness for preparation sessions after creating the topic and key facts outline. The number of sessions will depend upon the complexity of the issues identified in your witness case analysis and the abilities of the witness and attorney. Eventually you will be prepared for one final session. During that final session go over possible testimony at trial so as to make sure that you and the witness are comfortable with the process and, most importantly, that the witness understands what is going to happen. You must make certain that the witness knows and believes that their primary duty while on the stand is to tell the truth as they remember it, free from the influence of others, yourself included. The surest way to conduct a poor direct examination is to attempt to massage the testimony of the witness in a particular direction. The witness must understand, accept, and internalize the belief that their primary duty is to simply and effectively tell the truth. When the witness believes this, it frees them to have a conversation with the attorney for the benefit of the jury. It is a directed conversation, but the believability of what the witness says and the manner in which they say it will be greatly enhanced if the attorney has created a careful topic outline based upon a thorough case analysis, especially when the witness is committed to the truth as they remember it.

After you have identified which topics the witness will cover, you still must decide how the topics should be organized for the most effective presentation of the witness and the case. Maximum persuasion is the desired end result and again, case analysis should drive these decisions. That analysis must include how each witness supports the factual theory, legal theory and moral theme of the case. Of paramount importance is whether or not the witness's testimony will answer any of the deciding questions of fact faced by the jury. The topic outlines for each witness should contain the parts of your overall case analysis that the witness supports. A well prepared case analysis provides specific topics that can be lifted and reorganized for each witness, supporting your overall case theme and theory. The ultimate goal for every direct, cross and redirect examination is to persuade the jury to accept your answers to the deciding questions of fact, as well as the underlying contested fact questions.

Never lose sight of the fact that the jury is hearing this for the first time. You cannot expect them to make leaps of inference and logic that you have trained yourself to make through constant exposure to the witness and the case as a whole. Jurors are not incapable of understanding concepts, they just have not been exposed to the information in the way that you have. Do not make the mistake that many advocates make – do not assume the jury is stupid because they lack knowledge, educate them and you will reap the benefits.

> **Step 3: Organize the Presentation Order:**
>
> - Have a structure
> - Consider using timelines or chronologies
> - Presentation must make logical sense to a first time listener
> - Organize to maximize persuasion

When trying to determine what topics will accomplish this ultimate goal, consider what it is that you want to say in your closing. You must understand the connection between you witness's testimony and your closing argument. This should include issues that address both the strengths and weaknesses of your case. You can accomplish this through organization. Utilize the same tools that others use when they receive and digest information. Examples include structure so that each direct tells a story with a beginning, middle and end, time lines and chronologies (either by time or event). The important consideration is to use tools for organization that increase the ability of a new listener to understand your presentation.

3. Questioning Techniques for Direct Examination.

Unless you are laying a foundation or discussing preliminary or introductory matters, you are generally not allowed to lead witnesses on direct examination. The purpose of direct examination is to get evidence supporting your version of the facts from the individuals who have first hand knowledge of the event. In order to ensure that the information comes from the witness and not the attorney, open or non-leading questions are required. If the information does not come from the witness and their own observations, it is not sufficiently reliable to allow the finder of fact to consider it, and may not be either logically[2] or legally[3] relevant under the Federal Rules of Evidence. Federal Rule of Evidence 611 states that cross examination will be conducted by leading questions, and most jurisdictions have inverted that rule to require open-ended questioning during direct examination for the reasons stated herein. This has immediate structural implications for direct examination. The questioning techniques used during direct examination are designed to focus the attention on the witness while minimizing the presence of the lawyer and meeting the requirements of local practice and the rules.

Open-ended questions allow the witness to provide a complete answer on topics chosen by the advocate without the form of the question suggesting the answer to the witness. They work by identifying a topic of interest to the questioner and inviting the witness to testify fully regarding that topic. The quality and specificity of the answer is controlled by the nature of the open-ended question. A variety of open ended questions are normally used when conducting a direct examination. The type of open ended

> **Examples of Open Ended Questions:**
>
> (1) Wide Open Questions
> (2) Directive Questions
> (3) Open Questions
> (4) Probing or Testing Questions
> (5) Coupling Questions

question depends upon the demeanor and knowledge of the witness, what the attorney wants to discuss and the discretion of the presiding judge. The use of

---

[2] Logical relevancy is a minimal standard, but it does exist. Fed. R. Evid. 401 defines relevant evidence as "evidence having any tendency to make the existence of any fact that is of consequence . . . more probable or less probable than it would be without the evidence." Fed. R. Evid. 402 states that relevant evidence is generally admissible while irrelevant evidence is inadmissible. *See* Appendix III of this text.

[3] Fed. R. Evid. 403 provides a structure to allow the judge to exclude evidence that meets the relevancy standards of Fed. R. Evid. 401 and 402. Factors that allow exclusion include when (1) "probative value is **substantially outweighed** by the danger of unfair prejudice," (2) "confusion of the issues," may result (3) the jury may be misled, (4) "considerations of undue delay, waste of time, or needless presentation of cumulative evidence" warrant it. (Emphasis added.)*See* Appendix III of this text.

these different questioning forms allows the attorney to go from the broad to the specific and then shift focus to another topic, depending upon the planned structure of the direct examination and the answers provided by the witness.

Most effective wide open questions are used immediately following a Headline that has oriented the witness to the topic the advocate wishes to discuss. Wide open questions normally direct the witness to a specific **time**, **place**, **person**, or **event** identified in an earlier question or Headline. Once the wide open question orients the witness to the area the attorney is interested in talking about, the advocate then uses directive open questions to narrowly focus the topic the witness should address next. Directive open questions are normally coupled with a Headline so that the witness and fact-finder understand the scope and direction of the advocate's inquiry.

> **Wide Open Questions:**
> *Describe for us . . .*
> *Explain . . .*
> *Tell us about . . .*

> ### Examples of Directive Open Questions Used With a *Headline*:
>
> *I'd like to draw your attention to the letter you received that day.* What did you do with the letter?
>
> *Please direct your attention to the store on the corner of Fifth and Madison.* Did you or didn't you go into the store?
>
> *Let's now talk about the window of the store.* Could you see inside the store through the window?
>
> ### A Follow-Up Wide Open Question Would Be:
>
> *What did you see?*

Directive open questions coupled with a Headline are an effective and capable way to orient the witness to a very specific issue while ensuring that the fact-finder and the judge understand exactly what you are discussing. They are often followed by open questions that allow the witness to further explain the specific issue identified through directive open questions.

Open questions get out relevant information about a specific **time**, **place**, **person**, or **event** that the advocate wants to discuss in greater detail by allowing the witness to answer with more details (detail twice in one sentence). The structure of open questions allows for maximum explanation by the witness, by opening the door for the witness to answer completely based upon her own knowledge and experience.

Open Questions:

Who . . . ?

What . . . ?

When . . . ?

Where . . . ?

How . . . ?

The most specific and controlled type of open-ended questions are probing and testing questions. Advocates use these to elicit the last few bits of relevant information. While narrowly constructed, they are still open questions. They lead the witness to the specific fact you wish to discuss without suggesting the appropriate answer. These are focused questions beginning with a verb or other element that clarifies or explains an issue or point in the case. Lead the witness to a particular issue with these types of questions, but do not suggest the answer. The test for an appropriate probing or testing question is whether or not it focuses on a specific item requiring further inquiry to explain a relevant point for your case. Examples include: (1) *Did you . . . ?*, (2) *What about . . . ?* (3) *How about . . . ?* and (4) *Did you consider . . . ?*

After you have wrung every last bit of relevant information from the witness on a specific item, use coupling questions to emphasize the portions of the testimony of the witness that you want the jury to remember. Coupling questions also provide a flow and continuity to the direct examination. They allow the witness and the fact-finder to understand where the examination is going and to anticipate answers. It also mimics normal speech patterns, creating a sense of believability and credibility concerning the examination. A coupling question takes a word or words from the witness' answer and then uses it to

Coupling Questions:

Q: Mr. Witness, I draw your attention to what happened immediately after the gun went off. What did you see the defendant do next?

A: I saw the defendant drop the gun to the floor and walk quickly towards the exit of the restaurant.

Q: After the defendant let his gun drop to the floor and began to quickly walk towards the restaurant door, what did you do?

connect or couple the answer from the prior question to the current question.

This type of coupling arrangement allows the advocate to subtly underline the most important parts of a witness' testimony without shifting the focus away from the witness. It also uses repetition to teach the jurors the facts as related by the witness. Finally, when the words of an advocate mirror the testimony of credible witnesses it renders the advocate more credible in the eyes of the jury which is not a bad thing to be.

Attorneys are not prohibited from using open questions during other portions of the trial. There is a distinct difference between being allowed to do something and it being a good idea to do it. More than one advocate has snatched defeat from the jaws of victory by asking the wrong open ended question during cross examination. New advocates should concentrate on using open questions during direct examination and rarely, if ever, use them during cross examination. There are sound tactical and strategic reasons for adopting this strategy as a general rule.

B. THE LAW OF DIRECT EXAMINATION.

Federal Rule of Evidence 611[4] addresses witnesses. It establishes the manner and scope of witness testimony. The judge has a great deal of latitude when it comes to the form of questions posed by counsel. While Federal Rule of Evidence 611 provides guidelines and empowers the judge to enforce them, they are just that – guidelines. The most important paragraph is subsection (a).; It is a clear and definitive statement that the judge is in control and advocates should conduct questioning within the court to assist in ascertaining truth, avoiding waste of time, and protecting witnesses from harassment or undue embarrassment. Advocates that understand the breadth of the judge's authority can use that understanding when responding to objections in a manner that supports their position.

Both the Federal Rules of Civil Procedure[5] and the Federal Rules of Criminal Procedure[6] specify that the preferred means of testimony is in open court, unless otherwise required by statute in criminal cases, or at the discretion of the court and for good cause shown in civil cases. The stated preference is for in court testimony, with a greater restriction upon that right in civil cases when the confrontation clause is not potentially at issue. The confrontation clause bars most, if not all contemporaneous transmissions of testimony in a criminal case. Advocates addressing the possibility of out of court testimony in a criminal case would do well to consider those cases that have attempted to work around the confrontation clause.

---

[4] *See* Federal Rule of Evidence 611, a copy of which can be found in Appendix III.

[5] *See* Fed. R. Civ. P. 43(a).

[6] *See* Fed. R. Crim. P. 26.

Most litigation in this area has revolved around sexual assault and child victims. This preference, if not requirement, for open court testimony ensures that direct examination is not only about the words that come from the witness, but the manner in which those words are spoken. Where the attorney stands, how the witness appears, and the sound of their voices are more important because of this legal preference for in court testimony. The system understands that the jury measures credibility on substance, appearance, and delivery. The superior advocate will consider each of those issues when employing the skill, law, and

---

Article VI. Witnesses.
Rule 611.Mode & Order of Interrogation & Presentation:

(a) Control by court. The court shall exercise reasonable control over the mode and order of interrogating witnesses and presenting evidence so as to (1) make the interrogation and presentation effective for the ascertainment of the truth, (2) avoid needless consumption of time, and (3) protect witnesses from harassment or undue embarrassment.

(b) Scope of cross-examination. Cross-examination should be limited to the subject matter of the direct examination and matters affecting the credibility of the witness. The court may, in the exercise of discretion, permit inquiry into additional matters as if on direct examination.

(c) Leading questions. Leading questions should not be used on the direct examination of a witness except as may be necessary to develop the witness' testimony. Ordinarily leading questions should be permitted on cross-examination. When a party calls a hostile witness, an adverse party, or a witness identified with an adverse party, interrogation may be by leading questions.

Example 1: Federal Rule of Evidence 611.

---

art of direct examination.

Whenever witnesses testify and the testimony contains disputed facts, one of the primary questions that the jury will ask is who do they believe. Most courts provide the jury with a set of instructions designed to assist them in sorting through issues of credibility. Understanding how the judge will inform the jury about credibility issues should assist you in structuring your direct examination. The superior advocate uses the information provided in the instructions that she knows the judge will give to the jury to structure her direct examinations in accordance with the basic principles the judge will use to assist the jury in deciding who to believe.

Examples of Procedural Rules:

Federal Rule of Criminal Procedure 26: "In every trial the testimony of witnesses must be taken in open court, unless otherwise provided by a statute or by rules adopted under 28 U.S.C. §§ 2072–2077."

Federal Rule of Civil Procedure 43(a): "Form. In every trial, the testimony of witnesses shall be taken in open court unless a federal law, these rules, the Federal Rules of Evidence, or other rules adopted by the Supreme Court provide otherwise. The court may, for good cause shown in compelling circumstances and upon appropriate safeguards, permit presentation of testimony in open court by contemporaneous transmission from a different location."

Example 2: Federal Rule of Criminal Procedure 26 & Federal Rule of Civil Procedure 43(a).

C. THE ART OF DIRECT EXAMINATION.

1. Organization.

Your case analysis develops a persuasive factual theory, a sound logical legal theory, and invokes a compelling moral theme. Your factual theory explains the undisputed evidence and the opponent's evidence, shows why the other side is wrong, and establishes the facts necessary to carry your case. It does this by bearing the burden of fairness and common sense. To be effective, the factual theory relies upon the everyday experiences of the jurors. The judge instructs jurors that they should use their common sense during deliberations. Use that instruction when shaping your persuasive factual theory. Once you have chosen a factual theory everything else you do at trial must support that theory. Your legal theory applies the law to the factual theory, empowering the jury to decide in your favor. It gives the jury the legal means to decide the factual questions for your side. Think of your legal theory as the source of energy for your factual theory. It empowers the factual theory to move the jury based upon your moral theme.

A good moral theme creates emotional force. It invokes a sense within the jury of the innate "rightness" of your position. Effectively developed, it also provides the structure to package and present your factual theory. The best moral themes demand that the jury perform some specific action to right the wrong that has been committed against your client. Identify that specific action for your closing argument. It also exists beneath the surface of the entire trial. Call it to the attention of the jurors when appropriate. When done correctly the moral theme rises from the depths like a great beast, savaging the momentum and presentation of your opponent. The factual theory, when combined with the legal theory, provides the jury the tools to right the wrong expressed in your moral theme. An effective direct examination of a witness will contribute to one or more, and hopefully all three, of these areas.

You must plan each witness' testimony to include background information, substantive testimony and an appropriate ending point. The fact-finder should feel as though they are listening in on a conversation that focuses the witness on providing relevant and admissible information in an interesting and believable manner—one that also supports your theme and theory. The background information questions introduce the witness to the jury and explain the relevancy of their testimony. Spend sufficient time to ensure that the introduction of the witness and the development of her background contribute to your moral theme, factual theory, or legal theory without wasting time.

> **Planning & Presenting Direct Examination:**
>
> 1. Chronological examination.
> 2. The development of cause and effect.
> 3. Topical examination by subject matter.

You may have several different discrete sections of substantive testimony for each witness depending upon how they support your theme and theory. Different options exist for presenting substantive blocks regardless of the structure that you choose. Prudent opportunities for blocks of narrative must exist within each section. Appropriate ways to incorporate a narrative include conducting a chronological examination, use of cause and effect, and performing a topical examination by subject matter. Make certain that your direct examination ends on a question that focuses the jury on your theme or theory and is one that is not subject to suppression by a timely objection. It should also be a point that the opposing side cannot successfully attack through cross examination.

2. Physical Presence.

After deciding the organization of your direct, consider your location in the courtroom. In the beginning of this chapter we talked about how the focus during direct examination is on the witness and not the attorney. One way to increase the focus on your witness is to position yourself, when allowed by the

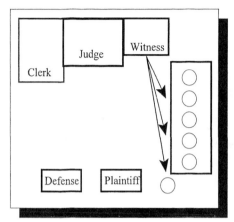

Figure 1: Advocate Position to Focus Attention on the Witness.

court, in a location that forces your witness to look at the jury. By taking a stand at the end of the jury box, you force your witness to speak loudly enough so that you may hear her, also ensuring that the jury can too without ever having to tell them to speak up. In addition, you provide the witness with her best opportunity to look the jury in the eye. Psychologically you have assumed a position as the "13th juror"—again, not a bad thing to be. The more the jury views you as just another person trying to find the truth of this particular dispute, the more likely they are to trust you and, more importantly, what you are saying. Positioning your body in the courtroom is a step in the right direction, particularly during direct when the focus is on your witness. By the same token, consider utilizing what are normally considered cross examination positions in the courtroom when impeaching your own witness or focusing the jury on what you are saying as opposed to what your witness is communicating.

In Figure 2, the advocate has assumed a position in the courtroom that focuses attention on her. It is impossible to successfully ignore an advocate who has taken a position of strength in the center of the courtroom. Use this technique to shift focus, break the monotony of a direct examination, or to focus the jury on the words coming from you. Do not over utilize this position, but have it in your kit bag to use at the appropriate time. When deciding when to move, make certain that your assumption of a new location is tied to a topic in your direct examination that will benefit from this shift in focus. Over time you will develop "comfort zones"—positions from which you will prefer to address certain issues within a particular trial. When done appropriately, returning to that spot in the courtroom during your closing argument will bring the jury back to the testimony given at that time. This can greatly increase the jury's memory of the testimony by providing them with a visual clue that ties into the words and demeanor of the witness. Let us move on now to the words used during direct examination.

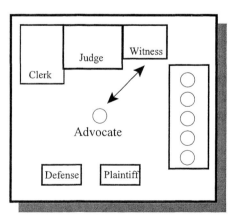

Figure 2: Advocate Position to Focus Attention on the Advocate.

3. Language.

Words are the tools of your chosen trade; choose them wisely. Whenever possible, use short, plain, concise words. One syllable words are best. "Car" is better than "vehicle," and much better than "motor vehicle." It suggests a picture to the jury and is the language of everyday life. "Vehicle" and "motor vehicle" are cop-speak that most jurors normally hear on TV. They have no place in your courtroom vocabulary. Always use the short, common words of everyday speech, preferably those that suggest mental pictures. These words increase the jury's understanding of the witness's testimony and allow for clearer communication by the witness.

Word Choice:		
vehicle	-	car
subsequent	-	after
prior	-	before
utilize	-	use
indicate	-	said
observe	-	see
reside	-	live
locate	-	find
inquire	-	ask
premises	-	place
assist	-	help
profession	-	job
residence	-	home
proceed	-	go

Some advocates fear the use of simple words. They are afraid that their use will remove persuasion from their voice and keep them from swaying the jury with the strength of their position. Nothing could be further from the truth. You must speak the language of your audience. Failure to use words that help create a mental picture can destroy the meaning of an otherwise generally accepted and clearly understood position. These words create wonderful visual images. In a classic example of this concept, George Orwell satirized academic scholarship by providing an academic translation of an earlier work, followed afterwards by the original text.[7]

Orwell's Translation:	**The Original Text:**
Objective consideration of contemporary phenomenon compels the conclusion that success or failure in competitive activity exhibits no tendency to be commensurate with innate capacity, but that a considerable element of the unpredictable must invariably be taken into account.	I returned, and saw under the sun, that the race *is* not to the swift, nor the battle to the strong, neither yet bread to the wise, nor yet riches to men of understanding, nor yet favor to men of skill; but that time and chance happeneth to them all.

---

[7] *Ecclesiastes* 9:11.

The difference between these texts is striking. The power of the original, along with its poetry and motion, is lost in the use of the large, nebulous words by Orwell. Keep it simple, and you will communicate your thoughts clearly.

Along with the use of simple words that create mental pictures, eliminate unnecessary words, redundancies, and doublespeak. Don't say "emergency situation," say "emergency." Have "innovations," not "new innovations." Doublespeak words deceive, distort, misrepresent, and confuse. Juries hate them, and opposing counsel love to point out their qualities.

uncontrolled contact with the ground	-	airplane crash
custodial engineer	-	janitor
diagnostic misadventure	-	malpractice
negative patient care outcome	-	patient died
non-decision making status	-	unconscious
extra-pair copulation	-	adultery
terminal living	-	dying
grain consuming animal units	-	livestock

Finally, rid your vocabulary of clichés that have lost their power and the clutter of normal colloquial speech. Words are clutter if they do not contribute to the narrative's persuasiveness, supply a reason for how someone acted, make an important fact more or less likely, impact witness credibility, believability, or reliability, or enhance your moral theme.

Consider the following example of a bad questioning technique on direct that does not use simple words:

Questioner: *When he departed the area, had you also departed, or embarked upon leaving, or had she, if she had expressed a desire to do so and been capable at that time, if given that she were not otherwise constrained by attendant circumstances, gone also, would he, then, assuming he displayed an awareness of that fact, have brought, you, meaning therewith you and she, along with him, in the car, to the bar?*

Opposing Counsel: *Objection your honor. I have no idea what counsel was asking, and I'm not sure he does either!*

Look at how well these simple questions work instead:

Questioner: *Where were you going that evening?*

Questioner: *Who was with you in the car?*

Questioner: *When did you get to the bar?*

Questioner: *What was the first thing you did when you got to the bar?*

Questioner: *Why did you do that?*

Avoid these pitfalls by using literary forms that enhance information retention in your direct examinations. They include repetition, parallelism, and the Rule of Threes. Repetition comes from our oral storytelling tradition and is likely the first way that each of us was taught by our parents. Parallelism takes facts that are logically parallel and places them alongside each other to show their relationship, connection, or contrast. Use parallel questions to bring out parallel facts or the lack of parallel facts, thereby supporting or contradicting persuasive factual or legal theories. The Rule of Threes presents ideas in a structure that implies a sense of completeness, significance, and believability. This rule applies to words, sentences, and paragraphs. Look again at this last paragraph to see the Rule of Threes in action.

As advocates, we often fear appearing stupid. We try to wrap ourselves in officious sounding words to avoid the appearance of a lack of knowledge. It does not work. We all have within us the ability to formulate dumb questions and large specious words will not eradicate your ability to appear stupid. However, practice can minimize this fear by exposing our stupidity to ourselves before we share it with others. For this very reason, I strongly suggest you practice your questions aloud.

> Was that the same nose you broke as a child?
>
> Now doctor, isn't it true that when a person dies in his sleep, in most cases at least, he just passes away quietly and doesn't know anything about it until the next morning?
>
> Do you have children or anything of that kind?
>
> Were you present in the courtroom this morning when you were sworn in?

With a bit of help and a fair amount of practice

you will be able to minimize your stupid questions, but you will never eliminate them entirely. You should celebrate that fact and not decry it. Stupid questions are part of what makes us human, and the ability to laugh at yourself when you ask a question that does not make sense is an invaluable skill that will pay dividends in front of any jury. Imperfection is an expression of your own humanity, and your connection to your own weaknesses will improve your ability to connect with the jury —not diminish it.

4. Examples of a Direct Examination.

The following excerpt is from a direct examination in a drug case. It is a workmanlike direct designed to get out facts quickly and succinctly. As you read through this direct think about the elements of a superior direct examination. Consider carefully where this direct follows the advice given here and where it does not. If you were conducting the direct examination of this detective, what changes might you make? Why? When you can answer those questions correctly, you are ready to apply the final step in developing superior direct examinations: your own understanding of human nature.

- Direct Examination of a Detective in a Drug Case -

Counsel for the State (Q): *Good afternoon, detective.*
Detective/Witness (A): *Good afternoon.*

Q: *Detective, where are you employed and in what capacity?*
A: *I'm a patrolman with the City Police Department.*

Q: *Okay. Directing your attention to December 4th, 1997, what capacity were you working then?*
A: *I was a detective with the Anti-crime Unit.*

Q: *Now, the Anti-crime Unit, what kind of unit is that?*
A: *It's mainly for narcotic surveillances and arrests.*

Q: *I see. How long were you a police officer?*
A: *Approximately ten years.*

Q: *And how long were you in the Anti-crime Unit?*
A: *Approximately five years.*

Q: *Did you take any special training when you were in the Anti-crime Unit?*
A: *Yes. I went to a state police narcotics school as well as a County top gun*

school and just the experience in working on the streets with the Anti-crime Unit.

Q: *Approximately how many arrests did you make?*
A: *Over a thousand.*

Q: *Now, directing your attention to December 4th, 2006 at about 11:30 a.m. Where did you go basically?*
A: *I was in the area of Cavalier Street, 15 Cavalier Street which is a street right off of Route 29.*

Q: *I see. And what was your purpose to going there?*
A: *We had information that people were selling narcotics in that area. So I went to that area to find a surveillance point.*

Q: *Where did you -- and did you find one?*
A: *Yes.*

Q: *Where?*
A: *I was in the area of 15 Cavalier Street.*

Q: *And what kind of an area is it? Are there houses, stores?*
A: *It's a -- there is apartment buildings on Cavalier Street but they're all abandoned.*

Q: *Okay. 15 Cavalier Street, what kind of a building was that?*
A: *It's a multiple apartment complex. There are many, many rooms in that in Cavalier Street.*

Q: *Is it occupied?*
A: *No.*

Q: *Okay. What floor did you go to?*
A: *Second floor.*

Q: *And did you use any device that would help you to see better?*
A: *Binoculars.*

Q: *Okay. So, when you set up on the second floor with your binoculars what did you see?*
A: *I observed --*

Q: *Could you keep your voice up?*

A: *Sure. I observed Jamie Roberts. She was standing in the middle of the street in 15 Cavalier Street and there was other people in the area, but there was a lot of abandoned cars in the area, and there's gentlemen working on the cars, fixing up the cars, and at one time I saw at one point I observed -- she was later identified as Cheryl Horton walk into the area and they had a short conversation, they went across the street into a grocery store and they came back, and at one point Jamie Roberts pulled out a packet of heroin out of her fifth pocket of her pants and handed it to Cheryl Horton and in return she received cash.*

Q: *Now what do you mean by the fifth pocket of your jeans?*

A: *The small change pocket in the jeans in the front of your pants.*

Q: *Okay. Could you maybe just show us?*

A: *The small pocket in the jeans. (Indicating.)*

Q: *Okay. Now, you have binoculars to see this?*

A: *Yes.*

Q: *And what exactly did you see?*

A: *They pulled out a packet of heroin and handed it to Cheryl Horton and in return she received cash.*

Q: *Okay. And what, if anything, did Jamie Roberts do then?*

A: *She walked over to a car that was parked in front of Cavalier Street, 15 Cavalier Street and Ms. Rogers was in the vehicle and she received the money that she had just gotten.*

Q: *Okay. What happened then?*

A: *Ms. Rogers gave Jamie Roberts some more packets of heroin and Jamie held the packets of heroin in the hand. There was four packets.*

Q: *How could you tell it was four packets?*

A: *With the binoculars. I could tell. She had them in the palm of her hand. She was counting them herself.*

Q: *So you saw her count four packets?*

A: *Yes.*

Q: *Okay. And who gave that to her?*

A: *Ms. Rogers.*

Q: *Okay. What happened then?*

A: *She went back into the area of the street and --and that's when another gentleman came up was Mr. Dupree, Chris Dupree, and they had a small conversation, and Ms. Roberts held out the packets of heroin in her hand and Mr. Dupree picked one of the packets of heroin out and held it up to the sun, flicked it to see if the package was full, if it was a good package, and he kept the package and in return gave Ms. Roberts cash.*

Q: *What did Ms. Roberts do then?*

A: *She went back to Ms. Rogers and Ms. Rogers she give her the money, but I guess Mr. Dupree needed change so Jamie or Ms. Rogers here was trying to get into her pocket but she couldn't so she got out of the car and gave Ms. Roberts some change and in return she gave the change to Chris Dupree.*

Q: *So Ms. Rogers had difficulty getting something out of her pocket?*

A: *Right. She was in the car so it was easier to get out and get into her pocket.*

Q: *And you saw money?*

A: *Yes.*

Q: *And you saw money come from Ms. Rogers?*

A: *Yes.*

Q: *And then what happened?*

A: *And she gave it to Ms. Roberts and in return gave the change to Mr. Dupree.*

Q: *Okay. Now, what -- Ms. Horton, what was she doing when all of this was going on?*

A: *She was in a parked car that was in front of Ms. Rogers, and it was an abandoned car and she was sitting in the passenger side of the vehicle snorting the bag of heroin.*

Q: *Could you see that?*

A: *Yes.*

Q: *Okay. And after you saw the change incident did you make any kind -- kind of communications to other officers?*

A: *I advised my lieutenant, Lieutenant Lister of the situation and other individuals of the Anti-crime Unit to come into the area, and as they would do that I would give a description of the people involved and where they were on the street.*

Q: *Did you have a radio?*
A: *Yes.*

Q: *Okay. Now, while you were waiting for your back up officers to come in did you see anything else?*
A: *Well, as she pulled into the area Ms. Roberts was walking back over, she was by Ms. Rogers and Cheryl Horton and she was showing Ms. Horton more packets of heroin, and when the officers came in she dropped a couple of packets on the ground.*

Q: *Now, Ms. Horton was in a car in front of Ms. Rogers, is that correct?*
A: *At one point, yes. And at one point she got out and jumped in the car with Ms. Rogers.*

Q: *And while she was in the car with Ms. Rogers Ms. Roberts came by?*
A: *Yes. And she was standing outside the car conversing and showing Ms. Horton a couple more bags of heroin.*

Q: *And then the officers came?*
A: *Yes.*

Q: *And what happened when the officers came?*
A: *A Like I said before, when she pulled up Ms. Roberts dropped a couple packets of heroin that she had in her hand on to the ground and she was placed under arrest. She also had another bag in her fifth pocket.*

Q: *What officer made that arrest?*
A: *Fucci.*

Q: *Okay.*
A: *And when she stopped Chris Dupree the package he had purchased, he had opened it, he was going to do it, and when the officer came he dropped it on the ground and the product fell on to the road.*

Q: *Okay. Okay. Who of the people you mentioned were arrested?*
A: *Chris Dupree, Cheryl Horton and Ms. Rogers.*

Q: *How about Jamie Roberts?*
A: *And Jamie Roberts.*

Q: *Okay. Now, they were all arrested?*
A: *Yes.*

Q: *And the substances, would you call that heroin, was that retrieved?*
A: *Yes. Not from Chris Dupree. It went on to the ground and it was destroyed when it hit the ground.*

Q: *But there were packets that Jamie Roberts had?*
A: *That's correct.*

Q: *Do you know how many?*
A: *Three.*

Q: *And where were they?*
A: *She dropped two and she had one in her fifth pocket, and the other one that she had, she had four all together, she sold one to Cheryl Horton. That was the bag she was smoking outside. It was a total of three.*

Q: *Okay. Now on the scene Jamie Roberts was read her rights, is that correct?*
A: *I believe so.*

Q: *And what if -- did --*
A: *Well, Lieutenant Lister said that she was read her rights at the scene because I was still in my surveillance spot, and when I returned to headquarters he said that she was read her rights, she understood her rights and said that she was selling heroin for Ms. Rogers.*

Q: *Okay. Now, the people that you saw, did you know who they were before you --*
A: *No.*

Q: *-- observed them?*
A: *No.*

Q: *You later identified them?*
A: *Yes.*

Q: *After they were arrested?*
A: *Yes.*

Q: *Okay. Now, was any -- was any drugs or anything found on Ms. Rogers?*
A: *Just cash. No drugs.*

Q: *How much cash?*
A: *I believe it was a hundred and twenty-four dollars.*

Q: *Okay. Now, do you see in court the lady that you call Ms. Rogers?*
A: *Yes.*

Q: *Could you point her out?*
A: *The lady sitting at the end of the table next to the attorney. (Indicating.)*

Counsel for the Defense: *The record can reflect he has identified Betty Rogers.*
The Court: *So noted.*

Q: *With your permission, your Honor, I would like him to use the diagram?*
The Court: *Very well.*

Q: *Okay. Could you show us Cavalier Street and 15 Cavalier Street?*
A: *Sure. (Drawing a diagram.)*

The Court: *Excuse me, officer.*
A: *Yes, sir.*
The Court: *Could you just back that up a little bit so I'd be able to see it? You can still face it towards the jury so that if you can just turn it that way a little bit more I'll be able to see it. I can still see it. Members of the jury, can you see the diagram? All right. Thank you, officer.*

Q: *Could you show us where 15 Cavalier Street is?*
A: *Right here. (Indicating.)*

Q: *And where were you in 15 Cavalier Street?*
A: *Approximately this area right here. (Indicating.)*

Q: *What floor?*
A: *Second floor.*

Q: *Okay. Now, could you identify the car that Ms. Rogers was sitting in?*
A: *(Indicating.)*

Q: *Okay. Now, Ms. Horton, when you observed her get into a car was that car nearby the car with Ms. Rogers?*
A: *Yes, it was right in front of himself marked in front of Ms. Rogers's car.*

Q: *Okay. Where was Jamie Roberts standing in the street when she talked to Ms. Horton?*
A: *Approximately right here. (Indicating.)*

Q: *And how about when she talked to Mr. Dupree?*
A: *Same area.*

Q: *Okay. Now, is there a grocery in the area or something like that?*
A: *Yes. This is the street. (Indicating.)*

Q: *When she first met Horton did they go anywhere near the grocery?*
A: *She went into the grocery store and came back.*

Q: *And when they came back that's when the sale went down?*
A: *Yes.*

Q: *Okay. Could you put your initials on -- initials and your date on the diagram?*
A: *(Complies.) Today is the 24th, correct?*

Q: *Right.*
STATE: *No further questions.*

The Court: *Defense?*
Counsel for the Defense: *Thank you, your Honor.*

D. RELEVANT EVIDENTIARY & PROFESSIONAL RESPONSIBILITY RULES.

1. Evidentiary Rule Matrix.

Table 1 serves as a starting point for additional inquiry into the relationships between specific tasks on direct examination and the rules of evidence. Your case analysis should assist you in identifying when these particular issues will arise. You should use the table to review your knowledge of the evidentiary rule so that you can include that in your legal theory of the case.

2. Professional Responsibility Rule Matrix.

Issue Arising During Direct Examination	Applicable Federal Rule of Evidence
Character traits of the victim or accused	404(a), 404(b) & 405
Character of a witness for truthfulness	608
Out of court statements offered for the truth of the matter asserted therein (hearsay)	801–807
Offering evidence of other crimes, wrongs and acts (FTA chapter 10)	404(b)
Prior convictions of a witness (FTA chapter 10)	609
Legal relevancy: Is the probative value substantially outweighed by the danger of unfair prejudice?	403
Are the questions logically relevant?	401 & 402
Competency of a witness	610
Personal knowledge of the witness	602
Questioning witnesses	611 & 614

Table 1: Potential Evidentiary Rules Applicable During Direct Examination

Table 2 serves as a starting point for additional inquiry into the potential professional responsibility issues that are implicated during direct examination. Counsel must ensure that they do not cross certain lines when investigating cases, preparing witnesses, and controlling direct testimony. The same issues also exist when listening to an opposing counsel's direct examination. You must pay particular attention to your jurisditions interpretation and application of the candor towards the tribunal standard found in rule 3.3. A thorough grasp of these issues will assist you in avoiding perjury and improper conduct. Your case analysis should assist you in identifying when these particular issues will arise. You should use the table to review your knowledge of the procedural rule so that you can include that in your planning for your directs.

* Unless otherwise specifically indicated, all professional conduct rules referenced are taken from the Delaware Supreme Court's professional responsibility rules. Those rules are almost identical to the model rules

Issue Arising During Direct Examination	Applicable Rule of Professional Responsibility*
(a)(1)–(3): A lawyer must not offer false evidence.	**RULE 3.3: Candor Toward the Tribunal**
(e): A lawyer must not "allude to any matter that [she] does not reasonably believe is relevant or that will not be supported by admissible evidence . . ." She must not "assert personal knowledge of facts in issue . . . or "state a personal opinion as to the justness of a cause, the credibility of a witness, the culpability of a civil litigant or the guilt or innocence of an accused."	**RULE 3.4: Fairness to Opposing Party & Counsel**
(a): A lawyer must not illegally "seek to influence a judge, juror, prospective juror or other official." (d): A lawyer must not intentionally disrupt the court and must conduct herself with respect for the court.	**RULE 3.5: Impartiality & Decorum of the Tribunal**
(a): A lawyer must not attempt to be an advocate and witness in the same trial (with some limited exceptions).	**RULE 3.7: Lawyer As Witness**

Table 2:The Most Prevalent Professional Conduct Rules During Direct Examination

promulgated by the American Bar Association and are public domain documents.

Points To Ponder . . .

1. If the purpose of direct examination is the unimpeded flow of information from the witness to the fact-finder, why not allow for narrative responses to questions? Why not just ask the witness to tell us what happened?

2. Should we allow jurors to question witnesses? Why or why not? What might be the impact of allowing jurors to pose questions to witnesses? How would you do it?

3. How could you develop the ability to present a direct examination in a manner that invites conversation and ease of understanding while maintaining control of the witness? Is witness control overrated or a necessary evil of the trial process?

CHAPTER SIX
CROSS EXAMINATIONS

"An evil soul producing holy witness
Is like a villain with a smiling cheek,
A goodly apple rotten at the heart.
O, what a goodly outside falsehood hath!"[1]

A. THE SKILL OF CROSS EXAMINATION.

1. Understanding Cross Examination.

Many advocates approaching cross examination view it with awe, fear and trepidation. They've seen the television shows where the witness breaks down and admits to committing the crime and realize in the pit of their stomach that juries have been conditioned to expect great things from cross examination. They fear they are not up to the

> Advocates are *not only allowed, but encouraged* to ask leading or closed questions during cross examination.

task and wonder how in the world they can ever adequately represent their client while employing all of the possibilities that cross examination is supposed to offer. These advocates often respond by embarking on a cross examination that reiterates the direct examination and then descends into a slash and burn campaign designed to destroy the credibility of the witness. This usually backfires, damaging instead the credibility of the advocate. Poorly done, cross examinations are often devastating for the advocate who performs them. Despite what many others have written, cross examination is actually a readily developed skill that lies within the abilities of any competent trial lawyer. What is required is preparation, attention to detail and a commitment to approaching cross

---

[1] WILLIAM SHAKESPEARE, THE MERCHANT OF VENICE, act 1, sc. 3.

examination through the lens of your case theme and theory. Advocates who plan cross examination with these precepts in mind are well along the way to mastering the art of cross examination. Everything is designed to make your case look better and your opponent's case worse, keep that in mind as you prepare cross and you will have an attainable goal. If you doubt that the bar has been set high then consider the words of those who have gone before:

> *"[Cross examination is] the greatest legal engine ever invented for the discovery of truth."*[2]

> *Cross examination is the principal means by which the believability of a witness and the truth of his testimony are tested."*[3]

> *The age old tool for ferreting out truth in the trial process is the right to cross examination. For two centuries past, the policy of the Anglo American system of evidence has been to regard the necessity of testing by cross examination as a vital feature of the law.*[4]

Your goals during cross examination are to: (1) control the witness; (2) establish facts that build to a Theme and Theory; and (3) establish facts that build up the credibility of your witnesses and diminish the credibility of your opponent's witnesses, including the witness being cross examined. In order to accomplish this you must know more than the witness does. That is only accomplished by a thorough, complete and continuing case analysis. When preparing specifically for cross examination, your first step is to identify and list the legal issues in the case that work with your case theme and theory. If you cannot do this, it is a red flag indicating that the theme and theory you have chosen does not fit the available facts. You must adapt your theme and theory to one that is supported by the facts. While doing this keep in mind the seven steps to creating a successful cross examination.

---

[2] 5 J. Wigmore, Evidence sec. 1367

[3] Davis v. Alaska, 415 US 308 (1974)

[4] Perry v. Leake, 109 S.Ct. 594, 601 n.7, 488 US 272 (1989)

> #### SEVEN STEPS TO A SUPERIOR CROSS EXAMINATION:
>
> - Start and end cross preparation with Case Analysis.
> - Every cross examination section must have a clearly defined purpose tied to theme, theory or credibility.
> - CONTROL THE WITNESS! Use leading, closed-ended, one fact questions, based on preparation and organization.
> - Organize the cross to accomplish your goals – replaying the direct examination is usually counterproductive.
> - Details give you control.
> - Impeach by the probabilities when warranted.
> - Use the witness' own words for control and effect.

2. Preparing Cross Examination.

Once you have identified the legal issues you must determine which of them represent the "Hard Questions of Fact" the jury must decide. These questions should be framed in the language of common sense and everyday life. Your job as an advocate is to translate the legal issue into a persuasive form for the jury. Brainstorm the good facts and bad facts associated with the witness from all available sources of information. For each good and bad fact you must identify a readily available witness, document or exhibit that supports the existence of that fact. For each witness you must list the good and bad facts with the location of the documentation that supports the fact in question. Done properly this will create a matrix that you can use to easily and quickly retrieve the evidence supporting each identified fact when necessary during cross examination. *This is a crucial point in the cross examination preparation process.* If you don't take the time to properly analyze the legal issues and facts that support them in light of your case theme and theory you are guaranteeing an ineffective and possibly self-destructive cross examination. You cannot arrive at a destination if you have not chosen one. Failure to properly analyze the case is a failure to choose a destination. If you do not, your opponent will and I guarantee that you won't enjoy the ride to that location.

Once you have compared the identified "Hard Questions of Fact for the Jury" with your list of good and bad facts for the witness you should choose the best points and worst points for each hard question of fact. You must then organize each of these clusters of good and bad facts into different sections of your cross examination. Applying the rule of threes to this process will organize your good and bad facts for maximum efficiency and persuasive power during the actual cross examination. After you've identified them you must cross reference those facts with the legal theory, factual theory and moral theme you developed during your case analysis.

> **Primary Goals of Cross Examination:**
>
> (1) Control the witness;
>
> (2) Establish facts that bolster your Theme and Theory; and
>
> (3) Establish facts that build up the credibility of your witnesses and diminish the credibility of your opponent's witnesses.

Look to see if any of these potential good or bad facts contradict your theme and theory, are of minimal persuasive value or are too dangerous to use during cross examination. Remember you are always following the first rule of trial advocacy – do nothing that is not in accordance with your case theme and theory. If the best facts for the witnesses support your theme and theory and do not contradict your version of the facts you should identify them as potential topic headlines for your cross examination outline. Make certain that you do not organize your cross examination in the same chronological fashion that the witness used on direct examination. The witness has practiced their direct and just delivered testimony. If you choose to use the same structure that the witness is familiar with you are increasing their sense of comfort and control – two feelings that you rarely, if ever, want to engender in an adverse witness. .

After identifying the topic headlines for your cross, you must employ advocacy techniques that maximize the persuasive impact of the answers to the questions you will ask to draw out those best facts. (1) cluster together all of the facts that enhance and support the topic, (2) lay out the facts one question at a time leading up to your final point, and (3) identify similar facts based upon your knowledge of human nature that support your final topic and ask questions about those before making your final point.

Each of these techniques is designed to create tension by building suspense and sparking the interest of the jury, while suggesting the answer that everyone expects is coming. There is nothing wrong with that expectation. If your case analysis was sufficient to the task, the story that you told in opening statement and develop through the testimony of your witnesses on direct examination has already laid a trail of bread crumbs leading to this moment in the cross examination of the witness. When you do this make certain that you have the available resources to impeach the witness if they stray from the good or bad facts that you previously identified through your case analysis. *This point is crucial. If the witness challenges you, and*

> **Maximizing the persuasive impact of answers on cross by:**
>
> (1) clustering together all of the facts that enhance and support the topic,
>
> (2) laying out the facts one question at a time leading up to your final point, and
>
> (3) identifying similar facts based upon your knowledge of human nature and then using them to make your final point.

the law allows you to respond to that challenge – you must. Failure to do so empowers the witness, weakens your theme and theory of the case and calls into question your credibility as an advocate in the eyes of the fact finder.

Consider the worst point identified by your case analysis. You must determine how you are going to handle this point. Can you put it into context in a way that neutralizes the point or explain it in a fashion that helps your theme and theory? If so you should include it in your cross and turn it to your advantage. If you can't put it into context or explain it then do not touch it in cross examination. The law of direct, cross and re-direct will not allow the opposing side to use it again on redirect if you leave it alone during cross. If it is not beneficial to your case it is bad enough that the jury heard it once, don't make the mistake of plowing ground that hurts you and then allowing the other side to cover it yet again on redirect.

If you are going to go after a "worst point" on cross make certain that you have a connection that is worthwhile to your theme and theory and strike that connection hard during your closing argument. If it does not meet the test of what you will say in closing then do not use it, even if you can explain it or put it in context. If you decide to go after one of these worst points on cross you should approach it by identifying a cluster of questions that you can ask to minimize, place in context or explain the worst fact. Do this to place the worst point in the best light possible as it relates to your theme and theory. To increase the persuasive nature of this type of cross examination you should break down the questions as simply as possible into one fact increments. This way you will control the witness and lead the jury to the conclusion that you want them to make about this particular issue. It is imperative that you have the supporting points to control the witness if they attempt to wander during your one fact build up.

After identifying the hard facts you must next organize the topics you need to cover in cross examination. The arrangement of topics must be effective and persuasive. Each topic either relates to a point in your favor or diminishes the opponent's position. The order of presentation is dictated by the impact you believe the witness should have. Determine if this particular witness has noncontroverted facts that support your theme and theory. If you have identified good facts that help, get them out of the witness quickly before you have to challenge and control the witness. Once you are forced to exert control over this witness through the use of pointed questions that may call for an impeachment that attacks the witness's character, you will never be able to go back and effectively get out the good facts that are not in controversy. A smooth cross examination can flow from the direct into the cross in a nonconfrontational manner - forcing the witness to agree with facts that help your case. Don't be the bad guy until the witness gives you a reason to be. When they later refuse to agree on facts that are in controversy, their disagreement and unwillingness to go your way will be emphasized for the jury. If you then have a set of facts to support your theory as to why they refuse to admit the truth as you see it, you can very successfully diminish the witness's credibility as to their entire testimony. Because cross is of an adverse witness, you may have to be creative to stay focused. You must stay organized, but let your cross be fluid to be most persuasive and get across the facts you want the jury to hear.

> **Starting the Cross:**
>
> Begin your cross exam with non-threatening or uncontroverted fact questions that support your theme and theory to keep the same momentum as on direct.

Remember that your primary goals during cross examination are to: (1) control the witness; (2) establish facts that bolster your Theme and Theory; and (3) establish facts that build up the credibility of your witnesses and diminish the credibility of your opponent's witnesses, including the witness being cross examined. One of the best ways to accomplish these goals is to begin the cross examination with a series of non threatening questions. Set a professional and businesslike tone with short, leading questions. Keep it to one fact per question. This gets the witness in a rhythm. They become used to answering "yes", "no", or some other short answer. This subconsciously conditions the witness to answer your questions without conflict. Make that first topic an easy one and it will give you witness control. This is a great place in the cross examination to identify those uncontroverted facts that this witness must admit to that support your case.

After you have identified how you will establish control of the witness next consider how to organize the rest of the cross. Whatever you choose, ***do not commit the cardinal sin of rehashing the direct examination by chronologically covering the same testimony that the jury just heard***. If you do the jury will hear it three times, once on direct, once on cross and then again on redirect. Any doubts they may have had about the veracity of the witness's version of events will be wiped away by this reverse use of the rule of threes. This is a common mistake made by most advocates. If the witness has practiced the direct so that they were fully prepared, why in the world would you think that asking them about it a second time would produce a result appreciably different from the direct? It will not, and you will look ineffective while your client's cause suffers.

Use the doctrine of primacy and recency to place your strongest points where the jury will be sure to notice them. This doctrine, when used in conjunction with a cross examination that is organized around substantive sections, each with a purpose and a connection to other sections, is very effective in producing witness control and a persuasive presentation of your case. If you decide to address weaker points during the cross examination, sandwich them between strong points to lend strength to them.

When attempting to cross effectively on these weak points, it helps to use the same words in your questions that are found in the previous statements of the witness. This narrowly defines the inquiry, and will prevent the witness from running for cover or explaining away the issue. This is particularly important when attempting to cross on a "weak point" that has the potential to hurt your case. You will only be able to effectively accomplish this if you prepare adequately. Using the witness's precise

> **Reasons for Cross Examination:**
>
> To elicit facts supporting your legal theory, factual theory or moral theme.
>
> To expose facts or bias that weakens your opponent's legal theory, factual theory or moral theme.
>
> To establish the credibility of your own witnesses or attack the credibility of opposing witnesses (when required by your legal theory, factual theory or moral theme).

words is a way to establish control and credibility. It puts the witness between a rock and a hard place – They either admit that you are correct or appear to prevaricate just because they don't want to admit the truth of what they said earlier. Either way you win.

3. Questioning Techniques: Leading, Closed-ended questions.

A closed-ended question is designed to identify the witnesses' knowledge of the facts or to challenge the credibility of a witness. The structure of the closed questions ensures that the witness can only respond with one possible truthful answer already known to the advocate posing the question. A variety of techniques are available to formulate Closed/Leading Questions. They include; (1) telling the witness instead of asking, (2) using taglines to force agreement by the witness, and (3) asking one fact questions.

> **Examples using taglines on cross:**
>
> "You got out of your car, didn't you?"
>
> "You closed the car door, correct?"
>
> "Isn't it true that you walked across the sidewalk?"

Two "styles" of phraseology are normally used when performing cross examination. The first is a leading question with a "tag" on the end of it. An example would be "You own a baseball bat, <u>don't you</u>." The "tag" is "don't you?" and takes many forms (e.g., didn't you?, isn't it true?, etc.). The other style is to drop the tag entirely. A leading question can still be asked with identical language without the tag. When you do this properly, there is a much greater emphasis on voice inflection. For example, "You own a baseball bat." Make this declarative sentence a leading question by placing the inflection on the word "bat."

Because leading questions are not truly inquisitive, voice inflection makes the critical difference. This is especially true with non-tag, leading questions. Thus, the question, "You own a baseball bat" can be leading or non-leading. If the inflection drops when saying "bat," it is leading. As discussed above, the falling inflection of the questioner does not reflect doubt or true inquisitiveness. If, however, your inflection rises on the "bat," it demonstrates the questioner is uncertain or at least inviting an explanation. A good cross-examination question marries proper form with tailored inflection. This skill comes with practice and is both fundamental and crucial.

When you make statements on cross examination that require agreement or disagreement by the witness, you establish a high degree of control and accuracy. The absence of taglines allows you to state the issue as though it is a fact that merely requires agreement or disagreement. This can be somewhat frightening and

> **Examples telling the witness instead of asking:**
>
> "You got out of your car."
>
> "You closed the car door."
>
> "You walked across the sidewalk."

awkward the first few times you try it. Some witnesses will stare at you blankly while others will ask, "Was that a question?" Do not allow this attempt at manipulation to work. Confidently look the witness in the eye and state your fact again, waiting in the silence for their response. They will respond – they have to. Count on that and use it to your benefit. Make certain that their response is in words and not through some sort of head gesture. The record of trial will not include head movement or grunts that may or may not indicate agreement or disagreement with your stated position. When witnesses try to avoid answering through noncommittal sounds or body movements, call them on it. Inform them that it is important that they speak clearly for the benefit of the court reporter and then make sure they do.

Each of these questioning techniques require agreement or disagreement by the witness. The difference between them is marked. First, your voice rises when you use a tagline. The rising inflection can indicate that you have some doubts as to the veracity of your position. It may invite the witness to challenge your position or imply to the jury that you really aren't sure if the question you are asking is correct. Second, the use of taglines can sometimes become an annoying habit. Jurors begin to listen for the taglines and keep count of how many times you may use the phrase during a given cross examination. Avoid anything that draws their attention away from the substantive issues you are raising. Since the purpose of your cross is to support your case theme and theory or to attack witness credibility, it is always substantive. Otherwise you should not be doing it. Finally, the choice of whether or not to use taglines is one of style and demeanor. Make certain that you experiment with both and then choose one that works for you.

Remember to ask one fact questions. Examples of one fact questions can be found throughout this chapter. Their use allows the advocate to control the witness and focus the inquiry so that it is understood by the jury. It becomes very difficult for a witness to prevaricate when only one factual issue is posed in the question. One fact questions are the building blocks that allow you to make your ultimate conclusion to the jury during closing argument when the witness is not there to argue about it.

Closed and leading questions are normally used during cross examination of adverse witnesses, when laying a foundation for the admissibility of evidence through any witness, or when the witness' demeanor or nature requires closed or leading questions in order to assist the finder of fact in getting to the testimony of the witness. This usually occurs when the witness has diminished communication ability due to their age or status as a victim of a violent crime. Always keep in mind that these Closed/Leading Questions are used to control witnesses, showcase the advocate, and to lay foundations for the admissibility of evidence. The focus for leading questions is on the advocate, not the witness. Closed questions allow the advocate to probe for logical weaknesses or fallacies in the witnesses' testimony, while also providing a vehicle to test the credibility of the witness through the crucible of cross examination.

B. THE LAW OF CROSS EXAMINATION.

Federal Rule of Evidence 611[5] addresses witnesses. It establishes the manner and scope of witness testimony, to include cross examination. While the form of cross examination as to questions is governed by Federal Rule of Evidence 611, many other evidentiary rules impact on your ability to refresh memory, attack the foundations of a witnesses testimony, admit character evidence, address prior criminal activity of a witness, or to impeach witnesses during cross examination. A complete understanding of the evidentiary rules governing these particular areas is necessary if you intend to develop into a complete advocate. Where appropriate in other chapters of this book the evidentiary rules that apply have been identified and explained. However, a course of study outside of trial advocacy is required to fully understand the procedural and substantive law that directly impacts what you can, and cannot, do at trial during cross examination. While such an inquiry is beyond the scope of this text and most trial advocacy courses, this chapter and others within

---

[5]   See Fed. Rule of Evid. 611, which can be found in Appendix III.

Article VI. Witnesses. Rule 611.
Mode and Order of Interrogation and Presentation:

(a) Control by court. The court shall exercise reasonable control over the mode and order of interrogating witnesses and presenting evidence so as to (1) make the interrogation and presentation effective for the ascertainment of the truth, (2) avoid needless consumption of time, and (3) protect witnesses from harassment or undue embarrassment.

(b) Scope of cross-examination. Cross-examination should be limited to the subject matter of the direct examination and matters affecting the credibility of the witness. The court may, in the exercise of discretion, permit inquiry into additional matters as if on direct examination.

(c) Leading questions. Leading questions should not be used on the direct examination of a witness except as may be necessary to develop the witness' testimony. Ordinarily leading questions should be permitted on cross-examination. When a party calls a hostile witness, an adverse party, or a witness identified with an adverse party, interrogation may be by leading questions.

Example 1: Federal Rule of Evidence 611 (2004).

Fundamental Trial Advocacy (FTA) provide you with a matrix of the common issues that arise during sections of a trial and the applicable rule of evidence at the end of each chapter. You should use these identified issues to supplement your personal study of the rules of evidence and procedure. Carefully combining your procedural knowledge with a well defined and practiced skill set will create superior advocacy.

Both the Federal Rules of Civil Procedure[6] and the Federal Rules of Criminal Procedure[7] specify that the preferred means of testimony is in open court unless otherwise specified by statute in criminal cases or at the discretion of the court, for good cause shown, in civil cases. The stated preference is for in court testimony, with a greater restriction upon that right in civil cases when the confrontation clause is not potentially at issue. The confrontation clause bars most, if not all contemporaneous transmissions of testimony in a criminal case. Advocates addressing the possibility of out of court testimony in a criminal case would do well to consider those cases that have attempted to work around the

---

[6] *See* Fed. R. Civ. P. 43(a).

[7] *See* Fed. R. Crim. P. 26.

confrontation clause, understanding that most litigation in this area has revolved around sexual assault and child victims.

This preference, if not requirement, for open court testimony ensures that cross examination allows the jury to not only hear the words spoken, but observe the physical responses to the questioning by both the lawyer and the witness. This includes the

> The jury measures witness and advocate credibility on substance, appearance and delivery.

location of the advocate in the courtroom, the different tones of voice they employ, and their physical reactions to the witness . The system understands that the jury measures credibility on substance, appearance and delivery. The superior advocate will consider each of those issues when employing the skill, law and art of cross examination.

Whenever witnesses testify one of the primary questions that the jury will ask is whom do they believe when the testimony contains disputed facts.

Examples of Procedural Rules:

Federal Rule of Criminal Procedure 26: "In every trial the testimony of witnesses must be taken in open court, unless otherwise provided by a statute or by rules adopted under 28 U.S.C. §§ 2072-2077.

Federal Rule of Civil Procedure 43(a): "Form. In every trial, the testimony of witnesses shall be taken in open court, unless a federal law, these rules, the Federal Rules of Evidence, or other rules adopted by the Supreme Court provide otherwise. The court may, for good cause shown in compelling circumstances and upon appropriate safeguards, permit presentation of testimony in open court by contemporaneous transmission from a different location."

Example 2: Federal Rule of Criminal Procedure 26, Federal Rule of Civil Procedure 43(a).

Most courts provide the jury with a set of instructions designed to assist them in sorting through issues of credibility and impeachment. These instructions are particularly important when dealing with a witness that has been subjected to a well developed cross examination. Issues of impeachment and credibility often go hand in hand in these situations. We will address impeachment instructions during the chapter on impeachment. Consider the credibility instruction provided here and how it might impact the planning and delivery of your cross examination, as well as the comments concerning credibility that you might make during closing arguments. The credibility of witnesses is a key issue during trial. Much of the use of cross examination revolves around assisting the jury in determining witness credibility. The superior advocate will use the information provided in the jury instructions on credibility to focus cross

---

1.01 General: Nature Of Case; Burden Of Proof; Duty Of Jury; Cautionary

....In deciding what the facts are, you may have to decide what testimony you believe and what testimony you do not believe. You may believe all of what a witness says, or only part of it, or none of it. In deciding what testimony to believe, consider the witnesses' intelligence, their opportunity to have seen or heard the things they testify about, their memories, any motives they may have for testifying a certain way, their manner while testifying, whether they said something different at an earlier time, the general reasonableness of their testimony and the extent to which their testimony is consistent with other evidence that you believe. Do not allow sympathy or prejudice to influence you. The law demands of you a just verdict, unaffected by anything except the evidence, your common sense, and the law as I give it to you.

Example 4: Excerpts from Model Civ. Jury Instr. 8th Cir. 1.01 (2005).

---

examination on exposing those issues the court will identify as impacting credibility.

Now that we have reviewed the three primary purposes of cross examination, the relevant law lets us turn our attention to developing effective cross examinations that support our factual theory, legal theory and moral themes.

C. THE ART OF CROSS EXAMINATION.

1. Fundamental Precepts.

While every cross examination is unique, there are certain fundamental precepts that counsel should always consider following when developing their cross examinations. They include:

"Cross-examination is a commando raid, not the invasion of Europe!"[8] The idea is to limit the number of points sought from each witness in order to maximize the effectiveness of those points that you do make. It serves as a screen to force advocates to truly consider the quality of what they are asking and the answers they expect to get. Too much information from one witness can obscure the facts from the testimony that may very well address your "Hard Questions of Fact" for the jury. Trying to cross a witness on every fact loses impact and frankly bores the fact finder, neither result you desire. Limit the issues you will address with a particular witness if you know important information may also be obtained from other witnesses. On the other hand, if you can cluster important points with more than one witness consider the rule of threes and the theories of primacy and recency when deciding what to keep and what to save for another witness. Only you will know what the most important facts are from your case analysis.

Use Primacy and Recency. Make your strongest points at the beginning and end of cross, sandwiching your less important points in the middle. When doing this consider if the need to initially establish control through questioning on uncontroverted facts is something that is sufficiently important to put up front in the cross.

Avoid the Ultimate Question! More than one advocate has snatched defeat from the jaws of victory by ruining a successful cross-exam when they erroneously believed that the witness would admit the critical, ultimate fact at issue. They reach for the Perry Mason or Matlock moment and fall, usually flat on their face. AVOID this temptation. While some counsel enjoy attacking on this point during cross,[9] the safer course for most advocates it to save that ultimate question for closing argument. There you will be able to argue the inference without giving the witness a chance to explain it away. Don't be greedy because you may bite off more than you can chew on something that gives you a terminal case of indigestion!

Single fact questions - No expansive narratives. Questions should be short, single-fact, and leading. Lead the witness, and the jury, to a desired response. Do not allow the witness to give expansive narratives. There is seldom a place

---

[8] See Irving Younger, The 10 Commandments of Cross Examination, available at NITA.org.

[9] See Terry McCarthy's lectures on the Science of Cross Examination.

for "How" or "Why" or "Tell the court" lines of questioning. When you ask that question you are effectively turning over control to the witness. . If you have hurt them or insulted them during the cross they are waiting for the chance to get even, don't give it to them.

Vary your questioning techniques! As we discussed previously, you can judiciously use tags to direct the questioning, but prefacing every question with "Isn't it true?" or ending every question with "wouldn't you agree?" can be very distracting. When used sparingly, taglines will help maintain control of the witness, the flow of cross examination and the topics discussed. The key word being sparingly.

Do not play with fire. Normally you should not ask questions to which you do not know the answer. Doing so places you in a position where you are at the mercy of a witness that has been called by the opposing side and is normally not inclined to assist you in your case. On rare occasions it may be necessary to ask the question for which you do not know the answer. If the worst possible answer to the question you are posing will leave you in a position that is not any worse than your current one then take the plunge. Sometimes the practice of law requires you at times to ask questions for which you do not know the answer. The proper methodology is to limit those instances, and proceed carefully when you must go fishing for information.

Develop a toolbox of control techniques. Canned responses that allow you to control hostile witnesses, are as simple as, "perhaps you didn't hear my question," "so the answer is yes," "maybe you could answer my question this time," "my question was ...", "I appreciate that you needed to say that, now could you please answer the question that I asked" and the time honored classic, "So we can agree that…" However, using these control techniques too liberally can also be distracting. Use them strategically to control an adverse witness. Never ask the judge to help you control the witness, when you do, you have just admitted to the entire room that you need assistance. Only do this when the witness's demeanor and actions have clearly established that they are not being reasonable or fair. Seek the judge's assistance only as a last resort.

2. Combining Skill with Art - Effective Crosses.

Cross examination is a goal-oriented process designed to accomplish one or more of three primary purposes, introducing a new fact to the jury, weakening or highlighting a fact that has already been introduced, or weakening or strengthening the credibility of a witness. A well done cross-examination consists of *selective* attacks on specific areas of the witness's testimony. Do not retell the whole thing again through cross examination. In order to accomplish these goals you should always apply three primary rules to cross examination.

The best way to ensure that you only address one fact with each question is to break your questions down into their smallest parts. Simple questions do not leave the witness with any option other than to answer or be obstructive. Either decision by the witness will be to your benefit. Simplicity destroys witness escape routes, builds precision, and ensures control by the advocate. This basic premise must be followed. One fact questions are the golden standard for cross-examination. When creating these questions use descriptive words that create a picture in the jury's mind. Consider the following:

> **Initial Question:**
>
> You saw a woman lying in a parking lot?

A better arrangement of short, one fact questions using simple leading questions, descriptive statements, while adding one new fact at a time would be:

> You saw a woman <u>hit by a car</u>?
> She was struck <u>by a Cadillac Escalade</u>?
> The woman was <u>lying on the asphalt</u>?
> In the parking lot?

Do not forget that you are not Clarence Darrow, Max Stern or Johnnie Cochran. Use leading questions on cross-examination. Leading questions give you control. They are questions that *declare* the answer. The best leading questions are short declarative statements of fact - with a "?" mark at the end. Look at the difference between these examples:

Good: Do you like to drink?

Better: You like to drink?

Best: You drink? *Followed by*: You like it?

Using a logical progression to reach a specific goal on cross-examination is the best construct for educating the jury. It allows you to forecast issues, foreshadow potential answers and create a sense of tension and finality as you lead them to the one unalterable conclusion posited by your logically progressing, one fact leading questions. In the eyes of others, a logical questioning progression makes the goal of the questions appear logically true. It also greatly reduces the witness's ability to evade. Finally it allows you to penalize the witness through sarcasm, impeachment and lack of credibility when they attempt to evade the logical progression of your questions.

An excellent way to create logical progression is to view your cross-examination as a series of vignettes, each with their own internal goal. Each of these vignettes is a *controlled* inquiry into a specific area. They are a series of questions designed to establish a *goal question*. You use these vignettes to advance your theory of the case one goal at a time. Imagine them as an inverted triangle, with the point oriented on the final goal question that everyone knows is coming.

In order to create functional vignettes you must identify your goal question, review all materials to see how many different ways you can prove the goal question, and then select the witness or witnesses that you should cross examine on that particular goal. When creating the structure of those questions, first move backwards in the sequence of questions until you reach a general point where the witness must agree with the question posed. From that starting point, draft a series of questions leading to the goal. Those questions should be general initially, but as the series of questions progress they should become increasingly specific in nature, right up to the goal question.

The progression creates context and makes the goal fact more persuasive. By using a series of questions, you support the goal fact with as much detail and supporting facts as you can to ensure the goal fact is believed and understood.

Single questions on a goal fact sacrifice the opportunity to surround the goal question with other questions that establish its veracity. Consider the following goal question, "The truck was blue?" You could handle it with a single fact leading question and do an adequate job of getting the information out, but it lacks emphasis. The use of simple, directed, supporting, facts changes the entire tenor of the goal question and the impact it will have on the jury. Consider how such a vignette could work:

> You were standing on the corner?
>
> The truck drove past you?
>
> The truck drove within five feet of you:
>
> It was about 3:00 PM?
>
> The sun was shining?
>
> You got a good look at the truck?
>
> You are certain of its color?
>
> **Goal question:** The truck was blue?

Sometimes it may be necessary to group vignettes together to properly lay the foundation for a series of goal questions that relate to one another. Use one goal question for each vignette and then group the related vignettes together to increase their effectiveness in explaining the complex issue. Start with the most general vignette first and then work toward the most specific. In the following examples a witness is being impeached on prior convictions and motive to fabricate. An adequate impeachment would include the following:

> Mr. Jones, you've been convicted of a felony?
>
> You were convicted of robbery?
>
> You pled guilty in exchange for a five-year deal?
>
> As part of the deal you agreed to testify against Mr. Smith?

A better impeachment would identify the following Goal Questions and begin to paint some picture of what happened. Consider the series of questions that take the time to paint a better picture. Note how the advocate here takes the facts that lead to the goal questions and uses them to form the vignette.

The best impeachment would create vignettes on each goal question and string them together in the cross. The first vignette should address the goal question - "You are an armed robber?" The difference between one question and this series of questions outlined below, although both lead to the same destination, is striking. One is conclusory and gets a fact before the jury. The second provides a wealth of information that paints a more complete picture for the jury. The persuasiveness of the second cross examination when compared to the first workmanlike and adequate

> You are an armed robber?
>
> You got caught red handed?
>
> You were facing 15 years confinement?
>
> You cut a deal?
>
> After the deal, you were looking at 5 years confinement?
>
> You became a cooperating witness?
>
> That was part of the deal?

> On July 15th you needed some money?
>
> So you picked up your gun?
>
> Your gun is a .44 magnum revolver?
>
> Your .44 was loaded?
>
> You went to the quick mart?
>
> You pointed your loaded .44 at the clerk?
>
> You told her to give you the money?
>
> You told her you'd kill her if she didn't?
>
> She was pregnant?
>
> She was very scared?
>
> She gave you the money?
>
> So you didn't kill her?
>
> You ran out of the quick mart?
>
> Goal Question: **"You are an armed robber?"**

goal question is striking.

Now let us create an effective cross examination for the second vignette goal question of "You got caught red handed?"

> On July 15th you needed some money?
>
> So you picked up your gun?
>
> Your gun is a .44 magnum revolver?
>
> Your .44 was loaded?
>
> You went to the quick mart?
>
> You pointed your loaded .44 at the clerk?
>
> You told her to give you the money?
>
> You told her you'd kill her if she didn't?
>
> She was pregnant?
>
> She was very scared?
>
> She gave you the money?
>
> So you didn't kill her?
>
> You ran out of the quick mart?
>
> Goal Question: **"You are an armed robber?"**

Next we will move on to our third vignette goal question of "You were facing 15 years confinement?"

> After being caught red handed, you saw an attorney?
>
> You were charged with armed robbery?
>
> You knew you were in a lot of trouble?
>
> Goal Question: **"You knew you were facing 15 years confinement?"**

This ability to identify proper vignettes with ultimate goal questions must include relating those goal questions to your theme and theory and then organizing them in sets that create synergy. It is the most fundamental skill of cross examination. When sequencing your vignettes and goal questions into a cohesive whole there are certain issues that you must consider. They include:

Checklist for sequencing your cross examination:

- Do not use chronological order in confrontational cross-examinations.
- Avoid chronological order in informational cross-examinations.
- Lay your theme early and often.
- Close cross-examination with a theme vignette.
- When attacking credibility, attack in the first vignette.
- Show bias, interest, or motive early in the cross-examination.
- End with a power vignette.
- Develop risky areas only after establishing control of the witness through safe vignettes.
- Never lead or end with a risky vignette.
- If you have more than one impeachment vignette, use the cleanest first.
- Disperse impeachment vignettes throughout the cross-examination.
- When expecting a no answer to one goal question, precede that chapter with a sure 'yes' answer.
- Bundle vignettes that need to be done together in order to complete a coherent picture of a single event.
- Prepared vignettes countering the power of the opponent's case are best performed in the middle of cross-examination.

Once you have decided upon the structure of your vignettes you must next consider the actual form of the questioning. Looping is a questioning technique designed to highlight important facts from a previous question while addressing an additional fact in the current question. The technique establishes a desired

---

The car was speeding?

The speeding car drove through the intersection?

The speeding car passed the children and hit the crossing guard?

fact or phrase, uses that fact within the next leading question, and then moves to a different subject.

You can take the looping technique and use it to combine different one fact questions into one question. Use this to link two facts together or to contrast one fact against another. This example addresses height differences as it relates to an alleged assault. The two facts you wish to establish are that (1) Mr. Smith is six-foot-four, and (2) Mr. Saunders is five-foot-six?

You can effectively loop fact 1 and fact 2 into a question that contrasts the differences between them. For example:

> Six-foot-four Mr. Smith beat five-foot-six Mr. Saunders?
>
> Six-foot-four Mr. Smith beat five-foot-six Mr. Saunders with his fists?
>
> Six-foot-four Mr. Smith beat five-foot-six Mr. Saunders with his fists until he was unconscious?

Use looping to highlight and contrast inconsistent facts. Consider the facts that (1) Mr. Connors is your friend, and (2) Mr. Connors stole $100 from you. The contrasting question could be:

> Mr. Connors is your friend, but he stole $100 from you?

Advocates also create spontaneous looping questions. These use the advocate's listening skills to extract useful words or phrases from the witness's answer and then place them into the next question. This is an excellent tool for controlling a difficult witness. It reveals the witness's character, and can create a dynamic where the advocate can dominate. It can be either a single or double loop construct. Simply listen to any answer from the witness that is not a yes or no. Then lift the useful word, usefulness being defined as assisting in the Theme or Theory of your case, and make it part of the next question. Then move safely to a different subject.

The following example of spontaneous looping occurs in a case addressing an alleged acquaintance rape in the victim's condo. While this type of subject is sensitive in nature and sometimes difficult to deal with, it is necessary to consider examples such as this if we are truly to become the best advocate that we can be. These cases go to trial and the victims of such crimes are poorly served when we lack the courage to develop the skills necessary to deal with them. Nonetheless, please be aware that the following questions deal with sexual misconduct and may be found disturbing to some. The advocate here has three goals; (1) show that the victim did not lock her door when she went to bed, (2) the victim had previously had consensual intercourse with the accused on five separate occasions, and (3) the accused told the victim that he would be back later that night. Look at how the vignettes and goal questions, along with the responses from the witness, allow for spontaneous looping that supports the theme and theory of the case.

First goal question – "The victim didn't lock her door when going to bed."

> Q: You live in the condo?
> A: *Yes.*

> Q: Both men and women live in your condo?
> A: *Yes.*

> Q: You usually lock the door when you go to bed?
> A: *Yes.*

> Q: The accused didn't break into your room on July 1st?
> A: *No.*

> Q: **"You didn't lock your door when you went to bed?"**
> A: *No.*

Second goal question – "You've had consensual intercourse with the accused, in your condo, on five previous and separate occasions."

> Q: He had been to your Condo before that night?
> A: Yes.

> Q: You've had consensual sexual intercourse with the accused before

July 1st?

A: Yes.

Q: Five times before?

A: Yes.

Q: Always in your condo?

A: Yes.

Q: **"You've had consensual intercourse with the accused in your condo on five previous and separate occasions?"**

A: Yes, but *our relationship was over.*

The alleged victim has given an answer that now allows the advocate to combine a spontaneous loop with the third goal question – "When he left, he told you he would be back later?"

Q: *Your relationship was over, but* he was in your condo earlier that evening?

A: Yes.

Q: At about 6:00 PM?

A: Yes.

Q: *Your relationship was over, but* he stayed for about 45 minutes?

A: Yes.

Q: *Your relationship was over, but* you talked to each other for 45 minutes?

A: Yes.

Goal Question: ***"Your relationship was over, but* when he left, he told you he would be back later?"**

A: Yes.

Now that the advocate has combined the spontaneous loop with their third goal question it is time to exploit them for maximum effect.

Q: *Your relationship was over, but* he came to your room that evening?

A: Yes.

Q: *Your relationship was over, but* when he left, he told you he would return?

A: Yes.

Q: *Your relationship was over, but* you went to bed when you were expecting him to return?

A: Yes.

Q: *Your relationship was over, but* you didn't lock the door when you went to bed?

A: No.

The use of vignettes, grouping strategies and looping in this fashion creates a cross examination that is controlled, persuasive and effective. Now that we have discussed what to ask and when to ask it, let us talk about where you should be located when you ask it. A new advocate may be uncomfortable with the repetetive nature of these questions, and fear an objection. The questions should be sufficiently dissimilar to avoid or defeat an "asked and answered" objection.

3. Physical Presence.

Words are powerful in the courtroom, but body position can create an additional opportunity for advocacy. During direct examination we discussed standing at the end of the jury box, attempting to become the "13th juror" while focusing the attention of the jury on the witness. The position of the advocate during cross examination is designed to accomplish exactly the opposite effect. Now we want the attention of they jury to be on the advocate. Some claim that advocates are testifying during cross examination. That is not correct. Your are positing statements of fact that the witness verifies or denies. The witness's response determines the use of what you ask, not the fact that you said it. Conceptulizing cross examination as though the advocate is testifying is a sloppy mechanism that leads to incorrect use of any answers given by the witness during your closing argument. Be creative but dilligent and your crosses will sing with the theme and theory of your case.

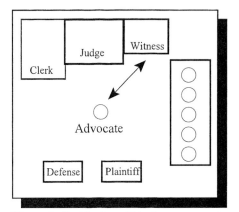

Figure 1 - Positioning within the courtroom to focus jury attention on the advocate.

Questions from the location identified in Figure 1 are by their very nature designed to focus the attention of the jury on the advocate and the tension between the advocate and the witness. When you stand here you have assumed a position of authority with the witness. All eyes are on you. Move closer to the witness question by question, exerting the appearance of physical dominance, to the extent allowed by local rules, or you can rhetorically turn to the jury as you ask your goal question, looking them directly in the eyes as you gauge their response to the witness's answer. From this position you can make whatever movement is necessary depending upon the feel within the courtroom.

3. Examples of a Cross Examinaton.

The following excerpt is from the cross examination of a police officer in a drug case. It is considered by most to be an adequate cross designed to point out issues supporting a defense theory of biased police work. After studying this chapter you may not longer find this particular cross examination to be as adequate as others might. Read through this cross think about the elements of a superior cross examination you have learned. Consider carefully where this cross follows the advice of this text and where it does not. If you were conducting the cross examination of this detective, what changes might you make? Why? When you can answer those questions correctly, you are ready to apply the most important process when creating superior cross examinations–your own understanding of human nature. You will also be capable of cross examining in a much clearer and developed fashion than the advocate below.

Q: Officer, in the course of the work that you do you prepare police reports?
A: Yes.

Q: And preparing police reports is part of your responsibilities as a law enforcement officer?
A: Yes.

Q: And when you first go to the police academy one of the things you learn is how to write police reports?

A: They give us a basic information on how to prepare a report, yes.

Q: Writing police reports is important?

A: Yes.

Q: Police reports are an official record of what happened?

A: Yes.

Q: And you use police reports to refresh your recollection?

A: That's correct.

Q: And other law enforcement officers involved with the same case also use police reports for background?

A: Yes.

Q: And, in fact, you've been using and are using a police report in this particular case?

A: Yes.

Q: And that would be a report which you wrote?

A: That's correct.

Q: It's important for police reports to be accurate?

A: Yes.

Q: It's important for police reports to have all significant details?

A: Yes.

Q: And the report that you prepared was accurate?

A: Yes.

Q: The report that you prepared had all significant details?

A: Yes.

Q: Officer --

DEFENSE: May I approach the witness, your Honor?

THE COURT: Of course.

Q: I'm going to show you what's been marked as exhibit D1- for

identification. I ask if you would please look at it and tell the jury whether that, in fact, is a copy of the police report that you prepared in this matter?
A: Yes.

Q: Okay. And that's a copy of the same item that you've been using to refresh your own recollection?
A: Yes.

Q: You were on the Anti-crime Unit for five years?
A: Yes, sir.

Q: Did you like it?
A: Yes.

Q: How did you -- how does it compare with your present assignment?
A: I don't understand the question how does it compare?

Q: Did you like it better or did you -- do you like your present assignment better?
A: Both jobs I'm a policeman. I love being a policeman. Wherever they put me I'll have fun.

Q: You've -- you've made over one thousand arrests?
A: Yes.

Q: How do you feel about the people when you have to arrest them?
A: My inside feelings?

Q: Your inside feelings?
A: Part of the job.

Q: Just part of the job?
A: Yes.

Q: You don't like them, you don't dislike them?
A: No.

Q: Just doing your job?
A: That's correct.

Q: And it's not your job to like people that are involved with drugs?
A: What was that question again?

Q: It's not part of your job to like people that are involved with drugs?
A: If they're cooperative with me, if they sell drugs, if they're cooperative and friendly towards me I have no problem with that.

Q: But it's not your job to like them, would you agree with that?
A: No, it's part of my job to be fair and -- and like them. I mean they're doing something wrong they're doing something wrong, that doesn't -- I don't take it personally.

Q: Okay. It's not your job to dislike them?
A: Correct.
Q: You agree?
A: Correct.

Q: And it is not your job to like them either?
A: (Nods.)

Q: Your job is to enforce the law, do you agree?
A: Yes.

Q: Okay. And when you see a crime being committed you do your job?
A: That's correct.

Q: And on December 4th, you were doing your job?
A: Yes.

Q: You were enforcing the law?
A: Yes.

Q: And you started your surveillance around 11:30 in the morning?
A: That's correct.

Q: The area of your surveillance was 15th Cavalier Street?
A: Yes.
Q: You saw Jamie Roberts?
A: Yes.

Q: She was standing in the middle of the road?
A: Yes.

Q: Cheryl Horton comes along?

A: Yes.

Q: Cheryl Horton goes up to Jamie Roberts?
A: Yes. I'm not sure if you're continuing your sentence or asking me a question.

Q: No. That's a question?
A: Okay. Yes.

Q: Okay.
A: All right.

Q: And they converse?
A: Yes.

Q: That's the way you described it in your report?
A: Yes.

Q: In fact, that just means they talked?
A: That's correct.

Q: Okay. And then you see Cheryl and Jamie walk to the grocery store that you put on that diagram?
A: Yes.

Q: They walked together?
A: Yes.

Q: And then they walked back to Cavalier Street – 15ᵗʰ Cavalier Street?
A: Correct.

Q: They walk back together?
A: Yes.

Q: And Jamie pulls a packet of heroin from her pocket?
A: That's correct.

Q: And Jamie gives the heroin to Cheryl?
A: That's correct.

Q: And Cheryl pays Jamie for the heroin?
A: Yes.

Q: And then Cheryl walks to a brown vehicle?
A: That's correct.

Q: And at that point Cheryl still has the heroin that she just got from Jamie?
A: That's correct.

Q: And Cheryl goes inside the brown vehicle?
A: Yes.

Q: And at that point Cheryl still has the heroin that she got from Jamie?
A: Yes.

Q: And Cheryl sits down inside the brown vehicle?
A: Yes.

Q: And at that point Cheryl still has the heroin that she got from Jamie?
A: Yes.

Q: And then you see Cheryl doing the heroin that she had just purchased?
A: Yes.

Q: And doing means using?
A: Yes.

Q: And at that point Cheryl still has the heroin?
A: Yes.

Q: She has the heroin in her hands and she's putting it into her body?
A: That's correct.

Q: And you saw her doing that?
A: Yes.

Q: And there's no doubt in your mind?
A: No.

Q: And then Cheryl moves to the car where Betty Rogers is?
A: Yes.

Q: And -- and Jamie Roberts shows Cheryl more packets of heroin?
A: That's correct.

Q: Back up units arrive?
A: Yes.

Q: And one of the back up personnel is Lieutenant Schuster?
A: That's correct.
Q: And at some point in time either then or later on you learn that Roberts told Schuster that Roberts was selling the heroin for Betty Rogers?
A: Yes.

Q: And everyone that you've been talking about is arrested and brought to headquarters?
A: Yes.

Q: And Cheryl Horton is charged with loitering?
A: I believe so, yes.

Q: The charge against Cheryl Horton, loitering, is a disorderly person's offense?
A: That's correct.

Q: Disorderly person's offense means it is not indictable?
A: That's correct.

Q: Since it's a disorderly person's offense it's something that would never be presented to a grand jury?
A: That's correct.

Q: It's something that would be handled in the Municipal Court of whatever town the incident happened?
A: Yes.

Q: And this incident happened in New Brunswick?
A: Yes.

Q: So this is an incident that would be handled for Cheryl Horton in the New Brunswick Municipal Court?
A: Yes.

Q: By the way, officer, whatever happened to this loitering complaint that you signed against Cheryl Horton?
A: I don't recall.

Q: Was it ever disposed of?
A: I'm not sure. I would have to check our city records.

Q: Were you ever called upon to testify in the matter?
A: I don't recall so, no.

Q: If you had testified would you remember?
A: Probably not. Not if it was -- this -- this was in 1994 and we're in 1997 now and we have a lot of municipal cases. Just to remember one case would be -- you know -- hard to do.

Q: Now, in your report I believe you mentioned that Jamie -- strike that. The car that Betty Rogers was sitting in, that was a Cougar, correct?
A: Yes.

Q: It was a blue Cougar?
A: That's correct.

Q: And Betty Rogers was sitting in the passenger seat of that car?
A: That's correct.
Q: And Jamie Roberts came to that car that you could tell a total of three times, is that correct?
A: Yes.

Q: And on one of these occasions Betty Rogers collects some cash from Jamie Roberts?
A: Yes.

Q: And at the same time Betty Rogers gives heroin to Ms. Roberts?
A: Yes.

Q: And Ms. Roberts returns to the middle of the street?
A: Yes.

Q: And she sells a packet, Roberts sells a packet to Chris Dupree?
A: Yes.

Q: And then Jamie Roberts returns to the blue Cougar?
A: Yes.

Q: This would be her second visit?

A: I believe so.

Q: And Betty Rogers is still in the passenger seat?
A: Yes.

Q: And Betty Rogers collects cash?
A: Yes.
Q: And then Betty Rogers leaves the car to get change for Ms. Roberts?
A: Yes.

Q: And until this point Betty Rogers has been sitting in the passenger seat?
A: Yes.

Q: Now, officer, at some point in time you became aware that Betty Rogers was asked for permission to search the car that she was in?
A: I didn't receive that. I was still in my surveillance spot.

Q: All right. But at some point in time someone asked her for permission to search the car?
A: I'm not sure. I was in the surveillance spot. I don't know of any conversation on the street.

Q: You don't know whether she was asked for permission to search the car?
A: No.

Q: Are you aware of the fact that her car was searched?
A: No.

Q: Officer, do you remember being called in front of the Middlesex County grand jury to testify in this case?
A: Yes. I have the transcript in front of me.

Q: And the grand jury sits in the administration building in New Brunswick?
A: Yes.

Q: The administration building is right next to this courthouse?
A: Yes.

Q: And you go up I believe it's the 10th floor?
A: 10th.

Q: 10th floor?

A: Yes.

Q: And you indicate that you have a transcript of your testimony in front of the grand jury?
A: Yes.

DEFENSE: May I approach the witness, your Honor?
THE COURT: Yes.

Q: Officer, I'm showing you what's been marked for identification as D2- and I ask if you would please look at it and see if that is another copy of the same transcript of your testimony?
A: Yes.

Q: You recognize that?
A: Yes.

Q: Do you have your own copy that you can refer to?
A: Yes.

Q: Officer, if you would, please turn to page nine of your grand jury transcript. Are you there, officer?
A: Yes.

Q: And do you agree that page nine is one of the pages with your own testimony on it?
A: Yes.

Q: Do you see, officer, at line sixteen there's a question, "Was the car searched?" And your answer at line seventeen is "Yes."?
A: Yes.

Q: And do you see, officer, at line eighteen there is a question, "Was there any more found in it?" And your answer is "No, she gave consent, Betty Rogers gave consent to search the car."?
A: Yes.

Q: That's your answer?
A: Yes.

Q: Okay?
A: This refreshes my memory.

Q: Thank you. Now, my earlier questions, officer, related to your preparation of criminal investigation -- of police reports, correct?
A: Yes.

Q: And one of the types of police reports that you prepare is called a criminal investigation report?
A: Yes.

Q: And that's the same report that we have been -- that you've been using here to refresh your recollection?
A: That's correct.

Q: And that's the same report that was marked for identification in this case as –
STATE: D1.

Q: -- as D1? This is D1 your criminal investigation report?
A: Yes.

Q: Okay. And you have a copy of D1- in front of you right now?
A: I have the continuation page, yes.

Q: The continuation page is the page that has the entire narrative?
A: That's correct.
Q: Now, when you've finished preparing a criminal investigation report, officer, if you're not satisfied with what it says you can make changes to it, can't you?
A: Yes.

Q: And if you're not satisfied with it you can change it to say whatever you think it should say?
A: The facts of the case, yes.

Q: Your criminal investigation report, D1-contained all the significant information in this case?
A: Yes.

Q: And there is no reference in D1- to your finding drugs -- to anyone finding drug paraphernalia on the person of Betty Rogers?
A: No.

Q: And if you or any of your fellow officers had found drug paraphernalia on the person of Betty Rogers you would have considered that significant to the case?
A: Yes.

Q: And if you had found paraphernalia on the person of Betty Rogers you would have put that in your report?
A: Yes.

Q: There's no reference in the report to anyone finding drug paraphernalia in the car that Betty Rogers was in?
A: No.

Q: This is the same car that with your memory now refreshed you recall was, in fact, searched?
A: Yes.

Q: By the way, was it you that searched the car, officer?
A: No.

Q: You know who did it?
A: No.

Q: If drug paraphernalia had been found in the car of Betty Rogers that would have been significant to the case?
A: Yes.

Q: And if you became aware that drug paraphernalia had been found in Betty Rogers's car that would have been in your police report?
A: Yes.

Q: You recovered three packets of heroin plus an empty, is that correct?
A: Yes.
Q: And it's your testimony that all four of these items that you recovered came from Betty Rogers?
A: Yes.

Q: You never checked to see whether any of those packets had latent fingerprints of Betty Rogers?
A: No.

Q: You never tried to check to see whether any of those packets had latent fingerprints of Betty Rogers?

A: No.

Q: You never submitted the packets to a fingerprint detective to see whether they held the latent prints of Betty Rogers?

A: No.

D. RELEVANT EVIDENTIARY AND PROFESSIONAL RESPONSIBILITY RULES.

1. Evidentiary Rule Matrix.

Table 1 serves as a starting point for additional inquiry into the relationships between specific tasks on cross examination and the rules of evidence. Your case analysis should assist you in identifying when these particular issues will arise. You should use the table to review your knowledge of the evidentiary rule so that you can include that in your legal theory of the case. Particular attention should be paid to understanding the fundamental rules concerning impeachment and their interactions with the other rules of evidence.

Issue Arising During Cross Examination	Applicable Federal Rule of Evidence
Character traits of the victim or accused	404(a), 404(b), 405
Character of a witness for truthfulness	608
Out of court statements offered for the truth of the matter asserted therein (hearsay)	801 - 807
Offering evidence of other crimes, wrongs & acts. (FTA chapter 10).	404(b)
Prior convictions of a witness. (FTA chapter 10).	609
Legal relevancy - Is the probative value substantially outweighed by the danger of unfair prejudice et al.	403
Are the questions logically relevant.	401, 402
Competency of a witness.	610
Personal knowledge of the witness.	602
Questioning witnesses.	611, 614

Table 1 - Potential Evidentiary Rules Applicable During Cross Examination

2. Professional Responsibility Rule Matrix.

Table 2 serves as a starting point for additional inquiry into the potential professional responsibility issues that are implicated during cross examination. Counsel must ensure that they do not cross certain lines when investigating cases, preparing witnesses and performing cross. The same issues also exist when listening to an opposing counsel's cross examination. You must pay particular attention to your jurisditions interpretation and application of the fairness towards opposing counsel rule found in 3.4. A thorough grasp of these issues will assist you in determing whether your conduct and that of your opponent's raise any ethical issues. Your case analysis should help in identifying when these particular issues will arise. You should use the table to review your

Issue Arising During Cross Examination	Applicable Rule of Professional Responsibility**
(a)(1-3) A lawyer must not offer false evidence.	**RULE 3.3 CANDOR TOWARD THE TRIBUNAL**
(e) A lawyer must not allude to any matter that she does not reasonably believe is relevant or that will not be supported by admissible evidence. She must not assert personal knowledge of facts in issue and never state a personal opinion as to justness of a cause, the credibility of a witness, the culpability of a civil litigant or the guilt or innocence of the defendant.	**RULE 3.4 FAIRNESS TO OPPOSING PARTY AND COUNSEL**
(a) A lawyer must not illegally seek to influence a judge, juror, prospective juror or other official. (d) A lawyer must not intentionally disrupt the court and must conduct herself with respect for the court.	**RULE 3.5 IMPARTIALITY AND DECORUM OF THE TRIBUNAL**
(a) A lawyer must not attempt to be an advocate and witness in the same trial (with some limited exceptions).	**RULE 3.7 LAWYER AS WITNESS**

Table 2 - Most Prevalent Professional Conduct Rules during Cross Examination

knowledge of the ethical rules so that you can include them when planning cross examinations.

*** Unless otherwise specifically indicated all professional conduct rules referenced are taken from the Delaware Supreme Court's professional responsibility rules. Those rules are almost identical to the model rules promulgated by the American Bar Association and are public domain documents.*

Points to Ponder...

1. If cross examination is the greatest legal engine ever created for discovering the truth, why is it necessary to control the means and methods of cross examination through FRE 611 to avoid witness embarrassment? Isn't the purpose of an effective cross examination often witness embarrassment and the destruction of credibility?

2. What are the advantages of a chronological cross examination? What are the disadvantages?

3. If cross examination is designed to get to the truth then why do trial advocacy professors teach that the focus of cross is the attorney? Does this make sense?

CHAPTER SEVEN
EXHIBITS

"To see sad sights moves more than to hear them told."[1]

A. THE SKILL OF EXHIBITS.

"Ours is the age of visual media. A whole generation of Americans has been raised and educated primarily by seeing."[2]

In order to effectively learn to handle exhibits at trial you must first understand that evidence offered at trial falls into three categories - (1) testimonial, (2) demonstrative, and (3) real. Real evidence consists of two further sub-categories, (1) fungible and (2) non-fungible. The first step in determining your foundational requirements for admissibility is to identify the type of evidence you intend to offer. The required foundation questions depend on the type of evidence offered and the purpose of the offered evidence. Categorizing the evidence is the single most important step in this process. Each type of evidence must be properly authenticated and admitted through the testimony of a sponsoring witness. Foundational requirements are derived from the evidentiary rules addressing each particular type of evidence. The foundation must be "laid" through the questions of the offering counsel and the responses of the witness. An improper foundation will prompt an objection and may prevent the offered evidence from being accepted by the court. The type of evidentiary objections that must be overcome are derived from the nature of the evidence counsel is seeking to admit, the foundational questions asked, and the responses received. Finally, sometimes evidence may fall into more than one category. Counsel must properly offer the evidence to ensure that they can use it for their intended purpose. This becomes important during jury deliberations since most jurisdictions do not allow demonstrative evidence back into the jury

---

[1]WILLIAM SHAKESPEARE, THE RAPE OF LUCRECE. *See* http://www.bartleby.com/70/49.html

[2] *See* THOMAS MAUET, TRIAL TECHNIQUES, (Aspen Publishers, Inc. 6th ed. 2002).

deliberation room.

SEVEN FUNDAMENTAL PRINCIPLES WHEN DEALING WITH EXHIBITS:

Use them. Opening, direct, cross, and closing.

Know the type of exhibit you have and the limitations on their use.

Identify your foundational requirements early and have them on hand in the courtroom for reference.

Practice, practice, practice.

Script foundations for persuasive impact as well as legal requirements.

Do not be afraid to voir dire.

BARPH when necessary.

Attorneys are required to ask foundational questions in order to establish the admissibility of evidence. These foundational questions are derived from the common law, evidentiary law and local court practices. They serve as a short cut for answering challenges to a piece of evidence based upon potential objections. Foundational questions normally deal with best evidence issues, authenticity, relevancy, personal knowledge and hearsay. "The requirement of authentication or identification as a condition precedent to admissibility is satisfied by evidence sufficient to support a finding that the matter in question is what its proponent claims." Federal Rule of Evidence 901 addresses authentication. For example, only a witness with personal knowledge of the scene may authenticate a diagram. They must be able to testify that the diagram is a "fair and accurate" depiction of the scene in question. The proponent of the diagram should ensure that the witness also explains labels and other markings present on the diagram prior to admitting it and using it.

Regardless of the type of proffered evidence it is the judge who determines the sufficiency of the authentication. That issue is a question of fact under Federal Rule of Evidence 104(a). In addition to the authentication requirement, the proponent of demonstrative evidence must be prepared to respond to other evidentiary objections raised by opposing counsel that may bar the admissibility of the

Easy Guide to Courtroom Objections (BARPH):

B – est Evidence

A – uthentication

R – elevance

P – ersonal Knowledge

H - earsay

evidence. An easy acronym to use when addressing possible evidentiary objections to exhibits is BARPH. Counsel should always lay all foundational elements when dealing with exhibits. These foundational questions can be used to not only authenticate the evidence, but to persuade the jury that the evidence is worthy of consideration.

Let us use our our earlier example of a diagram to discuss how you would admit it. First the diagram must be shown to the sponsoring witness, giving them the opportunity to examine it. Next you should ask the witness if the diagram is a "fair and accurate" depiction of the scene at that time. Unless exact distances are crucial the diagram need not be to scale, although this is a common objection that you will have to deal with if you have not

> **Using exhibits at trial:**
>
> 1. Introduce the exhibit.
> 2. Lay the foundation for admission.
> 3. Authenticate the exhibit.
> 4. Offer into evidence.
> 5. Have witness mark the exhibit as needed.
> 6. Publish the exhibit to the jury.

created a diagram that is to scale. The lack of scale may be established on either direct or cross-examination. If the diagram is drawn to scale, it should be noted on the record and the scale clearly shown on the diagram.

Once you have established that the diagram is relevant and authentic you offer it into evidence. You must then use it in the testimony of the witness and

> ### *Elements for the Foundation of a diagram.*
>
> *The diagram depicts a certain area or object;*
>
> *The witness is familiar with that area or object;*
>
> *The witness explains the basis for his knowledge of the area or object;*
>
> *The witness affirms the accuracy of the diagram.*

Foundation 1 - laying a foundation for a diagram

publish it to the jury. Publication may be accomplished in a variety of ways. You can provide copies to the jury, blow the exhibit up so that everyone may see it or place it in a location where the jury is able to reference as the witness testifies. There is room for creative advocacy during publication. Advocates should make certain that the jury can see and the exhibit, that the witness has access to it and that the judge can see it. Opposing counsel should request permission of the judge to move around the courtroom so that they may also observe the use of the diagram. The following questions normally meet the foundational requirement for various types of exhibits. Each jurisdiction may modify or rearrange these foundational questions, but they serves as a competent and complete basis from which to begin. As you read through them carefully note the specific differences for each type of exhibit. The foundational requirements vary because the evidentiary rules necessary to authenticate the evidence and establish its relevancy are influenced by the physical nature of the offered exhibit.

A photograph is authenticated by a witness who attests that the photograph accurately and fairly depicts the scene in question. There is no need to address the mechanics of exposing or developing the film, or the working condition of the camera. Also, it is important to note that a photograph does not need to be authenticated by the photographer, but must be authenticated by a witness with personal knowledge of the scene depicted in the photograph.

Elements for the Foundation of a photograph.

The witness is familiar with the object or scene;

The witness explains the basis for his familiarity with the object or scene;

The witness recognizes the object or scene in the photograph;

The witness testifies the photograph is a "fair," "accurate," "true," or "correct" depiction of the object or scene at the relevant time.

Foundation 2 - laying a foundation for a photograph

Non-fungible evidence is evidence that has a unique characteristic that allows it to be identified by individuals who have personal knowledge of that unique characteristic. Conversely, fungible evidence is evidence that does not have a unique characteristic rendering it readily identifiable. Fungible evidence requires additional foundational steps before it can be admitted, usually involving some type of chain-of-custody. Classic examples of non-fungible evidence include a gun with a serial number or other unique items seized for their evidentiary value.

Sometimes a non-fungible piece of evidence can also contain fungible evidence. An example of that would be a bloody knife. The knife has unique

---

Elements for the Foundation of a Non-fungible item of Evidence.

The object has a unique characteristic;

The witness observed the characteristic on a previous occasion;

The witness identifies the exhibit presented as the object;

The witness rests the identification on his present recognition of the characteristic; and

To the best of the witness' knowledge, the exhibit is in the same condition as it was when the witness initially saw or received the object.

Foundation 3 - laying the foundation for non-fungible evidence

characteristics that make it identifiable and a non-fungible piece of evidence, but the blood on the knife is fungible. The blood does not have unique characteristics and so a court would be concerned with its chain of custody before allowing its admission. Fungible evidence is easily modified, adulterated or replaced by people having access to it. In order to guarantee its relevance and

---

Elements of the Foundation: Fungible item of Evidence.

The witness is familiar with the item of evidence;

The witness acquired this familiarity by obtaining the item;

The witness uniquely marked the item of evidence to enable him to identify it later;

The witness properly safeguarded the item while it was in his possession to prevent the evidence from being lost or altered;

The witness ultimately disposed of the item (retention, destruction, or transfer to another individual);

To the best of his knowledge, the witness can positively identify the item of evidence as that which he previously had custody over; and

That the item of evidence is in the same condition as it was when he had custody previously.

Foundation 4 - laying the foundation for a fungible item of evidence

authenticity, fungible evidence must be carefully guarded to prevent contamination or destruction. Chain of custody procedures as captured by chain-of-custody documents accomplish this purpose.　To admit fungible evidence the

---

Elements of the Foundation: Chain-of-custody document.

The witness has personal knowledge of the business' filing or records system

It was a proper file or entry;

the witness recognizes the exhibit as the record (chain-of-custody document) he removed from the file; and

the witness specifies the basis on which he recognized the exhibit.

The witness removed the record (chain-of-custody document) in question from a certain file;

It was a proper file or entry;

the witness recognizes the exhibit as the record (chain-of-custody document) he removed from the file; and

the witness specifies why he recognizes the record.

Foundation 5 - Laying a foundation for a chain-of-custody document

---

chain of custody of documents relating to the evidence must be offered and admitted before the fungible evidence can be offered and admitted.

Establishing a proper chain of custody for fungible evidence is a condition precedent to its admissibility. This is a precise and important skill that a competent trial attorney must master. Improperly authenticated evidence may result in getting crucial evidence excluded from trial that could deal a fatal blow to your case. While this skill is important, it is relatively easy to master. All that is required is attention to the local rules of court, an understanding of how the rules of evidence impact foundational questions and a commitment to preparation that includes taking examples of foundational requirements for your intended exhibits into court with and having them readily available if you run into difficulties when laying your foundations.

Once counsel establishes the authenticity of a business record they must next establish that the contents of the chain-of-custody document are admissible as an exception to the hearsay rule, usually under the business records exception found in Federal Rule of Evidence 803(6). After laying the foundations for the fungible evidence and the chain-of-custody documents counsel can then move

---

Elements of the Foundation: Chain-of-custody document(Hearsay).

The chain-of-custody document was prepared by a person having a relationship with the agency preparing the chain-of-custody document;

The person had a duty to record the information on the chain-of-custody document;

The person had personal knowledge of the facts or events recorded in the chain-of-custody document;

The chain-of-custody document was prepared contemporaneously with the event(s);

It was a routine practice of the business to prepare chain-of-custody documents;

The chain-of-custody document was reduced to written form; and

The chain-of-custody document was prepared in the regular course of business.

Foundation 6 - Laying a foundation for a chain-of-custody document (Hearsay exception)

to admit both into evidence. Let us now consider how other rules of evidence and the procedures involved in admitting exhibits create additional legal issues and advocacy opportunities.

B. THE LAW OF EXHIBITS - VOIR DIRE & OBJECTIONS.

When an exhibit is offered into evidence opposing counsel must decide whether or not to object. The initial thought process should consider how allowing this evidence to be admitted will affect your chosen theme and theory. If it doesn't hurt let it in, especially if you have found a way to make it work to your advantage. If it does hurt, opposing counsel may (1) Voir Dire on the Exhibit, (2) Object as to the foundation, or (3) Object based upon BARPH.

Easy Guide to Courtroom Objections (BARPH):

B – est Evidence

A – uthentication

R – elevance

P – ersonal Knowledge

H - earsay

Opposing counsel may request to Voir Dire the witness on the exhibit for the purposes of developing an objection as to the exhibit's admissibility. This Voir Dire on an exhibit is a cross-examination of the witness that is limited in scope to questions addressing only the potential admissibility of the exhibit. Questions concerning the weight that the evidence might be given are outside the scope of the Voir Dire and should instead be asked during normal cross-examination of the witness. Since Voir Dire on an exhibit occurs during the direct examination of a witness by opposing counsel, judges are careful to restrict the scope of Voir Dire on Exhibits. Save your questions designed to attack the weight that the exhibit should be given for your cross examination.

A common objection often made during the Voir Dire is that it is "Outside the Scope of the direct." When a judge sustains this objection you can be confident that she perceives that you are asking questions about weight and not admissibility. Another common objection is "Your honor that goes to weight and not admissibility." That is another way of saying outside of the scope that is accepted in most jurisdictions. Normally, questions asked during Voir Dire on the Exhibit will not be allowed during cross, but creative counsel can easily tie what was earlier an admissibility issue to a greater weight issue later. If counsel choose to not request Voir Dire on an exhibit then they must either agree to its admission or object.

When counsel stands and says: "Objection – Insufficient Foundation." The judge must either: (a) Rule on the objection; or (b) respond to the objecting counsel by asking how the foundation is insufficient. If the Court sustains the objection without an explanation, the proponent of the exhibit may inquire for the reasons for the ruling under the Federal Rules of Evidence. When the objection is other than foundational the counsel opposing admissibility should stand and say "Objection," and then give a BRIEF statement of the grounds for the objection without testifying through the use of a rambling objection that is really designed to make arguments to the jury. The judge will either: (a) Rule on the objection; or (b) Ask the Proponent of the exhibit how they respond to opposing counsel's objection concerning the admissibility of the exhibit. If the Court sustains the objection, the proponent is not barred from continuing to attempt to lay an adequate foundation to get the exhibit into evidence.

C. THE ART OF EXHIBITS.

1. Persuasive use of exhibits.

Although foundations for a diagram are relatively easy to establish, the effective use of diagrams and other exhibits as persuasive tools depends upon how well counsel prepare for, and practice, their use. In this day and age one technique is to consider using the highest possible quality computer generated graphics. We live in the video age and slick presentations are now expected on our cell phones, let alone in court. The routine use of computer-generated products has created high expectations for all graphic products among our community. You should strive to meet or exceed those expectations in order to increase the effectiveness of your exhibits. A shabby diagram may well be interpreted as an indication that your case or investigation is also less than average, especially if your opposing counsel has chosen the high-tech route. A powerful diagram will continue selling your case long after the witness has left the stand. Diagrams should appear in opening statements, be used by witnesses during testimony and referred to during closing arguments. In jurisdictions that allow demonstrative evidence into the jury room, exhibits will continue to speak until the case is decided, long after counsel's final closing exhortations have faded from the courtroom and the minds of the jurors.

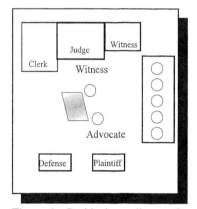

Figure 1 - Positioning a diagram for persuasive impact

Regardless of the type of diagram, demonstrative aid or exhibit you are using, its presentation must be fluid. This requires a commitment to practicing with the exhibit, both alone, and with the witness that will authenticate it. Different courtrooms are going to require different types of demonstrative evidence to be truly effective. Take the time to learn what delivery systems will be available in court. Once you have found the one that works best for you create your exhibits, practice, modify and then practice some more until you and the witness are comfortable in the type, manner and effectiveness of the presentation. Position the exhibit, yourself and your witness so that the jury and the judge can see the exhibit and you are able to use it effectively.

One collateral benefit of diagrams and other demonstrative evidence is they may permit you to have the witness to testify more than once about issues related to the diagram. First, have the witness tell the story during direct examination without the assistance of a diagram or other demonstrative aid. Next, lay the foundation for the exhibit, being careful to explain through your foundational questions how the use of the exhibit will further develop the witness's testimony. The witness must relate elements of their previous testimony a second time while laying the foundation for the exhibit and explaining its relevance. Finally, have the witness develop their testimony in greater detail, relying upon and using the exhibit to explain what happened. While you may run the danger of a cumulative objection, proper organization of questions should overcome and even prevent this problem.

Remember to always inform the judge when you intend to use

demonstrative evidence and give her an opportunity, along with opposing counsel, to view the demonstrative aids you intend to use. Judges hate surprises. You should never hide demonstrative aids or exhibits until the last minute in a futile attempt to surprise the opposing side, the surprise may be your own when the judge sustains their objection and does not allow you to use them.

2. Examples of Sample Foundations.

The following two examples show how to employ the techniques discussed in this chapter. Note the degree of control and direction that the advocate has over their witness even though this is direct examination. You are able to sprinkle a certain number of leading questions during direct examination when you are laying a foundation for the admissibility of an exhibit. When used artfully these leading questions reinforce control, establish pace and let the witness know with little to no uncertainty the direction that the advocate wishes to take.

For a Diagram:

Q.   *Mr. Witness, WHERE did the robbery occur?*
A.   *At the ATM machine located in the Grocery Store Parking Lot across from the Mini-Mall on State Street.*

Q.   *Please look at the diagram located on the easel to your left, it is marked Prosecution Exhibit 1 for Identification. Do you recognize this diagram?*
A.   *Yes.*

Q.   *WHAT is it?*
A.   *It is a diagram of the area around the ATM machine where I was robbed.*

Q.   *HOW do you recognize it?*
A.   *I've lived in this neighborhood for fifteen years and have done most of my ATM banking through that machine for the last eight years. I am very familiar with that area.*

Q.   *HOW often do you use this ATM?*
A.   *I used it about three times a week for the last eight years before the robbery. Since the robbery I haven't been able to go back to that spot.*

Q.   *Is this diagram a fair and accurate representation of the area around the ATM?*

A.   *Yes, it looks good to me.*

[This completes the foundation of an unmarked diagram. If the diagram has been pre-marked by counsel, it is now necessary to have the witness explain the labels that have been superimposed on various objects on the diagram. That explanation could go as follows:]

Q.   **Mr. Witness, HOW did you get to the ATM on the night of the robbery?**
A.   *I drove my car there.*

Q.   **WHERE did you park your car when you got there?**
A.   *In the Grocery Store parking lot on State Street, about 40 feet from the ATM Machine.*

Q.   **Is the position of your parked car shown on this diagram, P.E. 1 for ID?**
A.   *Yes, it is shown as a car with the word "Car" next to it on the diagram.*

Q.   **HOW is the ATM machine marked on the diagram?**
A.   *There is a picture of a building with the letters "ATM" next to it.*

Q.   **You testified earlier that it was dark outside when you arrived at the ATM. Was the area around the ATM also dark?**
A.   *No. It was lit fairly well by the streetlight located about fifteen feet from the ATM.*

Q.   **Please point out the location of the street lamp for the jury.**
A.   *Okay. There is a picture of a street lamp which is labeled "Light" on the diagram.*

Q.   **Mr. Witness, what happened after you arrived at the ATM?**
A.   *Well, my friend stayed in the car and I went to the machine to withdraw some cash. As I was entering my PIN number, a man in a ski mask came around the side of the machine and pointed a gun at me. He said that he would kill me if I didn't give him all my money.*

Q.   **Your honor, request permission to have the witness approach the diagram.**
J.   *Go ahead.*

Q.   **Using the blue marker, please place an "X" where you were standing when the masked man approached you.**
A.   *All right.*

Q. ***The witness marked P.E. 1 for ID, as directed. Now using the red marker, draw an arrow to indicate the approach used by the gunman before he robbed you.***

A. *Right here.*

Q. ***The witness marked P.E. 1 for ID with a red arrow as directed.*** [Counsel may offer the diagram into evidence at this time or any time before PASSING THE WITNESS. The diagram may not be further marked after it is admitted. Opposing counsel may ask that the judge instruct the JURY that the diagram is not to scale.]

Sample foundation for a Photograph:

Q. ***Mr. Witness, where do you work?***

A. *I work at the Grocery store on State Street across from the Mini-Mall.*

Q. ***I am showing opposing counsel what has previously been marked as Prosecution Exhibit 1 for Identification.*** [Show it to opposing counsel.] ***Your Honor, may I approach the witness?*** [Most jurisdictions require counsel to do this when initially approaching each witness, but you only need to ask once per witness.]

J. You may approach the witness counsel.

Q. I now hand you P.E. 1 for Identification. What is it?

A. It is a picture of the ATM Machine located in our Grocery store parking lot.

Q. How do you recognize it?

A. I have worked at that store as the assistant manager in charge of the night shift for the last twelve years. I was there when it was installed and have used it many times. I took this picture of the machine at the request of the store owner about 6 months ago. We were worried about the safety of our customers when they used it.

Q. From what angle was this photograph taken?

A. The picture is centered on the middle of the front of the ATM machine where customers use it. You can see the Grocery store in the background.

Q. Does this photo fairly and accurately depict the ATM Machine as it appeared six months ago?

A. Absolutely.

Q.   Your Honor, I offer P.E. 1 for Identification into evidence as P.E. 1.

These two examples are excellent starting points for developing your own techniques when laying foundations for admitting exhibits. Remember to review the foundational requirements that may be unique to your particular jurisdiction when preparing for trial. Place scripts within your trial notebook that allow you to quickly and efficiently ask the appropriate foundational questions when you come to that point in your direct examination. If the judge sustains an objection do not allow it to fluster you. Simply regroup and go through your foundational questions again. If the judge sustains another foundational objection it sometimes helps to show the judge that you are actually reading the foundational questions from an approved example in your jurisdiction. You have the ability to take the drudgery that is sometimes associated with laying foundations for exhibits and turn it into yet another opportunity for persuasive advocacy.

3. Example of an exhibit being introduced and used in an actual trial.

The following excerpt is from the direct examination of a police officer in a drug case. It is an adequate attempt to admit an exhibit, but the degree to which the exhibit is subsequently used by counsel is lacking. As you read through this direct think about the elements of a superior use of exhibits you have learned in this chapter. Consider carefully where this direct follows the advice of this text and where it does not. If you were conducting the direct examination of this detective, what changes might you make? Why? When you can answer those questions correctly you are ready to admit exhibits and use them effectively during all portions of the trial.

Q: With your permission, your Honor, I would like him to use the diagram?
THE COURT: Very well.

Q: Okay. Could you show us Cavalier Street and 15 Cavalier Street?
A: Sure. (Drawing a diagram.)

THE COURT: Excuse me, officer.
THE WITNESS: Yes, sir.
THE COURT: Could you just back that up a little bit so I'd be able to see it? You can still face it towards the jury so that if you can just turn it that way a little bit more I'll be able to see it. I can still see it. Members of the jury, can you see the diagram? All right. Thank you, officer.

Q: Could you show us where 15 Cavalier Street is?
A: Right here. (Indicating.)

Q: And where were you in 15 Cavalier Street?
A: Approximately this area right here. (Indicating.)

Q: What floor?
A: Second floor.

Q: Okay. Now, could you identify the car that Ms. Rogers was sitting in?
A: (Indicating.)

Q: Okay. Now, Ms. Horton, when you observed her get into a car was that car nearby the car with Ms. Rogers?
A: Yes, it was right in front of himself marked in front of Ms. Rogers's car.

Q: Okay. Where was Jamie Roberts standing in the street when she talked to Ms. Horton?
A: Approximately right here. (Indicating.)

Q: And how about when she talked to Mr. Dupree?
A: Same area.

Q: Okay. Now, is there a grocery in the area or something like that?
A: Yes. This is the street. (Indicating.)

Q: When she first met Horton did they go anywhere near the grocery?
A: She went into the grocery store and came back.

Q: And when they came back that's when the sale went down?
A: Yes.

Q: Okay. Could you put your initials on -- initials and your date on the diagram?
A: (Complies.) Today is the 24th, correct?

Q: Right.
STATE: No further questions.

Reviewing the direct examination excerpt directly above it is relatively clear that the advocate failed to accurately make the record while using this diagram. There is little indication of how the markings were made and it is difficult if not impossible to tell whether or not the diagram had any persuasive impact. If you were going to redo this direct examination how would you change it based upon what you have learned to this point in the book? What impact might the use of different colored markers or specific sticky notes or emblems have on its persuasive power. You should begin to see now how the use of an exhibit is a multi-sensory experience that should engage the jury, not put them to sleep.

D. RELEVANT EVIDENTIARY AND PROFESSIONAL RESPONSIBILITY RULES.

1. Evidentiary Rule Matrix.

Table 1 serves as a starting point for additional inquiry into the relationships between specific tasks dealing with exhibits and the rules of evidence. Your case analysis should assist you in identifying when these particular issues will arise. You should use the table to review your knowledge of the evidentiary rules so that you can include their development and application in your legal theory of the case.

Issue Arising Dealing with Exhibits	Applicable Federal Rule of Evidence
Authentication and identification rules	901 - 902
Best evidence rules	1001 - 1004
Business records	803(6)
Contents of writings, recordings and photographs	1001 - 1008
Documents and instruments	901 - 902
Public records	803(8)
Real and demonstrative evidence	901

Table 1 - Potential Evidentiary Rules Applicable with Exhibits

2. Professional Responsibility Rule Matrix.

Table 2 serves as a starting point for additional inquiry into the potential professional responsibility issues that are implicated during direct examination when exhibits are involved. Counsel must ensure that they do not cross certain lines when investigating cases, preparing witnesses and controlling direct testimony. The same issues also exist when listening to an opposing counsel's direct examination. You must pay particular attention to your jurisditions

Issue Arising When Using Exhibits	Applicable Rule of Professional Responsibility**
(a)(1-3) A lawyer must not offer false evidence.	**RULE 3.3 CANDOR TOWARD THE TRIBUNAL**
(e) A lawyer must not allude to any matter that she does not reasonably believe is relevant or that will not be supported by admissible evidence. She must not assert personal knowledge of facts in issue and never state a personal opinion as to justness of a cause, the credibility of a witness, the culpability of a civil litigant or the guilt or innocence of the defendant.	**RULE 3.4 FAIRNESS TO OPPOSING PARTY AND COUNSEL**
(a) A lawyer must not illegally seek to influence a judge, juror, prospective juror or other official. (d) A lawyer must not intentionally disrupt the court and must conduct herself with respect for the court.	**RULE 3.5 IMPARTIALITY AND DECORUM OF THE TRIBUNAL**
(a) A lawyer must not attempt to be an advocate and witness in the same trial (with some limited exceptions).	**RULE 3.7 LAWYER AS WITNESS**

Table 2 - Most Prevalent Professional Conduct Rules with Exhibits

interpretation and application of the candor towards the tribunal standard found in rule 3.3. A thorough grasp of these issues will assist you in avoiding perjury and improper conduct. Your case analysis should assist you in identifying when these particular issues will arise. You should use the table to review your knowledge of the ethical rules so that you can include that in your planning for your directs.

*** Unless otherwise specifically indicated all professional conduct rules referenced are taken from the Delaware Supreme Court's professional responsibility rules. Those rules are almost identical to the model rules promulgated by the American Bar Association and are public domain documents.*

Points to Ponder...

1. Why do the foundational questions not mirror the law of evidence? Is there a cogent reason for allowing common law and local practices to rule here?

2. Should demonstrative evidence be allowed back into the jury room? What limitations should be placed on a jury's use of admitted evidence during deliberations?

3. Why should the jury be allowed to consider and reconsider admitted evidence while they aren't allowed to listen to recorded testimony over and over again? Does this distinction make sense? What would you do if you were writing the rules now from scratch?

CHAPTER EIGHT
OBJECTIONS

"Men may construe things after their fashion,
Clean from the purpose of the things themselves."[1]

A. *THE SKILL OF OBJECTIONS.*

Most new advocates list objections as one of the areas of trial practice with which they are least comfortable. This discomfort comes from the fast paced nature of objections during the trial and the lack of connectivity between evidentiary law and trial skills when the advocate first learned about objections. Fortunately both of these issues can be overcome through practice and study.

The ability to make and respond to objections is a key skill for the trial advocate. To properly exercise this skill you must not only understand the rules of evidence, but also have a system that allows you to recall needed information amidst the heat of trial. A list of common objections and the corresponding rules of evidence in your trial notebook will help. One such possible list is included as an appendix to this book. Practice with the rules is another step toward competency in the area of trial advocacy. You should not despair, making good objections is a skill you can develop and given that most evidentiary ruling by the court are reviewed at the appellate under and abuse of discretion standard it is important that you win the battle at trial.

The first step along the path to mastering objections is to develop the ability to identify objectionable questions and evidence as they are actually presented during trial. Once you learn how to do this it is simple a matter of then deciding whether the question is objectionable, and is it to your strategic or tactical advantage to object. Case analysis should assist you in determining

---

[1] WILLIAM SHAKESPEARE, JULIUS CAESAR, act 1, sc. 3.

when you want to fight over an objectionable piece of evidence or testimony and when you want to let it go because it helps your case. You should always evaluate the situation before deciding whether or not to object. Ask yourself it the evidence is probably going to come in anyway. For example, if the objection is strictly to a lack of proper foundation, your objection will merely allow opposing counsel to fix the problem, making additional advocacy points while doing so. If that is the case then why object? You may wind up keying the jury members to the importance of evidence you would rather they not focus on. Objections are both strategic and tactical. A thorough case analysis and preparation of your direct and cross examinations will alert you to possible objections from opposing counsel, as well as arm you with objections you will anticipate to make against opposing counsel. These objections are planned in depth and fall into the strategic category.

Others arise in the heat of the moment and more fairly can be said to fall into the tactical category of objections. Sometimes something will simply not sound right and you will be on your feet objecting while still formulating the specific basis for your objection. One aspect of objecting that you may consider is whether an objection will make your opponent lose momentum or get flustered. While it is improper to make an objection solely to disrupt your opponent, it is proper to object whenever you have a good faith basis. Be cautious in this area. Tactical objections may work against you by making you appear overly contentious to the jury. It may also annoy the judge. Consider the judge to be a lion in a cage, if you are going to poke it with a stick, make sure it is on an issue that matters and the reaction that you get is not too severe.

The mechanics of making an objection depend upon your local jurisdiction and the preferences of the trial judge. Some judges will require you to state the basis and the applicable rule of evidence. Others only need to hear the word "objection," and they will start to interrogate opposing counsel. Be aware, especially as defense counsel, that appellate courts will often find waiver of an issue if the objection is not sufficiently specific. This may sometimes

> ## The following general guidelines should apply when making objections:
>
> 1. Stand up.
> 2. Say: "Objection, your honor, the question is" (leading, improper, argumentative, etc.).
> 3. Grab your objection reference guide in case the judge wants further information.
> 4. Listen to the judge or your opponent and prepare to respond.

require a citation to relevant case law. Waiver occurs in some jurisdictions if the objection is not renewed each time the disputed evidence or testimony is offered. Conversely, you can request that the judge note your continuing objection to evidence of the same type. When in doubt – object!

When you hear an objection you should think about what you just said, and why it may be objectionable. Reasons might include; (1) How the question was phrased (leading, argumentative, vague, ambiguous, compound) , (2)What you were asking the witness (answered a question that you already asked, gave a conclusion or opinion that is improper, answered with hearsay, gave a narrative response, disclosed privileged information), or perhaps (3) You have gotten ahead of yourself (assuming a fact not in evidence, incomplete or improper foundation, bolstering a witness before credibility is attacked). Wait to hear what the judge says. He may overrule the objection outright. If he invites a response, state your position. If the problem is a matter of phrasing, or you tried to enter evidence before the foundation was complete, ask for leave to rephrase the question or to complete the foundation. If you do not understand the objection, but the point that you were attempting to make was critical, ask the judge for clarification before responding.

> **The following general guidelines should apply when responding to objections:**
>
> 1. Stop talking and listen to the judge.
>
> 2. Do not immediately concede or offer to rephrase.
>
> 3. Be prepared to answer the judge's concerns.
>
> 4. Do not be argumentative in front of the jury.
>
> 5. Answer the judge, not opposing counsel.

B. THE LAW OF OBJECTIONS.

There are two general types of trial objections, form and substance. "Objections to Form" attack the way counsel *asked* the question. Federal Rule of Evidence 611(a) and (c) empowers the trial court to control the mode and order of interrogation, and to limit the use of leading questions. "Objections to Substance" attack the admissibility of the testimony elicited. All of these objections are derived directly from the law of evidence. The most common objections are outlined below with the form of the objection, an explanation of the basis for the objection, possible responses to the objection by a trial judge or by opposing counsel and, where applicable, more recent federal decisions addressing the objection.

1. Objections to form.

Ambiguous, Confusing or Unintelligible Question – F.R.E. 611(a).

Objection: *The question is ambiguous/confusing/unintelligible.*

Response: *I will rephrase.*

Explanation: A question is ambiguous if it may be interpreted in several ways, or if it is so vague or unclear that it may confuse the jury, judge or the witness.

Argumentative Question - F.R.E. 611(a).

Objection: *The question is argumentative.*

Response: *Rephrase the question.*

Explanation:· A question is argumentative if it is an attempt to make a jury argument, to summarize, draw inferences from, or comment on the evidence, or to ask the witness to testify as to his own credibility. A question can also be argumentative if it is unduly hostile or sarcastic.

Asked and Answered or Unduly Repetitious - F.R.E. 403, 611(a).

Objection: *The witness has already answered the question.*

Response: *The witness has not yet answered this particular question.*

Explanation: Repetitious questions are unlikely to elicit additional evidence of probative value. See United States v. Collins, 996 F .2d 950, 952 (8th Cir. 1993), cert. denied, 114 S. Ct. 412 (1993) (objection to question posed during re-direct examination on basis that it had been asked and answered on direct examination sustained).

Assumes Facts Not in Evidence - F.R.E. 601, 611(a).

Objection: *Assumes facts not in evidence.*

Responses: *(1) The existence of this fact may be inferred from evidence which has been admitted, (2) if permitted to answer the fact will be in evidence, or(3) the fact will be proved during the testimony of Witness X. We will "tie it up" later.*

Explanation· A question that assumes facts not yet in evidence effectively allows counsel to testify as to those facts without personal knowledge.

Multifarious; Compound Question - F.R.E.611(a).

Objection: *Compound Question.*

Response: *I will rephrase the question.*

Explanation: A question combining more than one inquiry is likely to be confusing and misleading to both the witness and the fact-finder.

Harassing the Witness - F.R.E. 403, 611(a)(3).

Objection: *Harassing the witness.*

Response: *I will rephrase the question.*

Explanation: A question that is asked to harass or embarrass a witness, for example, a question that unnecessarily delves into a witness's personal life, is impermissible.

Leading Question - F.R.E.611(c).

Objection: *Leading.*

Responses: *(1) The question is not a leading question simply because it elicits a yes or no answer. It is generally to elicit preliminary or background information from a witness through leading questions, (2) the witness is an adverse party, or the witness is hostile, (3) leading questions are allowed of one's own witnesses on cross- examination if the witness is called by the adverse party, or (4) I'll rephrase the question.*

Explanation: A leading question is one that suggests to the witness the answer desired by the examiner. Leading questions are generally impermissible on direct examination.

Calls for Narrative Answer - F.R.E. 403, 611(a).

Objection: *I object. The question calls for narrative testimony and deprives us of an Objection: Calls for a narrative. Counsel is trying to admit inadmissible evidence.*

Response: *I will rephrase the question.*

Explanation: Narrative, unspecific, or long "rambling" answers are not per se objectionable, but are likely to contain hearsay or other inadmissible evidence to which counsel is deprived of an opportunity to object. See United States v. Pless, 982 F.2d 1118, 1123 (7th Cir. 1992) ("there is nothing particular, unusual, or incorrect, in a procedure of letting a witness relate pertinent information in a narrative form as long as it stays within the bounds of pertinence and materiality").

Mischaracterizes or Misquotes the Witness or Prior Evidence - (F.R.E. 611(a).

Objection: *I object. The question mischaracterizes, misstates, or misquotes the prior testimony...*

Response: *I'll rephrase the question.*

Explanation: Questions that misquote previous testimony or evidence are likely to mislead or confuse the jury.

2. Objections to substance.

Lack of Authentication – F.R.E. 901, 902.

Objection: *I object. The evidence has not been properly authenticated.*

Response: *The item is sufficiently authenticated by _____ (a method listed in Rule 901(b)).*

Examples of sufficient authentication include:

- Testimony of a witness with knowledge.

- Non-expert opinion on the genuineness of handwriting.

- Comparison by trier of fact or expert witness to authenticated specimens.

- Distinctive characteristics of the item offered.

- Voice identification by opinion based upon hearing the voice under circumstances connecting it with the alleged speaker.

- Public records or reports.

- The item is self-authenticating under Rule 902.

Examples of self authenticating evidence under Rule 902 include:

Domestic public documents under seal.

- Domestic public documents not under seal if officer certifies that the signature is genuine.

- Foreign public documents.

- Certified copies or public records.

- Official publications.

- Newspapers and periodicals.

- Acknowledged or notarized documents.

- Commercial paper and related documents.

Explanation: Authentication is not satisfied if insufficient evidence has been offered to support a finding that the matter in question is what its proponent claims is it. See United States v. McGlory, 968 F .2d 309,328-29 (3d Cir. 1992), cert. denied, 507 U.S. 962 (1993) (to show authenticity there must be a prima facie showing of authenticity to the court; the jury will ultimately determine the authenticity of the evidence).

Best Evidence Not Offered - F.R.E. 1001, 1002, 1003, 1004.

> Objection: *I object. The evidence is not the best evidence.*

> Response: *The evidence qualifies as an original, or as a duplicate.*

Explanation: The best evidence rule requires the original writing, recording, or photograph to prove the content of the writing, recording, or photograph. F.R.E. 1001 defines original and duplicate. An "original" is the writing or recording itself, any counterpart intended to have the same effect, the negative or print therefrom if the evidence is a photograph, and any printout or other output shown to accurately reflect the data of an original that is stored in a computer.

A "duplicate" is "a counterpart produced by the same impression as the original, or from the same matrix, or by means of photography, including enlargements and miniatures, or by mechanical or electronic re-recording, or by chemical reproduction, or by other equivalent techniques." Duplicates are admissible to the same extent as originals.

> Response: *The rule is inapplicable because the proponent is not seeking to prove the content of the item.*

> Response: *The original is not obtainable and secondary evidence is therefore admissible.*

Explanation: Secondary evidence is admissible if the original has been lost or destroyed except for when the loss or destruction was done in bad faith by the proponent. Other examples for when secondary evidence is admissible from FRE 1004 include: (1) the original is unobtainable by any available judicial process or procedure, (2) the original is under the control of the opponent and the opponent does not produce the original when put on notice that it will be subject of proof at a hearing, (3) the item is offered for a collateral purpose. See United States v. Haddock, 956 F.2d 1534, 1545 (10th Cir. 1992) ("due to modern and accurate reproduction techniques, duplicates and originals should normally be treated interchangeably").

Improper Use of Character Evidence - F.R.E.404, 405, 608.

> Objection: *I object. The question calls for inadmissible character evidence.*

Response: *The person's character trait is "in issue."*

Explanation: A person's character is "in issue" when it is an element of a charge, claim, or defense. For example, in a claim of negligent entrustment, the trait of incompetence of the person to whom the defendant entrusted the dangerous instrumentality to is an element of the claim and is "in issue." Proof of character may then be made by opinion or reputation testimony, or by evidence of specific instances of conduct. Character evidence is generally inadmissible to show that a person acted in conformity with that character on a particular occasion. Character evidence may be proved only by reputation or opinion testimony, not by specific acts, except where a trait of the person's character is "in issue," or for the purpose of impeachment or rehabilitation on cross-examination.

Objection: *I object. Evidence of specific acts is impermissible to prove character.*

Response: *The character evidence is offered for the purpose of impeachment or rehabilitation on cross-examination and is therefore admissible under F.R.E. 608.*

Explanation: A witness that has testified as to the character of a person may be asked on cross-examination about specific acts of that person in the form of "have you heard?" or "do you know?" questions to test the factual basis of their testimony on direct examination. A witness may always be asked on cross-examination about specific instances of his or her own conduct that are probative of untruthfulness. Counsel must have a good faith basis for making the inquiry. (F.R.E. 608).

Objection: *I object. The question calls for inadmissible character evidence.*

Response: *The person's character trait is "in issue" because it is an element of a charge, claim, or defense.*

Explanation: The specific act is offered to prove something other than character. Evidence of other crimes, wrongs, or acts may be admissible to prove motive, opportunity, intent, preparation, plan, knowledge, identity, or absence of mistake or accident. (F.R.E. 404(b)). See United States v. Roberts, 887 F.2d 534 (5th Cir. 1989) (character trait was in issue on a question of whether defendant formed the requisite intent, and evidence of personality traits was therefore properly admitted); United States v. McGuiness, 764 F. Supp. 888 (S.D.N.Y. 1991) (evidence of defendant's previous refusal to accept bribes not admissible to prove character of defendant and action in conformity with that character);

United States v. Nazarenus, 983 F .2d 1480 (8th Cir. 1993) (extrinsic evidence of defendant's driving habits inadmissible to impeach defendant as specific acts may not be proved by extrinsic evidence for the purpose of attacking or supporting the witness's credibility). (F.R.E.608(b)).

Bolstering the Credibility of a Witness - F.R.E. 607, 608, 801(d)(1)(B).

Objection: *I object. Counsel is bolstering the witness.*

Response: *The witness's credibility has been attacked and this evidence is proper rehabilitation.*

Explanation: F.R.E. 608(a) permits evidence of a witness's character for truthfulness only after the witness's character for truthfulness has been attacked. Bolstering refers to a proponent's attempt to offer otherwise inadmissible character evidence solely for the purpose of enhancing his witness's credibility when the witness has not yet been impeached. See United States v. Hedgcorth, 873 F .2d 1307,1313-1314 (9th Cir. 1989), cert. denied, 493 U.S. 857 (1989) (testimony as to defendant's character for truthfulness properly excluded where government had not attacked defendant's character for truthfulness).

Impeachment on a Collateral Matter - F.R.E. 403, 608.

Objection: *I object. Extrinsic evidence of specific instances is inadmissible to impeach a witness on collateral matters.*

Responses: *(1) The extrinsic evidence is independently relevant to a substantive issue in the case, (2) the evidence is offered to prove bias, which is not a collateral matter, or (3) evidence of specific acts of a witness are admissible when offered to prove something other than a witness's untrustworthy character.*

Explanation: This objection arises most commonly when a party seeks to impeach a witness by introducing extrinsic evidence that contradicts an answer given by the witness. See United States v. Abel, 469 U.S. 45 (1984) (bias is not collateral); Foster v. General Motors Corp., 20 F.3d 838, 839 (8th Cir. 1994) (evidence relevant to a material issue is admissible).

Conclusion of Law or Ultimate Issue - F.R.E. 701, 702, 704.

Objection: *I object. The witness is testifying to an ultimate issue.*

Response: *The expert or lay witness has knowledge or expertise of the matter, and the evidence is helpful. An adequate foundation has been laid.*

Explanation: Testimony phrased in conclusory terms is less helpful than testimony that provides information to the jury so that it may draw its own conclusions. Conclusions of law are generally inadmissible. Lay or expert witness testimony must be based on the lay witness's perception or must be within the scope of the expertise of an expert witness, and must be helpful to the fact finder. Opinions on an ultimate issue are generally admissible. (F .R.E. 704). See United States v. Lockett, 919 F.2d 585, 590 (9th Cir. 1990) (expert opinions about guilt or innocence inadmissible); Kostelecky v. NL Acme Tool / NL Industries, Inc., 837 F.2d 828, 830 (8th Cir. 1988) ("evidence that merely tells the jury what result to reach is not sufficiently helpful to the trier of fact to be admissible").

Cross-Examination Beyond the Scope of Direct - F.R.E. 611(b).

Objection: *I object. The question asked goes beyond the scope of the matters raised on direct.*

Response: *The question is permissible because the subject matter of direct includes all inferences and implications arising from direct.*

Explanation: Cross-examination that raises subjects not raised on direct is generally inadmissible.

Cumulative - F.R.E. 403.

Objection: *I object. The evidence is cumulative.*

Response: *A party has a right to present a persuasive case and the cumulative evidence concept should not interfere with that right.*

Explanation: If the evidence is needlessly cumulative or repetitious, it may be excluded. See Davis v. Mason County, 927 F.2d 1473 (9th Cir. 1991), cert. denied, 502 U.S. 899 (1991) (testimony of expert witness properly excluded on ground that two other experts had testified on the same topic).

Hearsay - F.R.E. 801, 802, 803, 804.

Objection: *I object. The question calls for hearsay.*

Responses: *(1) The-statement is not hearsay because it is not offered to prove the truth of the matter asserted, (2) the statement is not hearsay under the rules... (3) I am offering it for a non-hearsay purpose, or (4) the statement is hearsay, but is specifically exempted by the rules...*

Explanation: Hearsay is inadmissible unless it falls within an established exception. Key hearsay exceptions, as listed in F.R.E. 801, 803 and 804, include:

- Prior statements by witness.
- Admissions by party-opponent offered against party-opponent.

- Present sense impressions.

- Excited utterances.

- Statement of the declarant's then existing state of mind.

- Statements for the purpose of medical diagnosis or treatment.

- Recorded recollections.

- Records of regularly conducted activity.

- Public records and reports.

- Learned treatises.

- Former testimony of unavailable declarant.

- Statement under belief of impending death where the declarant is unavailable.

- Statement against interest of an unavailable declarant.

Impermissible Hypothetical Question - F.R.E. 705.

Objection: *I object. Counsel is posing a hypothetical question that contains facts not in evidence.*

Response: *A hypothetical question need not refer to all of the relevant facts in evidence. The witness is an expert witness, and an expert may base an opinion on facts that are not admitted into evidence, as long as they are the type reasonably relied upon by experts in forming opinions on the subject.*

Explanation: A hypothetical question is inadmissible if it contains facts that are not already in evidence, that will not be introduced before the close of evidence, or that are not reasonably drawn from such facts.

See: Toucet v. Maritime Overseas Corp., 991 F.2d 5,10 (1st Cir. 1993) (a hypothetical question should include only those facts suggested by the evidence).

Witness is Incompetent or Lacks Personal Knowledge - F.R.E. 601 -606

Objection: *I object. The witness is incompetent or lacks sufficient capacity to testify, or no showing has been made that the witness has personal knowledge about this matter.*

Responses: *(1) Rule 601 abolishes objections to a witness's competence, (2) The witness is competent under state law, (3) A personal assertion by the witness is sufficient to show personal knowledge,. (4) I will ask additional questions sufficient to lay the foundation to establish personal knowledge.*

Explanation: All persons are presumed competent to testify except as otherwise provided in the rules. However, incompetence of a witness may be the basis for an objection in two situations: where state law supplies the rule of decision with respect to an element of a claim or defense, and the witness is incompetent under state law; or where insufficient evidence has been introduced to support a finding that the witness has personal knowledge of the matter. See United States v. Phibbs, 999 F .2d 1053 (6th Cir. 1993) (admission of testimony from witness with history of mental problems was not error as all persons are presumed competent to testify); Kemp v. Balboa, 23 F .3d 211 (8th Cir. 1994) (nurse not allowed to testify because she lacked personal knowledge as to the facts stated in medical records which she had not prepared).

Misleading - F.R.E. 403.

Objection: *I object. The evidence will mislead the jury. Or, if a bench trial, I object, the evidence is misleading.*

Response: *The probative value of the evidence outweighs the danger of misleading the jury or the court.*

Explanation: The danger of misleading the jury usually refers to the possibility that the jury will attach undue weight to the evidence. If the probative value of the evidence is substantially outweighed by the danger of misleading the jury, the evidence may be excluded. See Rogers v. RaymarkIndus., 922 F.2d 1426 (9th Cir. 1991) (evidence of observations taken at defendant's asbestos plant was properly excluded because plaintiffs complaint was based on activities at a different plant and there was no evidence of similarity among the plants).

Prejudicial Effect Outweighs Probative Value - F.R.E. 403.

Objection: *I object. The probative value of this evidence is outweighed by the danger of unfair prejudice.*

Response: *All probative evidence is prejudicial. The rule does not afford protection from evidence that is merely detrimental to a party's case. In this instance the probative value of the evidence outweighs the danger of unfair prejudice.*

Explanation: Evidence is unfairly prejudicial if it suggests a decision on an improper basis, most commonly an emotional basis. If the probative value of the evidence is substantially outweighed by the danger of unfair prejudice, the evidence may be excluded. See United States v. Skillman, 922 F.2d 1370, 1374 (9th Cir. 1990), cert. dism'd, 502 U.S. 922 (1991) (rule only protects against evidence that is unfairly prejudicial).

Confusion of the Issues - F.R.E. 403.

Objection: *I object. The evidence will confuse the issues.*

Response: *The probative value of the evidence outweighs the risk of confusion.*

Explanation: Evidence is confusing if it tends to distract the jury from the proper issues of the trial. If the probative value of evidence is outweighed by the danger of confusion, it may be excluded. See Ramos-Melendez v. Valdejully, 960 F.2d 4, 6 (1st Cir. 1992) (evidence of other suits against defendant properly excluded as distracting the jury from the issues at hand).

Privilege - F.R.E. 501.

Objection: *I object. The question calls for privileged information.*

Response: *The privilege asserted is not one created by constitution, court, or state rule, or one recognized by common law. The communication at issue is not privileged.*

Explanation: Privileged information based on the attorney-client privilege, doctor patient privilege, spousal privilege, and other privileges recognized by Common or statutory law is inadmissible. Privilege law is generally governed by the principles of common law as interpreted by the United States courts, but in civil actions, state privilege law applies with respect to an element of a claim or defense as to which state substantive law governs.

The privilege has been waived. See: United States v. Moscony, 927 F.2d 742, 751 (3d Cir. 1991), cert. denied, 501 U.S. 1211 (1991) (although Congress did not enact the Supreme Court's proposed privilege rules which discussed individual privileges, courts often refer to those rules for guidance).

Speculation - F.R.E. 602, 701, 702.

Objection: *I object. The question calls for the witness to speculate.*

Response: *I will rephrase the question to establish the witness's personal knowledge or basis for the witness's statement.*

Explanation: A question which asks a witness to speculate as to what occurred or what caused an event may conflict with the requirement that a witness have personal knowledge of a matter testified to, or in the case of an expert witness, may be an impermissible attempt to elicit an opinion beyond the scope of the witness's expertise.

C. THE ART OF OBJECTIONS.

Whenever opposing counsel violate the rules of evidence as to either the form of the question or the nature of the evidence they are attempting to admit, opposing counsel must decide whether or not to object. You should consider whether making the objection will assist you in advancing your theme and theory identified through case analysis or help you in preventing your opponent from furthering their theme and theory. If either of these two predicate possibilities exist then it may be appropriate to object. On the other hand, if it does not hurt consider passing on the potential objection. Especially if you have found a way to make the objectionable issue work to your advantage. If you are not sure, but it simply does not sound right when you hear then consider using BARPH.

An alternative to BARPH is to structure your objections for maximum persuasion. The judge is your target, so stop and think for a moment of how the objections might appear from the judge's perspective. We will use something as simple as a letter that talks about the lack of character of the accused for our example. Let us say that the letter was written by the alleged victim in a homicide case. The defense counsel who is trying to keep this evidence out has a variety of objections that are potentially available. The order in which she chooses to raise those objections is crucial. Consider the following:

Prosecutor(P): Ma'am I hand you what has been marked as PE 1 for ID. Do you recognize it?

Witness(W): Yes.

P: What is it?

W: It is a letter written by my dear sweet murdered daughter. She was talking about her sorry husband in it.

Defense(D): Objection - This violates 403. May I be heard?

Judge(J): Briefly counsel.

D: Your honor this note has a high probability of unfairly prejudicing my client. Any probative value is substantially outweighed by the danger of unfair prejudice.

J: Overruled. You may proceed state.

P: I offer PE 1 for ID into evidence as PE 1.

J: Admitted as marked.

Consider what would have happened if the young defense counsel had planned her objections to create a greater degree of concern about the ultimate substantial danger of unfair prejudice. In order to accomplish this she needs to stack and arrange her objections so that she gets the judge's attention. It might go like this:

Prosecutor(P): Ma'am I hand you what has been marked as PE 1 for ID. Do you recognize it?

Witness(W): Yes.

P: What is it?

W: It is a letter written by my dear sweet murdered daughter. She was talking about her sorry husband in it.

Defense(D): Objection - May I be heard?

Judge(J): Briefly counsel. Basis?

D: Your honor counsel has not laid a proper foundation.

J: Overruled. You may proceed state.

D: Objection - best evidence rule.

J: Explain.

D: Your honor this letter is a copy of an original that is not available for comparison.

J: I'm going to overrule that objection as well. You may proceed state.

D: Objection - authentication. May I be heard?

J: All right counsel.

D: Your honor the state has not properly authenticated this letter to show that it was in fact written by the alleged victim. We would request they do so before you admit it.

J: Okay. Lay a foundation state.

P: (state lays a foundation). I offer...

D: *Objection - authentication and hearsay.*

J: *Counsel I am overruling the authentication objection. State how do you respond to the hearsay objection?*

P: *Your honor it is a dying declaration.*

D: *Your honor how can a letter be a dying declaration? The state has not laid sufficient foundation to support that hearsay exception.*

J: *I disagree counsel. Objection as to hearsay is overruled.*

D: *Objection - impermissible character evidence.*

J: *Counsel this getting old. How is this letter impermissible character evidence?*

D: *It relates alleged prior misconduct by my client that the jury could improperly consider.*

J: *How do you respond state?*

P: *Your honor we offer it under the 404(b) exception and request a limiting instruction to the jury as to its permissible use under 105.*

J: *Based upon that offer I overrule the objection.*

D: *Your honor may I be heard.*

J: *Extremely briefly counsel.*

D: *Your honor we have established concerns with admitting this letter that include foundation, authentication, hearsay and impermissible character evidence. Although you have overruled each of these objections their cumulative effect is to point out quite clearly the substantial danger of unfair prejudice to my client if this letter is admitted. We request you exclude it under 403.*

J: *(rubbing his eyes) Counsel I'll consider your objection over lunch. We are in recess.*

　　　　The defense counsel in this second example may very well lose the 403 objection, but they have made an excellent record. They have also raised so many concerns that the judge may decide to exclude this piece of evidence.

This technique is useful when you want to send the signal to the judge that this particular issue is important and worthy of careful consideration. This approach will only work if you save it for the right moment. If you throw every objection available out indiscriminately then the judge will eventually tune you out.

> **When arranging or stacking objections you should consider:**
>
> 1. Logical relevance(401).
> 2. Authentication(900).
> 3. Foundation.
> 4. Hearsay(when applicable)(800).
> 5. Character(when applicable)(400).
> 6. Opinion (when applicable)(700).
> 7. Legal relevance(403).

Regardless of whether you are BARPHing or stacking, you should stand and say objection and then briefly state the basis for your concern. You should focus on the judge and her reactions, never looking at opposing counsel. The judge will either rule on your objection outright or ask opposing counsel to respond. Listen carefully both to what opposing counsel says and the judge's response. If opposing counsel cannot give the judge a valid basis to overrule the objection then you should keep remain quiet. Do not snatch defeat from the jaws of victory when objecting by talking too much. If you lose the objection you can make an offer of proof, and when necessary refer back to that lost objection when attempting to admit or suppress other evidence.

In addition to dealing with objections off the cuff, the superior advocate will plan for potential objections in depth on those important, if not dispositive, legal and factual issues identified during case analysis. This is accomplished by (1) identifying potentially objectionable issues through case analysis, (2) researching the basis and strength of your objection (with favorable case law identified and prepared), (3) analyzing potential responses by opposing counsel and then (4) preparing your counter-response. This type of in depth planning of objections creates the sense on the part of the judge that you know what you are talking about. They will take you seriously because their primary concern is protecting the record. When you can get inside of the decision making loop the judge uses to protect the record you are well on your way to winning the evidentiary battle over objections.

Points to Ponder...

1. If objections allow counsel to mislead the jury and frustrate the opposing side why do we allow them in their current form? Is there a viable alternative means? What impact would that have?

2. Should we prevent counsel from wasting time and insulting the court with spurious objections? How would you accomplish that?

3. Is it proper to assume that one of the purpose of objections is to misdirect attention or to break the flow of opposing counsel's work? If so why, if not, why not?

CHAPTER NINE
MOTIONS PRACTICE

"I am a humble suitor to your virtues;
For pity is the virtue of the law,
And none but tyrants use it cruelly."[1]

A. THE SKILL OF MOTIONS PRACTICE.

1. Case Analysis and Motions Practice.

Advocates use motions practice to identify the law that will apply and the evidence that will be admitted during the trial. The legal decisions by the judge have a tremendous impact on the manner in which you will either defend or prosecute any case. Much as you use instructions to mold your closing argument, motions are used to set the stage for the development of your final legal theory, factual theory and moral theme. They are also used during the trial to deny opposing counsel the opportunity to use evidence that you believe to be inadmissible or to force counsel to live with an interpretation of the law that does not support their theme and theory. Since motions serve as the gate through which disputed evidence or potentially applicable law must pass in order to be used at trial, a complete and thorough understanding of how to approach motions practice is important. You must understand it from not only a case analysis perspective, but from a "common sense" this is what I do and this is when I do it perspective.

The case analysis and case preparation discussions in chapter 3[2] of this

---

[1] WILLIAM SHAKESPEARE, TIMON OF ATHENS, act 3, sc. 5.

[2] See Chapter 3 Case Analysis and accompanying text.

book outline the relationship between motions and the various sections of the trial process. You must identify your legal issues and the facts, both disputed undisputed, that impact on the judge's decision as to those legal issues. Some of these legal issues will not be controversial, and you will readily be able to forecast the admissibility or inadmissability of some types of evidence based upon settled law. However, in other areas the legal issue you have identified is either one of first impression, or more commonly, one whose application is greatly influenced by factual determinations. A classic example of such a scenario is the case law dealing with applications of the 4th amendment of the United States Constitution. Using our case preparation methodology as a logical framework for deciding how to prepare and present a motion for the suppression of evidence illegally seized might work like this:

Written Motion	Offer evidence during motion hearing	Argument during the motion
Identify facts - uncontroverted and controverted. Identify applicable law. Argue law to facts. Offer to produce evidence. Request relief.	Police Officer - call, examine based upon departmental procedures and failure to follow. Show no warrant. Show bias against defendant. Defendant - Call for limited purpose of showing right was expressed. Witness 1 - call to show police ignored refusal to consent to search.	Legal Theory - deny state evidence of crime seized in house. Factual theory - police did not follow departmental procedures used to ensure compliance with constitution. Moral Theme - we cannot reward state for violating constitutional rights

There is nothing particularly earth shattering in the example above. It merely identifies the legal theory, organizes the facts needed to support the legal theory and then previews the motions hearing in writing to the court. The Rule of Threes adequately organizes and presents this information in a fashion helpful to the judge. It is also helpful to the advocate because it provides a template for organizing, analyzing and presenting a motion. The same thought process applies regardless of the legal issue. Certain fundamental tasks must always be accomplished to guarantee success in motions practice. Once you have identified these fundamental tasks you merely need to develop the skills that will allow you to be successful in these tasks. That is a question of preparation, not knowledge. One of the first steps you must take in order to be fully prepared

---

Seven Fundmental Tasks of Successful Motions Practice:

1. Know the local rules for filing deadlines, both according to the legal issue when appropriate and according to time.

2. Draft sound legal motions in writing when required. Use law, facts and inference to your advantage.

3. Identify the source of your evidence for the motions hearing and have it available in an appropriate form to admit before the judge. Do not forget the effect of Federal Rule of Evidence 104, or its state equivalent.

4. Do not forget to balance your law, facts and moral theme, even when dealing with motions. There is always a reason for the legal protection. Remind the judge of that necessity when necessary.

5. Know whom you are trying to persuade - the judge.

6. Do not argue with opposing counsel, argue to the judge.

7. Know when a ruling is preserved on appeal and when you must raise it again during the case in chief. Understand the tactical and strategic reasons behind any decision to raise such issues at trial.

---

for motions practice is to develop the written advocacy tools to properly frame your issues so that the actual hearing maximizes the opportunity to persuade the judge to rule in your favor.

2. *Writing Motions.*

You begin preparing for motions practice by reading and understanding the law in light of the precise issue you intend to raise. You must identify this target before taking any additional steps. Your targeted issue drives the substance and structure of your motion and must be chosen before you begin to write. You should also check the timeliness requirement for the issue you have chosen when beginning. This information can bye found in the local rules of

> **Tips for Effective Written Motions:**
>
> Do the "spadework." There is not excuse for a lack of research.
>
> Organize the facts.
>
> Apply the law to the facts.
>
> Evidence, evidence, evidence.
>
> Candid with the court - do not oversell your position!
>
> Timeliness of the motion.
>
> Burden of Proof.
>
> Know the local rules.

court requirements for motions. In most jurisdictions some issues, such as jurisdiction over the case, are waived once you make an appearance. Be sure to keep in mind the local rules and their impact on motions practice as you go forward. The sequence of events for motions practice varies from judge to judge, but is usually relatively predictable within a circuit. Typically, the judge sets a date for submission of written motions and written responses. This allows the judge and opposing counsel time to understand the issues fully prior to the hearing.

You should identify and understand the burden of proof before raising the motion. During the hearing this is probably the first question a judge will ask. Not understanding the burden is embarrassing in open court and more importantly impacts your written motion and the evidence you will offer. Normally the party making the motion or raising the objection has the burden of proof.

Once you have identified your targeted issued you must organize your facts. A good starting point is to write out your statement of facts - what you believe the facts to be that are relevant to the targeted issue. Ensure that your written motion sets forth all of the relevant facts in short, topically-organized and numbered paragraphs. For each assertion you make in your statement of facts you must have evidence supporting it. Often the temptation arises to merely adopt the statement of facts prepared by your opponent. You should rarely, if ever, adopt an opposing counsel's rendition of the facts, unless they are actually helpful to your case.

As you summarize the facts tailor them towards the conclusion you seek in your legal analysis. You will quickly realize that some facts are more important than other. After the statement of facts comes a careful presentation of all applicable law, including any law that is contrary to your position. You should concisely state your argument and your opponent's argument, clarifying the disputed issues. Be careful to correctly state the applicable standard or rule of law for the judge and then discuss your strongest cases, taking the time to distinguish any contradictory cases. Do not simply quote those strongest cases but discuss them so that the judge understands how they apply. While doing so you should make sure your argument places the relevant facts into legal principles the judge can decide. Stating the relief that you seek will assist in accomplishing this task. When appropriate you may also propose alternative solutions to the court. Finally you should check with your local court rules for a sample motion submission to ensure that your written motions are in the proper format. The judge will appreciate you taking the time to use the local rules that she enforces.

As part of the motions hearing the judge will expect you to present evidence. Usually the judge will not accept an offer of proof as evidence. When you make an offer of proof to the judge it is just that - an offer. It does not constitute evidence unless the opposing side is willing to stipulate that your version of the facts is correct. As you decide what format to use to introduce evidence in support of your motion keep in mind that the court is not bound by the rules of evidence in the motion phase. Under Federal Rule of Evidence 104(a) evidence may take the form of testimony, stipulations of fact, depositions, and exhibits.

Candor and honesty are essential to effective advocacy. You should never shade the facts in an attempt to win a motion. If the other side is competent they will immediately point out your conduct, and you now have not only an evidentiary problem but an ethical one as well. This does not mean that you cannot diffuse ambiguities or unfavorable facts by openly disclosing and confronting them. You should do so, with a purpose based upon your preparation. Do not assume the court will overlook the ambiguities or unfavorable facts. If the judge latches onto one of them and you have not addressed it you are done in the eyes of the court. Remember always that the advocate that candidly includes contrary but distinguishable legal authority will retain more credibility with the court than advocates who fail to do so.

3. Motions Hearing.

Prior to the Motions Hearing, mark the written motions and responses as required by the local court rules. During the hearing the judge will state that the purpose of this particular session is to litigate motions. The judge will then identify any appellate exhibits previously provided or offered to the court. If she does not do this you should respectfully remind her which exhibits have been admitted. The judge may next inquire into who has the burden and what the standard of proof is for this particular issue. After identifying the burden the judge is normally ready to hear the motion. Most judges give both sides an opportunity to briefly state their position before the presentation of evidence. Normally the moving party has the burden and presents its evidence first. The opposing party then presents its evidence, if any. Afterwards rebuttal and surrebuttal evidence, if any, is presented. The advocates then argue their positions to the judge. The judge deliberates on the motion and ultimately makes a ruling, either orally or in writing. This sequence may vary from judge to judge and such variance has no effect on the validity of the ultimate ruling. Remember also that a judge is typically more proactive and inquisitive during motions practice than in open court session before a jury. You should be prepared for the judge to attempt to focus counsel on the pertinent issues and be unhappy with wasted time.

> **Seven Steps of Motions Practice:**
>
> - State your position
> - Present your facts persuasively
> - Present case law consistent with your theory
> - Distinguish adverse case law
> - Apply the law to the facts
> - Restate your position
> - Request relief
>
> These steps apply to any motion including Motions in Limine and Judgements of Acquittal (made by Defense counsel after the Prosecution closes their case-in-chief and renews after Defense case-in-chief, prior to closing arguments).

Although your argument must be tailored for motions practice, the basic concepts of persuading the judge to rule in your favor apply. Typically, a good motions argument will initially state your position, move to the facts, present the law, apply the law to the facts and, finally, restate your position on the requested relief. Knowing your judge and the local rules will provide greater insight on the general scheme for the motion argument.

B. THE LAW OF MOTIONS PRACTICE.

Federal rule of evidence 104 establishes the authority of the judge to decide questions of admissibility in a motions hearing. This rule gives the judge authority to make decisions during motions without regards to the limitations on admissibility that the other federal rules of evidence might place upon the offered evidence. The only limitation on what evidence the judge may consider

---

Federal Rule of Evidence 104. Preliminary Questions

(a) Questions of admissibility generally.—Preliminary questions concerning the qualification of a person to be a witness, the existence of a privilege, or the admissibility of evidence shall be determined by the court, subject to the provisions of subdivision (b). In making its determination it is not bound by the rules of evidence except those with respect to privileges.

(b) Relevancy conditioned on fact.—When the relevancy of evidence depends upon the fulfillment of a condition of fact, the court shall admit it upon, or subject to, the introduction of evidence sufficient to support a finding of the fulfillment of the condition.

(c) Hearing of jury.—Hearings on the admissibility of confessions shall in all cases be conducted out of the hearing of the jury. Hearings on other preliminary matters shall be so conducted when the interests of justice require, or when an accused is a witness and so requests.

(d) Testimony by accused.—The accused does not, by testifying upon a preliminary matter, become subject to cross-examination as to other issues in the case.

(e) Weight and credibility.—This rule does not limit the right of a party to introduce before the jury evidence relevant to weight or credibility.

---

is found in the rule on privileges. The courts have determined that we will not destroy the privilege protections when deciding motions. The rule also allows for the conditional admissibility of evidence even though counsel has not yet established that it will be relevant. Conditional relevancy exists so that the court can control the flow of the trial and keep cases moving forward in a timely manner. It also reflects the modernization of trial process as part of the federal rules of evidence. Finally the rule allows the accused to testify for the limited purpose of addressing the subject of the motion without otherwise waiving his right to silence in a criminal case.

While federal rule of evidence 104 authorizes the trial judge to decide preliminary issues of admissibility, the impact of that authority and the limitations upon its exercise are discussed in federal rule of evidence 103. Rule 103 establishes that once the judge rules conclusively on an issue raised during a motions hearing that issue is preserved on appeal for the losing side. Prior to this recent change to the federal rules of evidence the losing party was required to object when the evidence addressed during the pretrial motion was actually admitted at trial. The change obviates the need for counsel to object a second time when the evidence is offered in the presence of the jury. Advocates should check to determine whether or not the rules of evidence in their jurisdiction has adopted a similar standard. If not the motions hearing does not end the issue when it comes to objecting. In order to ensure that the issue is preserved on appeal the losing advocate must make the record and object again when the evidence is proffered in open court.

This change to federal rule of evidence 103 settled an issue that had

---

Rule 103. Rulings on Evidence

(a) Effect of erroneous ruling.—Error may not be predicated upon a ruling which admits or excludes evidence unless a substantial right of the party is affected, and

(1) Objection.—In case the ruling is one admitting evidence, a timely objection or motion to strike appears of record, stating the specific ground of objection, if the specific ground was not apparent from the context; or

(2) Offer of proof.—In case the ruling is one excluding evidence, the substance of the evidence was made known to the court by offer or was apparent from the context within which questions were asked. Once the court makes a definitive ruling on the record admitting or excluding evidence, either at or before trial, a party need not renew an objection or offer of proof to preserve a claim of error for appeal.

(b) Record of offer and ruling.—The court may add any other or further statement which shows the character of the evidence, the form in which it was offered, the objection made, and the ruling thereon. It may direct the making of an offer in question and answer form.

(c) Hearing of jury.—In jury cases, proceedings shall be conducted, to the extent practicable, so as to prevent inadmissible evidence from being suggested to the jury by any means, such as making statements or offers of proof or asking questions in the hearing of the jury.

(d) Plain error.—Nothing in this rule precludes taking notice of plain errors affecting substantial rights although they were not brought to the attention of the court.

created much confusion within the practice. Advocates often use pre-trial motions to address inflammatory evidence that they hope to exclude. If they lose, they do not want to underline that fact from a persuasive perspective when the jury is receiving the evidence. Some jurisdictions required that before the change to federal rule of evidence 103. Those advocates practicing in state court should check and see if your jurisdiction follow the new rule 103, the old rule 103, or some local variant thereof.

C. *THE ART OF MOTIONS PRACTICE.*

If the pretrial motion is the best way to get a handle on issues that will affect the way you plan for trial, then the degree of persuasion that you bring to the pretrial motion is every bit as important as the persuasive techniques you use when communicating with the jury. While the ability to organize information and to tie the issue to your legal theory, factual theory and moral theme are always important, the primary difference during motions practice is the focused nature of the particular issue you are addressing and the audience you must convince. A motion is in an application to the judge for particular relief based upon your understanding of the facts of your case, and how the law applies to those facts.

Both sides should consider getting advanced rulings on the admissibility of their own evidence if admissibility is in doubt. Consider challenging the admissibility of your opponent's evidence in advance. Knowing whether key pieces of evidence are admissible will impact your theory of the case. A motion in limine asks the judge to rule on an evidentiary matter outside the hearing of the jury either before trial or during a recess. Check local court rules concerning motions in limine; some jurisdictions require advanced notice. Although often associated more with defense motion practice, motions in limine are available for both parties. Most jurisdictions allow motions to be oral or, at the discretion of the judge, in writing. An effective motion states the grounds upon which it is made and sets forth the ruling or relief sought. You should employ all of the techniques discussed elsewhere regarding eye contact, voice modulation and the use of exhibits, but the key persuasive techniques you choose to use must reflect your knowledge of the audience - a judge.

Judges have discretion to decide pretrial motions when made, or may chose to defer a decision until the issue or evidence arises during the trial. That deferral is normally not allowed if a party's right to review or appeal would be adversely affected. Where factual issues are involved in determining a motion, the judge is normally required to state the essential findings of fact on the record in most jurisdictions. If a motion is denied, you have the ability to have the judge reconsider a past ruling upon request, or sua sponte, at any time prior to the end of trial. Judge's are concerned with judicial economy - moving the case along in a fair but efficient fashion. They do not waste time and do not want you to waste their time either. A fifteen minute soliloquy on the wonders of the right to privacy under the United States Constitution will not be appreciated. Relevant and applicable case law, hopefully with precedential value will be.

It is important that you understand the procedures involved with motions practice in order to maximize your ability to persuade the judge. Judge's look for the fair, honest and reliable advocate. They want to be certain that when you argue a case, cite to authority or delineate negative cases that you are an honest broker. Honesty is a by product of both attitude and preparation. One is of limited value to the court without the other. The honest, but bumbling advocate is of no use to a judge ruling on a pre-trial motion. If they doubt your competency with the law they will not rule in your favor, even if they like you. The judge is concerned with protecting the record and not being overturned on appeal. They view everything you tell them through the lens of the appellate process. If you know this, you can arrange your facts, your law and your presentation to make the judge comfortable with the idea that the "safest" path to a non-appealable decision is by deciding the motion in your favor.

A competent advocate must be familiar with the procedures to complete his or her preparation for trial. The bulk of motion practice procedure is set forth in the local rules of court, and your familiarity with those rules and compliance with their procedures will be perceived by the trial judge as evidence of your competency. Sources of procedural guidance include regional or appellate court rules, as well as those specific ones published by your respective judge. The Rules of Professional Responsibility governing attorneys engaging in motions practice are inextricably intertwined with procedural rules. While oral motions are allowed, written motions are often more persuasive, articulate, and organized. To maximize persuasion and preserve issues on appeal written motions should be the rule rather than the exception whenever possible. The writing process forces the advocate to craft carefully their rendition of the facts and the law to increase persuasion and the chances of a favorable ruling on the motion.

When the time comes to actually argue the motion be prepared. The party that raised the motion normally states the relief sought to the judge to begin the motion hearing. The opposing advocate is allowed to briefly respond, and then the party that has the burden of proof admits evidence to support their position. The other counsel will then have an opportunity to proffer additional evidence, after which the judge will normally allow both sides to argue. Sometimes the judge will also allow the party that brought the motion, usually a criminal defense attorney, to make a rebuttal argument. Afterwards a ruling is entered and the case proceeds to the next issue. During this process the judge is your audience, not the opposing counsel. Remain silent when the other side is speaking. Give to the other advocate the same degree of respect that you would want when it is your turn to speak. Advocates interrupt each other when they are trying to prevent the opposing counsel from making a point that hurts their position. Do not fall into this habit. Wait for the judge to speak, speak when it is your turn and respond when allowed to do so. All arguments are made directly to the judge, never to opposing counsel. Nothing is gained by getting into an argument with an advocate for the other side. You have a referee and an umpire there - use her. By acknowledging the power and authority of the judge through the respectful nature of your conduct you increase your believability and reliability. These are key factors that the judge will consider when deciding which advocate to trust.

The advice in the proceeding paragraph is predicated on the idea of a judge that is attempting to discharge their duties in accordance with the judicial code of conduct. If that is not the case, then the ability to persuade falls into a different category. In those rare instances you may find yourself with the might of the both the opposing side and the bench arrayed against you. The record is your friend when this occurs. The more behaviors and actions that are unfair which you can place on the record the better your chance of winning on appeal. You will note that the audience you are attempting to persuade has changed now. If the trial judge is not being fair then your audience becomes the appellate court. This may make for an unpleasant trial experience, but advocates understand the necessity of properly identifying their audience as they choose the manner in which they will proceed. That advice holds true in motions practice just as it does elsewhere in the trial process.

D. TABLE OF MOTION ISSUES AND EVIDENTIARY RULES.

Table 1 serves as a starting point for additional inquiry into the relationships between specific tasks during motions practice and the rules of evidence. Your case analysis and motion preparation should assist you in identifying when these particular issues will arise. Use the table to review your knowledge of the evidentiary rule so that you can include the impact these rules have on the structure of motions practice in your jurisdiction.

Issue Arising Dealing with Motions	Applicable Federal Rule of Evidence
Authority to decide preliminary issues of admissibility.	104
Impact when accused's chooses to testify during motions hearing.	103
When is an issue preserved for appeal?	103
How to handle privileges during motions.	501
Real and demonstrative evidence	901

Table 1 - Potential Evidentiary Rules Applicable During Motions

Points to Ponder...

1. What tactical or strategic advantages do you perceive in motions practice? What pitfalls exist?

2. Are motions practice issues the types of questions that your client should have veto power over? Should you make motions that your client does not want you to make? Can you think of a situation where that might occur?

3. Does motions practice allow you to place ticking appellate time bombs in the record of trial? Is it a way to manipulate the judge or opposing counsel? Can you use it to take up opposing counsel's time so that don't have as much of an opportunity to prepare for trial? Should you?

CHAPTER TEN
IMPEACHMENT

"Breaking his oath and resolution
Like a twist of rotten silk."[1]

A. THE SKILL OF IMPEACHMENT.

1. Understanding Impeachment.

You learned in chapter 6 that the one of the three goals during cross examination is to establish facts that build up the credibility of your witnesses and decrease the credibility of your opponent's witness. Impeachment is the tool advocates use to accomplish this third goal. The fundamental purpose of impeachment is to discredit a witness as a reliable source of information. There are

> **Goals during cross examination:**
>
> (1) control the witness;
>
> (2) establish facts that build to a Theme and Theory; and
>
> (3) establish facts that build up the credibility of your witnesses and diminish the credibility of your opponent's witnesses.

five common methods of impeachment. There are some common legal and practical considerations that must be addressed before choosing which type of impeachment to employ. Initially you must know everything that the witness knows, and what the witness does not know, in order to be successful during impeachment. You will only be in this position if you have prepared sufficiently, and a continuing case analysis is the best means available to an

---

[1] WILLIAM SHAKESPEARE, CORIOLANUS, act 5, sc. 6.

advocate that guarantees sufficient knowledge to ensure success. There are five primary means of impeachment. Each has a slightly different legal basis, and

---

FIVE PRIMARY MEANS OF IMPEACHMENT:

- *Prior untruthful acts.* FRE 608(b).
- *Prior conviction.* FRE 609.
- *Prior inconsistent statement.* FRE 613.
- *Bias, prejudice or motive.* Common law.
- *Defects in Capacity to Observe, Recall or Relate.* Common Law.

---

the manner in which you accomplish each type of impeachment is tied to the reason you are legally allowed to impeach the witness.

As soon as a witness testifies, his credibility becomes an issue. Because credibility is intrinsically tied to testifying it is always logically relevant. The limitations of the Federal Rules of Evidence on impeachment establish the degree to which the credibility of a witness is legally relevant. Advocates must be able to articulate how a particular fact or set of facts tend to impeach the credibility of a witness and satisfy the logical relevancy requirements of the Federal Rules of Evidence. Bear in mind that probative impeachment evidence that is both logically and legally relevant may be excluded by the judge based on federal rule of evidence 403 if its probative value is substantially outweighed by the danger of unfair prejudice.

Witness credibility has three facets at trial--bolstering, impeachment, and rehabilitation. Advocates are not allowed to bolster the believability of their witness by offering to prove the witness's character for truthfulness before it has been attacked through impeachment by opposing counsel. Bolstering is generally prohibited. Advocates are permitted to accredit the witness by eliciting general background information and qualifications as a preliminary step of direct examination. This is an essential step for expert witnesses, and will be discussed in detail in chapter 12. After a witness has been impeached, the proponent may attempt to rehabilitate his credibility by giving him the opportunity to explain or deny an apparent inconsistency, prior bad act, or prior untruthfulness. Impeachment is not limited to opposing counsel. Under federal rule of evidence 607, "the credibility of a witness may be attacked by any party, including the party calling the witness."

For reasons of judicial economy, certain matters offered for impeachment of a witness may not be proven by extrinsic evidence because they raise questions which are too collateral to the issues in the trial. If courts allowed this sort of inquiry, examinations would consist of mini-trials within trials. This is referred to as the **Collateral Fact Rule.** If a matter is deemed collateral, the court will only permit inquiry on cross-examination. Prior untruthful acts of the witness are generally considered collateral, whereas prior convictions and proof of bias are rarely collateral. When an issue is collateral, extrinsic proof cannot be offered to establish the veracity of the impeachment. Some forms of impeachment may be proven by extrinsic evidence, while others only permit inquiry on cross-examination. Regardless of which impeachment technique is used, counsel must have a good faith belief that the impeaching facts are true.

These techniques are designed to create tension by building suspense and sparking the interest of the jury, while suggesting the answer that everyone expects. There is nothing wrong with that expectation during impeachment. You must make certain that you have the available resources to impeach the witness when they stray from the good or bad facts that you identified through your case analysis. **This point is crucial. If the witness challenges you, and the law allows you to respond to that challenge – you must.** The only thing worse than no impeachment is a bad one. Failure to properly control empowers the witness, weakens your theme and theory of the case and calls into question your credibility as an advocate in the eyes of the fact finder.

2. Preparing Impeachment.

Impeachment is not an end in itself. Counsel must always analyze not only whether impeachment of a particular witness will help their case, but how it will help the case. A clear theory of your case and your opponent's case is

---

Determining if you should impeach a witness:

Has the witness's testimony factually supported your case?

Will my chosen method of impeachment destroy the witness's entire credibility or only undermine their truthfulness on the impeached points?

Can I effectively impeach?

Will the jury see the impeachment as significant or only a lawyer trick?

How does the witness present - basically truthful or basically untruthful?

critical before you can adequately determine whether or not an impeachment is warranted and will be effective. An effective impeachment depends upon accurate knowledge of the law, good technique, and projection of the right attitude. Impeachment only matters when the jury knows that it has occurred and understand what it means. Counsel should always strive for clarity and simplicity because clarity and simplicity will assist the jury in understanding and using the impeachment for its intended purpose.

It is often to your long term benefit at trial to approach witnesses in a non-threatening way when possible. Using this technique will ensure you do not offend the jury's sense of fair play and perception of the witness. It also allows you to conduct a fair and competent cross examination without poisoning your relationship with what might otherwise be a cooperative witness. If the witness has testified in a way that exposes him to impeachment, consider whether clarification or refreshing his recollection will accomplish the same purpose that a full blown impeachment would produce. If the witness has hurt your case and you decide to impeach him, you must further consider what tone and style of impeachment will be most effective. If the witness is cocky, partisan, or simply lying, then a hard-hitting, aggressive tone may be appropriate. If the witness seems sincere, then a gentler approach may be warranted.

B. THE LAW OF CROSS EXAMINATION AND IMPEACHMENT.

Federal Rule of Evidence 611[2] addresses witnesses and establishes the manner and scope of witness testimony during cross examination. While the form of cross examination as to questions is governed by Federal Rule of Evidence 611, many other evidentiary rules impact on your ability to impeach witnesses. You must fully understand the doctrine behind the evidentiary rules governing impeachment to effectively learn this skill. You should begin your inquiry by developing a deeper basis of knowledge concerning prior untruthful acts under federal rule of evidence 608(b),[3] prior convictions under federal rule of evidence 609,[4] and prior inconsistent statements under federal rule of evidence 613.[5] Additionally you must master the common law concerning bias,

---

[2] See Federal Rule of Evidence 611 in Appendix III.

[3] See Federal Rule of Evidence 608(b) in Appendix III.

[4] See Federal Rule of Evidence 609 in Appendix III.

[5] See Federal Rule of Evidence 613 in Appendix III.

motive and defects in capacity to observe, recall or relate information. An in depth study of these evidentiary rules is beyond the capacity of this text, but in the following pages when each type of impeachment is discussed the chapter will provide a copy of the rule and the fundamental questioning steps you must

---

Article VI. Witnesses. Rule 611.
Mode and Order of Interrogation and Presentation:

(a) Control by court. The court shall exercise reasonable control over the mode and order of interrogating witnesses and presenting evidence so as to (1) make the interrogation and presentation effective for the ascertainment of the truth, (2) avoid needless consumption of time, and (3) protect witnesses from harassment or undue embarrassment.

(b) Scope of cross-examination. Cross-examination should be limited to the subject matter of the direct examination and matters affecting the credibility of the witness. The court may, in the exercise of discretion, permit inquiry into additional matters as if on direct examination.

(c) Leading questions. Leading questions should not be used on the direct examination of a witness except as may be necessary to develop the witness' testimony. Ordinarily leading questions should be permitted on cross-examination. When a party calls a hostile witness, an adverse party, or a witness identified with an adverse party, interrogation may be

---

Example 1: Federal Rule of Evidence 611 (2004).

take to establish a valid impeachment under that particular legal basis for impeachment. Using the text will make you competent, but it will not make you superior when it comes to impeachment. Impeachment is legally relevant activity at trial because the rules of evidence and the common law make it so. The law of evidence allows you to specifically point out certain defects in the testimony of witnesses. You should consider the evidentiary rules mentioned above and sprinkled through out this chapter as examples of the legal relevance standard that must exist before the court will allow you to impeach.

C. COMBINING THE SKILL, LAW, AND ART OF IMPEACHMENT.

Words are powerful in the courtroom during impeachment, but they are only part of the equation. Language choice, physical demeanor and body

position also impact on the perception and
viability of the impeachment. The
combination of all of these factors can turn
a difficult issue from a factual perspective
into an "I'm really sorry I have to point this
out but..." impeachment that makes all of
the points necessary for your case analysis
without directly attacking the witness. It is
a question of choice, of feel and of
perceptions. While we want the jury's
attention to be focused on the advocate
during cross examination, there are times

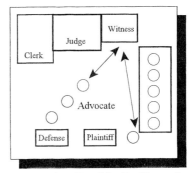

Figure 1 - Possible Positions for
Advocates During Impeachment

during impeachment when the witness has no good answer for the question you
have put to them. In that moment you want the jury focused on the witness, not
the advocate. You can sense during the impeachment if that moment is going
to come. If it is available you should seize it. When that happens focus the jury
on the witness using the same physical location techniques from direct
examination.

1. Prior Untruthful Acts.

Federal rule of evidence 608(b) permits counsel to impeach a witness
by cross-examining her concerning certain prior bad acts. Only those prior acts
which are probative of the witness's character for truthfulness may be used to
impeach under this rule. Impeachment by prior untruthful acts is limited to cross
examination. When you impeach for this purpose extrinsic evidence is not
allowed. If the witness denies or minimizes the deceptive nature of the act for
which you are attempting to impeach her, you cannot use extrinsic evidence to
refute her answer, or to establish the untruthful nature of the witness's prior act.
You are stuck with her answer. Although extrinsic evidence is not admissible
to prove the prior untruthful act, counsel may be required to disclose the basis
for believing that the act occurred. The inability to articulate a good faith basis
for an inquiry under federal rule of evidence 608(b) may result in a mistrial or
other judicial sanction. Additionally, the judge may forbid inquiry into prior
untruthful acts if they violate the requirements of federal rule of evidence 403.
The most common objections raised when advocates attempt to impeach a
witness with prior untruthful bad acts deal with the fact that the impeachment
is either unduly prejudicial or a waste of time. Judges pay particular attention
to this issue when the individual being impeached is the defendant.

You should always investigate each witness thoroughly for the potential
existence of this type of evidence. Prior untruthful acts happened in the past,

and they are not the sort of issues that witnesses like to disclose. Sometimes you will have to dig deep to find material that will help. It is difficult to investigate the personal lives of witnesses to discover this sort of information, but their official records and employment history can be quite accessible and helpful. One place to consider spending a good deal of time developing is the work environment. Supervisors of witnesses usually have an opinion regarding the witness's truthfulness or untruthfulness. Exploring the basis for these opinions can provide fruitful impeachment material.

During trial, form your questions carefully. There are several ways to approach the prior untruthful act. If you know the witness will admit the prior act, it may be possible to impeach with a few direct, dramatic questions. More commonly, you will need to pursue a more oblique approach, committing the witness to specific facts surrounding the prior incident before confronting her with the specific untruthful act. If you demonstrate to the witness your knowledge of the prior act through detailed, succinct, leading questions, she will be reluctant to deny your account. It is especially difficult for the witness if your questions refer to witnesses who could corroborate your allegations. The witness doesn't understand that you are barred from presenting extrinsic proof of the prior untruthful act. The subtle handling of documents during cross-examination may also lead the witness to believe that you possess documentary proof of the prior act.

Since you are not permitted to present extrinsic evidence of the prior bad act, you are stuck with the witness's denial. You may, however, test the witness's commitment to his denial. An initial denial may need clarification to ensure that you are referring to the same event as the witness. If you persist after a denial, you may draw an "asked and answered" objection from opposing counsel. Be prepared to explain to the judge that you are simply attempting to refresh the witness as to the surrounding facts or clarifying the incident to which you are referring.

Special care is warranted when using prior bad acts to impeach the accused in a criminal case. You should alert the judge and opposing counsel as to your intent to impeach the accused with such information. This gives the opposing counsel an opportunity to object to such impeachment prior to cross-examination. The judge will appreciate the opportunity to weigh the matter in advance outside the presence of the jury. Since the judge is the gatekeeper in determining whether or not you will be allowed to ask these questions it makes perfect sense to not try and hide the ball. For tactical reasons you may wish to delay such notice until after the accused has testified, because the very decision to get on the stand may be influenced by the knowledge that you have this type of impeachment information. In that case simply ask the judge for a hearing outside the presence of the jury to address possible impeachment after the direct examination of the accused and before you begin your cross.

As with other forms of impeachment, you must ensure that your impeachment is consistent with your plan for the witness. It is generally a good idea to consider eliciting favorable information from the witness before casting doubt on her veracity. It is often better to raise impeachment after the witness has offered testimony which conflicts with your theory of the case. Thus, the cross-examination could begin by having the witness affirm favorable testimony; then proceed to attack his unfavorable testimony; then impeach the witness to show that he does not always tell the truth. Remember that some witnesses help you more than hurt you and you may be better off foregoing impeachment opportunities.

Consider the following example:

Q. Isn't it true that you once lied to your insurance company by filing an incorrect claim about an allegedly stolen car stereo?

A. I don't know what you are talking about.

* If you receive this type of answer how much further can you go? You should ask these follow up questions to clarify the incident in question and to test the witness's commitment to his answer.

Q. GEICO refused to renew your car insurance recently, isn't that correct?

A. They canceled it because I had too many points on my license.

*Take the time to check the jury; do they seem to believe you or do they think you are cashing in on this guy's poor driving record to inappropriately call into question his credibility?

Q. You filed a claim with GEICO based on the alleged theft of your car stereo, right?

A. Right.

Q. At the time you filed the claim your policy was still in effect?

A. Yes.

Q. **GEICO refused to pay your claim?**

A. Yeah, they refused.

Q. **Your car stereo was never stolen?**

A. No.

Q. **Isn't it true that you filed a false claim for your car stereo with GEICO?**

A. No.

Q. **It's true isn't it that GEICO canceled your policy right after you claimed your stereo was stolen?**

A. No.

Q. **We can at least agree that GEICO canceled your policy after you filed your stolen stereo claim?**

A. Yes. But that was not the reason they cancelled it.

* You have probably gone as far as you can go with this impeachment. If the jury has been following you, they should get the clear impression that this witness is not truthful.

2. Prior Convictions.

The admissibility of prior untruthful acts are normally decided during a motion in limine. Resolution of issues of admissibility under federal rule of evidence 609 often requires judicial balancing. Both the proponent and the opponent of the witness should consider a motion in limine to obtain a ruling prior to trial so that they can make tactical decisions regarding the examination of the witness based upon potential impeachment. On the other hand, counsel may consider waiting for the

> **You May Impeach Concerning Prior Convictions by:**
>
> Cross examining the witness with the conviction,
>
> Entering the authenticated record of the conviction,
>
> Testimony by someone present when witness was convicted.

other side to raise the issue of the prior conviction if they believe it to be clearly admissible. In some jurisdictions discovery rules may require disclosure of this information even if you do not seek a ruling through a motion in limine. The impeaching party has the ability to choose the form of impeachment. Options include eliciting the fact of the *conviction* on cross-examination; admitting into evidence an authenticated record of the conviction; or by testimony of someone present when the witness was convicted.

This rule permits counsel to use either cross-examination or extrinsic evidence to prove the prior conviction. When the witness admits the facts pertaining to the conviction on cross-examination, however, the judge may exclude further evidence on the grounds that it is cumulative. While there is more than one way to prove a prior conviction, cross-examination of the witness about the conviction is the preferred method. If the witness denies, mischaracterizes, or minimizes the nature of the conviction, then the impeachment value of the record is magnified. Always be prepared to do it both ways. When preparing for possible impeachment with a conviction remember that a properly certified record of conviction is a self-authenticating document and needs no sponsoring witness. If opposing counsel objects to the record of conviction on hearsay grounds, cite to federal rule of evidence 803(8); that should be sufficient to overcome a hearsay objection.

It is important to note that most courts do not permit counsel to explore the details of the prior conviction. Getting in the conviction itself is enough for impeachment, but the details do not come in, i.e. you cannot ask what led her to commit the crime of the past conviction, etc. Some courts permit proof of the sentence imposed. The record of previous conviction usually indicates the sentence imposed. If the record is admissible, then cross-examination about the sentence imposed should also be admissible. Determine how far the judge will permit you to go by asking him during the pretrial hearing.

When sorting out which convictions may be used to impeach a witness under federal rule of evidence 609 it is helpful to sort the convictions into either crimes of dishonesty and false statement (usually referred to as crimen falsi crimes) and all other crimes. Crimen falsi crimes are admissible to impeach any witness, including the accused, regardless of the punishment authorized or actually imposed.[6] Convictions for other crimes, depends upon whether the crime was punishable by death, or confinement in excess of one year. If so impeachment by conviction may be admissible subject to the discretion of the court. The law of the jurisdiction in which the conviction was obtained governs the determination of maximum punishment. Maximum punishment is determined based upon the statutory possibility, not the actual punishment received. For instance, a conviction for robbery that carried a maximum

---

[6] See Fed. R. Evid. 609(a)(2).

sentence of 5 years would be a qualifying conviction, even if the court only sentenced the accused to less than one year confinement.

The "other crimes" category of convictions is subject to judicial balancing under federal rule of evidence 403 for all witnesses other than the accused when determining admissibility. When the accused is the witness then his conviction is admissible for impeachment purposes only if the judge determines that the probative value outweighs the prejudicial effect to the accused.[7] For convictions other than crimen falsi crimes there is a 10 year window. If the conviction was obtained or the sentence of confinement, to include any probation, was completed more than 10 years ago it is not admissible for impeachment purposes. However, the judge can still admit such evidence if the proponent of the evidence gives written notice and the judge determines that the probative value of the evidence substantially outweighs the prejudicial effect.[8] Note that this test differs from the normal federal rule of evidence 403 balancing test, with a preference for excluding the evidence under this standard. Keep in mind that pendency of an appeal will not render such convictions inadmissible, but pardon, annulment, or certificate of rehabilitation may bar use of such evidence. It is also important to note that evidence of juvenile adjudications is generally not admissible.[9]

Consider the following example where the witness admits to the previous conviction:

Q. Mr. Bones, isn't it true that you were convicted in state court nine years ago?

A. Yes.

Q. That court convicted you for filing a false claim with the state unemployment agency?

A. Yes, sir.

Q. And you were convicted of making a false claim for lying on several forms filed with the state?

A. Yes.

---

[7] See Fed. R. Evid. 609(a)(1).

[8] See Fed. R. Evid. 609(b).

[9] See Fed. R. Evid. 609.

Q. Nothing further, your honor.

Now consider this second example where the witness is not inclined to admit to the earlier conviction. Note how the advocate handles this process.

Q. Are you the same Mr. Bones who was previously convicted in federal court in December 20XX?

A. Well, I don't know if it was a federal court.

Q. Isn't it a fact that you were convicted of conspiracy to destroy the original manuscript of the Declaration of Independence in 20XX?

A. It should have never been signed!

Q. Please answer the question. Were you convicted of conspiracy to destroy the Declaration of Independence?

A. No, I was not.

Q. Isn't it a fact that you were sentenced to five years confinement for conspiracy to destroy the Declaration of Independence?

A. Uh, no, it was only two years.

Q. So, you now admit that you were convicted of that crime?

A. Well, yes, but it wasn't a "federal" court I wasn't sentenced to five years in jail.

Q. Your honor, the state moves to admit P.E. 10 for ID into evidence as P.E. 10.

J. Defense?

DC. We object to this exhibit on the grounds of hearsay and lack of authentication.

J. State?

State. Your honor P.E. 10 for ID is a self-authenticating document under

FRE 902(4) and also falls within the hearsay exception under FRE 803(8).

J.   The objection is overruled.   P.E. 10 for ID will be admitted as P.E. 10. You may proceed.

Q.   **I am handing the witness P.E. 10. Mr. Bones , this is an official record of your conviction. Please take a moment to read block "5e" of that record of conviction. Tell the court what block f states as the sentence you were given for the conspiracy to destroy the Declaration of Independence.**

A.   It says that I was sentenced to five years confinement.

Q.   **Thank you.   Nothing further.**

3. Prior Inconsistent Statements.

The use of the Prior Inconsistent Statements (PIS) for impeachment purposes only is governed by federal rule of evidence 613. When impeaching under this rule you can only use the facts of the impeachment to argue witness credibility in closing argument. You may not use the impeachment to suggest an alternative factual position – unless the witness adopts your position or an additional evidentiary rule allows for the admittance of the out of court statements which forms the basis of your impeachment. The form of the PIS can be varied. Possible options include written statements, transcripts of prior testimony, oral statements made by the witness, omissions of a material nature from a prior statement, and assertive or communicative conduct. The focus of the inquiry is whether or not you have a good faith basis to believe that the statement was made by the witness. If you do then it is potentially impeachment material.

Before federal rule of evidence 613 was adopted a common law requirement existed that you had to give the witness an opportunity to see the prior written statement before you could cross examine them on its contents. While federal rule of evidence 613 disposed of this requirement, some state jurisdictions still expect it. You should check your local rules before impeaching without first showing the written statement to the witness. In any event, you must disclose the written statement to opposing counsel upon their request. Most competent counsel routinely request disclosure of all impeachment materials during discovery. When impeachment occurs under the auspices of federal rule of evidence 613 it is admitted for the limited purpose of showing a lack of credibility. If the impeaching counsel wishes to argue that evidence substantively then it must also either be adopted as fact by the witness or be otherwise admissible under an appropriate hearsay rule.

The prior inconsistent statement may be admitted as extrinsic evidence only if (1) the witness denies making the prior statement or denies that it is inconsistent, (2) the inconsistency goes to a noncollateral matter, (3) and the statement is otherwise admissible under the hearsay rules. If the witness acknowledges the prior statement, then it is not allowed into evidence because it has been adopted by the witness. If counsel is able to introduce the prior statement the witness must be given the opportunity to explain or deny the statement. From a practical perspective impeachment with a prior inconsistent statement always begins with examination of the witness concerning the prior statement.

When a prior inconsistent statement is used, the judge shall give a limiting instruction to the jury upon request by the opposing party. The prior inconsistent statement is not substantive evidence and cannot be relied upon to prove an element of the offense or a defense. The statement, if admitted, will be accompanied by a limiting instruction from the judge stating it can be considered only on the issue of the witness's credibility. A prior inconsistent statement offered solely to impeach the witness under federal rule of evidence 613 is hearsay and not admissible for the truth of the matter contained therein. However, a prior inconsistent statement is not hearsay if declarant and witness are the same and the prior statement was made under oath and subject to cross-examination.[10] A prior inconsistent statement is also not hearsay if it is a party-opponent admission.[11]

> **Using the "3 C's:"**
>
> Commit to the in court testimony,
>
> Credit the earlier statement,
>
> Confront with the inconsistency.

When conducting prior inconsistent statement impeachment on cross-examination use the 3-step process commonly referred to as the "3 C's." The order of the three steps may vary depending on the witness, but is most situations you (1) commit the witness to their in court testimony, (2) credit the earlier statement of the witness, and (3) confront the witness with the inconsistency. The degree to which you emphasize each step in the "3 C's" is driven by the strength of your available information. It may be that you can spend a great deal of time crediting the earlier statement because of the circumstances under which it was made. Other times the difference between the prior statement and the

---

[10] See Fed. R. Evid. 801(d)(1)(A).

[11] See Fed. R. Evid. 801(d)(2).

current in court testimony is so great that you spend a good deal of time working on the confrontation. You choose which to emphasize based upon the strength of your case and the reason for your impeachment.

PIS using the 3 C's:

Commit the witness to what she said on direct: "*You told us on direct examination that you saw the accused with a knife, correct?*"

Credit the witness's prior statement and its accuracy: "*You made a statement about this case on July 4th last year?*

Things were fresh in your mind when you made that statement?

You swore to tell the truth before you gave that answer?

When you gave that statement you had never been interviewed by a prosecutor?

When you gave that statement you had not had the opportunity to discuss what happened that night with others who were there?

You have had that opportunity since you gave that statement?"

Confront the witness with the prior statement: "*You said in your July statement, and I quote, 'The accused was not carrying any weapon that I could see.' Those were your words?*"

Once you have mastered the basics of how to impeach with a prior inconsistent statement you should next begin to develop some tools that allow you to maximize the persuasive impact of the impeachment. Advocates may commit, credit, and confront in a number of ways. Consider the following examples:

Witness impeaches himself. Advocates may highlight the relevant portion of the witness's statement, mark the document as an exhibit for identification (always coordinate with the court reporter when marking an exhibit in advance), and present the document to the witness. The witness will then identify the document and confirm that it is his statement. Counsel may confront the witness with the conflicting language by having the witness read aloud the portion that counsel selected. Counsel may also have the witness read the preceding question (if the statement is in question-and-answer format) and then his own answer to that question. Be sure to control the witness during this maneuver. Focus the witness to do exactly what you want with clear, succinct and direct words.

Advocate impeaches the witness. Advocates may simply have the witness confirm the existence of the prior statement, reinforce its credibility, and verify the conflicting testimony by quoting it to the witness. This approach removes the necessity of fumbling with the document, since it does not need to be handed to the witness.

Graphic aid impeaches the witness. Advocates may wish to convert the documentary statement into a clear graphical aid and then project the document onto a screen. This way the jurors themselves can actually see the words that damn the witness.

Statement impeaches the witness. When the witness denies making the statement, and the statement does not relate to a collateral matter, counsel may, after the witness has departed, present another witness who overheard the witness's out-of-court statement or who took the written statement from the witness. In such a case, the statement may be admitted for the limited purpose of showing that it was made, unless the statement is admissible as substantive evidence (*see* FRE 801).

Make certain that you creatively adapt your techniques for validating the prior statement to the particular form of that prior statement. The important facts advocates should rely upon while validating the prior statement vary, depending on the form of the statement. If the prior statement was a sworn statement, then it is important to elicit the fact that the witness had the opportunity to review the statement, initialed each page, took an oath, and signed his name.

Now that you know how to impeach with a prior inconsistent statement the next question is when should you impeach? A good rule of thumb is to impeach only on significant inconsistencies. Nit-picking about minor variations on insignificant details is often unimpressive as an impeachment technique. If you do not have a valid impeachment that either advances your theme and theory, hurts your opponent's theme and theory or reduces the credibility of the witness then do not impeach. Juries understand that there will be minor variations in detail each time a human tells a story. Repeated attempts to call the witness a liar on the basis of these variations will be perceived as overreaching, rather than effective impeachment of the witness's credibility. You do not want to be the advocate who completes what they believe to be a competent impeachment by prior inconsistent statement only to look up and see the members of the jury looking at you with a "why did you bother" look on their faces. Make certain there is a true factual inconsistency rather than a mere semantic difference. You can clarify the facts during the **commit** phase of the impeachment to make certain you are in the right area. This is a technique that quickly becomes old if it is overused. Finally, you should always be prepared to prove the inconsistent statement with extrinsic evidence. When interviewing a witness before trial, have a witness present who can later be called to testify about inconsistent statements made in the interview. You should also, whenever possible, reduce significant pretrial statements to writing and have the witness swear to their truthfulness.

4. Bias, Motive.

Bias, prejudice, or any motive to misrepresent may be shown to impeach the witness either by the witness or by evidence otherwise adduced. Such evidence is relevant because it may show that the witness is not an impartial observer or witness of the truth. As long as the impeaching counsel can articulate a theory of why the witness may be predisposed to favor the other side, the evidence should be admissible. Common law allows this under the theory of bias, prejudice or motive. Each of these issues is not collateral to the testimony of the witness, even when the witness in question is not the victim.

The foundation required to establish bias, motive or prejudice is case specific and does not require any specific foundational elements. Proof of bias, prejudice or motive to lie may be established by direct or circumstantial evidence. To impeach the witness, you must persuade the fact-finder that the witness has some reason to perceive or recall events in a skewed manner, or to abandon his oath and become a partisan for one side.

Evidence of bias is not limited only to cross-examination of the witness. While the best evidence often may be concessions from the witness himself, supplemental proof may be necessary to give it full impact. Counsel will ordinarily be given wide latitude in proving facts which establish bias. Even if the witness admits his bias, or facts from which bias may be inferred, the judge may permit extrinsic evidence of the same facts, unless such evidence is cumulative. For example, if the witness acknowledges his friendship with the accused, the judge may still allow other witnesses to drive the fact home with specific examples of acts of friendship.

You cannot use it if you do not have it. The key to successful use of bias impeachment is thorough pretrial investigation. Interview every witness, talk to neighbors and social contacts. Ask your investigators to assist with this effort, even though it goes beyond element-based evidence gathering. You need to know as much as possible to prepare for effective impeachments in this area.

Develop a standard checklist for bias, prejudice and motive to lie. Certain bases for bias, prejudice and motive to lie recur often and are a good starting place for analysis. Consider these:

Fruitful Areas of Possible Bias:

Lay witnesses: family relationships, grudges, prior conflicts, romantic interests, friends, racism, common memberships, superior-subordinate relationships, officer-enlisted relationships, threats and coercion, peer pressure.

Experts: defense or prosecution orientation, hourly rate, depth of expertise, academic or real-world experience.

Police: pressure to obtain convictions, fear of disclosing departure from regulations.

Suspects: promise of clemency, threat of adverse action, immunity, avoiding suspicion.

Accused: desire to avoid conviction and punishment.

Do not choose to impeach witnesses about issues that are obvious to everyone in the courtroom. We all know that mothers love their sons. What benefit do you receive by impeaching a mother about her familial love when she has testified? You may have pointed that fact out to the jury, but does it matter? In the absence of evidence to the contrary there is little if any reason to belabor the obvious. It is often better to subtly establish facts from which bias can be inferred, rather than confronting the witness directly. Save the ultimate point for your closing argument. Establish the predicate facts that add up to bias, prejudice or motive to lie, but "do the math" for the jury during your closing argument. If you are foolish enough to ask the witness to sum it up for you they will, but you will not like their math. Witnesses usually respond with a dramatic reaffirmation of their oath or a statement of their heartfelt pain in admitting mistakes for the good of the "truth." When you allow this you have just let the witness shift the focus from the points you have made to the points they feel are important.

Consider the following example:

*Q. **Mr. Jones, you and the defendant, Mr. Smith, work on the same line in the cardboard factory?***

A. Yes.

Q. You are both quality control inspectors on the end of the line?

A. Yes.

Q. What is your current position on the line?

A. I am the assistant quality control manager.

Q. You are the assistant quality control manager. Who is the quality control manager?

A. Mr. Smith.

Q. How long have you been his assistant?

A. About eight years.

Q. You got the job when Mr. Smith recommended you for it?

A. Yes.

Q. Who writes your quarterly employee reports?

A. Mr. Smith does.

Q. You work with him on a daily basis?

A. Yes.

Q. You and the defendant are a good quality control team?

A. Best in the plant.

Q. You and the defendant spend time together after work?

A. Sure, all the time.

Q. You go to movies together?

A. Sometimes.

Q. You go to ball games together?

A. We've been to a few.

Q. You are both on the company softball team?

A. Yes.

Q. You guys practice year round, don't you?

A. Yes.

Q. In fact you are the team's star catcher?

A. Yes.

Q. And the defendant is your pitcher?

A. He's the best.

Q. You get along well with Mr. Smith, don't you?

A. What do you mean?

Q. You are good friends?

A. Yes.

Q. He's one of your best friends, isn't he?

A. I guess so.

Q. And you certainly don't want him to go to jail, do you?

A. No.

Q. You don't believe he should be tried, do you?

A. No.

Q. You weren't in the bowling alley the night Mr. Smith hit Mr. Johnson with a spare bowling pin?

A. No.

Q. All you know about the incident has been told to you by Mr. Smith?

A. I guess so.

5. Defects in Capacity.

While there is not a specific federal rule of evidence that addresses the ability of counsel to impeach a witness based upon defects in observation, such defects are not collateral and inquiry is generally permissible. When preparing the cross-examination of a witness who will provide testimony about a visual observation advocates must consider both the internal and the external factors that may affect the accuracy of such testimony. Internal factors are those physical and mental aspects of the witness that may have impacted their ability to fully and accurately observe, recall, or relate the questioned events. External factors are factors that exist outside of the witness but that had an impact on the ability of the witness to observe the questioned events. The advocate calling the witness will normally try to emphasize the positive internal and external factors supporting the credibility of the witness's observations. They may also try to remove the sting of negative factors by fronting them on direct. When impeaching advocates should try to demonstrate as many unreliable factors as possible and arrange them in a way that impacts on the overall credibility of the witness's testimony.

The most obvious example of internal physiological factors is poor eyesight, usually combined with a failure to wear prescription eye wear. Other visual factors include color blindness, physical disabilities, age, and night vision. Sometimes a witness has prior training that increases their ability to adequately recall and relate incidents they have observed. The classic example is an experienced police officer or other trained observers. Internal psychological factors include perception, memory and the witness's ability to communicate. Perception is effected by a variety of factors, such as distorted focus on certain elements of the scene to the exclusion of others. Examples of this type of distorted focus includes a preoccupation with the weapon in an

---

How to respond to objects when crossing on defects in capacity:

"A witness may not testify to a matter unless evidence is introduced sufficient to support a finding that the witness has personal knowledge of the matter." *See federal rule of evidence 602.*

"The credibility of a witness may be attacked by any party, including the party calling the witness." *See federal rule of evidence 607.*

"Leading questions are permitted on cross-examination." *See federal rule of evidence 611(c).*

---

assault rather than the facial features of the assailant. Personal expectations, such as bias, stereotypes, interpretations and assumptions also affect the perceptual process. This has led courts to develop model instructions to jurors to assist them in weighing the credibility of eye witness identifications.

External or environmental factors include such things as exposure time, line of sight, obstructions, lighting, weather, speed of movement, and distance. The traumatic nature of the event observed is also an important external factor that may impact the witness's ability to observe or remember. Advocates weave external and internal factors together, pointing out to the jury those issues that call into question the validity of the testimony of the witness. This is an artful way of saying that the witness believes what they are telling you, but you should not. When done properly impeachment as to defects in capacity allow you to convince the jury to not believe a witness without ever needing to call the witness a liar. They are instead merely mistaken. This is an easier position to take and a more realistic bar to reach for during this type of cross examination.

4.14 Eyewitness Identification

In any criminal case, the government must prove beyond a reasonable doubt that the defendant was the perpetrator of the crime[s] alleged. You have heard testimony of eyewitness identification. In deciding how much weight to give to this testimony, you may take into account the various factors mentioned in these instructions concerning credibility of witnesses. In addition to those factors, in evaluating eyewitness identification testimony, you may also take into account:

1. the capacity and opportunity of the eyewitness to observe the offender based upon the length of time for observation and the conditions at the time of observation;

2. whether the identification was the product of the eyewitness's own recollection or was the result of subsequent influence or suggestiveness;

3. any inconsistent identifications made by the eyewitness;

4. whether the witness had known or observed the offender at earlier times; and

---

Example of Eyewitness Identification Instructions - Model Crim. Jury Instr. 9th Circ. 4.14 (2003)

Because these types of impeachment need not be as confrontational as when you directly challenge the truthfulness of a witness, advocates should carefully consider the tone they choose to adopt while examining the witness.

It is not necessary to adopt a hostile or sarcastic tone when cross-examining a witness who is called to testify as to a visual observation. In fact, a friendly tone may produce better results in most cases. Even if the witness has given testimony that is adverse to your cause, the goal of such cross-examination is simply to elicit facts that affect the witness's ability to observe, interpret, and recall relevant facts accurately, not to beat them up on the stand.

Witnesses are naturally reluctant to concede the inaccuracy of their observations and recollections, especially after they have testified on direct. Avoid the temptation to ask a question that directly challenges the accuracy of the witness by reciting the factors bearing on accuracy and then challenging the witness to agree that his original report or testimony was wrong. In addition to being argumentative, such ultimate questions usually produce unsatisfactory responses. When confronted with a direct challenge to their veracity, most witnesses forcefully reassert the certainty of their observations and memory. As a general rule, save the reliability argument for summation.

When preparing for impeachment concerning defects in capacity take the time to carefully scrutinize the witness's prior statements. You should examine the record for statements by the witness that show a greater certainty about their observations at trial than immediately after the event when they observed it. The intervening preparation for trial can often inadvertently (or purposefully) focus the memory of the witness in a fashion not consistent with their initial unadulterated observations. These inconsistencies may not be sharp enough to clearly qualify as prior inconsistent statements, but they do tend to show that the witness has lost their objectivity over time. When necessary you can impeach on this issue, again without ever calling the witness a liar, but showing the jury why their current testimony is just not as useful as what they said earlier.

In addition to careful review of any documents, you must take the time to examine the scene. Conduct your own examination of the scene where the relevant observations took place. Whenever possible ensure that similar lighting conditions and other environmental factors mirror those of the time of the observations. You can have someone reenact the actions and then consider from a variety of distances and angles what could, or could not, have actually been observed. Finally you should and have an assistant reenact the action. Measure distances and views from various angles. Consider using a diagram to enhance the testimony in court. All of these preparatory steps will greatly assist you in identifying external factors bearing on reliability.

D. *TABLE OF POTENTIAL IMPEACHMENT ISSUES.*

Issue Arising During Impeachment	Applicable Federal Rule of Evidence
Character traits of the victim or accused.	404(a), 404(b), 405
Character of a witness for truthfulness.	608
Out of court statements offered for the truth of the matter asserted therein (hearsay).	801 - 807
Offering evidence of other crimes, wrongs & acts. (FTA chapter 10).	404(b)
Prior convictions of a witness.	609
Legal relevancy - Is the probative value substantially outweighed by the danger of unfair prejudice et al.	403
Are the questions logically relevant.	401, 402
Competency of a witness.	610
Personal knowledge of the witness.	602
Questioning witnesses.	611, 614

Table 1 - Potential Evidentiary Rules Applicable During Cross Examination

Table 1 serves as a starting point for additional inquiry into the relationships between specific tasks on impeachment and the rules of evidence. Your case analysis should assist you in identifying when these particular issues will arise. You should use the table to review your knowledge of the evidentiary rules so that you can include them in your legal theory of the case and witness examination preparation. An understanding of how these evidentiary rules work is absolutely crucial in order to create an effective impeachment.

For an identification and discussion of the relevant professional responsibility rules dealing with impeachment see chapter 6, Cross Examinations.

Points to Ponder...

1. How do you square the limitations on Cross Examination through FRE 611 with the FRE's rules on impeachment? Do we just treat liars differently? Should we?

2. Are all witnesses presumed to be truthful as well as competent? How would our system be different if we assumed everyone lied unless verified? Should we, if our purpose is a search for the truth?

3. In Europe the witness reviews their testimony at its conclusion and then swears or affirms its accuracy. Would you prefer that sort of approach in a common law court? Why have we gone the other way? Do you approve?

CHAPTER ELEVEN
PAST RECOLLECTIONS

"Remember thee?
Ay, thou poor ghost, whiles memory holds a seat
In this distracted globe. Remember thee?
Yea, from the table of my memory
I'll wipe away all trivial fond records,
All saws of books, all forms, all pressures past
That youth and observation copied there,
And thy commandment all alone shall live
Within the book and volume of my brain."[1]

A. THE SKILL, LAW AND ART OF REFRESHING MEMORY.

Witnesses at trial are in a strange and different land. For the advocate the courtroom is home. They know it, understand it, and have spent countless hours in practice and study. All withe goal of being be able to stand and deliver in the well of the courtroom when the time is right. Witnesses approach the courtroom experience from a different place. Unless they are professional witnesses, such as law enforcement personnel or experts, they do not have much experience with testifying. Their concepts of what to expect have been driven by books, movies and television. As a result a lot of stress is associated with testifying, even when the witness intends to tell the truth. That stress and worry leads to mistakes. Such mistakes include forgetting information or misstating information. The forgetful witness is a common feature of trial practice. Witnesses are not necessarily lying when they cannot remember an issue, they just cannot recall what it is the advocate is desperately trying to get them to say. Often this leads to additional stress, making it even more difficult to remember

---

[1] WILLIAM SHAKESPEARE, HAMLET, act 1, sc. 5.

what happened. Fortunately the federal rules of evidence recognize this very human response and provide a template for dealing with the effects of allowing recollections to be refreshed.[2]

Rule 612. Writing Used To Refresh Memory

Except as otherwise provided in criminal proceedings by section 3500 of title 18, United States Code, if a witness uses a writing to refresh memory for the purpose of testifying, either— (1) while testifying, or (2) before testifying, if the court in its discretion determines it is necessary in the interests of justice, an adverse party is entitled to have the writing produced at the hearing, to inspect it, to cross-examine the witness thereon, and to introduce in evidence those portions which relate to the testimony of the witness. If it is claimed that the writing contains matters not related to the subject matter of the testimony the court shall examine the writing in camera, excise any portions not so related, and order delivery of the remainder to the party entitled thereto. Any portion withheld over objections shall be preserved and made available to the appellate court in the event of an appeal. If a writing is not produced or delivered pursuant to order under this rule, the court shall make any order justice requires, except that in criminal cases when the prosecution elects not to comply, the order shall be one striking the testimony or, if the court in its discretion determines that the interests of justice so require, declaring a mistrial.

Federal Rule of Evidence 612 - See Appendix III

When faced with a witness who cannot recall a particular fact, advocates can try to refresh her memory by referring to a writing, a document, or other aid. This is commonly known as "refreshing recollection." The goal is to simply assist the witness is remembering what they already know by using a document or other object to "jog" their memory and remind them of the facts. There are few, if any, limitations on the means advocates can use to refresh a witness's recollection. Some common aids include letters, objects, documents, magazines, newspaper clippings, income tax returns, smells, police reports, notes, photographs, prior testimony, and tape recordings. While the limitations on the type of item that can be used are relatively small, it is important that advocates procedurally follow the steps laid out when refreshing recollection. The primary concern is to make certain that after the witness's memory if

---

[2] See Fed. R. Evid. 612.

refreshed they testify based upon what they remember, and not what is in the document. To that end certain foundational steps must be used by the advocate when refreshing recollection.

Foundation for Refreshing Recollection:

Witness states she cannot recall a fact or event;

Witness states that a particular writing or other aid could help jog her memory;

Witness is given the writing to read silently to herself;

Witness returns the writing to counsel;

Witness states that the writing has refreshed her memory; and

Witness testifies to the fact or event, without further aid of the writing.

In actual practice refreshing recollection usually is accomplished as follows:

Q. **Agent Edwards, what was the address of the house where you first encountered the accused on the date of his apprehension?**

A.   I can't remember. I know it was in Niles Township, but I can't remember anything more specific.

Q. **Is there anything you could review which would help you remember?**

A.   Yes. I made a report shortly after the apprehension.

Q. **Agent Edwards, I'm handing you what has been marked as Prosecution Exhibit 5 for Identification, a copy of which I am handing to the defense. What is it?**

A.   It's a copy of the report I made regarding this case.

Q. **Please read it over silently to yourself. (pause)**

Q. **I have retrieved Prosecution Exhibit 5 for Identification from the witness. Agent Edwards, does that refresh your memory?**

A.   Yes.

Q. **What is the address of the house where you first encountered the accused on the day of his apprehension?**

A.   It was 1551 Ferndale Blvd.

When done properly refreshing recollection is a seamless process that allows the advocate to remind the witness of what they already know without making a big deal out of it. It is not a disaster that the witness cannot remember, but merely a normal human reaction to a stressful situation. The advocate who cannot calmly handle refreshing recollection runs the risk of creating an impression in the jury's mind that the witness is trying to "pull a fast one" or is less credible because of the need to refresh

> **Suggested Keywords to Prompt the witness for Refreshing Memory:**
>
> Do you recall anything else?
>
> Would anything help you to refresh your recollection?
>
> Is their anything that would assist you in prompting your memory of what happened that day?
>
> What would help remind you of those facts?

recollection. This is a skill that is easily mastered if you practice it. With that precept in mind you must explain the elements of the foundation for recorded recollection to your witness before trial and rehearse with them so that both of you are comfortable with the process. Make sure they know that there is nothing wrong with failing to remember and reading a piece of paper on the stand to refresh their memory.

You should decide which cue words you will use to prompt the witness. Suggestions include: "Do you recall anything else?"; "Not that I remember." "Would anything help you to refresh your recollection?" "Yes." "What is that?" Practice those specific phrases with your witnesses during preparation.

SEVEN PRINCIPLES OF PAST RECOLLECTIONS:

Witnesses will forget essential facts.

Memorize the foundational elements for refreshing memory and past recollection recorded or know where to find those foundations when your memory fails.

Memory can be refreshed by any document.

Past recollection recorded must be a document made or adopted by the witness when the matter is fresh in the witness's memory.

Documents used merely to refresh memory are not admitted into evidence.

Documents qualifying as past recollection recorded may be admitted but are only read to the fact-finder unless offered by the adverse party.

Plan, prepare and practice with each witness.

Do not be afraid to use this technique. It is in no way sneaky or under-handed. It is instead a legitimate advocacy tool and especially appropriate for witnesses testifying about technical data, easy-to-forget matters such as dates, license plates, serial numbers and scientific data, as well as for the young or nervous witness.

The only danger areas in refreshing recollection from an objections perspective occur when advocates fail to follow procedures properly. Be exact about the procedure. Withdraw the document so the witness testifies from memory (albeit her refreshed memory) and not from the piece of paper. Distinguish the use of a document to refresh memory from use of the document as a substitute for testimony, which will require an exception to the hearsay rules.

When you are refreshing memory, the testimony, not the document, is the evidence; but you still mark the document as an exhibit and it becomes part of the record although it is not admitted into evidence. You must show a copy of the document you use to refresh the witness's memory to opposing counsel. More importantly, opposing counsel can introduce into evidence the portions your witness relies upon. You must ensure that it does not contain embarrassing or unhelpful information to your case. Do not try to be sneaky and use an excerpt from a document if the full document will harm your case. Although the full document is potentially admissible, you should be careful to mask the document so that irrelevant or privileged information cannot be read. Have a masked copy and an original ready for inspection.

When you are on the opposing side, always take the time to read the entire document. Be sure to object if refreshing the witness's memory sounds unduly suggestive or prompts the witness in a way you think the jury ought to know. If you are given the opportunity to be present during an out-of-court witness refreshment, do not decline and go to lunch. You never know what you might learn. Finally, remember even though the writing is read into evidence, it is not taken back with the jury members into deliberations unless offered by the adverse party.

B. THE SKILL, LAW AND ART OF PAST RECOLLECTION RECORDED.

Sometimes, despite your best efforts to refresh recollection you are unsuccessful. When that happens the witness cannot independently remember a particular fact about which he has been called to testify. If a written record of the earlier fact or event exists the writing may qualify as an exception to the hearsay rule and be introduced into evidence as past recollection recorded. It can then be considered substantively by the jury.[3]

803(5) Recorded recollection.—A memorandum or record concerning a matter about which a witness once had knowledge but now has insufficient recollection to enable the witness to testify fully and accurately, shown to have been made or adopted by the witness when the matter was fresh in the witness' memory and to reflect that knowledge correctly. If admitted, the memorandum or record may be read into evidence but may not itself be received as an exhibit unless offered by an adverse party.

In order to admit evidence pursuant to federal rule of evidence 803(5) the advocate must lay a proper foundation to show that the witness cannot remember, but earlier in time could remember and that a record of that memory was made. The following elements establish the foundation for introducing evidence of a past recorded fact as an exception to the hearsay rule for a witness's present recall of that fact.

Foundation for Past Recollection Recorded:

Witness cannot remember a fact or event on the stand;

Witness had firsthand knowledge at one time;

That knowledge is reflected in a memorandum or record made at or near the time the fact or event occurred, made or adopted by the witness;

Record was accurate and complete when made;

Record is in same condition now as when made; and

Witness still cannot completely and accurately recall the fact or event even after reviewing the record.

Example of a Sample Foundation:

---

[3] See Fed. R. Evid. 803(5).

Q.   *Mr. Simpson, did you see the automobile as it sped away?*

A.   *I was on the ground, but I looked up and saw the license plate.*

Q.   *What was the tag number?*

A.   *I don't recall. I know it was a Missouri tag, but I can't remember the numbers.*

Q.   *Is there anything that would help you to recall?*

A.   *Yes, I thought the number would be important so I scribbled it down a few minutes later when I found some paper.*

NOTE: At this point, you would lay the same foundation you would to refresh recollection under FRE 612.

Q.   *I'm handing you what's been marked as Defense Exhibit D for Identification, a copy of which I have provided the government. What is it?*

A.   *It's the note I made of the license number.*

Q.   *Please take a moment to read it over.(pause)*

Q.   *I'm retrieving Defense Exhibit D for Identification from the witness. Now, Mr. Simpson, please tell the jury the number of the license plate.*

A.   *Sir, I know it's going to sound strange, but I still can't remember.*

Q.   *Mr. Simpson, think again about Defense Exhibit D for Identification, When did you write this note?*

A.   *About 10 minutes after the car sped away with the guys who stole my wallet.*

Q.   *Are you sure it is accurate?*

A.   *Yes. I kept repeating the license number to myself until I had a pencil and paper.*

Q.   *I'm handing you again Defense Exhibit D for Identification. Your honor, I ask the court's permission for Mr. Simpson to testify from past recollection recorded using Defense Exhibit D for Identification.*

J.   *Objection?*

Pr. None.

J.   The witness may testify.

Q.   Tell the jury the numbers on the license plate.
A.   It was a Missouri plate with the number TGV 8765.

DC. Your honor, the defense offers Defense Exhibit D for Identification into evidence as Defense Exhibit D and asks that it be published to the jury. *Pr. The government objects your honor. The evidence is the witness's testimony, not the actual exhibit.*

J.   Agreed. The exhibit will not be published.

Unlike refreshing memory, in past recollection recorded you are offering an out-of-court statement (the contents of the contemporaneous writing) as evidence for the truth of its contents. This creates a hearsay that is not present when the memory is merely refreshed. The focus of analysis is on the ultimate source of the information. If it comes from the witness's memory then there is no hearsay issue, although there may very well be potential cross examination concerning defects in capacity as discussed in chapter 6. If the source of the information is an out of court statement then there is a hearsay issue and the statement must fall into a hearsay exception. The hearsay statement is admissible under past recollection recorded because it carries sufficient circumstantial guarantees of trustworthiness that are derived from the fact that the statement was made or near the time of the incident. It is important to note that the witness on the stand need not necessarily have been the one who made the writing. As long as the witness adopted the written document it suffices for purposes of 803(5). The test is whether or not the witness adopted the record, if made at or near the time of the event, and the witness testifies, the record accurately reflects the facts.

When dealing with these issues it always looks better to the jury if your witness can testify from present memory. If the witness cannot remember, first try to refresh their memory. If the witness still cannot remember, then lay the foundation for past recollection recorded. When you refresh memory keep in mind that although the witness may read from the document, the evidence is testimonial – the oral statement of the witness - not documentary. The writing itself should not be admitted into evidence unless offered by the opposing counsel. However, if you have to use past recollection recorded then the document is the evidence, not the testimony of the witness.

C. RELEVANT EVIDENTIARY AND PROFESSIONAL RESPONSIBILITY RULES.

1. Evidentiary Rule Matrix.

Table 1 serves as a starting point for additional inquiry into the relationships between specific tasks for past recollections and the rules of evidence. Your case analysis should assist you in identifying when these particular issues will arise. You should use the table to review your knowledge of the evidentiary rule so that you can include that in your legal theory of the case. Particular attention should be paid to understanding the fundamental rules concerning refreshing memory.

Issue Arising During Past Recollections	Applicable Federal Rule of Evidence
Out of court statements offered for the truth of the matter asserted therein (hearsay).	801 - 807
Recorded recollection of a witness.	803(5)
Legal relevancy - Is the probative value substantially outweighed by the danger of unfair prejudice et al.	403
Are the questions logically relevant.	401, 402
Prior Inconsistent Statements/ Impeachment (FTA chapter 10).	613
Personal knowledge of the witness.	602
Past recollection of a fact in issue.	612

Table 1 - Potential Evidentiary Rules Applicable During Past Recollections

2. Professional Responsibility Rule Matrix.

Table 2 serves as a starting point for additional inquiry into the potential professional responsibility issues that are implicated during past recollection recorded. Your case analysis should help in identifying when these particular issues will arise.

Issue Arising During Past Recollections	Applicable Rule of Professional Responsibility**
(a)(1-3) A lawyer must not offer false evidence.	**RULE 3.3 CANDOR TOWARD THE TRIBUNAL**
(e) A lawyer must not allude to any matter that she does not reasonably believe is relevant or that will not be supported by admissible evidence. She must not assert personal knowledge of facts in issue and never state a personal opinion as to justness of a cause, the credibility of a witness, the culpability of a civil litigant or the guilt or innocence of the defendant.	**RULE 3.4 FAIRNESS TO OPPOSING PARTY AND COUNSEL**
(a) A lawyer must not illegally seek to influence a judge, juror, prospective juror or other official. (d) A lawyer must not intentionally disrupt the court and must conduct herself with respect for the court.	**RULE 3.5 IMPARTIALITY AND DECORUM OF THE TRIBUNAL**
(a) A lawyer must not attempt to be an advocate and witness in the same trial (with some limited exceptions).	**RULE 3.7 LAWYER AS WITNESS**

Table 2 - Most Prevalent Professional Conduct Rules during Past Recollections

*** Unless otherwise specifically indicated all professional conduct rules referenced are taken from the Delaware Supreme Court's professional responsibility rules. Those rules are almost identical to the model rules promulgated by the American Bar Association and are public domain documents.*

Points to Ponder...

1. Should we allow witnesses to read from prior written statements when they can no longer remember details? How far should we go?

2. Why do we not have the same hearsay concerns with past recollection recorded that we do with other recorded out of court statements?

3. Is there a competency issue when a witness fails to remember? Should counsel be allowed to challenge the competency of witnesses based upon their memory? What effect would such a standard have?

CHAPTER TWELVE
EXPERTS

"We must not make a scarecrow of the law,
Setting it up to fear the birds of prey,
And let it keep one shape, till custom make it
Their perch and not their terror."[1]

A. *THE SKILL OF EXPERT WITNESSES.*

When presenting an expert witness to the jury, advocates should make certain they take the time to (1) tell the jury why the expert is here, (2) establish conclusively the foundations for the expertise of the expert, (3) tender the expert as an expert in the specific area identified to the jury and laid the foundation for, (4) ask the expert to provide the major opinions needed (5) explore the specific basis for these opinions (usually research or learned treatise in the field of expertise), (6) diffuse weaknesses, and then (7) restate the main opinion. If you follow these seven steps you will competently prepare and present expert testimony that is tied to your case theme and theories. In order to do so you must spend a significant amount of time educating yourself on the way in which your expert's testimony will assist the jury in understanding the issue in controversy. The first step in accomplishing this is to fully understand how the qualification process works and the steps to take to lay appropriate foundations for the admissibility of your expert's testimony.

1. *Qualifying an expert witness.*

As you begin to prepare to examine and cross examine expert witnesses

---

[1] WILLIAM SHAKESPEARE, MEASURE FOR MEASURE, act 2, sc.1.

you should review the lessons learned in the earlier chapters on dealing with witnesses. The same advocacy principles apply equally when dealing with excerpt witnesses, but you must also master the legal issues surrounding the admissibility of expert testimony. Both advocacy principles and legal principles must be combined when dealing with expert witnesses. The core legal principles regulating expert testimony fall into three primary categories: (1) will the expert be allowed to testify, (2) what is permissible testimony, and (3) how broad is the scope of cross-examination of the expert witness. Qualifying an expert witness is the first step that an advocate must master in order for the court to allow the expert to testify as an expert. To testify as an expert, a witness must be qualified by reason of knowledge, skill, experience, training, or education in a field of specialized knowledge.

To qualify a witness as an expert, you must call that witness to the stand and elicit testimony about his or her credentials, unless opposing counsel stipulates to the witness's qualifications. Counsel should rarely stipulate to their expert's qualifications. It is much more effective to have the jury hear the impressive credentials of your witness instead of a cold, dispassionate, and unemotional instruction from the judge that "the witness is qualified as an expert. If your judge "encourages" you to stipulate an acceptable alternative is to have a copy of the witness's resume or c.v. vitae

> **A qualifications checklist for Experts may include the following:**
>
> - Business or Occupation
> - Education
> - Previously Recognized As an Expert
> - Experiences in their speciality
> - Licenses
> - Professional Associations
> - Other Background
> - Publications, lectures, consulting work

admitted as an exhibit for the jury to read during deliberations or to ask for the most favorable instruction possible concerning the witness's expertise.

After you have established the credentials of your expert you must officially tender them to the court and have them accepted in order for them to be able to provide expert level testimony. When tendering the witness, they should be offered with sufficient specificity to clearly identify their area of expertise. Be specific. Do not, for example, qualify the witness as an expert in "child abuse or chemistry" but in the area your case needs help, such as child abuse accommodation by reporting victims, or biochemical drug testing of urine samples. The devil is in the details. When you offer a witness as an expert, the court may allow opposing counsel to voir dire as to the foundation of the witness's expertise.

2. *Attacking the qualifications of an expert witness (voir dire for purposes of forming an objection).*

Preparation is the key for effective voir dire when attacking the credentials of an expert or when attempting to limit the scope of an expert's court accepted expertise. When preparing to voir dire in this situation, address each of the following issues long before the witness actually takes the stand. First you need to know the subject area of the expert. Interview the witnesses and talk to your own experts in the area. You cannot effectively voir dire an expert witness if you don't understand the subject matter. You should also review all documentation within the file and that you have received through discovery. Next you should connect your case analysis to the expertise of the witness. Develop an understanding of how your evidence ties into the testimony of the expert.

Finally you need to carefully identify the basis of the expert's testimony. Did he actually perform any tests or is he merely commenting on the work of others. That type of comment often raises quality control issues. Has he interviewed everyone involved? Did he spend sufficient time familiarizing himself with the case? Is he basing his theories or opinion solely on government provided evidence or has he conducted his own tests? Is he aware of the defense's alternative theory, if not why not? Is he a "professional" expert? The answer to these questions will provide fruitful grounds to challenge either the qualifications of the witness or the validity of their testimony.

Occasionally you may strategically decide not to voir dire the expert, or even attack their testimony. When to let it go is an important decision. Consider the following to assist you in making that determination. Sometimes there is no reason to challenge the expert. If he doesn't hurt you, is not involved in your theory or is so qualified that you aren't going to get anywhere then merely let the witness slide into expert status. Be careful. Opposing counsel will try to stretch the bounds of the witness's expertise. It is extremely embarrassing to miss this point and have the court recognize the expert for an area that you were not expecting. Do not let this happen. Limit, limit, limit, the testimony to established areas of knowledge and pertinence.

Proper preparation will allow you to effectively use the voir dire process to break up the rhythm of the opponent's case, confuse the basis of the expert's opinion, and limit the expert witness's opinion while putting forth an alternative theory for your client. Preparation is the key to effective voir dire and cross examination of any witness, particularly one that is an expert.

B. THE LAW OF EXPERT WITNESSES.

1. Expert Witness or Expert Assistance, Does it matter?

Deciding how and when to employ experts is a tactical and strategic decision that has factual, theoretical and legal implications for your case. One of the first decisions you must make is how to categorize the expert. If the expert is a member of the defense team and is brought on to assist you in understanding the case, they are covered by attorney-client privilege and their comments to you, reports they produce and their conversations with the client are not discoverable by the opposing side. Once you decide to make them a witness however, the attorney-client dissipates. This creates a potential problem for attorneys who do not consider that possibility ahead of time. You could wind up disclosing things you do not want to, or alternatively having an expert that you cannot turn into a witness because the disclosure of privileged information would destroy your case. If this issue is thought out ahead of time during your case analysis, it can, to a certain extent be ameliorated through careful planning.

Rule 702. Testimony by experts
If scientific, technical, or other specialized knowledge will assist the trier of fact to understand the evidence or to determine a fact in issue, a witness qualified as an expert by knowledge, skill, experience, training, or education, may testify thereto in the form of an opinion or otherwise.

Federal Rule of Evidence 104(a) establishes that the trial judge decides preliminary questions concerning the relevance, propriety and necessity of expert testimony, the qualification of expert witnesses, and the admissibility of his or her testimony. The courts have provided judges with six factors that they must consider. They are:

- **Qualified Expert**. To give expert testimony, a witness must qualify as an expert by virtue of his or her "knowledge, skill, experience, training, or education." *See* FRE 702.

- **Proper Subject Matter**. Expert testimony is appropriate if it would be "helpful" to the trier of fact. It is essential especially if the trier of fact could not otherwise be expected to understand the issues and rationally resolve them. *See* Fed. R. Evid. 702.

- **Proper Basis**. The expert's opinion may be based on admissible evidence "perceived by or made known to the expert at or before the hearing" or inadmissible hearsay if it is "of a type reasonably relied upon by experts in the particular field in forming opinions or inferences upon the subject. . . ." The expert's opinion must have an adequate factual basis and cannot be simply a bare opinion. *See* Fed. R. Evid. 702 and 703.

- **Relevant**. Expert Testimony must be relevant. *See* Fed. R. Evid. 402.

- **Reliable**. The expert's methodology and conclusions must be reliable. *See* FRE 702.

- **Probative Value**. The probative value of the expert's opinion, and the information comprising the basis of the opinion must not be substantially outweighed any unfair prejudice that could result from the expert's testimony. *See* Fed. R. Evid. 403.

2. The Expert's Qualification to Form an Opinion.

During a trial, the concept of Knowledge, Training, and Education foundation can be established in the following ways. You must show the following with every expert witness. This information is normally found in the curriculum vitae of the expert and is fertile grounds for foundational questions during the direct examination. Qualifications are normally discussed while laying the foundation for the acceptance of an expert during direct examination.

Rule 702. Testimony by experts

….a witness qualified as an expert by knowledge, skill, experience, training, or education, may testify thereto in the form of an opinion or otherwise.

Examples of fertile areas used to establish the qualifications of an expert witness include degrees attained from educational institutions; other specialized training in the field; the witness is licensed to practice in the field and has done so (if applicable) for a long period of time; teaching experience in the field; the witness' publications; membership in professional organizations, honors or prizes received, previous expert testimony.

Skill and Experience Foundation – The following examples explain ways to lay the foundation for an expert with specialized knowledge.

- Testimony by FBI agent concerning his "crime scene analysis" of a double homicide. Testimony included observations that killer was an "organized individual" who had planned and spent some time in preparation for crime, was familiar with crime scene and victims, and acted alone. Such evidence was not too speculative for admission under Fed. R. Evid. 702.

- In another instance, a judge erred when he refused to allow the defense clinical psychologist to testify about the relevance of specific measurements for a normal prepubertal vagina, solely because the psychologist was not a medical doctor. As the court noted, testimony from a qualified expert, not proffered as a medical doctor, would have assisted the jury in understanding the government's evidence.

- A Judge did not err in qualifying a highway patrolman who investigated over 1500 accidents, as an expert in accident reconstruction.

3. *Proper Subject Matter ("Will assist the fact-finder").*

The current standard is whether the testimony assists the trier of fact, not whether it embraces an "ultimate issue" so as to usurp the jury's function. At the same time, ultimate-issue opinion testimony is not automatically admissible. Opinions still must be relevant and helpful as determined through Rules 401-403 and 702.

Rule 704. Opinion on Ultimate Issue

Testimony in the form of an opinion or inference otherwise admissible is not objectionable because it embraces an ultimate issue to be decided by the trier of fact.

One recurring problem is that expert should not opine that a certain witness's rendition of events is believable or not. We are skeptical about whether any witness could be qualified to opine as to the credibility of another. **An expert may not become a "human lie detector."** Questions like whether the expert believes the victim was raped, or whether the victim is telling the truth when she claimed to have been raped (i.e. was the witness truthful?) are impermissible. However, the expert *may* opine that a victim's testimony or history is consistent with what the expert's examination found, and whether the behavior at issue is *typical* of victims of such crimes. Focus on symptoms, not conclusions concerning veracity.

Consider the following applications of this rule:

•   A judge improperly applied "necessary testimony" standard rather than a "helpful testimony" standard in excluding forensic psychiatrist expert testimony that accused did not form specific intent to kill or injure children. The court noted that the federal rules of evidence liberally allow for expert testimony that will assist the trier of fact.

•   In one case the court held that the expert's focus should be on whether children exhibit behavior and symptoms consistent with abuse, but was reversible error to allow social worker and doctor to testify that the child-victims were telling the truth and were the victims of sexual abuse. **Questions such as whether the victim's behavior is consistent with individuals who have been raped, or whether injuries are consistent with a child who has been battered, however, are permissible**. For example an expert may testify as to what symptoms are found among children who have suffered sexual abuse and whether the child-witness has exhibited these symptoms.   However, testimony that expert explained to the child the importance of being truthful and, based on child's responses, recommended further treatment, was an affirmation that expert believed the victim, which improperly usurped the responsibility of the fact-finder. In this instance the court ruled that the expert went too far.

- In another case a government expert testified that preteen and teenage boys (the victims) were the least likely group to report abuse because of shame and embarrassment and fear of being labeled a homosexual. She opined that false allegations from that group were "extremely rare" and outside of her clinical experience. Such testimony was improperly admitted, although harmless.

- On the other hand, a social worker's testimony that a rape victim was not vindictive and wanted to stay away from the accused was not improper comment on credibility.

- On appeal for the first time, the defense objected to testimony of government expert on "child abuse accommodation" syndrome. Defense claimed that it amounted to labeling the accused as an abuser and vouching for the credibility of the victims because the expert got all her information from the victims. The appellate court rejected that argument and noted that the expert testimony was limited to factors and that the facts of this case were consistent with those factors.

- A defendant was charged with indecent acts with his daughter. The defendant made a partial confession to the police and at trial stated that any contact with his daughters was not of a sexual nature. On rebuttal the government called an expert in child abuse who testified that, in her opinion, the victim suffered abuse at the hands of her father. The defense did not object. On appeal the court noted that error was not constitutional. None the less, the court held that the error had a substantial influence on the findings and reversed the conviction.

4. Basis For the Expert's Testimony

Fed. R. Evid. 703 provides:

The facts or data in the particular case upon which an expert bases an opinion or inference may be those perceived by or made known to the expert, at or before the hearing. If of a type reasonably relied upon by experts in the particular field in forming opinions or inferences upon the subject, the facts or data need not be admissible into evidence.

The language of the rule is broad enough to allow three types of bases: facts personally observed by the expert; facts posed in a hypothetical question; and hearsay reports from third parties. **Expert testimony must be based on the facts of the case, but not necessarily the first hand observations of the expert**.

In an example, the fact that an expert did not interview or counsel victim did not render expert unqualified to arrive at an opinion concerning rape trauma syndrome. The defense objected to social worker's opinion that victim was exhibiting symptoms consistent with rape trauma accommodation syndrome and suffered from PTSD on basis that opinion was based solely on observing victim in court, reading reports of others and assuming facts as alleged by victim were true. Objection went to weight to be given expert opinion, not admissibility.

If the expert opinion is based on personal observations, then the foundational elements must include (1) Where and when the expert witness observed the fact; (2) Who was present; (3) How the expert witness observed the fact; (4) A description of the observed fact. These facts may not even necessarily be found within the record of the court. Facts presented out-of-court (non-record facts), are allowed if they are "of a type reasonably relied upon by experts in the particular field" (this is allowed even if inadmissible because it is not being offered for its truth but the experts testimony based on that evidence).

It is also permissible for expert opinions to be based on hearsay reports by third parties. "The rationale in favor of admissibility of expert testimony based on hearsay is that the expert is fully capable of judging for himself what is, or is not, a reliable basis for his opinion. This relates directly to one of the functions of the expert witness, namely to lend his special expertise to the issue before him." *United States v. Sims*, 514 F.2d 147, 149 (9th Cir.), *cert. denied*, 423 U.S. 845 (1975). Beware: there is a potential problem of smuggling in otherwise inadmissible evidence.

Compare the above cases to *Hutchinson v. Groskin*, 927 F.2d 722 (2d Cir. 1991) (testimony that expert's opinion was "consistent with" prognoses of 3 nontestifying physicians, not disclosed during discovery, conveyed hearsay testimony to the jury*) with Primavera v. Celotex Corp.*, 608 A.2d 515 (Pa. Super. Ct. 1992) (sustaining expert's reliance on hearsay reports since they were the kind of data ordinarily used by practitioners, and because the expert *used* the reports to arrive at and explain his opinion, not as a "mere conduit or transmitter" of the hearsay), *appeal denied*, 622 A. 2d 1374 (Pa. 1993).

The elements of the foundation based on hearsay reports by third parties include:

(1) The source of the third party report;
(2) The facts or data in the report;
(3) If the facts are inadmissible, a showing that they are nonetheless of the type reasonably relied upon by experts in the particular field.

---

5. *Relevance and Reliability.*

Expert testimony, like any other testimony, must be relevant to an issue at trial in order to be admissible. *Daubert, v. Merrell Dow Pharmaceuticals, Inc.* 509 U.S. 579 (1993) and Federal Rules of Evidence 401 and 402, establish the baseline requirements for admissible expert testimony. In *Daubert v. Merrell Dow Pharmaceuticals Inc.*, 509 U.S. 579 (1993), the Supreme Court held that nothing in the Federal Rules indicates that "general acceptance" is a precondition to admission of scientific evidence. Instead, the rules assign the task to the judge to ensure that expert testimony rests on a reliable basis and is relevant. The judge assesses the principles and methodologies of such evidence pursuant to Fed. R. Evid. 104(a). The role of the judge as a "gatekeeper" leads to a determination of whether the evidence is based on a methodology that is "scientific," and therefore reliable. The judgment is made before the evidence is admitted, and entails "a preliminary assessment of whether the reasoning or methodology is scientifically valid." The trial court is given broad discretion in admitting expert testimony; rulings are tested only for abuse of discretion. *General Electric Co. v. Joiner*, 118 S. Ct. 512 (1997).

The Supreme Court discussed a nonexclusive list of factors to consider in admitting scientific evidence, which included the *Frye v. United States*, 293 F. 1013 (D.C. Cir. 1923) test as a separate consideration.

Daubert Factors:

(1) Whether the theory or technique can be and has been tested;

(2) Whether the theory or technique has been subjected to peer review and publication;

(3) Whether the known or potential rate of error is acceptable;

(4) Whether the theory/technique enjoys widespread acceptance.

It is important to note that after *Daubert,* "helpfulness" alone will not guarantee admission of evidence because it does not guarantee "reliability." The Supreme Court recently resolved whether the judge's gatekeeping function and the *Daubert* factors apply to non-scientific evidence. In *Kumho Tire v. Carmichael,* 119 S. Ct. 1167 (1999), the Court held that the trial judge's gatekeeping responsibility applies to *all types* of expert evidence. The Court also held that to the extent the *Daubert* factors apply, they can be used to evaluate the reliability of this evidence. Finally, the Court ruled that factors other than those announced in *Daubert* can also be used to evaluate the reliability of non-scientific expert evidence.

6. Examples of matters for Experts.

The following examples are derived from actual cases where these issues concerning expert testimony have arisen, they are not all inclusive, but serve instead as potential examples. Advocates should focus on the *Daubert* factors when determining the validity of a proposed expert.

- **Child Abuse Accommodation Syndrome**. In a trial for child sex abuse crimes, evidence was received on how the victim exhibited "Child Sexual Abuse Accommodation Syndrome" (children change or recant their stories, delay or fail to report abuse, accommodate themselves to the abuse). While such evidence is controversial, it may be admitted where it explains the abused child's delay or recantation, as was the case here.

- **Drug Testing**. Defense claimed that the lab's use of GC/MS/MS to determine the existence of LSD in urine failed under *Daubert*. The appeals court hinted that there may be problems but reversed the case because the government failed to show that the 200 PG/ML established by the agency adequately accounted for innocent ingestion.

- **Dysfunctional Family Profile Evidence**. It was an error to present expert testimony that defendant's family situation was ripe for child sexual abuse, purporting to present characteristics of a family that included a child sexual abuser, then pursued a deductive scheme of reasoning that families with the profile present an increased risk of child sexual abuse and that the defendant's family fit the profile.

  - In another case, there was no abuse of discretion in allowing a government expert to testify concerning a dysfunctional family "profile" and whether the defendant's family displayed any of its characteristics. The expert's testimony went to support credibility of daughter's accusations and to explain her admitted unusual behavior. Unlike the case above, evidence here was used to explain the behavior of the victim on the assumption she was abused by *someone*, not necessarily the accused. Using "profile' evidence to explain the counter-intuitive behavioral characteristics of sexual abuse victims was permissible.

- **Eyewitness Identification**. *United States v. Garcia*, 44 M.J. 27, *cert. denied*, 117 S. Ct. 174 (1996). Abuse of discretion, though harmless, to limit testimony concerning the unreliability of eye witness identification by preventing testimony on the inverse relationship between confidence and accuracy in identifications and theories of memory transference and transposition. Judge excluded the testimony of defense expert in eyewitness identification on 403 grounds. The court said this per se denial was an abuse of discretion, but was harmless. The case was reviewed and affirmed. Court did not address the correctness of that part of the lower courts decision. It also did not illuminate how *Daubert* factors applied to this kind of expert testimony. The court did not announce any per se rule on the admissibility of this type of expert testimony.

- **False Confessions**. A court held that the judge did not abuse his discretion in excluding the testimony of an expert in false confessions. The court reasoned that no witness could serve as a human lie detector, and in this case, the evidence was unreliable because there was no correlation between the expert's studies and the accused in this case. In the future, no per se exclusion may be admissible if testimony is limited to factors and there is a close correlation between the study group and the accused at trial.

- **Hypnosis**. Hypnosis can be admissible if the judge finds that the use of hypnosis was reasonably likely to result in recall compatible in accuracy to normal human memory. *Rock v. Arkansas*, 483 U.S. 44 (1987). Proponent must show by clear and convincing evidence a satisfaction of the following procedural safeguards: (1) Conducted by an independent, experienced hypnotist; (2) Hypnotist was not regularly employed by the parties; (3) Information revealed to the hypnotist was recorded; (4) Detailed statement must be obtained from the witness in advance; and (5) Only hypnotist and subject were present during session.

- **Ineffective Assistance**. Accused charged with molesting his young stepdaughter. Judge ordered government to provide expert assistance to the defense. At trial, the defense did not call the expert. The appellate court remanded for further inquiry on the ineffective assistance issue because the defense did not call the expert.

- **Psychological Autopsy**. No error in allowing forensic psychologist to testify about suicide profiles and that his "psychological autopsy" revealed it was unlikely the deceased committed suicide. Applying *Daubert* and *Kumho Tire* the appellate court affirmed the trial judge's decision to exclude an experts opinion that the accused was not an exhibitionist. The court noted that there was no body of scientific knowledge to support the expert's claim that the MMPI could be used to conclude that an individual was not an exhibitionist and could not have committed a crime.

- **Rape Trauma Syndrome**. Rape Trauma is a subcategory of PTSD in the DSM-IV. The psychiatric community recognizes the DSM-IV as valid and reliable. Evidence may assist the fact-finder by providing knowledge concerning victim's reaction to assault. Rape trauma syndrome evidence could assist the trier of fact in determining the issue of consent. This would be particularly true where such members would likely have little or no experience with victims of rape. . . [The RTS evidence] serves as a helpful tool by providing the fact-finders with knowledge regarding a victim's psychological reactions to an alleged sexual assault.)

- RTS testimony to rebut an inference that a victim's conduct was inconsistent with a claim of rape where she did not fight off the attacker, made inconsistent statements concerning the assault, did not make a fresh complaint, and recounted the incident in a calm and "unnatural" manner was impermissible testimony.

- A Psychologist impermissibly expressed an opinion concerning a rape victim's credibility by discussing the performance of the victim on a "Rape Aftermath Symptoms Test," (RAST) and by stating that the victim did not fake or feign her condition. The expert thus became a "human lie detector." The RAST failed to meet the requirements for admissibility of scientific testimony (lack of foundation). Despite lack of defense objection, the court found plain error and sets aside findings and sentence.

- **Sleep Disorders**. Defendant was charged with sodomizing another male while the victim was asleep. Defense wanted to admit the testimony of two experts to testify about the victim's alleged sleep disorders. Judge excluded the testimony and the appellate court affirmed. Court held that under *Daubert*, the expert's methodologies were unreliable and not helpful because the victim had not been interviewed.

7. Polygraph Evidence.

FRE 707. Polygraph Examinations.

Notwithstanding any other provision of law, the results of a polygraph examination, the opinion of a polygraph examiner, or any reference to an offer to take, failure to take, or taking of a polygraph examination shall not be admitted into evidence. Nothing in this section is intended to exclude from evidence statements made during a polygraph examination which are otherwise admissible.

The original "Frye" test dealt with the use of a primitive form of polygraph examination equipment that was based upon blood pressure and reactions. From 1923 to 1987, the Frye test excluded polygraph evidence because it was not generally accepted within the scientific community. When Federal Rule of Evidence 707 was passed, the admissibility of polygraph examinations suddenly came into question. In *United States v. Scheffer,* 118 S. Ct. 1261 (1998) the Supreme Court overruled an opinon by the Court of Appeals of the Armed Forces that affirmed the use of polygraph evidence at trial. In an 8 to 1 opinion the Court said that a per se exclusion on polygraph evidence does not unconstitutionally abridge the right of an accused to present a defense. They left open for another day the potential use of this type of evidence by the government. This left some unresolved issues: (1) Would a more compelling case lead to a different result; (2) The opinion posited that a per se ban is somewhat inconsistent with *Daubert*; (3) There was no indication of what level of acceptance would be required to satisfy *Daubert* for polygraphs.

C. THE ART OF EXPERT WITNESSES.

One of the primary functions of the advocate is to package the presentation of the expert. The advocate must ensure that the expert is not only believable, but that the presentation captures the jury's attention in a positive and interesting way. Evidence that is ignored because it is boring, obtuse or

---

Seven Basic Principles of Direct Examination of Experts:

(1) Tell the jury why the expert is here.

(2) Establish conclusively the foundations for the expertise of the expert.

(3) Tender the expert as an expert in the specific area you have identified to the jury and for which you have laid the foundation.

(4) Ask the expert to provide the major opinions you need.

(5) Explore the specific basis for these opinions (usually research or learned treatise in the field of expertise).

(6) Diffuse weaknesses.

(7) Restate the main opinion.

---

impenetrable is of no use to the trial attorney. The techniques found in chapter 5 on direct examination and chapter 7 on exhibits must be combined, along with the foundational requirements to qualify an expert, to create a package of testimony that is focused and intelligent, but also understandable to the average juror. You must judge your expert, determining their communication strengths and weaknesses.

Expert witnesses are like, yet unlike, all other witnesses called at trial. They have additional abilities to comment on evidence in ways that others do not and the jury can use their testimony in ways not authorized for other witnesses.

Seven Basic Principles of Cross Examining Experts:

(1) Preparation is the key.

(2) Limit the scope of direct testimony through voir dire & objections.

(3) Know the subject area of expertise.

(4) Gather all relevant evidence to support cross.

(5) Connect case analysis to the expertise of the witness.

(6) Identify the basis of the expert's testimony.

(7) Decide strategically whether to voir dire the witness when opposing counsel attempts to tender the witness as an expert.

Their special status also creates the possibility that they will have difficulty communicating with the average juror. You serve as the conduit through which the testimony of the expert witness flows. You control the speed, direction and destination of the testimony. A careful application of the organizational skills discussed earlier in chapters 3, 5 and 7, in conjunction with the additional teaching requirements that come with converting expert knowledge into lay speak will serve you well when presenting an expert's observations and conclusions.

D. RELEVANT EVIDENTIARY AND PROFESSIONAL RESPONSIBILITY RULES.

1. Evidentiary Rule Matrix.

Table 1 serves as a starting point for additional inquiry into the relationships between specific tasks on direct examination with experts and the rules of evidence. Your case analysis should assist you in identifying when these particular issues will arise and help you in developing a greater degree of comfort and expertise in the process. You should use the table to review your knowledge of the evidentiary rules so that you can include that in your legal theory of the case, particularly as you establish the qualifications for an expert.

Issue Arising During Direct Examination of Experts	Applicable Federal Rule of Evidence
Expert testimony	701 -705
Character of a witness for truthfulness	608
Out of court statements offered for the truth of the matter asserted therein (hearsay)	801 - 807
Legal relevancy - Is the probative value substantially outweighed by the danger of unfair prejudice, et al.	403
Are the questions logically relevant.	401, 402
Competency of a witness.	610
Personal knowledge of the witness. (See 701 - 705 for expert witness exception to this requirement).	602
Questioning witnesses.	611, 614

Table 1 - Potential Evidentiary Rules Applicable During Direct Examination of an Expert

2. Professional Responsibility Rule Matrix.

Table 2 serves as a starting point for additional inquiry into the potential professional responsibility issues that are implicated during direct examination of Experts. Counsel must ensure that they do not cross certain lines when investigating cases, preparing witnesses and controlling direct testimony. The same issues also exists when listening to an opposing counsel's direct examination.   You must pay particular attention to your jurisdictions interpretation and application of the candor towards the tribunal standard found in rule 3.3.   A thorough grasp of these issues will assist you in avoiding perjury and improper conduct. Your case analysis should assist you in identifying when these particular issues will arise.   You should use the table to review your knowledge of the procedural rule so that you can include that in your planning for your directs.

*** Unless otherwise specifically indicated all professional conduct rules
referenced are taken from the Delaware Supreme Court's professional
responsibility rules. Those rules are almost identical to the model rules
promulgated by the American Bar Association and are public domain
documents.*

Issue Arising During Direct Examination of an Expert	Applicable Rule of Professional Responsibility**
(a)(1-3) A lawyer must not offer false evidence.	**RULE 3.3 CANDOR TOWARD THE TRIBUNAL**
(e) A lawyer must not allude to any matter that she does not reasonably believe is relevant or that will not be supported by admissible evidence. She must not assert personal knowledge of facts in issue and never state a personal opinion as to justness of a cause, the credibility of a witness, the culpability of a civil litigant or the guilt or innocence of the defendant.	**RULE 3.4 FAIRNESS TO OPPOSING PARTY AND COUNSEL**
(a) A lawyer must not illegally seek to influence a judge, juror, prospective juror or other official. (d) A lawyer must not intentionally disrupt the court and must conduct herself with respect for the court.	**RULE 3.5 IMPARTIALITY AND DECORUM OF THE TRIBUNAL**
(a) A lawyer must not attempt to be an advocate and witness in the same trial (with some limited exceptions).	**RULE 3.7 LAWYER AS WITNESS**

Table 2 - Most Prevalent Professional Conduct Rules When Examining an Expert

Points to Ponder...

1. Can you prepare to cross exam an expert witness in the same manner that you do other witnesses? How do you pick your battles? How do you control someone who has more knowledge of the subject matter than you can ever reasonable achieve?

2. How do you introduce and expound on expert witness testimony persuasively when so much of it is scientific gobbledygook that most average citizens don't understand?

3. Should we develop new and different advocacy methodologies to deal with expert witnesses? What would you suggest? Should all witnesses be called by the "court" and equally available to all? What problems might arise from that approach?

CHAPTER THIRTEEN
CLOSING ARGUMENTS

"In law, what plea so tainted and corrupt
But, being seasoned with a gracious voice,
Obscures the show of evil?" [1]

A. THE SKILL OF CLOSING ARGUMENTS.

The entire weight of a trial - the testimony, the exhibits, the legal arguments, rests upon your shoulders when you begin to close. The eyes of your client or the needs of the people you represent are focused on your words. This is the point where the jury hopes for guidance, clarity and justice. If you have properly analyzed and prepared your case the majority of what you planned to have to talk about is present in the courtroom. Now is the time when you pull from the testimony the facts you need and juxtapose them with what the law requires or allows. Properly done the jury hears you argue in closing for what you previewed during opening statements and provided as evidence during the testimony of witnesses. We will discuss the art of presentation during closing arguments later in this chapter, but before you can focus on the performance you must have properly laid the foundations for success.

> ### The Rule of Threes:
>
> • Tell them what you are going to tell them (opening statement).
>
> • Tell them (case-in-chief).
>
> • Tell them what you told them and why it means you win (closing argument).

---

[1] WILLIAM SHAKESPEARE, THE MERCHANT OF VENICE, act 3, sc. 2.

You began laying the foundations for success in closing arguments in chapter 3 when you first learned about how closing argument drives the entire trial process, serving as the destination that the trial has been pointed towards. Every action taken during opening statements, motions arguments, instructions conferences, direct examinations and cross examinations have been designed to

> ## The Three Primary Steps in Case Analysis:
>
> - Identify and analyze the legal issues.
> - Identify and analyze the factual issues.
> - Develop a moral theme and legal theory.

maximize the persuasive power of your legal, factual and moral position as expressed during closing argument. During case analysis you identified what you needed to say and how you wanted to say it by applying the three primary steps of case analysis. You then developed the theories and themes to assist you in bringing the jury to the point where they would believe, accept and internalize your position. The goal was to empower the jury to argue for you in the deliberation room where all true final arguments are made. Now that it is time to create the final closing argument you should discover that the argument exists as an independent entity– a creation of your case analysis and preparation. The work you did up front pays off during closing arguments in that you know what you are going to talk about, the question is how.

Closing arguments must contain the words empowering the jury to decide the case in your favor. It melds the facts and the law of the case, casting them in a moral light. A good closing argument demands that the jury do nothing other than what you ask. If you have properly identified the legal issues, factual issues, and picked the right theme and theory, the Closing Argument comes as an organic expression of what you have shown to be true during the trial. If that is not the case you will struggle to find a Closing Argument that makes sense and fits the facts and law as admitted to the jury and ruled upon by the court. There is great danger in choosing a Closing Argument that is not grounded in the facts and law as perceived by the jury. You may sound like the second coming of Gerry Spence delivering it, but the jury will be left cold in the end, and will turn to the side whose argument makes the most sense, both rationally and emotionally. There are certain organizational techniques and tools that you must employ, but they are "much ado about nothing" without your internal understanding of what your position truly is and how your argument must flow from that place. The jury will know if you are not genuine, and will distrust you. Do not make this mistake. If you have not found the center of your position within your case you will not find the superior closing argument. If you cannot see yourself standing before the jury in that moment, with those words, then you have not done your job during case analysis and you are not yet ready to close.

Closing argument is the destination where you expect to take the jury through the course of the trial. It is imperative that you identify your closing argument's legal theories, factual theories and moral themes during case analysis. This must be done before you begin with any other portion of your case. It must also be continuously revisited as you prepare for trial. Use the expected closing argument as a sanity check on your case. If you find yourself straying from your original destination make certain that you ask yourself why. If you cannot answer the "why" question you are in definite danger of losing. Most cases are lost through a lack of organization and cohesive presentation. The dangers of losing focus are particularly high when the closing argument shifts based upon the presentation during the case.

Do not allow the opposing side to determine your destination because you did not take the time to do so during your case analysis. You must know where you are going in order to get there. *Go back now and retrieve the list of questions that you recorded the first time you read through the case file. Has your case analysis answered them?* Did the legal theory and moral theme that you chose adequately allow you to address the issues that you expect are in the jury's mind through the testimony of witnesses during the case in chief? Have you clearly identified the relevant instructions you expect the judge to give after closing argument? Only when you can answer these questions are you prepared to begin crafting your closing argument. As you begin to craft that argument keep in mind the application of the rule of threes that you will utilize during opening statement, direct examinations, and cross examinations. Do not abandon the use of this powerful advocacy tool during closing argument.

Your closing argument should use primacy and recency by beginning with a high impact point. The jurors are tired from sitting through a contested trial and you want to take this opportunity to focus them on what really matters. Normally this point should hit on your moral theme from the opening statement, capturing the essence of why an injustice will be done if your side does not win. It should capture the jury's attention, challenge their perceptions and by its very existence argue continually for your side, long after you have concluded your argument. You want that initial impact to resonate in the jury deliberation room where the true final arguments are made.

Make sure that you ARGUE! Tell the jurors why your side should win using the facts, the law and all reasonable inferences from the evidence. Use your knowledge of the case, as presented at trial, to connect through logical inferences disparate portions of your case. Place the issues in context during argument so that the jurors can draw the appropriate inferences from the evidence, the law and their own personal knowledge. It can be done through sarcasm, common sense observations or humor. The important point is that now is the time to connect what is known with what is not known, in light of the experiences and knowledge of the jury. They must rely upon their common sense and understanding of human nature to sort through all of the trial testimony. Use those facts to fashion a closing argument that echos their own experiences. It gives your interpretation credibility, and creates synergy for your side. At the same time, you need to **trust the jury.** Now is not the time to rehash the evidence ("Agent Charles told you..."). Avoid clichés, or use them with a novel twist. The first word of your argument should directly and powerfully relate to why your side wins.

Do not be afraid to show enthusiasm for your case. This does not necessarily mean cheerleading or table pounding like a caricature of a bad tv lawyer, but it does mean caring – or seeming to care – strongly about the case and the position you are advocating. Enthusiasm can be reflected in a number of ways, most obviously in inflection and word choice, but also your command of the courtroom, presentation of a case, and unapologetic advocacy for your client. If you do not care enough about this case to get excited and energized how can you expect the jury to care?

During the opening statement a member of your team should have taken careful notes about the promises made by opposing counsel. If they have not kept those promises then during your closing argument you should hold the other side's opening against them. Listen carefully during your opponent's opening and remind the jury, in your closing, of promises made in the opening that your opponent did not keep. When those promises show an attempt to hide the ball or manipulate the process drive that home, using it to attack the credibility of opposing counsel's case, but not necessarily the credibility of opposing counsel themselves. Sometimes you win merely by the other side losing.

You should wield exhibits in the courtroom early and often. If they were worth admitting into evidence, they're worth reinforcing at every opportunity, because people learn best through multiple senses. Blow them up, put them on powerpoint slides, make pictures. Do whatever it takes to engage multiple senses of the jury during your argument.

Never state your personal opinions. "I think the defendant..." Of course you think: you're an advocate! You need not even (and should not) say "the defense believes" or "it is the government position." Sometimes this is spillover from the opening statement, after which counsel may become too cautious about arguing. Assertions made during argument in a closing need no preface or attribution; they call it argument for that reason and it is total advocacy. What you think or believe is not important or relevant. What the evidence demands, what common sense shows and what a basic understanding of human nature requires is where you should spend your time. It gives you the most bang for your buck and drives home the mission of argument, which is to persuade.

Do not give a civics lesson. Every second spent talking about the function of a closing argument sounds defensive and condescending. You will lose your audience. It invites the jury to ignore you, and the judge is going to tell the jury what the purpose and limitations of a closing argument are anyway. Giving the civics lesson is almost like saying, "Well I've got to stand up and argue now, but please feel free to ignore anything I say." If you start off that way rest assured, they will ignore you. This is not to say that you should not mention legal concepts when a case turns on a significant legal point, just do it when it makes sense. Expect the jury to understand your well-planned, lucid explanation of the law and to appreciate it, when it is relevant to their job.

The other side will hammer at your weaknesses; when you have a particularly strong part to your case (extremely sympathetic victim, registered source with checkered past), you can hardly over-sell it, highlight

---

The Do's of Closing Argument:

- Deal candidly with your weaknesses.

- Be confident in arguing your position.

- Maintain eye contact, but not so much to make jurors uncomfortable.

- Structure your argument – don't simply re-hash the facts.

- Draw on the jury's common sense.

- Use visual aids or physical evidence from the trial.

- Address the standard of proof.

- (Prosecution) Use rebuttal argument to hammer home your strongest points, how you refuted the defense's contentions, and remain positive in your case!

those strengths. Remember the rule of threes and primacy and recency when you are determining how to emphasize your strengths and compensate for your weaknesses during closing. You should take the time during your closing argument to account for significant weaknesses, but not for every weakness. You have to decide which are important and which will slip by your opponent. The obvious weaknesses of your case – perhaps compromises made by your victim, lab errors, and admissions by your client – need to be addressed by you, but do so with a plan. It gives you an opportunity to establish candor and credibility with the jury and suggests a sense of balance. However you should couple the admission with a compensating fact that diminishes the damage and gives the jury an "out" or better context in which to place the weakness so that it has less of an impact on your case. Just as primacy and recency work for your strongest points, common sense should tell you to sandwich weaker points in the middle of your argument.

Counsel should know all or virtually all of the instructions the judge will use in a given case. Part of your analysis and preparation is the identification of probable instructions and the request for specific instructions. When you discuss them with the jury there is no need to preface that discussion with "the judge will instruct you" because (a) she might not, and may choose this opportunity to point that out, and (b) better that you steal the language of the instruction, so that when the judge utters it, she appears to be affirming your wisdom.

Advocates usually are given liberal rein to argue inferences from the evidence and matters outside of the evidence that are part of generally accepted knowledge. Counsel must be careful, however, only to rely on evidence that has been properly admitted for an appropriate purpose. Care must be taken to ensure that evidence that is admitted by the court with a limiting instruction is not used to argue a point for which it has not been allowed. One example would be to take evidence of a prior inconsistent statement that was admitted for the limited purpose of attacking a witness's credibility and then arguing the facts within that

> ### The Don'ts of Closing Argument:
>
> - Misstate the evidence or the law.
>
> - Argue facts not in evidence.
>
> - State your personal belief in the justice of your cause.
>
> - Personally vouch for the credibility of a witness.
>
> - Comment on the accused's exercise of a fundamental right (prosecution).
>
> - Make personal attacks on opposing counsel.

statement to prove an element or to disprove an element of an offense or cause of action. The extra burden on defense counsel is to abide by the ethical rule that forbids calling the attention of the jury to the absence of evidence when in fact that evidence was suppressed.

B. THE LAW OF CLOSING ARGUMENTS.

Most legal issues regarding closing arguments revolves around the problems dealing with the effects of impermissible argument. A review of the case law dealing with what constitutes impermissible argument provides us with some broad legal principles that advocates can rely upon in setting the limits as to what is appropriate argument in most jurisdictions. Advocates who find themselves in a position where they wish to push the boundaries of permissible argument would do well to take the time to review the case law in their jurisdiction regarding these suggested legal principles.

SEVEN LEGAL PRINCIPLES FOR PROPER CLOSING ARGUMENTS:

- You are confined to the record. If evidence is not admitted you cannot argue it.
- The trial court has supervisory authority over the scope and direction of closing argument, but should give deference to counsel unless the law is misstated.
- Prosecutors cannot argue merely to inflame or arouse passions. The courts will consider whether a substantial right of the accused was violated when reviewing this issue.
- Advocates cannot intentionally misstate evidence or attempt to lead the jury to draw improper inferences from admitted evidence.
- Personal beliefs and opinions of counsel are forbidden.
- Reasonable inferences are permissible and expected.
- It is improper to refer to evidence which was either successfully objected to as to admissibility, stricken from the record, or otherwise excluded.

The development of the case law concerning closing arguments has generally taken two paths. The first path is an analysis of whether or not the conduct of the advocate making the argument was not ethical. The courts often refer to rules of professional conduct and the American Bar Association guidelines for prosecution and defense conduct concerning closing arguments when trying to make this decision. Once a determination has been made as to whether or not the advocate violated ethical norms (at this point the advocate often has a bar related issue), the next question is whether or not that violation resulted in the loss of a substantial right of a party, usually the accused. If so then relief may be provided by the court.

C. THE ART OF CLOSING ARGUMENTS.

Legal and Factual Theories are the application of the relevant law to the specific facts of your case. They form the basis for the legal or procedural reasons that you win. Theory is how the jury is empowered by the law to decide the case in your favor. Moral Theme, on the other hand, is the emotional reason you should win. It is why the jury wants to decide the case your way. You must weave these three facets together when creating superior closing arguments. Themes are as varied as the people, places and situations they capture and represent. Theme provides the moral force that brings the case to life. A good theme not only gets the jury on your side, it creates a feeling of comfort within them about deciding things your way. If you cannot find a theme within your case that will resonate with the jury try to determine what sense of injustice exists? Is there a wrong that has been committed against your client will get the jury to decide the case for you? Examples of such themes include the government rushing to judgment because your client is a member of a minority, the innocent person wronged by circumstance, and someone else did it. Other examples include the destruction of a way of life or the health of an individual through the greed of a soulless corporation. The storylines are as varied and complex as the tales of humanity that surround us each day. If you watch television, go to the movies or read books they are there for each of us to find and use.

Make sure that you start strong and end strong. This is classic primacy and recency; people remember what they hear first and last. Think hard about the first words out of your mouth as well as your closing lines; an ideal closing argument should appear spontaneous, but should not actually be spontaneous. Not only must you be able to start and end strong, you also have to create a sense of the humanity of your client. Sometimes this requires you to humanize them in the eyes of the jury. Part of this is terminology, but it should be more than calling the defendant by name if you are defense counsel or "the defendant" if the government). Counsel should paint pictures of victims or the defendant by placing them in scenarios and filling in human details that bring them to life; jurors will remember these facts and it will help you get past the temptation to look at the case as (merely) a contest between lawyers.

Argue! The only purpose in getting out of your chair is to persuade the jury to do something. Every sentence in the argument, every word choice, every decision of what evidence to highlight, ignore, or explain away, every decision of what to talk about in what sequence should move the jury or judge toward that end. You'll know you are arguing when you:

- **Draw conclusions and make inferences based upon the available evidence.** The admitted evidence will always support any number of interpretations, from the plausible to the fanciful – argue yours. If you can't say it with a straight face how can the jury believe it?

- **Comment on witness demeanor.** Do not underestimate the extent to which judgments about credibility are based on effect, how a witness looks and sounds. Pounce on this. It is the way we normally judge the credibility of other people whom we meet in life. Jurors do the same thing.

- **Apply law (including instructions) to the facts.** It's not appellate argument but neither is it a plebiscite. Assume that jury's try to analyze the case in light of the law; make it easier for them.

- **Refute the opponent's case.** This is most critical for the defense in its lone closing argument. Skilled prosecution/ plaintiff's counsel will often give a "minimalist" closing argument and save their strongest arguments for rebuttal, the one argument of the day to which the defense does not get to reply.

D. THE SKILL, LAW, AND ART OF REBUTTAL ARGUMENTS.

Rebuttal arguments are the province of given plaintiff attorneys and prosecutors. When done correctly they can serve to strike devastating blows to the defense case. To be effective they must be focused and lethal, reiterating those key issues that will carry the day. Done well it is the final nail in the defense coffin. Done poorly it can so confuse the issues that the jury must struggle through the maze of defense tactics without clear guidance. Advocates often overlook this portion of effective trial advocacy because there is an element of afterthought to making such arguments. You should focus upon it, it is the final argument the jury hears before deliberations.

The rebuttal argument gives the prosecution or plaintiff an opportunity to regain the momentum, to reestablish focus on the key issues in the case, and to refute the defense's arguments on key issues. A purely reactive point-by-point response to defense arguments cannot accomplish this mission. The rebuttal must refute the defense arguments on key issues and forcefully reassert the theory of guilt or culpability. The leading causes of weak and ineffective rebuttal arguments are inadequate preparation and ineffective organization of the argument. Use the following structure to consistently fashion rebuttal arguments that are on point, effective and devastating to the defense case.

Start by preparing the rebuttal as an integral part of your case. It is often said that the preparation of a case should begin with an outline of the closing argument. If that is so, preparation must also begin with an outline of the rebuttal argument. The government or plaintiff gets to argue first and last. The benefits of primacy and recency should be fully exploited by careful planning. The first closing and the rebuttal must work together to maximize the persuasive presentation of the your case. The primary mission of the rebuttal is to restore commitment to the theories and them that were clearly constructed in the first closing. You should remember that it is a restoration project, not a new building. The structures of the two arguments must be carefully coordinated to contribute to the same persuasive goal.

> **Rebuttal is a restoration project, not a new building**

Counsel usually make one of the following mistakes when fashioning and delivering a rebuttal argument. The first is attempting to fully analyze and neutralize the defense arguments presented during their closing. While it is tempting to immunize the jury against defense arguments, too much attention on the defense case will distort the focus of your closing. You should focus on your affirmative burden, only occasionally warning about the defense tactics to come. This allows you to set up your rebuttal points in accordance with your warnings. Those warnings must be tied to your analysis of the case, and the key elements upon which the evidence will most likely turn. Save your full refutation on those issues for rebuttal, if the defense attempts to address them. You can use this tactic to shape the argument of the defense. If they do not rise to your challenge, then you can draw the jury's attention to their failure to adequately address the damming evidence facing their client.

Another is the temptation to sandbag the defense by saving everything for rebuttal. This tactic surrenders the advantage of primacy, and may also run afoul of the scope limitations on rebuttal argument. Rebuttal is generally limited to matters that are raised by the defense argument. If the defense counsel ignores the issues you are saving for rebuttal you may very well be precluded from arguing them during rebuttal. Defense counsel could also counter the sandbagging tactic by offering argument only on some of the charged offenses or by waiving argument entirely. This tactic surrenders primacy and the shaping of the final argument to the defense and is not a good idea!

You must control the agenda during closing arguments. The first closing must establish the key issues, so that the rebuttal begins by reminding the jury that resolving those issues will determine the verdict. You must organize your rebuttal around these issues if you want it to be effective. Resist the temptation to engage in a point-by-point response to the defense argument. That allows the defense to control the agenda and makes the rebuttal quickly deteriorate into an uncoordinated attack. The picture of counsel wildly flailing away at the defense argument is not a pretty one. A better method is to identify the three main issues in the case and to construct an outline for rebuttal based on each of those issues. You should anticipate and war game the defense arguments on those main points. If you are prepared, you can then listen and refine the rebuttal during the defense argument. If the defense fails to address one of the issues that you selected for rebuttal, you can then explain to the jury why that omission is so glaring. Having analyzed the key issues in the case, counsel can prepare an outline of rebuttal arguments before trial. Use the following template to control the agenda:

- **Introduction**. You must regain the momentum for your side during the opening seconds of the rebuttal argument. Identify the crucial shortcomings in the defense argument or turn the defense theme against them. Develop an arsenal of responses for standard defense themes and use them to fashion a one-line rebuttal introduction.

- **Restate your theme**. A strong first closing puts you in the best position for rebuttal. Having already made your case, you can confidently begin the rebuttal argument by recapping the most compelling evidence of guilt. If the defense has stressed the reasonable doubt standard, acknowledge the government's burden of proof and confidently embrace it. This restores the proper focus on what you perceive as the real issue or issues in the case and sets up the outline for rebuttal.

- **Key Point Rebuttal**. Having set the stage by restoring focus on the crucial issues, you are ready to proceed with the negative aspect of the rebuttal -- refuting selected arguments of the defense. The following three-step process:

Restate, Refute and Recap should be used to address each key point that you that you selected for rebuttal.

You cannot effectively refute an argument without clearly restating it. Any attempt to make a straw man out of the defense argument will undermine your credibility with the jury and will draw an objection from an attentive defense counsel. Refuting the defense argument is the heart of negative rebuttal. Refutation takes a variety of forms, but it all boils down to this: refute the fact or refute the inferences drawn from the facts. No matter which tactic you use you must always appeal to common sense and explain why your theory offers a better alternative. The quality of this part of the argument will dramatically increase if advocates devote time during case preparation to anticipating defense arguments and thinking through avenues of rebuttal. You should end by recapping the theory of your case. After each defense argument is identified and refuted, explain how that conclusion affects the big picture and why it makes your theory the only certain conclusion. At the end of your rebuttal you must appeal for the verdict you want from the jury. The final appeal for a verdict is the final word before instructions. Use it to make your final appeal to the jury or judge. This appeal combines the plea for justice, the restatement of your theme, and a summary of the reasons that compel a verdict in your favor. This portion of the argument should be committed to memory.

A defense attorney's issues concerning rebuttal argument deal primarily with how to devise strategies that reduce the impact of rebuttal argument. A strong and effective tactic for defense counsel is to use your closing as a tool. Hone in on promises not fulfilled by plaintiff's counsel. Implore the jury to listen for the "answers to unanswered questions by the plaintiff" or "ask them why" statements. Giving the jury a number of issues to think about while the plaintiff is putting on their rebuttal automatically puts plaintiff's counsel in a precarious situation. Do they take the bait and answer your questions? Or do they stay on message and ignore the issues as a whole? Either way you have planted those seeds in the juror's minds and they will remember them while deliberating. In addition, engaging the jury this way in an active role, instead of strictly a spectator role can be immensely effective.

It goes without saying that the most important witness for your side is often you. The way you act, your command of the courtroom and sheer presence can sometimes carry the day in the mind of an otherwise doubting juror. Take control of the space available to you during rebuttal argument. One excellent technique is to walk out to a position approximately six to eight feet in front of the jury. Plant yourself firmly on both feet, face the jury and then allow the silence to draw their eyes to you. Make eye contact! Once you are sure you have them, then, and only then, begin you rebuttal.

Focus on key issues from your argument. This is your rebuttal. You are the filter for what is important and what is not. Bring the jury back to the strength of your case, while highlighting the weakness of theirs. Do not allow the arguments of defense counsel to sidetrack you. The worst mistake you can make is to address, point by point, the defense's position. It can breathe life into what was otherwise a "dead Frankenstein monster." Every piece of your rebuttal should turn the jury back, like an inexorable tide, to the strength, right and justice of your argument. If you are going to address the defense argument directly, do it constructively. Use it to buttress your own position. Do not reiterate what the defense said. This requires that you develop the ability to think on your feet. Rebuttal is the opportunity for counsel to impress the jury with their ability to quickly and concisely destroy the defense's argument. Use your evidence and apply it to the defense argument. Imagine the defense argument as a wall of bricks, built with loving patience by counsel in front of the jury. It stands there, tall, freshly mortared, without a chink. By thinking on your feet you can walk up to that defense wall, reach out, and pull out the one brick that brings the entire structure crashing to the ground.

Remember, not only are you a witness for your case, so is your worktable, your papers, and the way you use the evidence. Your ability to have at your fingertips each and every item is expected of competent counsel, and devastating when coupled with a strong rebuttal. Organize, organize and then organize again. In the heat of rebuttal it is devastating to the defense to use their evidence, or your own, to destroy their point. It is devastating for your case if you reach for the evidence, and cannot find it there, or are unable to adequately use it because you just cannot get it together.

The same practice tips that apply to closing argument also apply to rebuttal. Primacy and Recency are one of the most important. The jury will focus on the first thing you say during rebuttal. It must grab them. When you signal them that you are ending your rebuttal they will focus in again. Draw the sword and firmly pierce the defense's case. If your rebuttal does not tie back into your them and theory you are merely wasting air. The jury has heard all of the evidence. Remind them of what is important. Bring them to the truth, and they will decide in your favor. You want the last words from your rebuttal, tied to the evidence whenever possible, ringing in their ears as they go back to the deliberation room to review that same evidence.

Do not forget that less is more. Trust the jury. They have heard the evidence and want to get their job done. Do not insult their intelligence by holding them captive. While you may love the sound of your own voice, the jurors will love the silence of the deliberation room even more. Lead them to the right conclusion. Don't drag them to it and then rub their faces in it for an extended period of time. You don't accomplish anything, and lose some measure of the respect they normally accord a professional. Finally, you should never waive rebuttal. There may be a rare case where waiving rebuttal is conceivable, but waiver often reflects either undue confidence or a lack of understanding of the dynamics of a trial. Both can be interpreted in a negative fashion by the jury. You have the chance to have the last word, do so.

E. EXAMPLES OF A CLOSING ARGUMENTS.

Enclosed below are sections of closing arguments. As you read through them ask yourself whether or not the lessons that I have taught you appear in the words of these advocates. Read them critically, as a judge, as a juror, and as a fellow member of bar. Identify where they may be improved, and where they sing. When you can hear the music in another's argument you are well on your way to making music in your own.

The Closing Argument of Christopher Darden in the O.J. Simpson Trial

You know, they asked me to do the summation Marcia Clark just did for you, but I told them, no, it's too long. I'm not the kind of person who likes to talk that long and Marcia isn't either, but she had to. And I think that one of the things that you probably gathered from hearing her today is that this case really is a simple case in this essence. When you get down to the bottom line, this case really is a simple case. All you have to do is use the tools God gave you, the tools he gave you to use or utilize whenever you're confronted with a problem or an issue. All you have to do is use your common sense. And the Defense would have you believe that this is a complex series of facts and evidence and law and science and all of that. Not really. Not really. You have to question or wonder how it is a lawyer can summarize a case in eight hours when presenting the case took eight months. It's a simple case, but there's been a lot of smoke, a lot of smokescreens, a lot of diversions, a lot of detractions, a lot of distractions, and in some respect, there's been an attempt to get you to lose focus of what the real issues are in this case. And that takes time. If I could give you any advice as jurors, any advice at all, I would say to you, use your common sense. When you get all of this evidence and go into the jury room and after you pick a Foreperson, take that common sense that God gave you, take the evidence that the Prosecution gave you and the Defense evidence, go into that jury room, sit down, spread it out. And using that common sense, ask yourself a question; what does the evidence show What does the evidence show?

Some people think that because the Defendant in this case is a celebrity, that perhaps he is someone above the law, that there ought to be special rules for him or that somehow he should be treated differently than any other Defendant. But that's not justice. And there are some people that think because Fuhrman is a racist, that we ought to chuck the law out of the window, throw it out of the window, perhaps it shouldn't be applied in this case. Well, that's wrong and that's not why we're here, because we don't ignore the law just because of the status of a Defendant, because of who he is or because of who he knows. That isn't justice. You're here to ensure justice, I'm here to ensure justice and we all know the rules. And the rules say and the law says that he should not kill, that he should not have killed these two people, and the law says that if you believe that he killed these two people and if you believe that it has been proven to you beyond a reasonable doubt, that you should find him guilty. You heard Marcia Clark and you've heard the evidence and you've seen the evidence, and you're reasonable people. And, you know, we know. I mean, if we're honest with ourselves, we know, If we are. And it's unfortunate what we know. But we know the truth, and the truth that we know is that he killed these two people.

There have been lots of issues, lots of issues that came up in this trial. This trial has been an amazing experience. I'm sure you would agree. But even though there are a lot of small issues, a lot of other issues, a lot of little distractions here and there, you're here to address a single issue. This is a single case, one issue; did the Defendant kill these two people. One Defendant, O.J. Simpson. You heard from the Defense in this case and they presented testimony about slurs, epithets as they call them, a bunch of nasty, hateful, low-down language used by Mark Fuhrman. And I'm not even going to call him Detective Fuhrman if I can help it because he doesn't deserve that title. He doesn't warrant that kind of respect, not from me. But this isn't the case of Mark Fuhrman. This is the case of O.J. Simpson. And let me say this to you, if you will allow me to. And I don't mean to offend you or demean you, and I hope that you don't feel that I am. But this is the case of O.J. Simpson, not Mark Fuhrman. The case of Mark Fuhrman, if there's to be a case, that's a case for another forum, not necessarily a case for another day, because today may be the day. But it is a case for another forum, another jury perhaps. This case is about this Defendant, O.J. Simpson, and the "M" word, murder; not about Mark Fuhrman and the "N" word. And you know what that is. I am going to ask you to consider the fact of his misstatements or lies or untruths, however you want to term it, because you have to consider that. That's the law. You have to consider everything Fuhrman said on the witness stand because that's evidence in this case. And I want you to consider it. I want you to consider all the evidence. So don't think that I'm saying, hey, just overlook it, just overlook what he said, just overlook the fact that he lied about having used that slur in the past 10 years. But I am asking you to put it in the proper perspective. You decide what it's worth. You decide what it means. If it helps you in assessing his credibility--and it should, or his lack of credibility, I don't know--then you use it. But please just remember, Fuhrman isn't the only issue in this case and his use of that word is not the only issue in this case. And you have to be concerned about that. I have to be concerned about it as a lawyer for the Prosecution in this case because it apparently was a very, very significant event for the Defense.

And when I spoke to you back in January, I told you--I promised you I think that I would expose to you the other side of this man, of this Defendant. I promised you that I would expose to you the private side of him, that part of him, the side of him that was capable of extreme rage, jealously and violence, and I said to you back then, I said to you and I asked that you consider the nature of their relationship, with Nicole, because to understand what happened at Bundy, you need to know what happened between them during the 17-year period that they were together off and on, because when you look at that, you see a motive for killing. I'm sure the Defense is going to get up here at some point and say, uh, that domestic violence evidence, it's irrelevant, and they may say to you that just because this Defendant had some marital discord or violence in his marriage to Nicole Brown, that it doesn't mean anything. Well, this isn't a "Just because" issue. This is a "Because" issue. It is because he hit her in the past and because he slapped her and threw her out of the house and kicked her and punched her and grabbed her around the neck, it's because he did these things to her in the past that you ought to know about it and consider it, and it's because he used a baseball bat to break the windshield of her Mercedes back in 1985 and it's because he kicked her door down in 1993. You remember the Gretna Green incident. Remember the 911 call. It's because of a letter he wrote him--he wrote to Nicole rather around June the 6th talking about the IRS. It's because he stalked her, because he looked through her windows one night in April of 1992. They may say the Defendant is just looking through a window late at night. We say that's stalking. It's because of all those things and because all of these things alongside the physical evidence at the scene, the bloody shoeprints in his size, the blood drops at Bundy, the blood on his sock, the blood trail at Rockingham, it's because when you look at all of that, it all points to him.

And as Miss Clark alluded to earlier, the killing was personal, the way it was done. The way it was done, this is personal. Somebody had a score to settle. Who had a score to settle with Nicole? When you look at all of that, you look at the domestic violence, the manner of the killing, the physical evidence, the history of abuse and their relationship, the intimidation, the stalking, you look at it, it all points to him. It all points to him. Now, they may not think this evidence is important. But it was important to Nicole Brown. You heard Detective Mark Fuhrman testify about the 1985 incident. Let me say Fuhrman, Fuhrman, Fuhrman, Fuhrman. All right. I've said Fuhrman about 50 times. Let me let you know this. We're not hiding Fuhrman. He's too big, especially now, to hide. So hey, Fuhrman testified. Fuhrman described for you a 1985 domestic violence, domestic abuse incident or incident of violence or incident of abuse or disturbing--what do you call it--disturbing the peace incident, whatever you want to call it. But in 1985, Detective Fuhrman was not a detective. I just called him Detective, geez. Fuhrman was a patrol officer. He went to 360 north Rockingham in response to a call. And you recall the testimony. He saw Nicole sitting on the--on a Mercedes as I recall.

The window was bashed out, the fenders were dented, there was a baseball bat nearby. The Defendant was walking along the driveway. Fuhrman had a conversation with the Defendant. Nicole was crying, her face was covered with her hair, she was holding her hands to her face. You remember that testimony. That was 10 years ago. 10 years ago, Fuhrman went to 360 north Rockingham in response to that call. That's 1985. 1994, Nicole's dead. When you look at the relationship between these two and you reflect back on the testimony from Christian Reichardt and you think about the 911 calls and Officer Edwards and you think about the day of the recital, you think about Denise Brown and what she had to say about the Defendant--remember that time at the red onion when he grabbed her by the crotch in front of a bar full of strangers and said, "This is where my babies come from. This is mine." Remember that testimony? This relationship between this man and Nicole, you know, it is like the time bomb ticking away. Just a matter of time, just a matter of time before something really bad happened. You know, you meet people in life and there are people with short fuses. You know, they just go off. And there are others with longer fuses, you know, takes them a little while longer to go off. And relationships are the same way sometimes, you know, especially a violent abusive relationship like this one. This thing was like a fuse, a bomb with a long fuse.

You see that fuse is lit in 1989. It was new years, new year's night. It was about 4:00 o'clock in the morning. And as I recall, we called to the witness stand a 911 operator. Her name was Sharon Gilbert. And that night--that morning, she received a call. The caller never identified herself. The line was left open. The call came in, the line was left open. The 911 operator stayed on the line and listened in. I stood before you back in January. I said to you if you listen carefully to that tape--and you'll have the tape in the jury room. You put it in a tape recorder. When you listen to it, listen carefully because you can hear in the background the sound of someone being struck or slapped. And that's what the

911 operator heard and she told you on the witness stand that she heard that. She heard the sound, the noise of someone being beaten and she put that out on the radio. You recall that? She put it out on the radio that there was a woman being beaten at 360 north Rockingham. They may say that this isn't important evidence. I say they're wrong. There's physical abuse here, wife beating here, spousal abuse, spousal battery going on and this is an emergency situation. And Sharon Gilbert, the 911 operator, puts this call out code 2, high, get somebody to 360 north Rockingham fast. And they do. And they do. About 4:00 o'clock in the morning, Officer Edwards arrived at 360 north Rockingham. You recall Officer Edwards. He and his partner, they drove up Rockingham--I'm sorry-- they drove up Ashford to pass the Ashford gate. They stopped at Rockingham where they saw the call box. He got out of his patrol car and he pushed the button at the call box, and a voice responded on the other side. It was the voice of the maid at that time, Michelle Aboudram. Officer Edwards identified himself, told Michelle that he was there in response to a 911 call and that he needed to speak to the person that made the call. Michelle said, "Hey, there's no problem here. Don't worry about it. Go on about your way." But Officer Edwards was persistent and he said, "No, no, no. I'm not leaving until I speak to the person that made that call." And as he spoke to Michelle Aboudram, someone ran out of the bushes in the dark. Do you recall that testimony? You heard it. It was here. Someone ran from the bushes in the dark. It was a woman, a woman with blond hair. She was wearing a bra. She was wearing a bra and pajamas or sweatpants. And that woman came running from the bushes in the darkness toward the gate where the call box was and she was yelling something. She was shouting something. Do you remember what she was shouting? Remember what the testimony was in this case? She was shouting, "He's going to kill me, he's going to kill me, he's going to kill me," and she shouted this four or five times as she arrived at that button and began pushing that button to get out of that gate, to get off that property, to get out of his house.

And as Officer Edwards stood there on the street side, on the Rockingham side of that gate, looking at her on the opposite side of the gate, what did he see? He saw that she was covered with mud. She was panicked. As Officer Edwards put it, she was hysterical. And she's hitting that button, hitting that button trying to open that gate to get out of there and she's yelling to him, "He's going to kill me." And what did Officer Edwards say? What did he say? "Who? Who is going to kill you?" He didn't see anybody running behind her. "Who? Who is going to kill you?" And what does she say? "O.J. O.J. O.J. Simpson." The gate finally opened, and she ran through the gate, she ran to Officer Edwards and she fell in his arms and collapsed and she said, "He is going to kill me," and she just kept repeating it. Well, at that point, Officer Edwards shined his flashlight on her face. Remember the testimony? When he shined that flashlight on her face, he saw that her eye was starting to blacken. The right side of her forehead was swollen. There was an imprint, some sort of a swollen mark on her right cheek-- cheek did I say?

And he also said that she had a hand print--he saw a hand print, a hand print on the left side of her neck, on the left side of her throat. A hand print. Someone had grabbed this woman, his wife by the neck hard enough to leave an imprint around her neck, an imprint in the shape of his hand. Let me say this to you. We submit to you that the hand that left that imprint five years ago is the same hand that cut that same throat, that same neck on June 12th, 1994. It was the Defendant. It was the Defendant then, it's the Defendant now. And at that point, Nicole Brown made a--she said a series of things to Officer Edwards. Remember, keep in mind that she was hysterical, she was upset and she was panicked, and I'm sure that she was in fear because she must have been in fear because she was running through the night covered with mud in a bra and in her pajamas. And she said to Officer Edwards--she said something very important to Officer Edwards. She said, "You never do anything about him. You come out here, you've been out here eight times and you never do anything about him." That's what she told Officer Edwards that day. She said, "You've been out here eight times."

And I don't know. This is the evidence in the case. You're going to have to decide what that means. You can interpret what he says. You don't have to just take it literally. You decide what that means. It could mean a couple things. And after he said that and after he complained to Officer Edwards about the fact he was going to be arrested for beating his wife, he says to Officer Edwards, "This is a family matter. It is a family matter and nothing more." Well, wife beating is not just a family matter, is it? I mean, is this something we ought to take seriously? That's one thing about spousal abuse. You know, it happens and it always happens behind closed doors. And you know what they say; nobody knows what goes on behind closed doors. And we don't know everything that went on behind the gates of this man's estate at Rockingham, but we do know this; that whatever it was, whatever went on there had gone on eight times prior to this time, right? We know that. But he says it's a family matter. He minimizes what has happened. He doesn't care about this woman. He doesn't care about what he did to her.

It seems as if she was more concerned about her kids than she was doing anything to the Defendant. She didn't--she didn't care about documenting her own injuries at that time. She just wanted to be with her kids. But Edwards took her to West L.A. Station and he took some Polaroid photographs of her. Remember those photographs? Back in February I think it was, I think I marked those People's 4 and 5. I want you to go back for a moment with me eight months ago. Take a look at these injuries. Keep in mind, these are Polaroids and they're eight years old. Look at these injuries. Just look at what you can see, which isn't much at this point. See the small cut to the right side from where we are on the right side of her upper lip? Look at the swollen left cheek. Look at the scar, the scratch, the bruise on the right side of her forehead. You see that? You've seen other pictures of her. You saw a picture of her when she was alive and smiling.

Look at that picture, the one you're looking at now. When you look at the one of her smiling, you look at those two pictures, you think it helps you discern just how badly bruised she was. At some point, he took her back home to be with her kids. The Defendant, well, they didn't catch him that night. And the next day, Nicole spoke to Ron Shipp and the next day as well, the Defendant spoke to Detective Farrell. Remember Detective Farrell, the detective investigating this case? He called Detective Farrell on the phone and apologized for the incident and expressed to Detective Farrell his dismay at the extent of her injuries. You remember that. He called Farrell and told him he didn't realize she had been injured that much. You didn't realize the full extent of her injuries at the time? I don't know. You tell me. That's a Polaroid. This is People's 29. She doesn't quite look like that in any other photograph you've seen in this case, does she?

She left. She filed for divorce, and he couldn't take it. You heard from Kathryn Bowe and her husband, Mr. Colby. Remember Mr. Colby? They lived at the corner on Gretna Green. In 1992, and I believe it was April 28th around 11:00 p.m. That night--it's here on the chart--they looked out the window and they saw a figure, a man, a man in the dark. In the darkness, they saw a man, and the man was out on the sidewalk and he was looking around and he was pacing a little bit up and down the sidewalk. He was pacing, walking up and down on the sidewalk. Know what it means when people pace. I do it a lot. But I don't know what this person was doing pacing out there on the sidewalk, but they thought this was unusual at 11:00 o'clock at night. Was it a Sunday night? I think it was a Sunday night.

And they watched this person and they watched this person, this man--by the way, this man was about six feet, six foot two, 200 pounds, African American. They watched this man in the dark in the night pacing up and down the sidewalk, and then they saw that man walk down the sidewalk, up the driveway and peer through the window of Nicole Brown's house on Gretna Green. Remember that testimony? He didn't handle that divorce--the filing of that divorce too well now, did he? Now, they may say, oh, well, he--you know, he looked through a window. Big deal. This is more than just looking through a window. This is stalking. When people come up to your window at 11:00 o'clock at night and they peek through it and they look through it and they watch you, there's something wrong here. There is something wrong here. This is obsessive conduct, ladies and gentlemen. This is obsessive conduct. This is stalking. And the Colby's saw this man, they saw him do that, they saw him walk back on the sidewalk, and they became so concerned about him that they telephoned the police. They called the police. And after they called the police, they continued to watch through this window to watch this man. They couldn't tell who the man was at that point in time, but after a few moments, they could. Who was that man? Him. It was the Defendant, O.J. Simpson, stalking Nicole. It's already April, April of 1992. Let me tell you something. By April of 1992, this woman knew she was going to die. She told Edwards that he was going to kill her. She told him that back in 1989, and apparently she believed that. You heard testimony from a D.A. Investigator in this case, my investigator from my office, Mike Stevens, and Mr. Stevens testified that in December of 1994 and with the permission of a Judge, he said that he went to a bank and he drilled a hole in a safe deposit box. You recall that testimony? And it was in that safe deposit box that he found a letter that we showed you a moment ago. Remember that, the letter where the Defendant says he doesn't know how he got so crazy? They found that letter and they found two other letters from the Defendant, from O.J. Simpson, to Nicole, attempting to get back with her, attempting to convince her to take him back, attempting to convince her that things would be better the next time. They found those letters in that safe deposit box and they found something else. They found a will. They found a will, this woman's will. It had been executed during 1990, which means she must have been about 30 years old. You know many people at the age of 30 who execute wills? But they find her will, his letters and something else. Do you have that?

There was some photographs, some photographs from back in 1989, because after he beat her in 1989, she called her sister, Denise, and Denise came over and she showed Denise the injuries this man inflicted on her and she asked Denise to take pictures of those injuries, and she put those pictures in that safe deposit box along with her will, along with her letters. Okay. She put those things there for a reason. I mean, they're just letters and they're just pictures. But if you are going to have a safe deposit box, you'd think that the things you put in that box are the things that you think are important. Now, I don't know how you want to interpret that conduct. You can interpret it any way you want. But let me suggest to you that you should interpret it this way. She is leaving you a road map to let you know who it is who will eventually kill her. She knew in 1989. She knew it and she wants you to know it. She knew who was going to do it to her, but she didn't know when. But whenever that event actually came, she wanted you to know who did it. Think about that. Just think about that.

A will, photographs of her being beaten. Okay. You tell me. There is one category entitled "The pathologically jealous." Remember? And O.J. Simpson said, "Well, maybe you know, maybe a little bit. Maybe I'm a little bit jealous, a little bit pathologically jealous." That is one of these things where you can't just be a little bit of. Either you are or you aren't. You know what I mean? You can't be somewhat jealous or partially jealous. Either you're jealous or you're not jealous. And this Defendant, he was jealous and he was out of control and he was consumed with passion for Nicole and he was obsessive because in April of 1992, he is peeking through windows. He has already beaten her. He has already beaten up her car. And he does some other things. In 1988 and 1989, I told you already that the testimony from Denise Brown was that he humiliated Nicole in public by grabbing her crotch in front of a bar full of strangers. And what else had he done? What else had he done? He's thrown Nicole and Denise out of his home one night. Remember that night, that night Denise said to him, "O.J., you take Nicole for granted," and he blew up. Remember, he blew up and he said, "Hey, I do everything for her." And he became enraged back then. He picked Nicole up, he threw her against the wall, he threw her out of the house. He threw Denise out of the house and he threw all the clothes downstairs and out of the house too. Remember that testimony? This is the private side of him. This is the other side. This is the side of this man that you don't see in the commercial. He is out of control. He cannot handle it and the fuse is burning.

The Closing Argument of Johnnie Cochran in the O.J. Simpson Trial

The Defendant, Mr. Orenthal James Simpson, is now afforded an opportunity to argue the case, if you will, but I'm not going to argue with you, ladies and gentlemen. What I'm going to do is to try and discuss the reasonable inferences which I feel can be drawn from this evidence.

Ultimately, it's what you determine to be the facts is what's going to be important, and all of us can live with that. You are empowered to do justice. You are empowered to ensure that this great system of ours works. Listen for a moment, will you, please. One of my favorite people in history is the great Frederick Douglas. He said shortly after the slaves were freed, quote, "In a composite nation like ours as before the law, there should be no rich, no poor, no high, no low, no white, no black, but common country, common citizenship, equal rights and a common destiny." This marvelous statement was made more than 100 years ago. It's an ideal worth striving for and one that we still strive for. We haven't reached this goal yet, but certainly in this great country of ours, we're trying. With a jury such as this, we hope we can do that in this particular case.

I'd like to comment and to compliment Miss Clark and Mr. Darden on what I thought were fine arguments yesterday. I don't agree with much of what they said, but I listened intently, as I hope you'll do with me. And together, hopefully these discussions are going to be helpful to you in trying to arrive at a decision in this case where you don't compromise, where you don't do violence to your conscious (sic), but you do the right thing. And you are the ones who are empowered to determine what is the right thing. Let me ask each of you a question. Have you ever in your life been falsely accused of something? Have you ever been falsely accused? Ever had to sit there and take it and watch the proceedings and wait and wait and wait, all the while knowing that you didn't do it? All you could do during such a process is to really maintain your dignity; isn't that correct? Knowing that you were innocent, but maintaining your dignity and remembering always that all you're left with after a crisis is your conduct during. So that's another reason why we are proud to represent this man who's maintained his innocence and who has conducted himself with dignity throughout these proceedings. Now, last night, as I thought about the arguments of my colleagues, two words came to mind. And I want to--I asked my wife this morning to get the dictionary out and look up two words. The two words were "Speculative" and "Cynical." Let me see if I can get those words that she got for me.

And I want you to tell me what does it mean to speculate, what does it mean to be cynical, as I thought about my colleagues' arguments and their approach to this case and their view of this case. "Cynical" is described as contemptuously distrustful of human nature and motives, gloomy distrustful view of life. And to speculate--to speculate, to engage in conjecture and to surmise or--is to take to be the truth on the basis of insufficient evidence. I mention those two definitions to you because I felt that much of what we heard yesterday and again this morning was mere speculation.

People see things that are totally cynical. Maybe that's their view of the world. Not everybody shares that view. Now, in this case--and this is a homicide case and a very, very, very serious case. And of course, it's important for us to understand that. It is a sad fact that in American society, a large number of people are murdered each year. Violence unfortunately has become a way of life in America. And so when this sort of tragedy does in fact happen, it becomes the business of the police to step up and step in and to take charge of the matter. A good efficient, competent, noncorrupt police department will carefully set about the business of investigating homicides. They won't rush to judgment. They won't be bound by an obsession to win at all costs. They will set about trying to apprehend the killer or killers and trying to protect the innocent from suspicion.

In this case, the victims' families had an absolute right to demand exactly just that in this case. But it was clear unfortunately that in this case, there was another agenda. From the very first orders issued by the LAPD so-called brass, they were more concerned with their own images, the publicity that might be generated from this case than they were in doing professional police work. That's why this case has become such a hallmark and that's why Mr. Simpson is the one on trial. But your verdict in this case will go far beyond the walls of Department 103 because your verdict talks about justice in America and it talks about the police and whether they're above the law and it looks at the police perhaps as though they haven't been looked at very recently. Remember, I told you this is not for the naive, the faint of heart or the timid. So it seems to us that the evidence shows that professional police work took a backseat right at the beginning. Untrained officers trampled--remember, I used the word in opening statement--they traipsed through the evidence.

Because of their bungling, they ignored the obvious clues. They didn't pick up paper at the scene with prints on it. Because of their vanity, they very soon pretended to solve this crime and we think implicated an innocent man, and they never, they never ever looked for anyone else. We think if they had done their job as we have done, Mr. Simpson would have been eliminated early on.

Now, at the outset, let's talk about this time line for the Defense. I said earlier that Mr. Darden did a good job in his argument, but one thing he tended to trip over and stumble over was when he started to talk about our case. He doesn't know our case like we know our case. It was interesting, wasn't it, because first he stood up and started talking about the time line being at 10:15. Then he said, well, they didn't prove anything, but, "Golly, well, it may have been as late as 10:30." That's interesting, isn't it? Never heard that before.

And so as we look then at the time line and the importance of this time line, I want you to remember these words. Like the defining moment in this trial, the day Mr. Darden asked Mr. Simpson to try on those gloves and the gloves didn't fit, remember these words; if it doesn't fit, you must acquit. And we are going to be talking about that throughout. So to summarize, if you take the witnesses that we presented who stand unimpeached, unimpeached, and if you are left with dogs starting to bark at 10:35 or 10:40, 10:40 let's say--and we know from the most qualified individuals, Henry Lee and Michael Baden, this was a struggle that took from five to 15 minutes. It's already 10:55. And remember, the thumps were at 10:40 or 10:45--O.J. Simpson could not be guilty. He is then entitled to an acquittal.

And when you are back there deliberating on this case, you're never going to be ever able to reconcile this time line and the fact there's no blood back there and O.J. Simpson would run into an air conditioner on his own property and then under her scenario, he still has the knife and the clothes. But what does she tell you yesterday? Well, he still has the knife and he's in these bloody clothes and presumably in bloody shoes, and what does he do? He goes in the house. Now, thank heaven, Judge Ito took us on a jury view. You've seen this house. You've seen this carpet. If he went in that house with bloody shoes, with bloody clothes, with his bloody hands as they say, where's the blood on the doorknob, where's the blood on the light switch, where's the blood on the banister, where's the blood on the carpet? That's like almost white carpet going up those stairs. Where is all that blood trail they've been banting about in this mountain of evidence? You will see it's little more than a river or a stream. They don't have any mountain or ocean of evidence. It's not so because they say so. That's just rhetoric. We this afternoon are talking about the facts. And so it doesn't make any sense. It just doesn't fit. If it doesn't fit, you must acquit.

And so she (Ms. Clark) talks about O.J. being very, very recognizable. She talks about O.J. Simpson getting dressed up to go commit these murders. Just before we break for our break, I was thinking--I was thinking last night about this case and their theory and how it didn't make any sense and how it didn't fit and how something is wrong. It occurred to me how they were going to come here, stand up here and tell you how O.J. Simpson was going to disguise himself. He was going to put on a knit cap and some dark clothes, and he was going to get in his white Bronco, this recognizable person, and go over and kill his wife. That's what they want you to believe. That's how silly their argument is. And I said to myself, maybe I can demonstrate this graphically. Let me show you something. This is a knit cap. Let me put this knit cap on (Indicating). You have seen me for a year. If I put this knit cap on, who am I? I'm still Johnnie Cochran with a knit cap. And if you looked at O.J. Simpson over there--and he has a rather large head--O.J. Simpson in a knit cap from two blocks away is still O.J. Simpson. It's no disguise. It's no disguise. It makes no sense. It doesn't fit. If it doesn't fit, you must acquit.

Consider everything that Mr. Simpson would have had to have done in a very short time under their timeline. He would have had to drive over to Bundy, as they described in this little limited time frame where there is not enough time, kill two athletic people in a struggle that takes five to fifteen minutes, walk slowly from the scene, return to the scene, supposedly looking for a missing hat and glove and poking around, go back to this alley a second time, drive more than five minutes to Rockingham where nobody hears him or sees him, either stop along the way to hide these bloody clothes and knives, et cetera, or take them in the house with you where they are still hoisted by their own petard because there is no blood, there is no trace, there is no nothing. So that is why the Prosecution has had to try and push back their timeline. Even to today they are still pushing it back because it doesn't make any sense. It doesn't fit.

As I started to say before, perhaps the single most defining moment in this trial is the day they thought they would conduct this experiment on these gloves. They had this big build-up with Mr. Rubin who had been out of the business for five, six, seven, eight years, he had been in marketing even when he was there, but they were going to try to demonstrate to you that these were the killer's gloves and these gloves would fit Mr. Simpson. You don't need any photographs to understand this. I suppose that vision is indelibly imprinted in each and every one of your minds of how Mr. Simpson walked over here and stood before you and you saw four simple words, "The gloves didn't fit." And all their strategy started changing after that. Rubin was called back here more than all their witnesses, four times altogether. Rubin testified more than the investigating officers in this case, because their case from that day forward was slipping away from them and they knew it and they could never ever recapture it. We may all live to be a hundred years old, and I hope we do, but you will always remember those gloves, when Darden asked him to try them on, didn't fit.

Consider the EAP b found under Nicole Brown Simpson's fingernails where they try to come in and tell you it is a degraded BA and a cross-examination. Again Blasier got Matheson to admit there was no specific support in any of the literature for a BA degraded into a B, and this was by all accounts a double-banded B. The reason they didn't want to pursue that, because she may have scratched somebody with a b type, but they never pursued those things. The second hat at Bundy. The Bundy location inside, when the Defense investigator finds this hat, nobody wanted to collect it. They refused in fact to collect it. When we in this trial, before you, discovered that evidence had been moved at Bundy and that a key piece of evidence, the piece of paper, had disappeared, they didn't do anything to find out about it that we know of. I am concerned about those kind of things.

So we heard last night and we are treated to this morning some very, very interesting observations by my learned colleague, Mr. Darden.

Now, this is interesting because Mr. Darden started off by saying, well, you know, we are going to put together this other piece, it is not really one of the elements of the crime of murder, motive, but we are going to talk to you about motive now. We are going to tell you and convince you about the motive in this case, and then he spent a long time trying to do that. As I say, he did a fine job and addressed the facts and conjured up a lot of emotion. You notice how at the end he kind of petered out of steam there, and I'm sure he got tired and he petered out because this fuse he kept talking about kept going out. It never blew up, never exploded. There was no triggering mechanism. There is nothing to lead to that. It was a nice analogy, almost like that baby analogy, the baby justice and the house of fire. You don't have to go through the house of fire. You have to keep yourself on the prize, the house of justice, a city called Justice, and that is what this is leading to, so this is what it is all about. The court--Mr. Darden looks up there, says, well, gee, judge, whatever limited purpose, but let's talk about the limited purpose for which all of his argument was about. When you talk about this evidence of other crimes, such evidence was received--excuse me, sir--and may be considered by you only for the limited purpose of determining if it tends to show the characteristic method or plan or scheme about identity or motive. For the limited purpose for which you may consider such evidence, you must weigh it in the same manner as you do all other evidence in the case. You are not permitted to consider such evidence for any other purpose. So this isn't about character assassination of O.J. Simpson, as you might think at first blush. This is about Mr. Darden trying to conjure up a motive for you. And at the outset let me say that no, none, not one little bit of domestic violence is tolerable between a man and a woman. O.J. Simpson is not proud of that 1989 incident. He is not proud of it. But you know what? He paid his debt to that and it went to court. He went through that program. And the one good thing, and no matter how long Darden talked, from 1989 to now there was never any physical violence between O.J. Simpson and Nicole Brown Simpson.

It is wonderful that we live in the age of videotape because it tells you about who O.J. Simpson. Cindy Garvey tells you how O.J. Simpson was. He was this mean dark brooding person at this concert, that he was going to kill his ex-wife because he didn't like his seats. Because he didn't like his seats or because he didn't invite her to dinner. That is how silly what they are talking about in this case as he tries to play out this drama. But let me show you, rather than talk--a picture is worth a thousand words, so let me show you this video. You watch this video for a moment and we will talk about it. This is for Chris Darden. (At 4:19 P.M. a videotape was played.)

You will recognize some of the people in this videotape after awhile. Mr. Simpson kissing Denise Brown, Miss Juditha Brown, Mr. Louis Brown. Talking to a friend. That is his son Justin who he kisses, smiling and happily waving. Mr. Brown is happy. Laughing and falling down and laughing again, bending over laughing. You see that. You see that with your own eyes. You will have that back in this jury room. How does that comport with this tortured, twisted reasoning that he was angry in some kind of a jealous rage? Did he look like he was a jealous rage to you? Your eyes aren't lying to you when you see that. Thank heaven we have videotape. I didn't tell you about that in opening statement. Do you think that is pretty compelling? Thank heaven we have that. And we know in this city how important videotapes can be when people don't want to believe things even when they see on it videotapes and you saw that yourself.

And even after that video, like any proud papa, you know what O.J. Simpson did? Took a picture, a photograph with his daughter. Let's look at this photograph for a minute, if you want to see how he looks while he is in this murderous rage, while this fuse is going on that Darden talks about. Where is the fuse now, Mr. Darden? Where is the fuse? Look at that look on his face liked (sic) any proud papa. He is proud of that little girl and who wouldn't be proud of her.

Then we know that at nine o'clock he talked to Christian Reichardt, his friend Dr. Christian Reichardt, and you saw Chris Reichardt come in here and talk to you. I thought he made a very, very, very good witness from the standpoint of what he had to say. He told you that O.J. Simpson sounded even happier than usual. He was more jovial, he got his life back together and he was moving on. Isn't that interesting? Isn't that an interesting way of looking at circumstantial evidence. Let me show you how we differ in this case. A doctor witness comes in and says O.J. Simpson is jovial at nine o'clock on June 12th. Pretty good evidence, wouldn't you say? I think you would love to have that. Anybody would in a case where you are supposedly in a murderous rage. Instead of Chris Darden standing here and saying, well, that is pretty tough evidence for us to overcome, he says O.J. Simpson was happy because he was going to kill his wife. Now, if you believe that, I suppose I might as well sit down now and I am probably wasting my time. I don't think any of you believe that. That is preposterous. It flies in the face of everything that is reasonable. You have these two reasonable hypotheses, his isn't reasonable, but assume it is reasonable, you would have to adopt this, that he is jovial, he is happy. They make a date for that next Wednesday and O.J. Simpson returns from back east. You remember that. That is the testimony. Mr. Darden tries to make a big thing of the fact, well, gee, you know, golly, was he depressed about the fact that they had broken up or they had finally broke up? He said, yeah, he had been down. He never said he was depressed. Said he was down or upset and who wouldn't be. Remember the last questions I asked. If you had just ended a 17-year relationship and it was over, you would feel down for a short period of time until you got your life on track. You wouldn't go kill your ex-wife, the mother of your children. O.J. Simpson didn't try to kill or didn't kill Nicole Brown Simpson when they got a divorce, when they went through whatever they went through when Faye Resnick moved in.

In this case in opening statement I showed you Bob Shapiro's foresight and wisdom. He had these photographs taken I think on June 15th. Instead of praising this lawyer who was interested in the truth, the Prosecution says, well, they went to Dr. Huisenga. That wasn't really his doctor. Isn't that preposterous. Dr. Huisenga, by all accounts, is a qualified doctor. He was the raiders team doctor. I suppose he is supposes qualified. This is Mr. O.J. Simpson's body as it appeared on June 15th. Wouldn't you expect to see a lot of bruises and marks on that body? You see his back. Some of these aren't very flattering, but this is not about flattery; this is about his life. Now, on his hands--there is some slight abrasions on his hands, but nothing consistent with a fight like this. You know it. I know it. We all know it. We will talk more about this, this so-called fishhook cut and where he got that. It will become very clear when we talk about demeanor where that came from. Miss Clark wants to try and confuse that, but that is very, very clear. So with regard to Mr. Simpson's physical condition, I don't want to just tell you to take my word, stand here and say, oh, yeah, he was in great shape on that day or he looked good or whatever. Fortunately we had photographs again, we had graphic evidence of this man's body. This man had not been in a life and death struggle for five to fifteen minutes.

And just before we take the dinner break, let's talk briefly about these witnesses from the family and what they had to say. The first. We first called Arnelle Simpson, and you saw Arnelle on the stand. Arnelle Simpson, the Defendant's daughter, born the day he won the Heisman trophy.

And she told you how her father reacted when he got the news that his ex-wife had been killed. She told you. She had never before heard her father sound like that, how upset he was, how he lost control of himself, how distraught he was. You heard and you saw her on that stand. That is why we called her, so you would have better understanding, because we knew, I knew there would come a day that Marcia Clark would stand here and say, well, you know, he wouldn't react like he does when somebody gets this information, just like he did yesterday, because what Miss Clark forgot was I examined Detective Phillips. And you look back through your notes. The first thing that O.J. Simpson said to Detective Phillips was, "What do you mean she has been killed?" And then he kept repeating himself and repeating himself, and Phillips, to his credit, said he became very, very upset, kept repeating himself, and Phillips gave the phone to Arnelle Simpson.

So they can make--she can again theorize, fantasize all she wants. Well, he didn't ask, well, it was a car accident? Have you ever had some bad news given to you? There is no book that you go to. The only book you should go to is the bible or your God, whomever you believe in to help get you through it. There is nothing that says how you would handle yourself in those times. These Prosecutors don't understand that. They would stand here and tell you that that is preposterous. This man was upset. And you are going to see at everything he did from that moment that he found out that his ex-wife had been killed was consistent only with innocence absolutely that day. And so Arnelle Simpson helps us in that regard.

Now, when you want to think about the depths to which people will go to try to win, when you want to talk about an obsession to win, I'm going to give you an example. There was a witness in this case named Thano Peratis. This is a man who's their man who took O.J. Simpson's blood. This is a man who had a subpoena, at one point said he could have come down here and testify. They didn't call him. By the time we wanted to call him, he's unavailable because of his heart problem, remember? So what we did is, we read you his grand jury testimony I believe and we played for you his preliminary hearing testimony. And in that testimony, it's very, very consistent. He's been a nurse for a number of years. You saw him. He works for the city of Los Angeles. He says that when he took this blood from O.J. Simpson on June 13th, he took between 7.9 and 8.1 cc's of blood. That's what he said. That's real simple, isn't it? We knew that. He's sworn to tell the truth under oath both places, the grand jury and preliminary hearing. Pretty clear, isn't it? Pretty clear. You remember in my opening statement, I told you, you know, something's wrong here, something's sinister here, something's wrong, because if we take all their figures and assume they took 8 cc's of blood, there's 6.5 cc's accounted for, there is 1.5 cc's missing of this blood. There's some missing blood in this case. Where is it?

It took all four detectives, all four LAPD experienced detectives to leave the bodies. They had to notify the Coroner. They didn't have a criminalist to go over to notify O.J. Simpson. Who's fooling who here? This is preposterous. They're lying, trying to get over that wall to get in that house. You don't believe so? You're talking about saving lives. Remember what Arnelle said. First of all, they all make this big mistake. They forget and they say, "Well, when we leave from the back, we go right in that back door of the house there, go right in the back door." But they forgot. Arnelle Simpson comes in here and testifies you can't go in the back door because remember, Kato had put on the alarm. You had to go around the house to the front. Arnelle had to open the keypad to let them in, remember? You think who knows better? You'd think she knows better or they know better? She had to let them in. So they're worried about dead bodies and people being in that house and saving lives? Who goes in first? Arnelle Simpson goes in first. These big, brave police officers, and the young lady just walks in there first. They don't go upstairs looking. They just want to be inside that house and make her leave to give Fuhrman a chance to start what he's doing, strolling around the premises and doing what he's doing there.

Then we come, before we end the day, to Detective Mark Fuhrman. This man is an unspeakable disgrace. He's been unmasked for the whole world for what he is, and that's hopefully positive.

And they put him on the stand and you saw it. You saw it. It was sickening. And then my colleague, Lee Bailey, who can't be with us today, but God bless him, wherever he is, did his cross-examination of this individual and he asked some interesting questions. Some of you probably wondered, "I wonder why he's asking that." He asked this man whether or not he ever met Kathleen Bell. Of course, he lied about that.

Then Bailey says: "Have you used that word, referring to the `n' word, in the past 10 years? "Not that I recall, no. "You mean, if you call someone a Nigger, you had forgotten it?

"I'm not sure I can answer the question the way it's phrased, sir." And they go

on. He says, "Well--" And then pins him down. "I want you to assume that perhaps at some time since 1985 or `86, you addressed a member of the African American race as a Nigger. Is it possible that you have forgotten that act on your part? "Answer: No, it is not possible. "Are you, therefore, saying that you have not used that word in the past 10 years, Detective Fuhrman?

"Answer: Yes. That is what I'm saying. "Question: And you say under oath that you have not addressed any black person as a Nigger or spoken about black people as niggers in the past 10 years, Detective Fuhrman? "That's what I'm saying, sir. "So that anyone who comes to this court and quotes you as using that word in dealing with African Americans would be a liar; would they not, Detective Fuhrman? "Yes, they would".

Let's remember this man. This is the man who was off this case shortly after 2:00 o'clock in the morning right after he got on it. This is the man who didn't want to be off this case. This is the man, when they're ringing the doorbell at Ashford, who goes for a walk. And he describes how he's strolling. Let me quote him for you. Here's what he says:

"I was just strolling along looking at the house. Maybe I could see some movement inside. I was just walking while the other three detectives were down there." And that's when he walks down and he's the one who says the Bronco was parked askew and he sees some spot on the door. He makes all of the discoveries. He's got to be the big man because he's had it in for O.J. because of his views since `85. This is the man, he's the guy who climbs over the fence. He's the guy who goes in and talks to Kato Kaelin while the other detectives are talking to the family. He's the guy who's shining a light in Kato Kaelin's eyes. He's the guy looking at shoes and looking for suspects. He's the guy who's doing these things. He's the guy who says, "I don't tell anybody about the thumps on the wall." He's the guy who's off this case who's supposedly there to help this man, our client, O.J. Simpson, who then goes out all by himself, all by himself.

Now, he's worried about bodies or suspects or whatever. He doesn't even take out his gun. He goes around the side of the house, and lo and behold, he claims he finds this glove and he says the glove is still moist and sticky. Now, under their theory, at 10:40, 10:45, that glove is dropped. How many hours is that? It's now after 6:00 o'clock. So what is that? Seven and a half hours. The testimony about drying time around here, no dew point that night. Why would it be moist and sticky unless he brought it over there and planted it there to try to make this case? And there is a Caucasian hair on that glove. This man cannot be trusted. He is sinful to the Prosecution, and for them to say he's not important is untrue and you will not fall for it, because as guardians of justice here, we can't let it happen.

Why did they then all try to cover for this man Fuhrman? Why would this man who is not only Los Angeles' worst nightmare, but America's worse nightmare, why would they all turn their heads and try to cover for them? Why would you do that if you are sworn to uphold the law? There is something about corruption. There is something about a rotten apple that will ultimately infect the entire barrel, because if the others don't have the courage that we have asked you to have in this case, people sit sadly by. We live in a society where many people are apathetic, they don't want to get involved, and that is why all of us, to a person, in this courtroom, have thanked you from the bottom of our hearts. Because you know what? You haven't been apathetic. You are the ones who made a commitment, a commitment toward justice, and it is a painful commitment, but you've got to see it through. Your commitment, your courage, is much greater than these police officers. This man could have been off the force long ago if they had done their job, but they didn't do their job. People looked the other way. People didn't have the courage. One of the things that has made this country so great is people's willingness to stand up and say that is wrong. I'm not going to be part of it. I'm not going to be part of the cover-up. That is what I'm asking you to do. Stop this cover-up. Stop this cover-up. If you don't stop it, then who? Do you think the police department is going to stop it? Do you think the D.A.'s office is going to stop it? Do you think we can stop it by ourselves? It has to be stopped by you.

But the capper was finding those tapes, something that you could hear. Lest there be any doubt in anybody's mind, Laura McKinny came in here, and I can imagine the frustration of the Prosecutors, they've had the glove demonstration, they have seen all these other things go wrong and now they got to face these tapes.

We owe a debt of gratitude to this lady that ultimately and finally she came forward. And she tells us that this man over the time of these interviews uses the "N" word 42 times is what she says. And so-called Fuhrman tapes. And you of course had an opportunity to listen to this man and espouse this evil, this personification of evil. And so I'm going to ask Mr. Harris to play exhibit 1368 one more time. It was a transcript. This was not on tape. The tape had been erased where he said, "We have no niggers where I grew up." These are two of 42, if you recall. Then this was his actual voice. (At 10:00 A.M., Defense exhibit 1368, a videotape, was played.)

This is the word text for what he then says on the tape. Now, you heard that voice. No question whose voice that is. Mr. Darden concedes whose voice that is. They don't do anything. Talking about women. Doesn't like them any better than he likes African Americans. They don't go out and initiate contact with some six foot five inch Nigger who has been in prison pumping weights. This is how he sees this world. That is this man's cynical view of the world. This is this man who is out there protecting and serving. That is Mark Fuhrman.

F. RELEVANT EVIDENTIARY AND PROFESSIONAL RESPONSIBILITY RULES.

1. Evidentiary Rule Matrix.

Table 1 serves as a starting point for additional inquiry into the potential evidentiary pitfalls advocates should be aware of as they prepare and deliver their own closing arguments. The same issues also exist when listening to an opposing counsel's closing argument. A thorough grasp of these issues will assist you in avoiding objections when you are performing and identifying them when others are closing. Your case analysis should assist you in identifying when these particular issues will arise. You should use the table to review your knowledge of the procedural rule so that you can include that in your planning for your closing argument.

Although there are no FRE specifically for Closing Arguments, general evidentiary issues will always apply, especially the proper uses for admitted evidence.

Issue Arising During Closing Argument	Applicable Federal Rule of Evidence*
Properly address evidence admitted with a limiting instruction	105(b)
Out of court statements offered for the truth of the matter asserted therein (hearsay)	801 - 807
Properly arguing evidence of other crimes, wrongs & acts. (FTA chapter 10).	404(b)
Legal relevancy - Is the probative value substantially outweighed by the danger of unfair prejudice et al.	403
Are the questions logically relevant.	401, 402

Table 1 - Most Prevalent Evidentiary Rules during Closing Arguments

2. *Professional Responsibility Rule Matrix.*

Table 2 serves as a starting point for additional inquiry into the potential professional responsibility issues that are implicated during closing arguments. Counsel, particularly prosecutors, must ensure that they do not cross certain lines when arguing during closing. The same issues also exist when listening to an opposing counsel's closing argument. A thorough grasp of these issues will assist you in avoiding improper argument and identifying the improper argument of others. Your case analysis should assist you in identifying when these particular issues will arise. You should use the table to review your knowledge of the procedural rule so that you can include that in your planning for your closing argument.

Issue Arising During Closing Argument	Applicable Rule of Professional Responsibility**
(a)(1-3) A lawyer must not offer false evidence.	**RULE 3.3 CANDOR TOWARD THE TRIBUNAL**
(e) A lawyer must not allude to any matter that she does not reasonably believe is relevant or that will not be supported by admissible evidence. She must not assert personal knowledge of facts in issue and never state a personal opinion as to justness of a cause, the credibility of a witness, the culpability of a civil litigant or the guilt or innocence of the defendant.	**RULE 3.4 FAIRNESS TO OPPOSING PARTY AND COUNSEL**
(a) A lawyer must not illegally seek to influence a judge, juror, prospective juror or other official. (d) A lawyer must not intentionally disrupt the court and must conduct herself with respect for the court.	**RULE 3.5 IMPARTIALITY AND DECORUM OF THE TRIBUNAL**

Table 2 - Most Prevalent Professional Conduct Rules during Closing Arguments

** *Unless otherwise specifically indicated all professional conduct rules*

referenced are taken from the Delaware Supreme Court's professional responsibility rules. Those rules are almost identical to the model rules promulgated by the American Bar Association.

Points to Ponder...

1. Why should you trust the jury? What happens if you don't?

2. Do you really have to believe in your case? Isn't this too altruistic or idealistic? What are the benefits of belief? What is the downside?

3. What benefits do instructions provide when preparing arguments? How much should you rely upon them? How do you do that?

CHAPTER FOURTEEN
JURY SELECTION

"I not deny the jury,
Passing on the prisoner's life,
May in the sworn twelve have a thief or two
Guiltier than him they try.
What's open made to justice,
That justice seizes."[1]

A. *THE SKILL OF JURY SELECTION(VOIR DIRE).*

The primary purpose of voir dire is to obtain information about potential jurors. The information can be used to challenge (eliminate) potential jurors who are prejudiced, biased or inflexible. Voir Dire also allows the parties to intelligently exercise peremptory challenges. Voir dire can also be used to educate potential jurors as to particular factual and legal issues in the case; eliminate shock and surprises; obtain promises of fairness; and, develop a rapport with the jury pool. Finally, you can use it to preview the legal and factual issues in your case, foreshadowing your opening statement and closing arguments. The beauty of voir dire when well done is that the prospective jurors talk. It is the first and last time they will have the opportunity to speak before deliberations. You can learn a great deal from what is said, when it is said and how it is said.

You must accept that you will never be able to effectively identify and choose jurors that will decide the case your way. You do have the ability, however, to identify those jurors that are so biased against your case that you will not get a fair shake if they are on the jury. This seems like a paradigm shift, but it actually comports with the law, and is a manageable goal for voir dire. Bias is much easier to identify and query than friendship. It is much easier for

---

[1] WILLIAM SHAKESPEARE, MEASURE FOR MEASURE, act 2, sc. 1.

most people to tell you what they do not like as opposed to what they do like. This is also an excellent opportunity for you to get a sense of how individual jurors will respond to questions designed to identify bias for or against your legal theory, factual theory and moral theme. Bias against a fundamental concept upon which you have built your case analysis and case preparation is a clear indicator that a particular juror should not be selected to serve on your jury.

Voir dire questions should be selected carefully. You should refrain from asking questions which insult the intelligence of potential jurors and you should also carefully tailor your questions to the facts of each case. Be sensitive to the various education levels of the potential jurors and the practice requirements of the Trial Judge. Some judges will agree to review written questions before trial. Some judges require written questions, especially in very serious cases. This approach will permit you to identify and resolve any problem areas outside the presence of the potential jurors. Remember, in jurisdictions where judges are elected voir dire is one of the few instances where judges are allowed to "campaign" their voting base. Be sensitive to this potential issue – when in doubt never embarrass a potential juror.

WHY VOIR DIRE?

Identify jurors to challenge for cause.

Identify jurors to peremptorily challenge.

Educate potential jurors about facts in the case.

Educate potential jurors about the legal issues.

Eliminate shocks and surprises.

Obtain promises of fairness.

Develop rapport with the jury pool.

Sometimes, particularly in serious cases, the Trial Judge may allow questionnaires to the potential jurors. These questionnaires provide you with a great deal of information about the members before you ask a single question in court. Judges generally like questionnaires because they save court time and avoid embarrassing questions of the potential jurors. Also, jurors, being human beings, generally are more inclined to answer sensitive and personal questions candidly and honestly on a questionnaire than in the courtroom. Most "group" Voir Dire questions can be asked in questionnaires. Often the use of group questionnaires will identify potential areas of individual voir dire that would otherwise be missed during group questioning. When a juror answers a question that might call for individual voir dire, make sure that you do not ask the follow up questions during the group voir dire. For example, if a juror says he has knowledge of the case or knows a witness, do not ask what he has heard or what he thinks of a witness in front of the group. You should always ask follow-up questions in individual voir dire. By adhering to this advice you will avoid the possibility of tainting the entire pool of prospective jurors with an answer to a question you initially posed.

Individual voir dire is better than group voir dire at identifying jurors that should be challenged. Of course, there are inevitably a number of questions that must be posed to the potential jurors to obtain basic information from which you can ask follow up questions during individual voir dire. Members are reluctant to answer questions of a sensitive or personal nature in front of other members. Most judges now allow individual voir dire, especially after questionnaires have been circulated. Judges realize that many of the general questions asked during group voir dire have been covered by the questionnaires leaving the questions that probe information that could lead to challenges for cause for individual voir dire. Individual voir dire should be conducted much like the deposition of a witness. You should ask open-ended questions such as "what happened next..." and "how did that make you feel" and "explain that situation for us." Your goal should be to obtain as much information as possible about a potential disqualifying event or attitude. In other words, you should know what happened, when it happened, where it happened, how it happened, why it happened, and what effect the event had on the potential juror. Open-ended

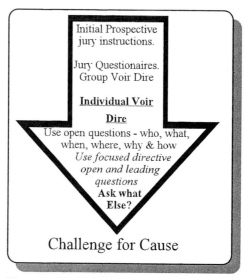

Figure 1 - The Voir Dire Process

questions let potential jurors answer questions using their own vocabulary and manner of expression. This gives you a better insight into their opinions. With that information you will be able to fully a factual basis to exercise challenges for cause when appropriate. It will also allow you to develop a gut instinct when deciding when and how to use your peremptory challenges.

You should ask the Judge to instruct the jurors about defenses or complicated issues of law before you consider asking questions about those areas. For example, if your defense will be self-defense, you should consider asking the Judge to give the instruction before you conduct voir dire so that you can ask intelligent questions about their attitudes concerning self-defense. Judges are sometimes jealous when attorneys try to instruct the jurors about the law. Having the Judge first instruct the jurors allows the Judge to perform their primary authority as the law giver in the trial. This can save time, and, more importantly, may deter the Judge from interrupting you in front of the jurors when you try to explain an issue of law in order to conduct an effective voir dire. A non-exhaustive list of potential voir dire areas and questions can be found later in this chapter. Again, many of these questions could be included in a questionnaire. You can then follow up your inquiry on individual voir dire as necessary based upon your identified legal and factual issues.

B. THE LAW OF JURY SELECTION(VOIR DIRE).

The primary legal issue that you must concern yourself with during jury selection is referred to as the *Batson* Requirements.[2] *Batson* is a U.S. Supreme court case which established that you cannot use your peremptory challenges to remove individuals from the jury pool based solely upon their race. You must have a neutral reason other than race for your decision to strike a particular juror. *Batson* applies to perempory challenges and not challenges for cause, although counsel must answer an objection to the exercise of a challenge for cause if race is raised as an alternative reason for the challenge. Each of you should take the time to fully review *Batson* and its progency before engaging in jury selection.

For purposes of trial advocacy training you should understand that you cannot exercise peremptory challenges in a discriminatory manner that are based on race or gender, and this prohibitions applies to both parties. However, this rule does not extend to the point that a requirement exists for the defendant and the challenged potential jurors to be of the same racial group before a *Batson* type challenge may be raised. For example, the prosecutor must articulate a gender-neutral reason to peremptorily challenge female jurors. Before exercising a peremptory challenge on a minority member, counsel must articulate race or gender neutral reasons that are unambiguous and supported by the record. They must be prepared to articulate as many race neutral reasons as

---

[2] Batson v. Kentucky, 476 U.S. 79 (1986). In this landmark case the United States Supreme Court applied the equal protection clause to an analysis of peremptory challenges by the prosecution in a criminal case. They established that once a defense counsel makes a prima facie showing that their appears a pattern of racial discrimination to prosecutorial peremptory challenges the burden shifts to the prosecution to establish a race neutral reason for the challenge. This standard has been extended to gender and ethnicity as well. It is not absolute, and there has been a great deal of discussion as to how far and it what direction Batson truly extends. At a minimum an understanding of this doctrine serves as an excellent starting point for new advocates who are dealing with the jury selection process. Identifying the land mines before you step on them is usually a good idea - understanding Batson and its progency will assist new advocates in doing exactly that.

possible in order to protect the record. Opposing counsel must force the challenging party to specify a race or gender neutral reason for the challenge in order to preserve the issue for appeal.

C. THE ART OF JURY SELECTION (VOIR DIRE).

1. Making a Good Impression.

Voir dire is your first opportunity to make a good impression on the jurors. As you strive to make this impression you must always keep in mind that every question you pose must be directly tied to one or more of the purposes of voir dire. You can rely upon your basic advocacy skills as you deal with this "group" experience. There are certain general techniques that apply almost universally, most of those are appropriate during jury selection. How you conduct yourself can either enhance or diminish your credibility in the eyes of all concerned. As mentioned in other portions of this book, eye contact is a fundamental means of making a connection with your audience. This is especially true for jurors. When you read questions while looking down at a piece of paper you are telling your audience that you are more interested in your written questions than their responses to those questions. Eye contact while you are posing the questions has several benefits. It allows you to connect with the jurors and it provides you with the opportunity to read the body language of the jurors when you ask your questions. Body language and facial expressions are keys that the observant advocate can use to direct additional inquiry. Watch for changes in facial expressions, body movements, avoidance of eye contact, hesitancy to respond, and other indications that a juror is uncomfortable or insincere in his or her response. Make a note of these so that you can use them to support a challenge for cause when needed.

2. Interacting With the Jury Pool.

Before you can determine how to ask questions and when to ask them, you must first develop a method for accurately recording responses, particularly during group voir dire. The best questions in the world are useless if you cannot, in the moment of group voir dire, record answers in a way that helps you determine whom you want to question during individual voir dire. You must be able to note answers and to follow up. When recording the responses you should also record the way the response was delivered. A basis for challenge may be found in not only the answer but also the delivery. One excellent method is to draw up a matrix and have co-counsel carefully record all responses from both parties and the judge. Use some type of shorthand and key so that you can quickly record answers and decipher what you are writing. On those occasions where you do not have co-counsel a matrix and seating chart is vital. You should also consider asking a co-worker or other support personnel to sit in the gallery and take notes if possible.

During voir dire your interactions with the jury assists you in weighing and measuring them at the same time that they are weighing and measuring the advocates in the case. Because of this dynamic you should not attempt to use trick questions to catch jurors. Such questions only serve to alienate potential jurors and causes them to distrust you, leading them to pick and root for the other side.

In the same vein, you must be careful to appropriately reference instructions during voir dire in the manner required by your jurisdiction. Some judges do not want attorneys talking about the law to the jury - period. In those courts you should avoid the dynamic of attempting to discuss the instructions you expect the judge to give during the course of the trial. When it is allowed you can use the instructions you expect the judge to give to reinforce legal concepts that you have chosen to build your case around. For example, in an case where accident may be raised as a defense you could ask the jury the following question to drive the point home: "If the Judge instructs you that the defense of accident is a complete defense to the indictment, please raise your hand if you can follow that instruction?" Finally, whenever dealing with the law you should be careful to never misquote or misstate it. If you do you will lose credibility with both the jury and the judge. One way to avoid this potential pitfall is to ask the judge to provide the instruction on the concept you wish to voir dire on before you begin. After the judge has read the instruction you can then voir dire, referencing back to the words of the judge as you question witnesses, getting them to agree to certain concepts your case analysis has identified as being crucial. Remember that is quite appropriate to use leading questions when you desire to educate the jury on legal and factual concepts, just be sure to not insult their intelligence when you do so.

3. Developing Challenges for Cause.

One of the primary purposes of voir dire is to develop a Challenge for Cause. When developing challenges for cause and advocate must be intimately familiar with the grounds for a challenge for cause and the potential juror's responses to the earlier written questionnaires. This basis of knowledge, when combined with the following techniques will assist advocates in developing strong challenges.

Take care to never use questions that are accusatory, reproaching or cause embarrassment, especially during group voir dire. Advocates should always begin by reviewing the questionnaires and probing a little deeper on those questionnaire issues by using non-leading and open-ended questions in general voir dire. During that time you should be careful to avoid going into detail with a potential juror on an issue that might ripen into a challenge for cause. Remember that you do not want to taint the other members of the group. If a response in general voir dire clearly establishes a ground for a challenge for cause, counsel should then ask the other potential jurors if they agree with the response. If others agree, then the number of potential jurors that could be challenged for cause has increased. These potential jurors should be queried further on individual voir dire. During individual voir dire you should consider shifting to the use of leading questions to nail down the potential challenge for cause you identified during group voir dire.

One common source of potential challenges that advocates should pursue is whether any potential juror have had any previous contact with counsel, witnesses, or the defendant or heard something about the case. Based upon this the potential juror may have either favorable or unfavorable opinions that may affect their ability to be fair and neutral. Just because they may have heard something about the case does not disqualify them per se. Instead, advocates should focus on whether the potential juror can set aside what they heard and make their decision solely on the evidence presented in court. Advocates will need to get potential jurors to state on the record how they would be able to set aside what they heard earlier.

Where a potential juror, or a family member or friend has been accused or convicted of a crime, or was the victim of a crime, counsel need to inquire into this area in individual voir dire. Again, counsel should not merely accept the assurances that the potential juror can set aside these facts and faithfully execute their duty as a juror. Counsel should seek to have them explain how he would do so. If a challenge for cause is denied in this area, counsel should generally exercise a peremptory challenge.

D. *SOME SUGGESTED VOIR DIRE QUESTION BY TOPIC.*

The following examples are provided to give you an idea of the starting point for voir dire questions that address certain issues that permeate most trials. They are predominately criminal in nature, because the vast majority of issues that arise out of voir dire at the appellate level are tied to a criminal case. As you read them ask yourself how you would need to modify them to ensure that they accurately reflect the issues you have identified during case analysis. This is a crucial point. You must take the final step of making suggested voir dire questions your own. The only way to do this is to marry them to specific legal, factual and moral issues. Your selection of an appropriate legal theory, factual theory and moral theme will assist you in finding not only the right voir dire questions substantively, but the right means of delivering them to the jury.

The Offense:

- You have all read the indictment. The Judge told you that these alleged offense are not evidence of guilt. Do you have a problem with that concept of the law?

- The offense alleged in this case is (OFFENSE). Do you feel that the nature of the offense would make it difficult for you to render a fair and impartial verdict in this case?

- (Defendant's name) is charged with several different offenses. Does the mere fact that he is facing multiple allegations lead you to believe that he is probably guilty of some or all of them?

Jurors as Victim of a Crime:

- Have you, a close friend or member of your family, ever been the victim of a (similar) offense?

- Have you, a close friend, or any member of your family, ever been a witness to an offense?

- Have you, a close friend, or any member of your family ever been accused of a (similar) offense?

Relationship with the opposing counsel other members of the team:

- Do you know (insert name)? If yes, ask:

- How do you know her? Professionally? Personally?

- Do you rely on her for advice on military justice matters?

- Have you ever received any legal assistance advice from her?

- How often do you consult with her?

- How long has she served as your legal advisor?

- Would you give her arguments more weight?

Knowledge of the case:

- Other than what you've learned so far in court today, do you know anything about this case?

- Do you regularly review the community newspaper or watch local news? Do you recall seeing anything about this case?

Knowledge of witnesses:

- During the course of the trial, we expect the following witnesses to be called. If you know any of these people, please raise your hand when the name is called. Then follow up on individual voir dire.

- Potential Juror #12, how do you know Witness Z?

- Do you believe that, by virtue of your relationship with Witness Z, you would give any greater or lesser weight to his testimony than to the testimony of a witness you did not know?

Knowledge of location:

- The indicted offenses are alleged to have occurred at (LOCATION). Are you familiar with (LOCATION)?

- How?

- If you were to receive testimony that (DEFENDANT) was present at (LOCATION), would that fact alone lead you to draw any ideas about him?

Objections to evidence:

- You are aware that trials are governed by certain rules, which are designed not only to assist you in reaching the truth, but also to ensure fairness to both sides. Can you accept this proposition?

- Would you agree that each side is entitled to have those rules enforced so that only proper matters are brought before you for consideration?

- Do you agree that the defense may properly object to evidence that the prosecution is trying to offer because that evidence does not comply with the rules governing trials?

- Would you hold it against the defense in your deliberations for attempting to prevent improper evidence from coming before you?

Weight of prosecution v. defense evidence:

- Do you believe that evidence presented by the prosecution is more reliable than evidence presented by the defense?

- If (DEFENDANT) decides to call witnesses or present evidence in his behalf, will you weigh this evidence just as you would evidence presented by the prosecution?

Burden of proof:

- The Judge will instruct (or has instructed you) that the government has the burden of proof in this case, the standard or proof is beyond a reasonable doubt, and the burden of proof never shifts to the defense. All elements of the crime charged must be proven beyond a reasonable doubt. If even one element is not proven beyond a reasonable doubt, you must vote not guilty. The defense need not introduce any evidence whatsoever.

- Do you have any problem with these legal concepts?

- Do you wish that the standard were less for the government?

- Do you believe that the defense should be required to answer the government's evidence, explain his case or present any evidence at all?

Presumption of innocence:

- The Judge will instruct (or has instructed you) that the (DEFENDANT) is presumed to be innocent of the charges the government has preferred against him.

- Do you agree that the presumption of innocence means that (DEFENDANT) remains an innocent man unless the prosecutor can prove guilt beyond a reasonable doubt?

- Do you, right now, have an opinion as to whether (DEFENDANT) is guilty of any of the offenses indicted?

Indictment as evidence of guilt:

- Do you believe that, because the government has indicted my client with an offense, he must be guilty of the crime?

Jury's basis for a decision:

- The judge will instruct you as to the law, but you are the sole and exclusive judges of the facts. Do you believe that the rule should be some other way? How would you do it?

Confidential informant:

- In a short two sentences explain how the confidential informant in your case began working for police, what the trouble the confidential informant was in and that he began working to get out of trouble – if all of this will come into evidence. If the evidence will not be admitted, you will not be able to explore this area. Explain in one sentence that the believability of the source is critical to the government's case (if this is true).

- Do you believe that you should consider the motive of the confidential informant to help the government as a factor in weighing his credibility?

Confessions (Consider each of the following when relevant to your particular case):

- Do you believe everything that you read in newspapers or magazines, hear on radio or see on television?

- Do you agree that many words of the English language have various meanings?

- Do you agree that a word may mean one thing to one person and another thing to another person?

- Do you agree that just because an individual is an American that does not mean that he is able to read and write English?

- Have you heard from whatever source that hundreds of high school graduates every year cannot read or write?

- Do you agree that someone, whose native language is not English, may have a very difficult time understanding English?

- Have you ever known someone who took the blame for something he did not do so that he could protect a friend/individual?

- Do you agree that there are reasons why someone would take the blame for something they did not do? For example, maybe they were protecting a loved one?

- Can you agree that circumstances could exist where a confession would not be the truth? Or would not be accurate? In other words, can you agree that someone would confess to a crime they did not commit?

- Have you heard of individuals giving false confessions?

- Do you agree that there may be circumstances surrounding an interrogation of an individual where the individual would say anything just to end the interrogation?

- Do you agree that an individual's breaking point varies from person to person? In other words, some people break easier under stress than others do?

- Would you agree that a statement given under stress could be unreliable or untrue?

- Would you agree that a statement taken after an individual has been interrogated for a long time, with little or no sleep, could have less reliability than from an individual who is not tired?

- Have you ever signed a document, then later discovered that you had signed something other than you thought you were signing?

- Is it reasonable to assume that people sometimes sign documents without reading them carefully? Or without reading them at all?

Defense theory of the case:

- Do you disagree with the proposition of law (state defense theory of case, e.g., that a man who is threatened with deadly force is entitled to use deadly force in his own defense?) NOTE: You may want to request that the judge give the jury the instruction prior to your voir dire.

Defendant's right to plead not guilty:

- (If plea is not guilty, and conviction is likely) As you are aware, (DEFENDANT), has pleaded not guilty to all the offenses. In the event that you were to find him guilty, would you in any way hold against him the fact that he pled not guilty?

Testimony of the defendant:

- If (DEFENDANT) were not to testify in his own defense, would you draw any negative inference from that fact or consider his failure to testify as an indication of guilt?

- Do you agree that (DEFENDANT) has no duty to present any evidence in trial to prove that he is innocent?

- Do you agree that it is the prosecutor's duty to present evidence in this trial?

- Do you agree with the proposition of law that says the burden of proving the defendant guilty beyond a reasonable doubt rests with the prosecution, and that the defendant need not introduce any evidence whatsoever?

- Knowing this, you do realize that (DEFENDANT) is not bound to explain his side of the case?

- Would you consider (DEFENDANT) failure to testify as an indication that he is guilty?

- In a trial, a defendant has the right not to testify, to not take the witness stand. Do you believe that a defendant that does not testify is more likely to be guilty than a defendant that does testify?

- If the defense does not present any witnesses of their own, but relies solely on the cross-examination of government witnesses, would that cause you to conclude (DEFENDANT) is guilty?

- If (DEFENDANT) were to testify, would you be inclined to disbelieve him solely because the state has indicted him?

- If (DEFENDANT) were to testify, would you listen to his testimony the same way that you would any other witness?

- Will you consider and judge (DEFENDANT) testimony by the same rules and standards you would use in judging the testimony of any other witness in this case?

- Would the fact that (DEFENDANT) was convicted of an offense in the past cause you to prejudge him and to disregard any of his testimony?

- Will you assume, because of his prior conviction, regardless of what his testimony is, that he is not telling the truth?

- You will be told that you can consider his prior conviction only in evaluating his credibility. Would you assume that because he has a prior conviction that he must be guilty of this offense?

Defendant's relatives will testify:

- You may hear from (DEFENDANT) relatives when the defense has an opportunity to present evidence. Would any of you disbelieve these witnesses merely because they are related to (DEFENDANT)?

- Do you believe that because (WITNESS) is the defendant's relative, his/her testimony is entitled to lesser belief than that of someone unrelated to the defendant?

Joint trial:

- There is more than one person on trial here. The judge will tell you these individuals must be given separate consideration. Will you assume the evidence admitted against only one of the defendant's should also be used against the others, just because they are being tried together?

- If the evidence convinces you of guilt beyond a reasonable doubt of one but not the other, will you have difficulty finding the other not guilty?

Sodomy and other consensual acts:

- Do you agree that the issue of consent is a very important factor to consider? Would you agree that consensual _____ sex is not necessarily indicative of a lack of moral character?

- Do you have religious or strong moral feeling against _____ sex?

- Do you believe that the only legitimate purpose of human sexual actions is to reproduce?

- Do you understand what a victimless offense is?

Interracial issues:

- Do you believe that interracial dating is improper?

- Do you believe that interracial marriage is improper?

- Do you feel that you would be unable to impartially serve in a case where the defendant and the alleged victim are of a different race?

- Do you agree that an individual who pursues an interracial relationship may experience problems with prejudice in the community? Do you agree that prejudice can affect your judgment?

- Are you uncomfortable with the idea of interracial dating/marriage?

- Do you have religious or moral objections to interracial dating or marriage?

- Do you agree that any discomfort you may feel concerning interracial relationships must be set aside in order to give (DEFENDANT) a fair trial?

Guns or other weapons:

- You will receive testimony in this trial that a (GUN)(KNIFE) was used in the alleged commission of this crime. Have you, your close friends or family members, ever had an experience with (WEAPON) that might make it difficult for you to sit on a case where (WEAPON) was involved?

- Do you actively participate in the debate over the political issue of gun control?

- Would you be prejudiced against an individual merely because he had owned or carried a firearm?

- Are you a member of the National Rifle Association?

- Do you feel that the sale of handguns should be prohibited?

- Do you object to anybody keeping a firearm in his own home for self-protection?

- Do you own a gun?

Cursing:

- You may hear swear or cuss words in this trial. Would you be so uncomfortable after hearing these words in this courtroom that you would have difficulty in impartially weighing the evidence in this case?

Narcotics:

- You may receive evidence that on the day in question, (DEFENDANT) used illegal drugs. Would this fact alone make it difficult for you to render a fair and impartial verdict?

Alcohol:

- Do you make it a point never to allow alcoholic beverages in your home?

- Do you have religious or moral beliefs against drinking alcoholic beverages?

- You will hear evidence that (WITNESS) is a chronic alcoholic. Is there any reason why you could not fairly judge the case of an individual who is an alcoholic?

Pornography:

- You may hear evidence concerning (DEFENDANT) (use, possession, reading, and viewing) pornographic (movies, magazines, materials). Do you have a religious or moral aversion to pornography?

- Should pornography be outlawed completely?

- Do you hold the belief that a person who (reads, possesses, watches) pornographic material is immoral?

- Do you believe that a person who (possesses, watches, reads) pornographic material is predisposed or inclined to commit (offense)?

- Do you feel that a people should be punished for (watching, possessing, and reading) pornographic material?

Publicity:

- Over the past several months there has been considerable publicity on television, radio magazines and newspapers concerning this (case) (type of offense). What specific facts do you remember from what you saw, heard or read? Do you feel that you could not sit as a juror on this case in view of the publicity you have seen, heard or read?

- Do you know anything about the facts of this case other than what you have heard in court today?

- Have you heard anybody discussing this case?

- (If the juror has knowledge) What did you (read, hear, discuss)?

- Have you formed an opinion as to the guilt or innocence of (DEFENDANT) from what you (heard, discussed, read)?

- In spite of what you have read or heard, do you think you could judge this case only on the facts that emerge in testimony and evidence in this courtroom, and not be influenced by anything you heard or read?

Emotional issues/abuse case:

- Do you agree that a situation involving _____ can be a highly emotional situation?

- Do you agree that it is only human to have some type of emotional reaction to this type of case?

- Do you agree with the proposition that being emotional can have some impact on your ability to rationally and objectively evaluate the facts or make a rational decision?

- Can you agree to minimize, as extensively as possible, your emotional feelings about this case, to ensure that (DEFENDANT) receives a fair and impartial trial?

- If the complaining witness takes the stand and becomes emotional, or even cries, while telling her story, would this fact, standing alone, convince you that she is telling the truth?

Adverse/gruesome photographs:

Photos – General issues

- Do you agree with the proposition that, based on how they are taken or developed, photographs may not accurately depict the subject of the photo?

- Do you agree that the circumstances under which a photograph was taken are important? Such as lighting or weather conditions?

- Photographs only depict the scene shown in the photo. Do you agree that testimony must be heard to determine how serious an injury is? For instance, an injury can look serious in a photo, but not be serious?

Autopsy Photos

- You will see autopsy photographs today. Have you seen an autopsy before or have seen photographs of an autopsy?

- Some of the photographs are very gruesome. This may cause some type of emotional response. SEE EMOTION LINE OF QUESTIONS.

- Autopsies are done after a person's death and are an accepted medical procedure to determine the cause of death. Do you understand that (DEFENDANT) did not cause this to be done to the body you see in the photos?

- Except for a medical opinion of the cause of death, do you agree that an autopsy is not reflective of what happened to the individual as is charged?

Photos – bruises and wounds

- You will see photos of (VICTIM'S) injuries. Do you agree that photographs cannot tell you how serious an injury is?

- Do you agree that, based on how a photograph is taken, it can distort or make the scene appear worse than it actually is?

- Do you agree that enlarging a photo would have a tendency to do this? In other words, enlargement makes a wound or bruise appear larger than is actually was?

Child Abuse – Sexual/physical:

- The case involves (physical, sexual) abuse of a child. Do you agree that these types of cases can be very emotional? SEE EMOTION QUESTIONS.

- Do you feel any pressure to convict because this case involves alleged acts of violence and sexual misconduct with a child?

- Would you automatically believe the testimony of the alleged victim in this case merely because she is a child?

Parental discipline:

- Do you believe that a parent has a right to use physical punishment in disciplining a child? Do you all agree that this could include spanking?

- Did you receive excessive punishment as a child?

Experts:

- Do you have training in, experience with, or interaction with someone in (area of expertise)?

- Can you accept the opinion of a psychiatrist, etc.?

- What is your opinion of (name of profession)?

- Will you consider the evidence given by (expert) in the same light as other evidence received here today?

- Will you give the testimony presented by the government's expert witness any more credibility, just because it is coming from someone called an expert?

- Do you agree that, as a human being, an expert can make mistakes?

- Do you agree that (name of expertise) is not an exact science? That the opinion the expert gives is just that, an opinion?

- That this opinion may not be exactly accurate or correct?

- Do you agree that the expert's opinion may vary depending on the facts that form the basis for that opinion?

- Do you agree that it is important for an expert to have all the relevant facts surrounding a situation before forming an opinion?

Mistaken identification:

- The defense in this case is one of mistaken identity. This is a proper and legitimate defense under the law. Do you have preconceived ideas that would make it difficult for you to consider a defense of mistaken identification?

- Do you agree that the identity of the person who commits a crime must be shown with such certainty as to eliminate any possibility of error?

- That is, it is not enough for the government to prove beyond a reasonable doubt that the offense was committed as alleged in the specification, but the government must also prove beyond a reasonable doubt that (DEFENDANT) was the person who committed it?

- Do you agree that the most honest witness may be mistaken or inaccurate in his or her recollection? Will you consider the witness's opportunity to observe, the lighting conditions, the rapidity with which the offense occurred?

Self defense:

- The defense in this case is self-defense. The judge will instruct you that if evidence of self-defense is present, the government must prove beyond a reasonable doubt that (DEFENDANT) did not act in self-defense. Would you have difficulty returning a verdict of not guilty if the government fails to prove beyond a reasonable doubt that (DEFENDANT) did not act in self-defense?

- Do you feel that you would be unable to follow the judge's instructions on self-defense because of your personal views on the subject? For example, are you a pacifist or do you hold any religious beliefs that would prevent you from accepting the general principle of self-defense?

- Do you disagree with the principle of law that says that a person is justified in injuring another human being if he believes that he is in actual danger of being seriously injured by his attacker?

- Do you feel that self-defense can never justify the willful taking of a human life?

- The judge will instruct you that a person has a right to use a (knife, gun, etc.) under certain circumstances. Would the fact that (DEFENDANT) used a (knife, gun) in self-defense make it difficult for you to return a verdict of not guilty if the government fails to prove beyond a reasonable doubt that (DEFENDANT) did not act in self-defense?

- Do you have any feelings against a person who uses a (knife, gun) to protect himself (or his family)?

- Do you have feelings or convictions about possession of weapons that would make it difficult for you to consider a defense of self-defense in this case?

- There will be no question in this trial that (DEFENDANT) (struck, stabbed, shot) (VICTIM). To juror: Do you believe that a person is justified in (striking, stabbing) an attacker if she believes that she is in actual danger of being seriously hurt by the attacker?

Use of a dangerous weapon:

- Should the judge instruct you that if (DEFENDANT) had a reasonable belief that he could use whatever force he believed necessary to stop the attack upon himself, to include (striking, stabbing, shooting) and not be guilty of the charge, would you be able to abide by that instruction?

- If the judge instructs you that a person has a right to use (knife, gun, etc) in self-defense under some circumstances, will you accept and follow this principle of law?

Insanity defense:

- Are you aware that the law does not hold a person responsible for his act, if he was insane at the time he committed the crime? Do you disagree with that proposition of law?

- If you find (DEFENDANT) was legally insane when he committed the crime, will you have any difficulty following the judge's instructions and rendering a verdict of not guilty?

- Do you feel that the insanity defense should be removed from our system?

- If a psychiatrist/psychologist testifies in this case, would you give less weight to his testimony merely because the defendant and his family retained and paid for his services?

Murder:

- Knowing that the charge against (DEFENDANT) is murder, could you give him the same fair trial that you would give him if he were charged with a lesser crime?

- Have you had close family or friends who died as a result of foul play?

- If the spouse of the deceased were to testify, would that testimony so influence you that you could not give (DEFENDANT) a fair trial?

- Can you accept the proposition that one person can accidently kill another person without being criminally liable?

Rape:

- One of the offenses alleged in this case is rape. Do you feel that the nature of the charge itself would make it difficult for you to render a fair and impartial verdict in this case?

- Do you believe the law of rape is unfair to the woman who claims she was raped?

- The judge will instruct you that consent is a defense to rape, and requires a verdict of not guilty. Would you be reluctant to apply the principle of law that says consent is a defense to rape?

- The judge will instruct you that the law does not permit a conviction for rape unless the victim makes her lack of consent known by taking appropriate resistance under the circumstances. Would you have difficulty applying this principle of law?

- Do you feel pressure to convict the defendant of rape because this case involved alleged sexual misconduct with another man's wife?

Character evidence:

- Witnesses will testify about the alleged victim's poor character for truth and veracity. Do you agree to consider this testimony in determining whether or not to believe the witness?

- If evidence of the defendant's good character for (insert relevant trait) is presented during the trial, are you willing to consider that evidence using the guidelines given to you by the Judge?

Driving while under the influence of alcohol:

- In addition to the blood alcohol test, are you willing to consider the testimony of witnesses who observed the defendant on the night in question in determining whether or not the defendant was under the influence of alcohol?

Accomplice testimony:

- Are you willing to find the defendant not guilty if he did not share the motive of the accomplice?

- Are you willing to find the defendant not guilty if he did not encourage or assist the accomplice?

- Can you agree that the mere presence at the scene of a crime is not a crime?

Closing questions:

- At this time would you, if you were in (DEFENDANT) position, be satisfied to have your fate decided by a juror who had your frame of mind?

- Do you agree that you will be fulfilling your sworn duty if you find (DEFENDANT) not guilty because the prosecutor failed to prove him guilty beyond a reasonable doubt?

Points to Ponder...

1. To what extent should judges control voir dire? Why have they generally assumed a much greater role in the voir dire process in the United States?

2. Is this development an indictment of the adversarial system?

3. Do the ethical concerns that apply to witnesses also apply to jury selection? Why should the hands of counsel be bound by good faith questions when trying to sort out who should sit in judgment of their peers?

CHAPTER FIFTEEN
TECHNOLOGY IN THE COURTROOM

"To see sad sights moves more than to hear them told."[1]

A. USING TECHNOLOGY.

Technology in the courtroom is relative. To a lawyer from the 1800s the ability to reproduce documents in typeset so that they were readily available to use with the jury was a possibility beyond their means. To advocates in the 21st century the ability to engage multiple senses for persuasive purposes its at an all time high. We can project life size images onto drop down screens, recreate accidents with computer graphics, tell stories through the use of presentation software. We focus and engage our juries in the process through the manipulation of sensory data, all under the complete control of the advocate. This ability is subject only to an advocates understanding of the technology and its appropriate use. For the relatively inexpensive investment of a laptop computer and the associated printers and display hardware an advocate has the ability to embark upon the use of technology in a manner that is revolutionizing how we persuade juries. It also creates an environment where more is possibly much less persuasively.

Technology in the courtroom is a tool that every advocate should learn to use. We educate, we teach, we persuade in the courts, and using technology

---

[1] WILLIAM SHAKESPEARE, The Rape of Lucrece.

allows advocates to engage jurors in a manner in which those jurors are accustomed. The combination of sight, sound and touch is a powerful one. Our jurors are a video generation, and when our presentations in court leverage that fact we are more persuasive. Advocates must accept that the use of technology is a "combat multiplier" in the courtroom. Like any multiplier it can become distracting and ineffective when used indiscriminately.

The law establishes the right of the advocate to use technology to persuade, subject to the rulings of the trial judge, but unfortunately advocates sometime may have the *right* to use technology, but lack the *ability* to do it effectively. This chapter serves as an introductory overview to the specific types of technology available for use in the courtroom. It is not a "how to" manual that will develop expertise with a particular delivery system. Reviewing this chapter should spark within you the beginnings of the creative process, empowering you to leverage technology for your client's benefit.

SEVEN FUNDAMENTAL PRINCIPLES WHEN DEALING WITH EXHIBITS:

Use them. Opening, direct, cross, and closing.

Know the type of exhibit you have and the limitations on their use.

Identify your foundational requirements early and have them on hand in the courtroom for reference.

Practice, practice, practice.

Script foundations for persuasive impact as well as legal requirements.

Do not be afraid to voir dire.

BARPH when necessary.

Most technological means of displaying and organizing exhibits are designed to focus attention and highlight issues. Often the technology is merely a delivery system, an argument through presentation, of the exhibit itself. You must be able to lay the appropriate foundation for the exhibit itself, and then establish for the judge how the technology you wish to use will assist the jury in understanding the evidence and deciding the case. The most prevalent argument from an evidentiary perspective normally addresses the substantial danger of unfair prejudice, confusion of issues, or waste of time under Federal Rule of Evidence 403. You should consider the seven fundamental principles of dealing with exhibits and apply them to your technological delivery system. If the use of technology does not fall in line with these principles then you are probably wasting not only your own time but the court's as well.

> **Easy Guide to Courtroom Objections (BARPH):**
>
> **B** – est Evidence
>
> **A** – uthentication
>
> **R** – elevance
>
> **P** – ersonal Knowledge
>
> **H** - earsay

Attorneys are required to ask foundational questions in order to establish the admissibility of evidence, and that requirement does not change when technology enters the picture. The foundational questions you must ask are still derived from the common law, evidentiary law and local court practices. The difference when dealing with new and novel uses of technology is that you must sometimes analogize to other foundational litanies. BARPH is a good place to begin when identifying potential objections to the use of technology. Foundational questions normally deal with best evidence issues, authenticity, relevancy, personal knowledge and hearsay. "The requirement of authentication or identification as a condition precedent to admissibility is satisfied by evidence sufficient to support a finding that the matter in question is what its proponent claims." Regardless of the type of proffered evidence it is the judge who determines the sufficiency of the authentication. That issue is a question of fact under federal rule of evidence 104(a). In addition to the authentication requirement, the proponent of demonstrative evidence must be prepared to respond to other evidentiary objections raised by opposing counsel that may bar the admissibility of the evidence, such as unfair prejudice under Federal Rule of Evidence 403.

> **Using technology at trial:**
>
> - Be familiar with the set up of the courtroom
> - Know the equipment
> - Sit in the jury box to ensure the jury can see the presentation
> - Make sure the color scheme improves visibility
> - Prepare for Possible Objections

B. TYPES OF TECHNOLOGY.

1. Presentation Software.

There are several different types of presentation software programs designed to highlight text, call out specific portions and manage the flow and presentation of exhibits to the jury during opening statements, witness examination and closing arguments. The most ubiquitous of these is the Microsoft program PowerPoint. PowerPoint allows the attorney to create a series of slides that serve as giant easels displaying bullet information, diagrams, pictures, documents or other information.

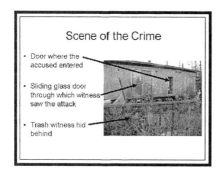

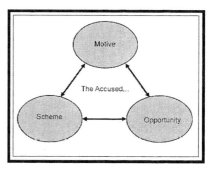

PowerPoint Slides	
Pros	**Cons**
<ul><li>Lets the jury use another sensory perception during your case.</li><li>Emphasizes important points.</li><li>Makes your case seem put together and well thought out.</li></ul>	<ul><li>Can be a stumbling point and a distraction if the advocate is not versed in its use.</li><li>Over reliance may weaken your case in the eyes of the jury.</li><li>Some jurors may see that as compensating for a weak case.</li><li>If done improperly, may bore jurors.</li></ul>

PowerPoint requires the user to carefully arrange the information. Once a PowerPoint Slide presentation has been prepared it is difficult to modify or to otherwise call up exhibits out of the expected order. It is, however, extremely easy to use, readily available, and in the hands of a competent advocate a devastatingly persuasive tool.

Other software presentation programs are also available. Many of these programs allow you to call out portions of exhibits on the fly. This means that you can highlight a small part of a document or other exhibit and with the click of a mouse have that portion blown up so that it is readily available for the jury's consideration. When choosing the type of software program you wish to use the technological friendliness of your local courts is one consideration, another is the amount of time you have to become fully trained in the software versus the initial ease of use.

2. ELMOs.

Another common piece of presentation equipment is a document camera, often referred to as an ELMO. ELMOs allow you to project a document or diagram onto a large screen. You can have witnesses annotate the document much as they would any other diagram. ELMOs are now available in most jurisdictions, and they serve as a more advanced type of projector for any written piece of paper or picture.

ELMOs	
Pros	**Cons**
• Easy to use—no transparency needed • Allows a witness to "step down" and interact with the exhibit	• Not all courtrooms will have a projector like this • If the courtroom only has an overhead projector, copy the exhibit onto a transparency

When using the ELMO or other projection equipment advocates should be careful not to turn their back on the jury while using the exhibit. This goes for the witness as well. You should also consider how the witness is to mark the exhibit. Options include colored markers, stickers and different colored labels. Just as with other diagrams, it is important to have a schematic that is persuasive and understandable.

Technology presentation packages are excellent for:

- Displaying maps (aerial, street maps, etc.)
- Recreating an accident
- Using flow charts to explain complicated issues
- Establishing timelines (with pictures)
- Displaying Autopsy/ injury photos
- Putting your "hook" phrase on a slide during opening & closing
- Focusing on key jury instructions during Closing Arguments
- Humanizing the deceased in a criminal or civil case
- Highlighting the confession of the Defendant with a callout box containing admissions
- Calling attention to the contract the defendant signed showing his responsibility to the homeowner
- Playing the videotaped will of the decedent

---

2. Video Based.

The third type of technology commonly making its way into the courtroom is the use of video based presentations. These presentations may be produced by camera or computer, and are admissible when used by experts to form opinions or by witnesses to explain their testimony. There must be a foundational connection between the video and the witness to admit it. Video presentations that have no foundation in the knowledge of the witness or the expert nature of the witness' testimony may be difficult to admit. The key issue that advocates must focus on when using video deal with authentication, personal knowledge and prejudice. It is best to provide the court with advance copies of video when you intend to admit so that the court has time to review the information and cogently rule on its admissibility.

C. RELEVANT EVIDENTIARY ISSUES AND PROFESSIONAL RESPONSIBILITY RULES.

1. Evidentiary Rule Matrix.

Table 1 serves as a starting point for additional inquiry into the relationships between specific tasks dealing with exhibits and the rules of evidence. The foundational requirements do not change when technology enters the courtroom, but you should be even more aware of potential prejudice issues based upon the ability to project exhibits and publish them in a graphic manner.

Issue Arising Dealing with Exhibits	Applicable Federal Rule of Evidence
Authentication and identification rules	901 - 902
Best evidence rules	1001 - 1004
Business records	803(6)
Contents of writings, recordings and photographs	1001 - 1008
Documents and instruments	901 - 902
Public records	803(8)
Real and demonstrative evidence	901
Substantial danger of unfair prejudice	403

Table 1 - Potential Evidentiary Rules Applicable to Exhibits Using Technology

2. Professional Responsibility Rule Matrix.

The following potential professional responsibility issues are implicated when technology is involved. Counsel must ensure that they do not cross certain lines when using technology to persuasively package their case. This includes the development of witness testimony in conjunction with the use of technology. The same issues also exist when listening to an opposing counsel's use of technology during direct examination, opening statement and closing argument. You should use the table to review your knowledge of the ethical rules so that you properly prepare for the use of technology during witness preparation and trial.

Issue Arising During Direct Examination using Exhibits	Applicable Rule of Professional Responsibility**
(a)(1-3) A lawyer must not offer false evidence.	**RULE 3.3 CANDOR TOWARD THE TRIBUNAL**
(e) A lawyer must not allude to any matter that she does not reasonably believe is relevant or that will not be supported by admissible evidence. She must not assert personal knowledge of facts in issue and never state a personal opinion as to justness of a cause, the credibility of a witness, the culpability of a civil litigant or the guilt or innocence of the defendant.	**RULE 3.4 FAIRNESS TO OPPOSING PARTY AND COUNSEL**
(a) A lawyer must not illegally seek to influence a judge, juror, prospective juror or other official. (d) A lawyer must not intentionally disrupt the court and must conduct herself with respect for the court.	**RULE 3.5 IMPARTIALITY AND DECORUM OF THE TRIBUNAL**
(a) A lawyer must not attempt to be an advocate and witness in the same trial (with some limited exceptions).	**RULE 3.7 LAWYER AS WITNESS**

Table 2 - Most Prevalent Professional Conduct Rules Concerning the Use of Technology

*** Unless otherwise specifically indicated all professional conduct rules referenced are taken from the Delaware Supreme Court's professional responsibility rules. Those rules are almost identical to the model rules promulgated by the American Bar Association and are public domain documents.*

Points to Ponder...

1. Why should we allow the "mumbo jumbo" of technology into the courtroom? Does the persuasive power of technology outweigh the dangers involved in its use?

2. Should demonstrative evidence based upon technology be allowed back into the jury room? What happens when the demonstrative technology is both substantive and demonstrative?

3. What is wrong with merely limiting witness testimony to words and the arguments of counsel to verbal structures? What would be lost? How would advocacy change if such limitations were imposed?

APPENDIX I
EXCERPTS FROM THE DELAWARE RULES OF PROFESSIONAL CONDUCT

The following excerpts from the Delaware Rules of Professional Conduct have been heavily edited for brevity and applicability to the specific rules identified in <u>Fundamental Trial Advocacy, 1st Edition</u>. The included rules and comments should be helpful to advocates when studying how the rules of professional conduct interact with the trial process. In some instances the comments for rules have been removed. In other sections both the rules and their comments were omittedd in their entirety for the sake of brevity and clarity. These rules are a beginning reference point and a refresher of text for those issues identified and discussed in the previous chapters. Before relying upon a final interpretation of the rule in question you should take the time to refer to the rules of professional responsibility for your jurisdiction. The American Bar Association will not provide edited versions of the Model Rules of Professional Conduct so this text has utilized those in the public domain, specifically the Delaware rules. These rules were based almost entirely upon the Model Rules of Professional Conduct promulgated and approved by the American Bar Association.

THE DELAWARE LAWYERS' RULES OF PROFESSIONAL CONDUCT
(Effective July 1, 2003)

Preamble: A lawyer's responsibilities.

[1] A lawyer, as a member of the legal profession, is a representative of clients, an officer of the legal system and a public citizen having special responsibility for the quality of justice.

[2] As a representative of clients, a lawyer performs various functions. As advisor, a lawyer provides a client with an informed understanding of the client's legal rights and obligations and explains their practical implications. As advocate, a lawyer zealously asserts the client's position under the rules of the adversary system. As negotiator, a lawyer seeks a result advantageous to the client but consistent with requirements of honest dealings with others. As an evaluator, a lawyer acts by examining a client's legal affairs and reporting about them to the client or to others.

[3] In addition to these representational functions, a lawyer may serve as a third-party neutral, a nonrepresentational role helping the parties to resolve a dispute or other matter. Some of these Rules apply directly to lawyers who are or have served as third-party neutrals. See, e.g., Rules 1.12 and 2.4. In addition, there are Rules that apply to lawyers who are not active in the practice of law or to practicing lawyers even when they are acting in a nonprofessional capacity. For example, a lawyer who commits fraud in the conduct of a business is subject to discipline for engaging in conduct involving dishonesty, fraud, deceit or misrepresentation. See Rule 8.4.

[4] In all professional functions a lawyer should be competent, prompt and diligent. A lawyer should maintain communication with a client concerning the representation. A lawyer should keep in confidence information relating to representation of a client except so far as disclosure is required or permitted by the Rules of Professional Conduct or other law.

[5] A lawyer's conduct should conform to the requirements of the law, both in professional service to clients and in the lawyer's business and personal affairs. A lawyer should use the law's procedures only for legitimate purposes and not to harass or intimidate others. A lawyer should demonstrate respect for the legal system and for those who serve it, including judges, other lawyers and public officials. While it is a lawyer's duty, when necessary, to challenge the rectitude of official action, it is also a lawyer's duty to uphold legal process.

[6] As a public citizen, a lawyer should seek improvement of the law, access to the legal system, the administration of justice and the quality of service rendered by the legal profession. As a member of a learned profession, a lawyer should cultivate knowledge of the law beyond its use for clients, employ that knowledge in reform of the law and work to strengthen legal education. In addition, a lawyer should further the public's understanding of and confidence in the rule of law and the justice system because legal institutions in a constitutional democracy depend on popular participation and support to maintain their authority. A lawyer should be mindful of deficiencies in the administration of justice and of the fact that the poor, and sometimes persons who are not poor, cannot afford adequate legal assistance. Therefore, all lawyers should devote professional time and resources and use civic influence to ensure equal access to our system of justice for all those who because of economic or social barriers cannot afford or secure adequate legal counsel. A lawyer should aid the legal profession in pursuing these objectives and should help the bar regulate itself in the public interest.

[7] Many of a lawyer's professional responsibilities are prescribed in the Rules of Professional Conduct, as well as substantive and procedural law. However, a lawyer is also guided by personal conscience and the approbation of professional peers. A lawyer should strive to attain the highest level of skill, to

improve the law and the legal profession and to exemplify the legal profession's ideals of public service.

[8] A lawyer's responsibilities as a representative of clients, an officer of the legal system and a public citizen are usually harmonious. Thus, when an opposing party is well represented, a lawyer can be a zealous advocate on behalf of a client and at the same time assume that justice is being done. So also, a lawyer can be sure that preserving client confidences ordinarily serves the public interest because people are more likely to seek legal advice, and thereby heed their legal obligations, when they know their communications will be private.

[9] In the nature of law practice, however, conflicting responsibilities are encountered. Virtually all difficult ethical problems arise from conflict between a lawyer's responsibilities to clients, to the legal system and to the lawyer's own interest in remaining an ethical person while earning a satisfactory living. The Rules of Professional conduct often prescribe terms for resolving such conflicts. Within the framework of these Rules, however, many difficult issues of professional discretion can arise. Such issues must be resolved through the exercise of sensitive professional and moral judgment guided by the basic principles underlying the Rules. These principles include the lawyer's obligation zealously to protect and pursue a client's legitimate interests, within the bounds of the law, while maintaining a professional, courteous and civil attitude toward all persons involved in the legal system.

[10] The legal profession is largely self-governing. Although other professions also have been granted powers of self-government, the legal profession is unique in this respect because of the close relationship between the profession and the processes of government and law enforcement. This connection is manifested in the fact that ultimate authority over the legal profession is vested largely in the courts.

[11] To the extent that lawyers meet the obligations of their professional calling, the occasion for government regulation is obviated. Self-regulation also helps maintain the legal profession's independence from government domination. An independent legal profession is an important force in preserving government under law, for abuse of legal authority is more readily challenged by a profession whose members are not dependent on government for the right to practice.

[12] The legal profession's relative autonomy carries with it special responsibilities of self-government. The profession has a responsibility to assure that its regulations are conceived in the public interest and not in furtherance of parochial or self interested concerns of the bar. Every lawyer is responsible for observance of the Rules of Professional Conduct. A lawyer should also aid in securing their observance by other lawyers. Neglect of these responsibilities compromises the independence of the profession and the public interest which

it serves.

[13] Lawyers play a vital role in the preservation of society. The fulfillment of this role requires an understanding by lawyers of their relationship to our legal system. The Rules of Professional Conduct, when properly applied, serve to define that relationship.

SCOPE

[14] The Rules of Professional Conduct are rules of reason. They should be interpreted with reference to the purposes of legal representation and of the law itself. Some of the Rules are imperatives, cast in the terms "shall" or "shall not." These define proper conduct for purposes of professional discipline. Others, generally cast in the term "may," are permissive and define areas under the Rules in which the lawyer has discretion to exercise professional judgment. No disciplinary action should be taken when the lawyer chooses not to act or acts within the bounds of such discretion. Other Rules define the nature of relationships between the lawyer and others. The Rules are thus partly obligatory and disciplinary and partly constitutive and descriptive in that they define a lawyer's professional role. Many of the Comments use the term "should." Comments do not add obligations to the Rules but provide guidance for practicing in compliance with the Rules.

[15] The Rules presuppose a larger legal context shaping the lawyer's role. That context includes court rules and statutes relating to matters of licensure, laws defining specific obligations of lawyers and substantive and procedural law in general. The Comments are sometimes used to alert lawyers to their responsibilities under such other law.

[16] Compliance with the Rules, as with all law in an open society, depends primarily upon understanding and voluntary compliance, secondarily upon reenforcement by peer and public opinion and finally, when necessary, upon enforcement through disciplinary proceedings. The Rules do not, however, exhaust the moral and ethical considerations that should inform a lawyer, for no worthwhile human activity can be completely defined by legal rules. The Rules simply provide a framework for the ethical practice of law.

[17] Furthermore, for purposes of determining the lawyer's authority and responsibility, principles of substantive law external to these Rules determine whether a client-lawyer relationship exists. Most of the duties flowing from the client-lawyer relationship attach only after the client has requested the lawyer to render legal services and the lawyer has agreed to do so. But there are some duties, such as that of confidentiality under Rule 1.6, that attach when the lawyer agrees to consider whether a client-lawyer relationship shall be established. See Rule 1.18. Whether a client-lawyer relationship exists for any specific purpose can depend on the circumstances and may be a question of fact.

[18] Under various legal provisions, including constitutional, statutory and common law, the responsibilities of government lawyers may include authority concerning legal matters that ordinarily reposes in the client in private client-lawyer relationships. For example, a lawyer for a government agency may have authority on behalf of the government to decide upon settlement or whether to appeal from an adverse judgment. Such authority in various respects is generally vested in the attorney general and the state's attorney in state government, and their federal counterparts, and the same may be true of other government law officers. Also, lawyers under the supervision of these officers may be authorized to represent several government agencies in intragovernmental legal controversies in circumstances where a private lawyer could not represent multiple private clients. These Rules do not abrogate any such authority.

[19] Failure to comply with an obligation or prohibition imposed by a Rule is a basis for invoking the disciplinary process. The Rules presuppose that disciplinary assessment of a lawyer's conduct will be made on the basis of the facts and circumstances as they existed at the time of the conduct in question and in recognition of the fact that a lawyer often has to act upon uncertain or incomplete evidence of the situation. Moreover, the Rules presuppose that whether or not discipline should be imposed for a violation, and the severity of a sanction, depend on all the circumstances, such as the willfulness and seriousness of the violation, extenuating factors and whether there have been previous violations.

[20] Violation of a Rule should not itself give rise to a cause of action against a lawyer nor should it create any presumption in such a case that a legal duty has been breached. In addition, violation of a Rule does not necessarily warrant any other nondisciplinary remedy, such as disqualification of a lawyer in pending litigation. The rules are designed to provide guidance to lawyers and to provide a structure for regulating conduct through disciplinary agencies. They are not designed to be a basis for civil liability. Furthermore, the purpose of the Rules can be subverted when they are invoked by opposing parties as procedural weapons. The fact that a Rule is a just basis for a lawyer's self-assessment, or for sanctioning a lawyer under the administration of a disciplinary authority, does not imply that an antagonist in a collateral
proceeding or transaction has standing to seek enforcement of the Rule.

[21] The Comment accompanying each Rule explains and illustrates the meaning and purpose of the Rule. The Preamble and this note on Scope provide general orientation. The Comments are intended as guides to interpretation, but the text of each rule is authoritative.

Rule 1.0. Terminology

(a) "Belief" or "believes" denotes that the person involved actually supposed the fact in question to be true. A person's belief may be inferred from circumstances.

(b) "Confirmed in writing," when used in reference to the informed consent of a person, denotes informed consent that is given in writing by the person or a writing that a lawyer promptly transmits to the person confirming an oral informed consent. See paragraph (e) for the definition of "informed consent." If it is not feasible to obtain or transmit the writing at the time the person gives informed consent, then the lawyer must obtain or transmit it within a reasonable time thereafter.

(c) "Firm" or "law firm" denotes a lawyer or lawyers in a law partnership, professional corporation, sole proprietorship or other association authorized to practice law; or lawyers employed in a legal services organization or the legal department of a corporation or other organization.

(d) "Fraud" or "fraudulent" denotes conduct that is fraudulent under the substantive or procedural law of the applicable jurisdiction and has a purpose to deceive.

(e) "Informed consent" denotes the agreement by a person to a proposed course of conduct after the lawyer has communicated adequate information and explanation about the material risks of and reasonably available alternatives to the proposed course of conduct.

(f) "Knowingly," "known," or "knows" denotes actual knowledge of the fact in question. A person's knowledge may be inferred from circumstances.
(g) "Partner" denotes a member of a partnership, a shareholder in a law firm organized as a professional corporation, or a member of an association authorized to practice law.

(h) "Reasonable" or "reasonably" when used in relation to conduct by a lawyer denotes the conduct of a reasonably prudent and competent lawyer.

(i) "Reasonable belief" or "reasonably believes" when used in reference to a lawyer denotes that the lawyer believes the matter in question and that the circumstances are such that the belief is reasonable.

(j) "Reasonably should know" when used in reference to a lawyer denotes that a lawyer of reasonable prudence and competence would ascertain the matter in question.

(k) "Screened" denotes the isolation of a lawyer from any participation in a matter through the timely imposition of procedures within a firm that are reasonably adequate under the circumstances to protect information that the isolated lawyer is obligated to protect under these Rules or other law.

(l) "Substantial" when used in reference to degree or extent denotes a material matter of clear and weighty importance.

(m) "Tribunal" denotes a court, an arbitrator in a binding arbitration proceeding or a legislative body, administrative agency or other body acting in an adjudicative capacity. A legislative body, administrative agency or other body acts in an adjudicative capacity when a neutral official, after the presentation of evidence or legal argument by a party or parties, will render a binding legal judgment directly affecting a party's interests in a particular matter.

(n) "Writing" or "written" denotes a tangible or electronic record of a communication or representation, including handwriting, typewriting, printing, photostating, photography, audio or video recording and e-mail. A "signed" writing includes an electronic sound, symbol or process attached to or logically associated with a writing and executed or adopted by a person with the intent to sign the writing.

Rule 1.1. Competence

A lawyer shall provide competent representation to a client. Competent representation requires the legal knowledge, skill, thoroughness and preparation reasonably necessary for the representation.

Rule 1.2. Scope of representation

(a) Subject to paragraphs (c) and (d), a lawyer shall abide by a client's decisions concerning the objectives of representation and, as required by Rule 1.4, shall consult with the client as to the means by which they are to be pursued. A lawyer may take such action on behalf of the client as is impliedly authorized to carry out the representation. A lawyer shall abide by a client's decision whether to settle a matter. In a criminal case, the lawyer shall abide by the client's decision, after consultation with the lawyer, as to a plea to be entered, whether to waive jury trial and whether the client will testify.

(b) A lawyer's representation of a client, including representation by appointment, does not constitute an endorsement of the client's political, economic, social or moral views or activities.

(c) A lawyer may limit the scope of the representation if the limitation is reasonable under the circumstances and the client gives informed consent.

(d) A lawyer shall not counsel a client to engage, or assist a client, in conduct that the lawyer knows is criminal or fraudulent, but a lawyer may discuss the legal consequences of any proposed course of conduct with a client and may counsel or assist a client to make a good faith effort to determine the validity, scope, meaning or application of the law.

Rule 1.3. Diligence
A lawyer shall act with reasonable diligence and promptness in representing a client.

Rule 1.4. Communication

(a) A lawyer shall:
(1) promptly inform the client of any decision or circumstance with respect to which the client's informed consent, as defined in Rule 1.0(e), is required by these Rules; (2) reasonably consult with the client about the means by which the client's objectives are to be accomplished; (3) keep the client reasonably informed about the status of the matter; (4) promptly comply with reasonable requests for information; and (5) consult with the client about any relevant limitation on the lawyer's conduct when the lawyer knows that the client expects assistance not permitted by the Rules of Professional Conduct or other law.

(b) A lawyer shall explain a matter to the extent reasonably necessary to permit the client to make informed decisions regarding the representation.

Rule 1.5. Fees - Omitted.

Rule 1.6. Confidentiality of information

(a) A lawyer shall not reveal information relating to the representation of a client unless the client gives informed consent, the disclosure is impliedly authorized in order to carry out the representation, or the disclosure is permitted by paragraph (b).

(b) A lawyer may reveal information relating to the representation of a client to the extent the lawyer reasonably believes necessary: (1) to prevent reasonably certain death or substantial bodily harm; (2) to prevent the client from committing a crime or fraud that is reasonably certain to result in substantial injury to the financial interests or property of another and in furtherance of which the client has used or is using the lawyer's services; (3) to prevent, mitigate, or rectify substantial injury to the financial interests or property of another that is reasonably certain to result or has resulted from the client's commission of a crime or fraud in furtherance of which the client has used the lawyer's services;

(4) to secure legal advice about the lawyer's compliance with these Rules; (5) to establish a claim or defense on behalf of the lawyer in a controversy between the lawyer and the client, to establish a defense to a criminal charge or civil claim against the lawyer based upon conduct in which the client was involved, or to respond to allegations in any proceeding concerning the lawyer's representation of the client; or (6) to comply with other law or a court order.

COMMENT

[1] This Rule governs the disclosure by a lawyer of information relating to the representation of a client during the lawyer's representation of the client. See Rule 1.18 for the lawyer's duties with respect to information provided to the lawyer by a prospective client, Rule 1.9(c)(2) for the lawyer's duty not to reveal information relating to the lawyer's prior representation of a former client and Rules 1.8(b) and 1.9(c)(1) for the lawyer's duties with respect to the use of such information to the disadvantage of clients and former clients.

[2] A fundamental principle in the client-lawyer relationship is that, in the absence of the client's informed consent, the lawyer must not reveal information relating to the representation. See Rule 1.0(e) for the definition of informed consent. This contributes to the trust that is the hallmark of the client-lawyer relationship. The client is thereby encouraged to seek legal assistance and to communicate fully and frankly with the lawyer even as to embarrassing or legally damaging subject matter. The lawyer needs this information to represent the client effectively and, if necessary, to advise the client to refrain from wrongful conduct. Almost without exception, clients come to lawyers in order to determine their rights and what is, in the complex of laws and regulations, deemed to be legal and correct. Based upon experience, lawyers know that almost all clients follow the advice given, and the law is upheld.

[3] The principle of client-lawyer confidentiality is given effect by related bodies of law: the attorney-client privilege, the work product doctrine and the rule of confidentiality established in professional ethics. The attorney-client privilege and work product doctrine apply in judicial and other proceedings in which a lawyer may be called as a witness or otherwise required to produce evidence concerning a client. The rule of client-lawyer confidentiality applies in situations other than those where evidence is sought from the lawyer through compulsion of law. The confidentiality rule, for example, applies not only to matters communicated in confidence by the client but also to all information relating to the representation, whatever its source. A lawyer may not disclose such information except as authorized or required by the Rules of Professional Conductor other law. See also Scope.

[4] Paragraph (a) prohibits a lawyer from revealing information relating to the representation of a client. This prohibition also applies to disclosures by a lawyer

that do not in themselves reveal protected information but could reasonably lead to the discovery of such information by a third person. A lawyer's use of a hypothetical to discuss issues relating to the representation is permissible so long as there is no reasonable likelihood that the listener will be able to ascertain the identity of the client or the situation involved.

[5] *Authorized disclosure.* -- Except to the extent that the client's instructions or special circumstances limit that authority, a lawyer is impliedly authorized to make disclosures about a client when appropriate in carrying out the representation. In some situations, for example, a lawyer may be impliedly authorized to admit a fact that cannot properly be disputed or to make a disclosure that facilitates a satisfactory conclusion to a matter. Lawyers in a firm may, in the course of the firm's practice, disclose to each other information relating to a client of the firm, unless the client has instructed that particular information be confined to specified lawyers.

[6] *Disclosure adverse to client.* -- Although the public interest is usually best served by a strict rule requiring lawyers to preserve the confidentiality of information relating to the representation of their clients, the confidentiality rule is subject to limited exceptions. Paragraph (b)(1) recognizes the overriding value of life and physical integrity and permits disclosure reasonably necessary to prevent reasonably certain death or substantial bodily harm. Such harm is reasonably certain to occur if it will be suffered imminently or if there is a present and substantial threat that a person will suffer such harm at a later date if the lawyer fails to take action necessary to eliminate the threat. Thus, a lawyer who knows that a client has accidentally discharged toxic waste into a town's water supply may reveal this information to the authorities if there is a present and substantial risk that a person who drinks the water will contract a life-threatening or debilitating disease and the lawyer's disclosure is necessary to eliminate the threat or reduce the number of victims.

[7] Paragraph (b)(2) is a limited exception to the rule of confidentiality that permits the lawyer to reveal information to the extent necessary to enable affected persons or appropriate authorities to prevent the client from committing a crime or a fraud, as defined in Rule 1.0(d), that is reasonably certain to result in substantial injury to the financial or property interests of another and in furtherance of which the client has used or is using the lawyer's services. Such a serious abuse of the client-lawyer relationship by the client forfeits the protection of this Rule. The client can, of course, prevent such disclosure by refraining from the wrongful conduct. Although paragraph (b)(2) does not require the lawyer to reveal the client's misconduct, the lawyer may not counsel or assist the client in conduct the lawyer knows is criminal or fraudulent. See Rule 1.2(d). See also Rule 1.16 with respect to the lawyer's obligation or right to withdraw from the representation of the client in such circumstances. Where the client is an organization, the lawyer may be in doubt whether contemplated conduct will

actually be carried out by the organization. Where necessary to guide conduct in connection with this Rule, the lawyer may make inquiry within the organization as indicated in Rule 1.13(b).

[8] Paragraph (b)(3) addresses the situation in which the lawyer does not learn of the client's crime or fraud until after it has been consummated. Although the client no longer has the option of preventing disclosure by refraining from the wrongful conduct, there will be situations in which the loss suffered by the affected person can be prevented, rectified or mitigated. In such situations, the lawyer may disclose information relating to the representation to the extent necessary to enable the affected persons to prevent or mitigate reasonably certain losses or to attempt to recoup their losses. Disclosure is not permitted under paragraph (b)(3) when a person who has committed a crime or fraud thereafter employs a lawyer for representation concerning that offense if that lawyer's services were not used in the initial crime or fraud; disclosure would be permitted, however, if the lawyer's services are used to commit a further crime or fraud, such as the crime of obstructing justice. While applicable law may provide that a completed act is regarded for some purposes as a continuing offense, if commission of the initial act has already occurred without the use of the lawyer's services, the lawyer does not have discretion under this paragraph to use or disclose the client's information.

[9] A lawyer's confidentiality obligations do not preclude a lawyer from securing confidential legal advice about the lawyer's personal responsibility to comply with these Rules. In most situations, disclosing information to secure such advice will be impliedly authorized for the lawyer to carry out the representation. Even when the disclosure is not impliedly authorized, paragraph (b)(2) permits such disclosure because of the importance of a lawyer's compliance with the Rules of Professional Conduct.

[10] Where a legal claim or disciplinary charge alleges complicity of the lawyer in a client's conduct or other misconduct of the lawyer involving representation of the client, the lawyer may respond to the extent the lawyer reasonably believes necessary to establish a defense. The same is true with respect to a claim involving the conduct or representation of a former client. Such a charge can arise in a civil, criminal, disciplinary or other proceeding and can be based on a wrong allegedly committed by the lawyer against the client or on a wrong alleged by a third person, for example, a person claiming to have been defrauded by the lawyer and client acting together. The lawyer's right to respond arises when an assertion of such complicity has been made. Paragraph (b)(5) does not require the lawyer to await the commencement of an action or proceeding that charges such complicity, so that the defense may be established by responding directly to a third party who has made such an assertion. The right to defend also applies, of course, where a proceeding has been commenced.

[11] A lawyer entitled to a fee is permitted by paragraph (b)(5) to prove the services rendered in an action to collect it. This aspect of the rule expresses the principle that the beneficiary of a fiduciary relationship may not exploit it to the detriment of the fiduciary.

[12] Other law may require that a lawyer disclose information about a client. Whether such a law supersedes Rule 1.6 is a question of law beyond the scope of these rules. When disclosure of information relating to the representation appears to be required by other law, the lawyer must discuss the matter with the client to the extent required by Rule 1.4. If, however, the other law supersedes this Rule and requires disclosure, paragraph (b)(6) permits the lawyer to make such disclosures as are necessary to comply with the law. See, e.g., *29 DEL. CODE ANN. § 9007A(c)* (which provides that an attorney acting as guardian ad litem for a child in child welfare proceedings shall have the "duty of confidentiality to the child unless the disclosure is necessary to protect the child's best interests").

[13] Paragraph (b)(6) also permits compliance with a court order requiring a lawyer to disclose information relating to a client's representation. If a lawyer is called as a witness to give testimony concerning a client or is otherwise ordered to reveal information relating to the client's representation, however, the lawyer must, absent informed consent of the client to do otherwise, assert on behalf of the client all nonfrivolous claims that the information sought is protected against disclosure by the attorney-client privilege or other applicable law. In the event of an adverse ruling, the lawyer must consult with the client about the possibility of appeal to the extent required by Rule 1.4. Unless review is sought, however, paragraph (b)(6) permits the lawyer to comply with the court's order.

[14] Paragraph (b) permits disclosure only to the extent the lawyer reasonably believes the disclosure is necessary to accomplish one of the purposes specified. Where practicable, the lawyer should first seek to persuade the client to take suitable action to obviate the need for disclosure. In any case, a disclosure adverse to the client's interest should be no greater than the lawyer reasonably believes necessary to accomplish the purpose. If the disclosure will be made in connection with a judicial proceeding, the disclosure should be made in a manner that limits access to the information to the tribunal or other persons having a need to know it and appropriate protective orders or other arrangements should be sought by the lawyer to the fullest extent practicable.

[15] Paragraph (b) permits but does not require the disclosure of information relating to a client's representation to accomplish the purposes specified in paragraphs (b)(1) through (b)(6). In exercising the discretion conferred by this Rule, the lawyer may consider such factors as the nature of the lawyer's relationship with the client and with those who might be injured by the client, the lawyer's own involvement in the transaction and factors that may extenuate the

conduct in question. A lawyer's decision not to disclose as permitted by paragraph (b) does not violate this Rule. Disclosure may be required, however, by other Rules. Some Rules require disclosure only if such disclosure would be permitted by paragraph (b). See Rules 1.2(d), 4.1(b), 8.1 and 8.3. Rule 3.3, on the other hand, requires disclosure in some circumstances regardless of whether such disclosure is permitted by this Rule. See Rule 3.3(c).

[16] *Acting competently to preserve confidentiality.* -- A lawyer must act competently to safeguard information relating to the representation of a client against inadvertent or unauthorized disclosure by the lawyer or other persons who are participating in the representation of the client or who are subject to the lawyer's supervision. See Rules 1.1, 5.1 and 5.3.

[17] When transmitting a communication that includes information relating to the representation of a client, the lawyer must take reasonable precautions to prevent the information from coming into the hands of unintended recipients. This duty, however, does not require that the lawyer use special security measures if the method of communication affords a reasonable expectation of privacy. Special circumstances, however, may warrant special precautions. Factors to be considered in determining the reasonableness of the lawyer's expectation of confidentiality include the sensitivity of the information and the extent to which the privacy of the communication is protected by law or by a confidentiality agreement. A client may require the lawyer to implement special security measures not required by this Rule or may give informed consent to the use of a means of communication that would otherwise be prohibited by this Rule.

[18] *Former client.* -- The duty of confidentiality continues after the client-lawyer relationship has terminated. See Rule 1.9(c)(2). See Rule 1.9(c)(1) for the prohibition against using such information to the disadvantage of the former client.

Rule 1.7. Conflict of interest: Current clients

(a) Except as provided in paragraph (b), a lawyer shall not represent a client if the representation involves a concurrent conflict of interest. A concurrent conflict of interest exists if: (1) the representation of one client will be directly adverse to another client; or (2) there is a significant risk that the representation of one or more clients will be materially limited by the lawyer's responsibilities to another client, a former client or a third person or by a personal interest of the lawyer.

(b) Notwithstanding the existence of a concurrent conflict of interest under paragraph (a), a lawyer may represent a client if: (1) the lawyer reasonably believes that the lawyer will be able to provide competent and diligent representation to each affected client; (2) the representation is not prohibited by law; (3) the representation does not involve the assertion of a claim by one client against another client represented by the lawyer in the same litigation or other proceeding before a tribunal; and (4) each affected client gives informed consent, confirmed in writing.

Rule 1.8. Conflict of interest: Current clients: Specific rules

(a) A lawyer shall not enter into a business transaction with a client or knowingly acquire an ownership, possessory, security or other pecuniary interest adverse to a client unless: (1) the transaction and terms on which the lawyer acquires the interest are fair and reasonable to the client and are fully disclosed and transmitted in writing to the client in a manner that can be reasonably understood by the client; (2) the client is advised in writing of the desirability of seeking and is given a reasonable opportunity to seek the advice of independent legal counsel on the transaction; and (3) the client gives informed consent, in a writing signed by the client, to the essential terms of the transaction and the lawyer's role in the transaction, including whether the lawyer is representing the client in the transaction.

(b) A lawyer shall not use information relating to representation of a client to the disadvantage of the client unless the client gives informed consent, except as permitted or required by these Rules.

(c) A lawyer shall not solicit any substantial gift from a client, including a testamentary gift, or prepare on behalf of a client an instrument giving the lawyer or a person related to the lawyer any substantial gift unless the lawyer or other recipient of the gift is related to the client. For purposes of this paragraph, related persons include a spouse, child, grandchild, parent, grandparent or other relative or individual with whom the lawyer or the client maintains a close, familial relationship.

(d) Prior to the conclusion of representation of a client, a lawyer shall not make or negotiate an agreement giving the lawyer literary or media rights to a portrayal or account based in substantial part on information relating to the representation.

(e) A lawyer shall not provide financial assistance to a client in connection with pending or contemplated litigation, except that: (1) a lawyer may advance court costs and expenses of litigations, the repayment of which may be contingent on the outcome of the matter; and (2) a lawyer representing an indigent client may pay court costs and expenses of litigation on behalf of the client.

(f) A lawyer shall not accept compensation for representing a client from one other than the client unless: (1) the client gives informed consent; (2) there is no interference with the lawyer's independence of professional judgment or with the client-lawyer relationship; and (3) information relating to representation of a client is protected as required by Rule 1.6.

(g) A lawyer who represents two or more clients shall not participate in making an aggregate settlement of the claims of or against the clients, or in a criminal case an aggregated agreement as to guilty or nolo contendere pleas, unless each client gives informed consent, in a writing signed by the client. The lawyer's disclosure shall include the existence and nature of all the claims or pleas involved and of the participation of each person in the settlement.

(h) A lawyer shall not: (1) make an agreement prospectively limiting the lawyer's liability to a client for malpractice unless the client is independently represented in making the agreement; or (2) settle a claim or potential claim for such liability with an unrepresented client or former client unless that person is advised in writing of the desirability of seeking and is given a reasonable opportunity to seek the advice of independent legal counsel in connection therewith.

(i) A lawyer shall not acquire a proprietary interest in the cause of action or subject matter of litigation the lawyer is conducting for a client, except that the lawyer may: (1) acquire a lien authorized by law to secure the lawyer's fee or expenses; and (2) contract with a client for a reasonable contingent fee in a civil case.

(j) A lawyer shall not have sexual relations with a client unless a consensual sexual relationship existed between them when the client-lawyer relationship commenced.

(k) While lawyers are associated in a firm, a prohibition in the foregoing paragraphs (a) through (i) that applies to any one of them shall apply to all of them.

Rule 1.9. Duties to former clients

(a) A lawyer who has formerly represented a client in a matter shall not thereafter represent another person in the same or a substantially related matter in which that person's interests are materially adverse to the interests of the former client unless the former client gives informed consent, confirmed in writing.

(b) A lawyer shall not knowingly represent a person in the same or a substantially related matter in which a firm with which the lawyer formerly was associated had previously represented a client: (1) whose interests are materially adverse to that person; and (2) about whom the lawyer had acquired information protected by Rules 1.6 and 1.9(c) that is material to the matter; unless the former client gives informed consent, confirmed in writing.

(c) A lawyer who has formerly represented a client in a matter or whose present or former firm has formerly represented a client in a matter shall not thereafter: (1) use information relating to the representation to the disadvantage of the former client except as these Rules would permit or require with respect to a client, or when the information has become generally known; or (2) reveal information relating to the representation except as these Rules would permit or require with respect to a client.

Rule 1.10. Imputation of conflicts of interest: General rule

(a) Except as otherwise provided in this rule, while lawyers are associated in a firm, none of them shall knowingly represent a client when any one of them practicing alone would be prohibited from doing so by Rules 1.7 or 1.9, unless the prohibition is based on a personal interest of the prohibited lawyer and does not present a significant risk of materially limiting the representation of the client by the remaining lawyers in the firm.

(b) When a lawyer has terminated an association with a firm, the firm is not prohibited from thereafter representing a person with interests materially adverse to those of a client represented by the formerly associated lawyer and not currently represented by the firm, unless: (1) the matter is the same or substantially related to that in which the formerly associated lawyer represented the client; and (2) any lawyer remaining in the firm has information protected by Rules 1.6 and 1.9(c) that is material to the matter.

(c) When a lawyer becomes associated with a firm, no lawyer associated in the firm shall knowingly represent a client in a matter in which that lawyer is disqualified under Rule 1.9 unless: (1) the personally disqualified lawyer is timely screened from any participation in the matter and is apportioned no part of the fee therefrom; and (2) written notice is promptly given to the affected former client.

(d) A disqualification prescribed by this rule may be waived by the affected client under the conditions stated in Rule 1.7.

(e) The disqualification of lawyers associated in a firm with former or current government lawyers is governed by Rule 1.11.

Rule 1.11. Special conflicts of interest for former and current government officers and employees

(a) Except as law may otherwise expressly permit, a lawyer who has formerly served as a public officer or employee of the government: (1) is subject to Rule 1.9(c); and (2) shall not otherwise represent a client in connection with a matter in which the lawyer participated personally and substantially as a public officer or employee, unless the appropriate government agency gives its informed consent, confirmed in writing, to the representation.

(b) When a lawyer is disqualified from representation under paragraph (a), no lawyer in a firm with which that lawyer is associated may knowingly undertake or continue representation in such a matter unless: (1) the disqualified lawyer is timely screened from any participation in the matter and is apportioned no part of the fee therefrom; and (2) written notice is promptly given to the appropriate government agency to enable it to ascertain compliance with the provisions of this rule.

(c) Except as law may otherwise expressly permit, a lawyer having information that the lawyer knows is confidential government information about a person acquired when the lawyer was a public officer or employee, may not represent a private client whose interests are adverse to that person in a matter in which the information could be used to the material disadvantage of that person. As used in this Rule, the term "confidential government information" means information that has been obtained under governmental authority and which, at the time this Rule is applied, the government is prohibited by law from disclosing to the public or has a legal privilege not to disclose and which is not otherwise available to the public. A firm with which that lawyer is associated may undertake or continue representation in the matter only if the disqualified lawyer is timely screened from any participation in the matter and is apportioned no part of the fee therefrom.

(d) Except as law may otherwise expressly permit, a lawyer currently serving as a public officer or employee: (1) is subject to Rules 1.7 and 1.9; and (2) shall not: (i) participate in a matter in which the lawyer participated personally and substantially while in private practice or nongovernmental employment, unless the appropriate government agency gives its informed consent, confirmed in writing; or (ii) negotiate for private employment with any person who is involved as a party or as lawyer for a party in a matter in which the lawyer is participating personally and substantially, except that a lawyer serving as a law clerk to a judge, other adjudicative officer or arbitrator may negotiate for private employment as permitted by Rule 1.12(b) and subject to the conditions stated in Rule 1.12(b).

(e) As used in this Rule, the term "matter" includes: (1) any judicial or other proceeding, application, request for a ruling or other determination, contract, claim, controversy, investigation, charge, accusation, arrest or other particular matter involving a specific party or parties, and (2) any other matter covered by the conflict of interest rules of the appropriate government agency.

Rule 1.12. Former judge, arbitrator, mediator or other third-party neutral

(a) Except as stated in paragraph (d), a lawyer shall not represent anyone in connection with a matter in which the lawyer participated personally and substantially as a judge or other adjudicative officer or law clerk to such a person or as an arbitrator, mediator or other third-party neutral, unless all parties to the proceeding give informed consent, confirmed in writing.

(b) A lawyer shall not negotiate for employment with any person who is involved as a party or as lawyer for a party in a matter in which the lawyer is participating personally and substantially as a judge or other adjudicative officer or as an arbitrator, mediator or other third-party neutral. A lawyer serving as a law clerk to a judge or other adjudicative officer may negotiate for employment with a party or lawyer involved in a matter in which the clerk is participating personally and substantially, but only after the lawyer has notified the judge or other adjudicative officer.

(c) If a lawyer is disqualified by paragraph (a), no lawyer in a firm with which that lawyer is associated may knowingly undertake or continue representation in the matter unless: (1) the disqualified lawyer is timely screened from any participation in the matter and is apportioned no part of the fee therefrom; and (2) written notice is promptly given to the parties and any appropriate tribunal to enable them to ascertain compliance with the provisions of this rule.

(d) An arbitrator selected as a partisan of a party in a multimember arbitration panel is not prohibited from subsequently representing that party.

Rule 1.13. Organization as client

(a) A lawyer employed or retained by an organization represents the organization acting through its duly authorized constituents.

(b) If a lawyer for an organization knows that an officer, employee or other person associated with the organization is engaged in action, intends to act or refuses to act in a matter related to the representation that is a violation of a legal obligation to the organization, or a violation of law which reasonably might be imputed to the organization, and is likely to result in substantial injury to the organization, the lawyer shall proceed as is reasonably necessary in the best interest of the organization. In determining how to proceed, the lawyer shall give due consideration to the seriousness of the violation and its consequences, the scope and nature of the lawyer's representation, the responsibility in the organization and the apparent motivation of the person involved, the policies of the organization concerning such matters and any other relevant considerations. Any measures taken shall be designed to minimize disruption of the organization and the risk of revealing information relating to the representation to persons outside the organization. Such measures may include among others: (1) asking for reconsideration of the matter; (2) advising that a separate legal opinion on the matter be sought for presentation to appropriate authority in the organization; and (3) referring the matter to higher authority in the organization, including, if warranted by the seriousness of the matter, referral to the highest authority that can act on behalf of the organization as determined by applicable law.

(c) If, despite the lawyer's efforts in accordance with paragraph (b), the highest authority that can act on behalf of the organization insists upon action, or a refusal to act, that is clearly a violation of law and is likely to result in substantial injury to the organization, the lawyer may resign in accordance with Rule 1.16.

(d) In dealing with an organization's directors, officers, employees, members, shareholders or other constituents, a lawyer shall explain the identity of the client when the lawyer knows or reasonably should know that the organization's interests are adverse to those of the constituents with whom the lawyer is dealing.

(e) A lawyer representing an organization may also represent any of its directors, officers, employees, members, shareholders or other constituents, subject to the provisions of Rule 1.7. If the organization's consent to the dual representation is required by Rule 1.7, the consent shall be given by an appropriate official of the organization other than the individual who is to be represented, or by the shareholders.

Rule 1.14. Client with diminished capacity

(a) When a client's capacity to make adequately considered decisions in connection with a representation is diminished, whether because of minority, mental impairment or for some other reason, the lawyer shall, as far as reasonably possible, maintain a normal client-lawyer relationship with the client.

(b) When the lawyer reasonably believes that the client has diminished capacity, is at risk of substantial physical, financial or other harm unless action is taken and cannot adequately act in the client's own interest, the lawyer may take reasonably necessary protective action, including consulting with individuals or entities that have the ability to take action to protect the client and, in appropriate cases, seeking the appointment of a guardian ad litem, conservator or guardian.

(c) Information relating to the representation of a client with diminished capacity is protected by Rule 1.6. When taking protective action pursuant to paragraph (b), the lawyer is impliedly authorized under Rule 1.6(a) to reveal information about the client, but only to the extent reasonably necessary to protect the client's interests.

Rule 1.15. Safekeeping property - omitted

Rule 1.15A. Trust account overdraft notification - omitted

Rule 1.16. Declining or terminating representation

(a) Except as stated in paragraph (c), a lawyer shall not represent a client or, where representation has commenced, shall withdraw from the representation of a client if: (1) the representation will result in violation of the rules of professional conduct or other law; (2) the lawyer's physical or mental condition materially impairs the lawyer's ability to represent the client; or (3) the lawyer is discharged.

(b) Except as stated in paragraph (c), a lawyer may withdraw from representing a client if: (1) withdrawal can be accomplished without material adverse effect on the interests of the client; (2) the client persists in a course of action involving the lawyer's services that the lawyer reasonably believes is criminal or fraudulent; (3) the client has used the lawyer's service to perpetrate a crime or fraud; (4) a client insists upon taking action that the lawyer considers repugnant or with which the lawyer has a fundamental disagreement; (5) the client fails substantially to fulfill an obligation to the lawyer regarding the lawyer's services and has been given reasonable warning that the lawyer will withdraw unless the obligation is fulfilled; (6) the representation will result in an unreasonable financial burden on the lawyer or has been rendered unreasonably difficult by the client; or (7) other good cause for withdrawal exists.

(c) A lawyer must comply with applicable law requiring notice to or permission of a tribunal when terminating a representation. When ordered to do so by a tribunal, a lawyer shall continue representation notwithstanding good cause for terminating the representation.

(d) Upon termination of representation, a lawyer shall take steps to the extent reasonably practicable to protect a client's interests, such as giving reasonable notice to the client, allowing time for employment of other counsel, surrendering papers and property to which the client is entitled and refunding any advance payment of fee or expense that has not been earned or incurred. The lawyer may retain papers relating to the client to the extent permitted by other law.

COMMENT

[1] A lawyer should not accept representation in a matter unless it can be performed competently, promptly, without improper conflict of interest and to completion. Ordinarily, a representation in a matter is completed when the agreedupon assistance has been concluded. See Rules 1.2(c) and 6.5. See also Rule 1.3, Comment [4].

[2] *Mandatory Withdrawal.* -- A lawyer ordinarily must decline or withdraw from representation if the client demands that the lawyer engage in conduct that is illegal or violates the Rules of Professional Conduct or other law. The lawyer is not obliged to decline or withdraw simply because the client suggests such a course of conduct; a client may make such a suggestion in the hope that a lawyer will not be constrained by a professional obligation.

[3] When a lawyer has been appointed to represent a client, withdrawal ordinarily requires approval of the appointing authority. See also Rule 6.2. Similarly, court approval or notice to the court is often required by applicable law before a lawyer withdraws from pending litigation. Difficulty may be encountered if withdrawal is based on the client's demand that the lawyer engage in unprofessional conduct. The court may request an explanation for the withdrawal, while the lawyer may be bound to keep confidential the facts that would constitute such an explanation. The lawyer's statement that professional considerations require termination of the representation ordinarily should be accepted as sufficient. Lawyers should be mindful of their obligations to both clients and the court under Rules 1.6 and 3.3.

[4] *Discharge.* -- A client has a right to discharge a lawyer at any time, with or without cause, subject to liability for payment for the lawyer's services. Where future dispute about the withdrawal may be anticipated, it may be advisable to prepare a written statement reciting the circumstances.

[5] Whether a client can discharge appointed counsel may depend on applicable law. A client seeking to do so should be given a full explanation of the consequences. These consequences may include a decision by the appointing authority that appointment of successor counsel is unjustified, thus requiring self-representation by the client.

[6] If the client has severely diminished capacity, the client may lack the legal capacity to discharge the lawyer, and in any event the discharge may be seriously

adverse to the client's interests. The lawyer should make special effort to help the client consider the consequences and may take reasonably necessary protective action as provided in Rule 1.14.

[7] *Optional Withdrawal.* -- A lawyer may withdraw from representation in some circumstances. The lawyer has the option to withdraw if it can be accomplished without material adverse effect on the client's interests. Withdrawal is also justified if the client persists in a course of action that the lawyer reasonably believes is criminal or fraudulent, for a lawyer is not required to be associated with such conduct even if the lawyer does not further it. Withdrawal is also permitted if the lawyer's services were misused in the past even if that would materially prejudice the client. The lawyer may also withdraw where the client insists on taking action that the lawyer considers repugnant or with which the lawyer has a fundamental disagreement.

[8] A lawyer may withdraw if the client refuses to abide by the terms of an agreement relating to the representation, such as an agreement concerning fees or court costs or an agreement limiting the objectives of the representation.

[9] *Assisting the Client upon Withdrawal.* -- Even if the lawyer has been unfairly discharged by the client, a lawyer must take all reasonable steps to mitigate the consequences to the client. The lawyer may retain papers as security for a fee only to the extent permitted by law. See Rule 1.15.

Rule 1.17. Sale of law practice - omitted

Rule 1.18. Duties to prospective client

(a) A person who discusses with a lawyer the possibility of forming a client-lawyer relationship with respect to a matter is a prospective client.

(b) Even when no client-lawyer relationship ensues, a lawyer who has had discussions with a prospective client shall not use or reveal information learned in the consultation, except as Rule 1.9 would permit with respect to information of a former client.

(c) A lawyer subject to paragraph (b) shall not represent a client with interests materially adverse to those of a prospective client in the same or a substantially related matter if the lawyer received information from the prospective client that could be significantly harmful to that person in the matter, except as provided in paragraph (d). If a lawyer is disqualified from representation under this paragraph, no lawyer in a firm with which that lawyer is associated may knowingly undertake or continue representation in such a matter, except as provided in paragraph (d).

(d) When the lawyer has received disqualifying information as defined in paragraph (c), representation is permissible if: (1) both the affected client and the prospective client have given informed consent, confirmed in writing, or: (2) the lawyer who received the information took reasonable measures to avoid exposure to more disqualifying information than was reasonably necessary to determine whether to represent the prospective client; and (i) the disqualified lawyer is timely screened from any participation in the matter and is apportioned no part of the fee therefrom; and (ii) written notice is promptly given to the prospective client.

Rule 2.1. Advisor

In representing a client, a lawyer shall exercise independent professional judgment and render candid advice. In rendering advice, a lawyer may refer not only to law but to other considerations, such as moral, economic, social and political factors, that may be relevant to the client's situation.

Rule 2.2. Intermediary (Deleted)

Rule 2.3. Evaluation for use by third persons - omitted

Rule 2.4. Lawyer serving as third-party neutral

(a) A lawyer serves as a third-party neutral when the lawyer assists two or more persons who are not clients of the lawyer to reach a resolution of a dispute or other matter that has arisen between them. Service as a third-party neutral may include service as an arbitrator, a mediator or in such other capacity as will enable the lawyer to assist the parties to resolve the matter.

(b) A lawyer serving as a third-party neutral shall inform unrepresented parties that the lawyer is not representing them. When the lawyer knows or reasonably should know that a party does not understand the lawyer's role in the matter, the lawyer shall explain the difference between the lawyer's role as a third-party neutral and a lawyer's role as one who represents a client.

Rule 3.1. Meritorious claims and contentions

A lawyer shall not bring or defend a proceeding, or assert or controvert an issue therein, unless there is a basis in law and fact for doing so that is not frivolous, which includes a good faith argument for an extension, modification or reversal of existing law. A lawyer for the defendant in a criminal proceeding, or the respondent in a proceeding that could result in incarceration, may nevertheless so defend the proceeding as to require that every element of the case be established.

Rule 3.2. Expediting litigation

A lawyer shall make reasonable efforts to expedite litigation consistent with the interests of the client.

COMMENT

[1] Dilatory practices bring the administration of justice into disrepute. Although there will be occasions when a lawyer may properly seek a postponement for personal reasons, it is not proper for a lawyer to routinely fail to expedite litigation solely for the convenience of the advocates. Nor will a failure to expedite be reasonable if done for the purpose of frustrating an opposing party's attempt to obtain rightful redress or repose. It is not a justification that similar conduct is often tolerated by the bench and bar. The question is whether a competent lawyer acting in good faith would regard the course of action as having some substantial purpose other than delay. Realizing financial or other benefit from otherwise improper delay in litigation is not a legitimate interest of the client.

Rule 3.3. Candor toward the tribunal

(a) A lawyer shall not knowingly: (1) make a false statement of fact or law to a tribunal or fail to correct a false statement of material fact or law previously made to the tribunal by the lawyer; (2) fail to disclose to the tribunal legal authority in the controlling jurisdiction known to the lawyer to be directly adverse to the position of the client and not disclosed by opposing counsel; or (3) offer evidence that the lawyer knows to be false. If a lawyer, the lawyer's client, or a witness called by the lawyer, has offered material evidence and the lawyer comes to know of its falsity, the lawyer shall take reasonable remedial measures, including, if necessary, disclosure to the tribunal. A lawyer may refuse to offer evidence, other than the testimony of a defendant in a criminal matter, that the lawyer reasonably believes is false.

(b) A lawyer who represents a client in an adjudicative proceeding and who knows that a person intends to engage, is engaging or has engaged in criminal or fraudulent conduct related to the proceeding shall take reasonable remedial measures, including, if necessary, disclosure to the tribunal.

(c) The duties stated in paragraph (a) and (b) continue to the conclusion of the proceeding, and apply even if compliance requires disclosure of information otherwise protected by Rule 1.6.

(d) In an ex parte proceeding, a lawyer shall inform the tribunal of all material facts known to the lawyer which will enable the tribunal to make an informed decision, whether or not the facts are adverse.

COMMENT

[1] This Rule governs the conduct of a lawyer who is representing a client in the proceedings of a tribunal. See Rule 1.0(m) for the definition of "tribunal." It also applies when the lawyer is representing a client in an ancillary proceeding conducted pursuant to the tribunal's adjudicative authority, such as a deposition. Thus, for example, paragraph (a)(3) requires a lawyer to take reasonable remedial measures if the lawyer comes to know that a client who is testifying in a deposition has offered evidence that is false.

[2] This Rule sets forth the special duties of lawyers as officers of the court to avoid conduct that undermines the integrity of the adjudicative process. A lawyer acting as an advocate in an adjudicative proceeding has an obligation to present the client's case with persuasive force. Performance of that duty while maintaining confidences of the client, however, is qualified by the advocate's duty of candor to the tribunal. Consequently, although a lawyer in an adversary proceeding is not required to present an impartial exposition of the law or to vouch for the evidence submitted in a cause, the lawyer must not allow the tribunal to be misled by false statements of law or fact or evidence that the lawyer knows to be false.

[3] *Representations by a Lawyer.* -- An advocate is responsible for pleadings and other documents prepared for litigation, but is usually not required to have personal knowledge of matters asserted therein, for litigation documents ordinarily present assertions by the client, or by someone on the client's behalf, and not assertions by the lawyer. Compare Rule 3.1. However, an assertion purporting to be on the lawyer's own knowledge, as in an affidavit by the lawyer or in a statement in open court, may properly be made only when the lawyer knows the assertion is true or believes it to be true on the basis of a reasonably diligent inquiry. There are circumstances where failure to make a disclosure is the equivalent of an affirmative misrepresentation. The obligation prescribed in Rule 1.2(d) not to counsel a client to commit or assist the client in committing a fraud applies in litigation. Regarding compliance with Rule 1.2(d), see the Comment to that Rule. See also the comment to Rule 8.4(b).

[4] *Legal Argument.* -- Legal argument based on a knowingly false representation of law constitutes dishonesty toward the tribunal. A lawyer is not required to make a disinterested exposition of the law, but must recognize the existence of pertinent legal authorities. Furthermore, as stated in paragraph (a)(2), an advocate has a duty to disclose directly adverse authority in the controlling jurisdiction that has not been disclosed by the opposing party. The underlying concept is that legal argument is a discussion seeking to determine the legal premises properly applicable to the case.

[5] *Offering Evidence.* -- Paragraph (a)(3) requires that the lawyer refuse to offer evidence that the lawyer knows to be false, regardless of the client's wishes. This duty is premised on the lawyer's obligation as an officer of the court to prevent the trier of fact from being misled by false evidence. A lawyer does not violate this Rule if the lawyer offers the evidence for the purpose of establishing its falsity.

[6] If a lawyer knows that the client intends to testify falsely or wants the lawyer to introduce false evidence, the lawyer should seek to persuade the client that the evidence should not be offered. If the persuasion is ineffective and the lawyer continues to represent the client, the lawyer must refuse to offer the false evidence. If only a portion of a witness's testimony will be false, the lawyer may call the witness to testify but may not elicit or otherwise permit the witness to present the testimony that the lawyer knows is false.

[7] The duties stated in paragraphs (a) and (b) apply to all lawyers, including defense counsel in criminal cases. In some jurisdictions, however, courts have required counsel to present the accused as a witness or to give a narrative statement if the accused so desires, even if counsel knows that the testimony or statement will be false. The obligation of the advocate under the Rules of Professional Conduct is subordinate to such requirements. See also Comment [9].

[8] The prohibition against offering false evidence only applies if the lawyer knows that the evidence is false. A lawyer's reasonable belief that evidence is false does not preclude its presentation to the trier of fact. A lawyer's knowledge that evidence is false, however, can be inferred from the circumstances. See Rule 1.0(f). Thus, although a lawyer should resolve doubts about the veracity of testimony or other evidence in favor of the client, the lawyer cannot ignore an obvious falsehood.

[9] Although paragraph (a)(3) only prohibits a lawyer from offering evidence the lawyer knows to be false, it permits the lawyer to refuse to offer testimony or other proof that the lawyer reasonably believes is false. Offering such proof may reflect adversely on the lawyer's ability to discriminate in the quality of evidence and thus impair the lawyer's effectiveness as an advocate. Because of the special protections historically provided criminal defendants, however, this Rule does not permit a lawyer to refuse to offer the testimony of such a client where the

lawyer reasonably believes but does not know that the testimony will be false. Unless the lawyer knows the testimony will be false, the lawyer must honor the client's decision to testify. See also Comment [7].

[10] *Remedial Measures.* -- Having offered material evidence in the belief that it was true, a lawyer may subsequently come to know that the evidence is false. Or, a lawyer may be surprised when the lawyer's client, or another witness called by the lawyer, offers testimony the lawyer knows to be false, either during the lawyer's direct examination or in response to cross-examination by the opposing lawyer. In such situations or if the lawyer knows of the falsity of testimony elicited from the client during a deposition, the lawyer must take reasonable remedial measures. In such situations, the advocate's proper course is to remonstrate with the client confidentially, advise the client of the lawyer's duty of candor to the tribunal and seek the client's cooperation with respect to the withdrawal or correction of the false statements or evidence. If that fails, the advocate must take further remedial action. If withdrawal from the representation is not permitted or will not undo the effect of the false evidence, the advocate must make such disclosure to the tribunal as is reasonably necessary to remedy the situation, even if doing so requires the lawyer to reveal information that otherwise would be protected by Rule 1.6. It is for the tribunal then to determine what should be done -- making a statement about the matter to the trier of fact, ordering a mistrial or perhaps nothing.

[11] The disclosure of a client's false testimony can result in grave consequences to the client, including not only a sense of betrayal but also loss of the case and perhaps a prosecution for perjury. But the alternative is that the lawyer cooperate in deceiving the court, thereby subverting the truth-finding process which the adversary system is designed to implement. See Rule 1.2(d). Furthermore, unless it is clearly understood that the lawyer will act upon the duty to disclose the existence of false evidence, the client can simply reject the lawyer's advice to reveal the false evidence and insist that the lawyer keep silent. Thus the client could in effect coerce the lawyer into being a party to fraud on the court.

[12] *Preserving Integrety of Adjunctive Process.* -- Lawyers have a special obligation to protect a tribunal against criminal or fraudulent conduct that undermines the integrity of the adjudicative process, such as bribing, intimidating or otherwise unlawfully communicating with a witness, juror, court official or other participant in the proceeding, unlawfully destroying or concealing documents or other evidence or failing to disclose information to the tribunal when required by law to do so. Thus, paragraph (b) requires a lawyer to take reasonable remedial measures, including disclosure if necessary, whenever the lawyer knows that a person, including the lawyer's client, intends to engage, is engaging or has engaged in criminal or fraudulent conduct related to the proceeding.

[13] *Duration of Obligation.* -- A practical time limit on the obligation to rectify false evidence or false statements of law and fact has to be established. The conclusion of the proceeding is a reasonably definite point for the termination of the obligation. A proceeding has concluded within the meaning of this Rule when a final judgment in the proceeding has been affirmed on appeal or the time for review has passed.

[14] *Ex parte Proceedings.* --] Ordinarily, an advocate has the limited responsibility of presenting one side of the matters that a tribunal should consider in reaching a decision; the conflicting position is expected to be presented by the opposing party. However, in any ex parte proceeding, such as an application for a temporary restraining order, there is no balance of presentation by opposing advocates. The object of an ex parte proceeding is nevertheless to yield a substantially just result. The judge has an affirmative responsibility to accord the absent party just consideration. The lawyer for the represented party has the correlative duty to make disclosures of material facts known to the lawyer and that the lawyer reasonably believes are necessary to an informed decision.

[15] *Withdrawal.* -- Normally, a lawyer's compliance with the duty of candor imposed by this rule does not require that the lawyer withdraw from the representation of a client whose interests will be or have been adversely affected by the lawyer's disclosure. The lawyer may, however, be required by Rule 1.16(a) to seek permission of the tribunal to withdraw if the lawyer's compliance with this Rule's duty of candor results in such an extreme deterioration of the client-lawyer relationship that the lawyer can no longer competently represent the client. Also see Rule 1.16(b) for the circumstances in which a lawyer will be permitted to seek a tribunal's permission to withdraw. In connection with a request for permission to withdraw that is premised on a client's misconduct, a lawyer may reveal information relating to the representation only to the extent reasonably necessary to comply with this Rule or as otherwise permitted by Rule 1.6.

Rule 3.4. Fairness to opposing party and counsel

A lawyer shall not:

(a) unlawfully obstruct another party's access to evidence or unlawfully alter, destroy or conceal a document or other material having potential evidentiary value. A lawyer shall not counsel or assist another person to do any such act;

(b) falsify evidence, counsel or assist a witness to testify falsely, or offer an inducement to a witness that is prohibited by law.

(c) knowingly disobey an obligation under the rules of a tribunal, except for an open refusal based on an assertion that no valid obligation exists;

(d) in pretrial procedure, make a frivolous discovery request or fail to make reasonably diligent efforts to comply with a legally proper discovery request by an opposing party;

(e) in trial, allude to any matter that the lawyer does not reasonably believe is relevant or that will not be supported by admissible evidence, assert personal knowledge of facts in issue except when testifying as a witness, or state a personal opinion as to the justness of a cause, the credibility of a witness, the culpability of a civil litigant or the guilt or innocence of an accused; or

(f) request a person other than a client to refrain from voluntarily giving relevant information to another party unless: (1) the person is a relative or an employee or other agent of a client; and (2) the lawyer reasonably believes that the person's interests will not be adversely affected by refraining from giving such information.

COMMENT

[1] The procedure of the adversary system contemplates that the evidence in a case is to be marshalled competitively by the contending parties. Fair competition in the adversary system is secured by the prohibitions against destruction or concealment of evidence, improperly influencing witnesses, obstructive tactics in discovery procedure, and the like.

[2] Documents and other items of evidence are often essential to establish a claim or defense. Subject to evidentiary privileges, the right of an opposing party, including the government, to obtain evidence through discovery or subpoena is an important procedural right. The exercise of that right can be frustrated if relevant material is altered, concealed or destroyed. Applicable law in many jurisdictions makes it an offense to destroy material for purpose of impairing its availability in a pending proceeding or one whose commencement can be foreseen. Falsifying evidence is also generally a criminal offense. Paragraph (a) applies to evidentiary material generally, including computerized information. Applicable law may permit a lawyer to take temporary possession of physical evidence of client crimes for the purpose of conducting a limited examination that will not alter or destroy material characteristics of the evidence. In such a case, applicable law may require the lawyer to turn the evidence over to the police or other prosecuting authority, depending on the circumstances.

[3] With regard to paragraph (b), it is not improper to pay a witness's expenses or to compensate an expert witness on terms permitted by law. The common law rule in most jurisdictions is that it is improper to pay an occurrence witness any fee for testifying and that it is improper to pay an expert witness a contingent fee.

[4] Paragraph (f) permits a lawyer to advise employees of a client to refrain from giving information to another party, for the employees may identify their interests with those of the client. See also Rule 4.2.

Rule 3.5. Impartiality and decorum of the tribunal

A lawyer shall not:

(a) seek to influence a judge, juror, prospective juror or other official by means prohibited by law;

(b) communicate or cause another to communicate ex parte with such a person or members of such person's family during the proceeding unless authorized to do so by law or court order; or

(c) communicate with a juror or prospective juror after discharge of the jury unless the communication is permitted by court rule;

(d) engage in conduct intended to disrupt a tribunal or engage in undignified or discourteous conduct that is degrading to a tribunal.

COMMENT

[1] Many forms of improper influence upon a tribunal are proscribed by criminal law. Others are specified in the ABA Model Code of Judicial Conduct, with which an advocate should be familiar. A lawyer is required to void contributing to a violation of such provisions.

[2] During a proceeding a lawyer may not communicate or cause another to communicate ex parte with persons serving in an official capacity in the proceeding, such as judges, masters or jurors, or with members of such person's family, unless authorized to do so by law or court order. Furthermore, a lawyer shall not conduct or cause another to conduct a vexatious or harassing investigation of such persons or their family members.

[3] A lawyer may not communicate with a juror or prospective juror after the jury has been discharged unless permitted by court rule. The lawyer may not engage in improper conduct during the communication.

[4] The advocate's function is to present evidence and argument so that the cause may be decided according to law. Refraining from abusive or obstreperous conduct is a corollary of the advocate's right to speak on behalf of litigants. A lawyer may stand firm against abuse by a judge but should avoid reciprocation;

the judge's default is no justification for similar dereliction by an advocate. An advocate can present the cause, protect the record for subsequent review and preserve professional integrity by patient firmness no less effectively than by belligerence or theatrics.

[5] The duty to refrain from disruptive, undignified or discourteous conduct applies to any proceeding of a tribunal, including a deposition. See Rule 1.0(m).

Rule 3.6. Trial publicity

(a) A lawyer who is participating or has participated in the investigation or litigation of a matter shall not make an extrajudicial statement that the lawyer knows or reasonably should know will be disseminated by means of public communication and will have a substantial likelihood of materially prejudicing an adjudicative proceeding in the matter.

(b) Notwithstanding paragraph (a), a lawyer may state: (1) the claim, offense or defense involved and, except when prohibited by law, the identity of the persons involved; (2) information contained in a public record; (3) that an investigation of a matter is in progress; (4) the scheduling or result of any step in litigation; (5) a request for assistance in obtaining evidence and information necessary thereto; (6) a warning of danger concerning the behavior of a person involved, when there is reason to believe that there exists the likelihood of substantial harm to an individual or to the public interest; and (7) in a criminal case, in addition to subparagraphs (1) through (6): (i) the identity, residence, occupation and family status of the accused; (ii) if the accused has not been apprehended, information necessary to aid in apprehension of that person; (iii) the fact, time and place of arrest; and (iv) the identity of investigating and arresting officers or agencies and the length of the investigation.

(c) Notwithstanding paragraph (a), a lawyer may make a statement that a reasonable lawyer would believe is required to protect a client from the substantial undue prejudicial effect of recent publicity not initiated by the lawyer or the lawyer's client. A statement made pursuant to this paragraph shall be limited to such information as is necessary to mitigate the recent adverse publicity.

(d) No lawyer associated in a firm or government agency with a lawyer subject to paragraph (a) shall make a statement prohibited by paragraph (a).

COMMENT

[1] It is difficult to strike a balance between protecting the right to a fair trial and safeguarding the right of free expression. Preserving the right to a fair trial

necessarily entails some curtailment of the information that may be disseminated about a party prior to trial, particularly where trial by jury is involved. If there were no such limits, the result would be the practical nullification of the protective effect of the rules of forensic decorum and the exclusionary rules of evidence. On the other hand, there are vital social interests served by the free dissemination of information about events having legal consequences and about legal proceedings themselves. The public has a right to know about threats to its safety and measures aimed at assuring its security. It also has a legitimate interest in the conduct of judicial proceedings, particularly in matters of general public concern. Furthermore, the subject matter of legal proceedings is often of direct significance in debate and deliberation over questions of public policy.

[2] Special rules of confidentiality may validly govern proceedings in juvenile, domestic relations and mental disability proceedings, and perhaps other types of litigation. Rule 3.4(c) requires compliance with such Rules.

[3] The Rule sets forth a basic general prohibition against a lawyer's making statements that the lawyer knows or should know will have a substantial likelihood of materially prejudicing an adjudicative proceeding. Recognizing that the public value of informed commentary is great and the likelihood of prejudice to a proceeding by the commentary of a lawyer who is not involved in the proceeding is small, the rule applies only to lawyers who are, or who have been involved in the investigation or litigation of a case, and their associates.

[4] Paragraph (b) identifies specific matters about which a lawyer's statements would not ordinarily be considered to present a substantial likelihood of material prejudice, and should not in any event be considered prohibited by the general prohibition of paragraph (a). Paragraph (b) is not intended to be an exhaustive listing of the subjects upon which a lawyer may make a statement, but statements on other matters may be subject to paragraph (a).

[5] There are, on the other hand, certain subjects which are more likely than not to have a material prejudicial effect on a proceeding, particularly when they refer to a civil matter triable to a jury, a criminal matter, or any other proceeding that could result in incarceration. These subjects relate to: (1) the character, credibility, reputation or criminal record of a party, suspect in a criminal investigation or witness, or the identity of a witness, or the expected testimony of a party of witness; (2) in a criminal case or proceeding that could result in incarceration, the possibility of a plea of guilty to the offense or the existence or contents of any confession, admission, or statement given by a defendant or suspect or that person's refusal or failure to make a statement; (3) the performance or results of any examination or test or the refusal or failure of a person to submit to an examination or test, or the identity or nature of physical evidence expected to be presented; (4) any opinion as to the guilt or innocence of a defendant or suspect in a criminal case or proceeding that could result in

incarceration; (5) information that the lawyer knows or reasonably should know is likely to be inadmissible as evidence in a trial and that would, if disclosed, create a substantial risk of prejudicing an impartial trial; or (6) the fact that a defendant has been charged with a crime, unless there is included therein a statement explaining that the charge is merely an accusation and that the defendant is presumed innocent until and unless proven guilty.

[6] Another relevant factor in determining prejudice is the nature of the proceeding involved. Criminal jury trials will be most sensitive to extrajudicial speech. Civil trials may be less sensitive. Non-jury hearings and arbitration proceedings may be even less affected. The Rule will still place limitations on prejudicial comments in these cases, but the likelihood of prejudice may be different depending on the type of proceeding.

[7] Finally, extrajudicial statements that might otherwise raise a question under this Rule may be permissible when they are made in response to statements made publicly by another party, another party's lawyer, or third persons, where a reasonable lawyer would believe a public response is required in order to avoid prejudice to the lawyer's client. When prejudicial statements have been publicly made by others, responsive statements may have the salutary effect of lessening any resulting adverse impact on the adjudicative proceeding. Such responsive statements should be limited to contain only such information as is necessary to mitigate undue prejudice created by the statements made by others.

[8] See Rule 3.8(f) for additional duties of prosecutors in connection with extrajudicial statements about criminal proceedings.

Rule 3.7. Lawyer as witness
(a) A lawyer shall not act as advocate at a trial in which the lawyer is likely to be a necessary witness unless: (1) the testimony relates to an uncontested issue; (2) the testimony relates to the nature and value of legal services rendered in the case; or (3) disqualification of the lawyer would work substantial hardship on the client.

(b) A lawyer may act as advocate in a trial in which another lawyer in the lawyer's firm is likely to be called as a witness unless precluded from doing so by Rule 1.7 or Rule 1.9.

COMMENT

[1] Combining the roles of advocate and witness can prejudice the tribunal and the opposing party and can also involve a conflict of interest between the lawyer and client.

[2] *Advocate-Witness Rule.* -- The tribunal has proper objection when the trier of fact may be confused or misled by a lawyer serving as both advocate and witness. The opposing party has proper objection where the combination of roles may prejudice that party's rights in the litigation. A witness is required to testify on the basis of personal knowledge, while an advocate is expected to explain and comment on evidence given by others. It may not be clear whether a statement by an advocate-witness should be taken as proof or as an analysis of the proof.

[3] To protect the tribunal, paragraph (a) prohibits a lawyer from simultaneously serving as advocate and necessary witness except in those circumstances specified in paragraphs (a)(1) through (a)(3). Paragraph (a)(1) recognizes that if the testimony will be uncontested, the ambiguities in the dual role are purely theoretical. Paragraph (a)(2) recognizes that where the testimony concerns the extent and value of legal services rendered in the action in which the testimony is offered, permitting the lawyers to testify avoids the need for a second trial with new counsel to resolve that issue. Moreover, in such a situation the judge has firsthand knowledge of the matter in issue; hence, there is less dependence on the adversary process to test the credibility of the testimony.

[4] Apart from these two exceptions, paragraph (a)(3) recognizes that a balancing is required between the interests of the client and those of the tribunal and the opposing party. Whether the tribunal is likely to be misled or the opposing party is likely to suffer prejudice depends on the nature of the case, the importance and probable tenor of the lawyer's testimony, and the probability that the lawyer's testimony will conflict with that of other witnesses. Even if there is risk of such prejudice, in determining whether the lawyer should be disqualified, due regard must be given to the effect of disqualification on the lawyer's client. It is relevant that one or both parties could reasonably foresee that the lawyer would probably be a witness. The conflict of interest principles stated in Rules 1.7, 1.9 and 1.10 have no application to this aspect of the problem.

[5] Because the tribunal is not likely to be misled when a lawyer acts as advocate in a trial in which another lawyer in the lawyer's firm will testify as a necessary witness, paragraph (b) permits the lawyer to do so except in situations involving a conflict of interest.

[6] *Conflict of Interest.* -- In determining if it is permissible to act as advocate in a trial in which the lawyer will be a necessary witness, the lawyer must also consider that the dual role may give rise to a conflict of interest that will require compliance with Rules 1.7 or 1.9. For example, if there is likely to be substantial conflict between the testimony of the client and that of the lawyer, the representation involves a conflict of interest that requires compliance with Rule 1.7. This would be true even though the lawyer might not be prohibited by paragraph (a) from simultaneously serving as advocate and witness because the lawyer's disqualification would work a substantial hardship on the client.

Similarly, a lawyer who might be permitted to simultaneously serve as an advocate and a witness by paragraph (a)(3) might be precluded from doing so by Rule 1.9. The problem can arise whether the lawyer is called as a witness on behalf of the client or is called by the opposing party. Determining whether or not such a conflict exists is primarily the responsibility of the lawyer involved. If there is a conflict of interest, the lawyer must secure the client's informed consent, confirmed in writing. In some cases, the lawyer will be precluded from seeking the client's consent. See Rule 1.7. See Rule 1.0(b) for the definition of "confirmed in writing" and Rule 1.0(e) for the definition of "informed consent."

[7] Paragraph (b) provides that a lawyer is not disqualified from serving as an advocate because a lawyer with whom the lawyer is associated in a firm is precluded from doing so by paragraph (a). If, however, the testifying lawyer would also be disqualified by Rule 1.7 or Rule 1.9 from representing the client in the matter, other lawyers in the firm will be precluded from representing the client by Rule 1.10 unless the client gives informed consent under the conditions stated in Rule 1.7.

Rule 3.8. Special responsibilities of a prosecutor

The prosecutor in a criminal case shall:

(a) refrain from prosecuting a charge that the prosecutor knows is not supported by probable cause;

(b) make reasonable efforts to assure that the accused has been advised of the right to, and the procedure for obtaining, counsel and has been given reasonable opportunity to obtain counsel;

(c) not seek to obtain from an unrepresented accused a waiver of important pretrial rights, such as the right to a preliminary hearing;

(d) make timely disclosure to the defense of all evidence or information known to the prosecutor that tends to negate the guilt of the accused or mitigates the offense, and, in connection with sentencing, disclose to the defense and to the tribunal all unprivileged mitigating information known to the prosecutor, except when the prosecutor is relieved of this responsibility by a protective order of the tribunal;

(e) not subpoena a lawyer in a grand jury or other criminal proceeding to present evidence about a past or present client unless the prosecutor reasonably believes: (1) the information sought is not protected from disclosure by any applicable privilege; (2) the evidence sought is essential to the successful completion of an ongoing investigation or prosecution; and (3) there is no other feasible alternative to obtain the information;

(f) except for statements that are necessary to inform the public of the nature and extent of the prosecutor's action and that serve a legitimate law enforcement purpose, refrain from making extrajudicial comments that have a substantial likelihood of heightening public condemnation of the accused and exercise reasonable care to prevent investigators, law enforcement personnel, employees or other persons assisting or associated with the prosecutor in a criminal case from making an extrajudicial statement that the prosecutor would be prohibited from making under Rule 3.6 or this Rule.

COMMENT

[1] A prosecutor has the responsibility of a minister of justice and not simply that of an advocate. This responsibility carries with it specific obligations to see that the defendant is accorded procedural justice and that guilt is decided upon the basis of sufficient evidence. Precisely how far the prosecutor is required to go in this direction is a matter of debate and varies in different jurisdictions. Many jurisdictions have adopted the ABA Standards of Criminal Justice Relating to the Prosecution Function, which in turn are the product of prolonged and careful deliberation by lawyers experienced in both criminal prosecution and defense. Applicable law may require other measures by the prosecutor and knowing disregard of those obligations or a systematic abuse of prosecutorial discretion could constitute a violation of Rule 8.4.

[2] In some jurisdictions, a defendant may waive a preliminary hearing and thereby lose a valuable opportunity to challenge probable cause. Accordingly, prosecutors should not seek to obtain waivers of preliminary hearings or other important pretrial rights from unrepresented accused persons. Paragraph (c) does not apply, however, to an accused appearing pro se with the approval of the tribunal. Nor does it forbid the lawful questioning of an uncharged suspect who has knowingly waived the rights to counsel and silence.

[3] The exception in paragraph (d) recognizes that a prosecutor may seek an appropriate protective order from the tribunal if disclosure of information to the defense could result in substantial harm to an individual or to the public interest.

[4] Paragraph (e) is intended to limit the issuance of lawyer subpoenas in grand jury and other criminal proceedings to those situations in which there is a genuine need to intrude into the client-lawyer relationship.

[5] Paragraph (f) supplements Rule 3.6, which prohibits extrajudicial statements that have a substantial likelihood of prejudicing an adjudicatory proceeding. In the context of a criminal prosecution, a prosecutor's extrajudicial statement can create the additional problem of increasing public condemnation of the accused.

Although the announcement of an indictment, for example, will necessarily have severe consequences for the accused, a prosecutor can, and should, avoid comments that have no legitimate law enforcement purpose and have a substantial likelihood of increasing public opprobrium of the accused. Nothing in this Comment is intended to restrict the statements which a prosecutor may make which comply with Rule 3.6(b) or 3.6(c).

[6] Like other lawyers, prosecutors are subject to Rules 5.1 and 5.3, which relate to responsibilities regarding lawyers and nonlawyers who work for or are associated with the lawyer's office. Paragraph (f) reminds the prosecutor of the importance of these obligations in connection with the unique dangers of improper extrajudicial statements in a criminal case. In addition, paragraph (f) requires a prosecutor to exercise reasonable care to prevent persons assisting or associated with the prosecutor from making improper extrajudicial statements, even when such persons are not under the direct supervision of the prosecutor. Ordinarily, the reasonable care standard will be satisfied if the prosecutor issues the appropriate cautions to law-enforcement personnel and other relevant individuals.

Rule 3.9. Advocate in nonadjudicative proceedings - omitted

Rule 4.3. Dealing with unrepresented person

In dealing on behalf of a client with a person who is not represented by counsel, a lawyer shall not state or imply that the lawyer is disinterested. When the lawyer knows or reasonably should know that the unrepresented person misunderstands the lawyer's role in the matter, the lawyer shall make reasonable efforts to correct the misunderstanding. The lawyer shall not give legal advice to an unrepresented person, other than the advice to secure counsel, if the lawyer knows or reasonably should know that the interests of such a person are or have a reasonable possibility of being in conflict with the interests of the client.

COMMENT
[1] An unrepresented person, particularly one not experienced in dealing with legal matters, might assume that a lawyer is disinterested in loyalties or is a disinterested authority on the law even when the lawyer represents a client. In order to avoid a misunderstanding, a lawyer will typically need to identify the lawyer's client and, where necessary, explain that the client has interests opposed to those of the unrepresented person. For misunderstandings that sometimes arise when a lawyer for an organization deals with an unrepresented constituent, see Rule 1.13(d).

[2] The Rule distinguishes between situations involving unrepresented persons

whose interests may be adverse to those of the lawyer's client and those in which the person's interests are not in conflict with the client's. In the former situation, the possibility that the lawyer will compromise the unrepresented person's interests is so great that the Rule prohibits the giving of any advice, apart from the advice to obtain counsel. Whether a lawyer is giving impermissible advice may depend on the experience and sophistication of the unrepresented person, as well as the setting in which the behavior and comments occur. This Rule does not prohibit a lawyer from negotiating the terms of a transaction or settling a dispute with an unrepresented person. So long as the lawyer has explained that the lawyer represents an adverse party and is not representing the person, the lawyer may inform the person of the terms on which the lawyer's client will enter into an agreement or settle a matter, prepare documents that require the person's signature and explain the lawyer's own view of the meaning of the document or the lawyer's view of the underlying legal obligations.

Rule 4.4. Respect for rights of third persons

(a) In representing a client, a lawyer shall not use means that have no substantial purpose other than to embarrass, delay or burden a third person, or use methods of obtaining evidence that violate the legal rights of such a person.

(b) A lawyer who receives a document relating to the representation of the lawyer's client and knows or reasonably should know that the document was inadvertently sent shall promptly notify the sender.

COMMENT

[1] Responsibility to a client requires a lawyer to subordinate the interests of others to those of the client, but that responsibility does not imply that a lawyer may disregard the rights of third persons. It is impractical to catalogue all such rights, but they include legal restrictions on methods of obtaining evidence from third persons and unwarranted intrusions into privileged relationships, such as the client-lawyer relationship.

[2] Paragraph (b) recognizes that lawyers sometimes receive documents that were mistakenly sent or produced by opposing parties or their lawyers. If a lawyer knows or reasonably should know that a such a document was sent inadvertently, then this Rule requires the lawyer to promptly notify the sender in order to permit that person to take protective measures. Whether the lawyer is required to take additional steps, such as returning the original document, is a matter of law beyond the scope of these Rules, as is the question of whether the privileged status of a document has been waived. Similarly, this Rule does not address the legal duties of a lawyer who receives a document that the lawyer knows or reasonably should know may have been wrongfully obtained by the sending

person. For purposes of this Rule, "document" includes e-mail or other electronic modes of transmission subject to being read or put into readable form.

[3] Some lawyers may choose to return a document unread, for example, when the lawyer learns before receiving the document that it was inadvertently sent to the wrong address. Where a lawyer is not required by applicable law to do so, the decision to voluntarily return such a document is a matter of professional judgment ordinarily reserved to the lawyer. See Rules 1.2 and 1.4.

Rule 5.1. Responsibilities of partners, managers, and supervisory lawyers

(a) A partner in a law firm, and a lawyer who individually or together with other lawyers possesses comparable managerial authority in a law firm, shall make reasonable efforts to ensure that the firm has in effect measures giving reasonable assurance that all lawyers in the firm conform to the Rules of Professional Conduct.

(b) A lawyer having direct supervisory authority over another lawyer shall make reasonable efforts to ensure that the other lawyer conforms to the Rules of Professional Conduct.

(c) A lawyer shall be responsible for another lawyer's violation of the Rules of Professional Conduct if: (1) the lawyer orders or, with knowledge of the specific conduct, ratifies the conduct involved; or (2) the lawyer is a partner or has comparable managerial authority in the law firm in which the other lawyer practices, or has direct supervisory authority over the other lawyer, and knows of the conduct at a time when its consequences can be avoided or mitigated but fails to take reasonable remedial action.

Rule 5.3. Responsibilities regarding non-lawyer assistants

With respect to a nonlawyer employed or retained by or associated with a lawyer:

(a) a partner in a law firm, and a lawyer who individually or together with other lawyers possesses comparable managerial authority in a law firm, shall make reasonable efforts to ensure that the firm has in effect measures giving reasonable assurance that the person's conduct is compatible with the professional obligations of the lawyer;
(b) a lawyer having direct supervisory authority over the nonlawyer shall make reasonable efforts to ensure that the person's conduct is compatible with the professional obligations of the lawyer; and

(c) a lawyer shall be responsible for conduct of such a person that would be a violation of the Rules of Professional Conduct if engaged in by a lawyer if: (1) the lawyer orders or, with the knowledge of the specific conduct, ratifies the conduct involved; or (2) the lawyer is a partner or has comparable managerial authority in the law firm in which the person is employed, or has direct supervisory authority over the person, and knows of the conduct at a time when its consequences can be avoided or mitigated but fails to take reasonable remedial action.

Rule 5.4. Professional independence of a lawyer

(a) A lawyer or law firm shall not share legal fees with a nonlawyer, except that: (1) an agreement by a lawyer with the lawyer's firm, partner, or associate may provide for the payment of money, over a reasonable period of time after the lawyer's death, to the lawyer's estate or to one or more specified persons; (2) a lawyer who undertakes to complete unfinished legal business of a deceased lawyer may pay to the estate of the deceased lawyer that proportion of the total compensation which fairly represents the services rendered by the deceased lawyer; (3) a lawyer who purchases the practice of a deceased, disabled, or disappeared lawyer may, pursuant to the provisions of Rule 1.17, pay to the estate or other representative of that lawyer the agreed-upon purchase price; (4) a lawyer or law firm may include nonlawyer employees in a compensation or retirement plan, even though the plan is based in whole or in part on a profit-sharing arrangement; and (5) a lawyer may share court-awarded legal fees with a nonprofit organization that employed, retained or recommended employment of the lawyer in the matter.

(b) A lawyer shall not form a partnership with a nonlawyer if any of the activities of the partnership consist of the practice of law.

(c) A lawyer shall not permit a person who recommends, employs, or pays the lawyer to render legal services for another to direct or regulate the lawyer's professional judgment in rendering such legal services.

(d) A lawyer shall not practice with or in the form of a professional corporation or association authorized to practice law for a profit, if: (1) a nonlawyer owns any interest therein, except that a fiduciary representative of the estate of a lawyer may hold the stock or interest of the lawyer for a reasonable time during administration; (2) a nonlawyer is a corporate director or officer thereof or occupies the position of similar responsibility in any form of association other than a corporation; or (3) a nonlawyer has the right to direct or control the professional judgment of a lawyer

Rule 5.5. Unauthorized practice of law; multijurisdictional practice of law -

omitted

Rule 5.6. Restrictions on right to practice - omitted

Rule 5.7. Responsibilities regarding law-related services - omitted

Rule 6.1. Voluntary pro bono publico service - omitted

Rule 6.2. Accepting appointments

A lawyer shall not seek to avoid appointment by a tribunal to represent a person except for good cause, such as:

(a) representing the client is likely to result in violation of the Rules of Professional Conduct or other law;

(b) representing the client is likely to result in an unreasonable financial burden on the lawyer; or

(c) the client or the cause is so repugnant to the lawyer as to be likely to impair the client-lawyer relationship or the lawyer's ability to represent the client.

Rule 6.3. Membership in legal services organization - omitted

Rule 6.4. Law reform activities affecting client interests - omitted

Rule 6.5. Non-profit and court-annexed limited legal-service programomitted

Rule 7.1. Communications concerning a lawyer's services - omitted

Rule 7.2. Advertising - omitted

Rule 7.3. Direct contact with prospective clients - omitted

Rule 7.4. Communication of fields of practice and specialization - omitted

Rule 7.5. Firm names and letterheads - omitted

Rule 8.1. Bar admission and disciplinary matters

An applicant for admission to the bar, or a lawyer in connection with a bar admission application or in connection with a disciplinary matter, shall not:

(a) knowingly make a false statement of material fact; or

(b) fail to disclose a fact necessary to correct a misapprehension known by the person to have arisen in the matter, or knowingly fail to respond to a lawful demand for information from an admission or disciplinary authority, except that this rule does not require disclosure of information otherwise protected by Rule 1.6.

Rule 8.2. Judicial and legal officials

(a) A lawyer shall not make a statement that the lawyer knows to be false or with reckless disregard as to its truth or falsity concerning the qualifications or integrity of a judge, adjudicatory officer or public legal officer, or a candidate for election or appointment to judicial or legal office.

(b) A lawyer who is a candidate for judicial office shall comply with the applicable provisions of the Code of Judicial Conduct.

Rule 8.3. Reporting professional misconduct

(a) A lawyer who knows that another lawyer has committed a violation of the rules of Professional Conduct that raises a substantial question as to that lawyer's honesty, trustworthiness or fitness as a lawyer in other respects, shall inform the appropriate professional authority.

(b) A lawyer who knows that a judge has committed a violation of applicable rules of judicial conduct that raises a substantial question as to the judge's fitness for office shall inform the appropriate authority.

(c) This Rule does not require disclosure of information otherwise protected by rule 1.6.

(d) Notwithstanding anything in this or other of the rules to the contrary, the relationship between members of either (i) the Lawyers Assistance Committee of the Delaware State Bar Association and counselors retained by the Bar Association, or (ii) the Professional Ethics Committee of the Delaware State Bar Association, or (iii) the Fee dispute Conciliation and Mediation Committee of the Delaware State Bar Association, or (iv) the Professional Guidance Committee of the Delaware State Bar Association, and a lawyer or a judge shall be the same as that of attorney and client.

Rule 8.4. Misconduct

It is professional misconduct for a lawyer to:
(a) violate or attempt to violate the Rules of Professional Conduct, knowingly assist or induce another to do so or do so through the acts of another;

(b) commit a criminal act that reflects adversely on the lawyer's honesty, trustworthiness or fitness as a lawyer in other respects;

(c) engage in conduct involving dishonesty, fraud, deceit or misrepresentation;

(d) engage in conduct that is prejudicial to the administration of justice;

(e) state or imply an ability to influence improperly a government agency or official or to achieve results by means that violate the Rules of Professional Conduct or other law; or

(f) knowingly assist a judge or judicial officer in conduct that is a violation of applicable rules of judicial conduct or other law.

APPENDIX II
ALPHABETICAL OBJECTION GUIDE

The following list of common objections is provided in alphabetical order. You should use this list to assist you in identifying the source of objections raised by others when you are not familiar with the rule that forms the basis for the objection.

1. AMBIGUOUS: Confusing question in that it is capable of being understood in more than one sense. FEDERAL RULE OF EVIDENCE 611(a).

2. ARGUMENTATIVE: (a) Counsel's question is really argument to the jury in guise of a question (Example: Counsel summarizes facts, states conclusion, and demands witness agree with conclusion); or (b), excessive quibbling with witness. FEDERAL RULE OF EVIDENCE 611(a).

3. ASKED AND ANSWERED: Unfair to allow counsel to emphasize evidence through repetition. (An especially useful objection during re-direct examination; greater leeway on cross-exam, however, to test recollection). FEDERAL RULE OF EVIDENCE 611(a).

4. ASSUMES A FACT NOT IN EVIDENCE: Fact not testified to is contained within the question. FEDERAL RULE OF EVIDENCE 103(c); 611(a).

5. AUTHENTICATION LACKING: Proof must be offered that the exhibit is in fact what it is claimed to be. FEDERAL RULE OF EVIDENCE 901(a).

6. BEST EVIDENCE RULE: If rule applies, original document must be offered or its absence accounted for. If contents of document are to be proved, rule usually applies. FEDERAL RULE OF EVIDENCE 1002. (See also 1003 and 1004).

7. BEYOND SCOPE (OF DIRECT, CROSS, ETC.): Question unrelated to examination immediately preceding, or to credibility. Questioner should be required to call witness as own. FEDERAL RULE OF EVIDENCE. 611(b).

8. BOLSTERING: Improper to bolster the credibility of a witness before credibility is attacked. FEDERAL RULE OF EVIDENCE 608(a).

9. COMPOUND: More than one question contained in the question asked by counsel. FEDERAL RULE OF EVIDENCE 611(a).

10. CONCLUSION: Except for expert, witness must testify to facts within personal knowledge; conclusions are for the jury and counsel during closing argument. FEDERAL RULE OF EVIDENCE 602; 701.

11. CONFUSING: Unfamiliar words, disjointed phrases, or question confuses the evidence. FEDERAL RULE OF EVIDENCE 611(a).

12. COUNSEL TESTIFYING: Counsel is making a statement instead of asking a question. FEDERAL RULE OF EVIDENCE 603.

13. CUMULATIVE: Military judge has discretion to control repetitive evidence. Repeated presentation of the same evidence by more exhibits or more witnesses is unfair, unnecessary and wastes time. FEDERAL RULE OF EVIDENCE 102, 611(a).

14. FOUNDATION LACKING: No proper foundation for testimony or exhibit. (Es; Offer of "recorded recollection" without showing memory failure; similar to objection for lack of authentication or personal knowledge.) FEDERAL RULE OF EVIDENCE 602; 901(a).

15. HEARSAY: (question) - Answer would elicit hearsay, and no exception has been shown. FEDERAL RULE OF EVIDENCE 802. HEARSAY- (answer) - Question did not call for hearsay, but witness gave it anyway. Move to strike and ask judge to instruct that response be disregarded. FEDERAL RULE OF EVIDENCE 802.

16. IMPEACHMENT BY PROPER MEANS: Methods of impeachment are limited and specific. FEDERAL RULE OF EVIDENCE 607-610.

17. "IMPROPER": When you are sure the question is improper, but cannot think of the correct basis for an objection, try, "Objection, Your Honor, improper question." The JUDGE may know the proper basis and sustain your objection, and if JUDGE asks for your specific basis, you have gained time to think of it. To be used very infrequently. FEDERAL RULE OF EVIDENCE 103(c); 611.

18. IMPROPER CHARACTERIZATION: The question or the response has characterized a person or conduct with unwarranted suggestive, argumentative, or impertinent language. (Example: "He looked like a crook.") FEDERAL RULE OF EVIDENCE 404-405; 611(a).

19. INCOMPETENT WITNESS: Lack of qualification, such as oath or mental capacity. Also applies if military judge or member is called as a witness. FEDERAL RULE OF EVIDENCE 104(a); 603; 605; 606.

20. IRRELEVANT: Would not tend to make any fact that is of consequence more probable or less probable. FEDERAL RULE OF EVIDENCE 402.

21. LEADING: Form of question tends to suggest answer (permitted, of course, on cross-exam). FEDERAL RULE OF EVIDENCE 611(c).

22. MISQUOTING WITNESS (or MISSTATING EVIDENCE): Counsel's question misstates prior testimony of witness. Similar to objection based on assuming fact not in evidence. FEDERAL RULE OF EVIDENCE 103©.

23. NARRATIVE: Question is so broad or covers such a large time period it would allow witness to ramble and possibly present hearsay or irrelevant evidence. The judge has broad discretion in this matter. FEDERAL RULE OF EVIDENCE 103(c); 611(a).

24. OPINION: Lay opinion or inference that is beyond the scope permitted by FEDERAL RULE OF EVIDENCE 701; personal knowledge lacking; or expert witness has not been qualified as such. FEDERAL RULE OF EVIDENCE 602; 701; 702.

25. PREJUDICE OUTWEIGHS PROBATIVE VALUE: Out of the members' hearing, argue that "the probative value of the evidence is substantially outweighed by its prejudicial effect." May apply to exhibits as well as testimony. (Don't let the members hear you say that the evidence is prejudicial. They may be impressed.) FEDERAL RULE OF EVIDENCE 403.

26. PRIVILEGED: Answer would violate valid privilege (lawyer-client, husband-wife, clergyman, etc.) FEDERAL RULE OF EVIDENCE 501.

27. SPECULATION AND CONJECTURE: Question requires witness who lacks personal knowledge to guess. FEDERAL RULE OF EVIDENCE 602.

28. UNRESPONSIVE: Answer includes testimony not called for by the question. Especially applicable to voluntary response by hostile witness. NOTE: An objection based <u>solely</u> on this ground is generally deemed appropriate only if made by the examining attorney; thus opposing counsel should state some additional basis for the objection. FEDERAL RULE OF EVIDENCE 103(c); 611(a).

APPENDIX III
FEDERAL RULES OF EVIDENCE

The following federal rules of evidence are valid as of December 31, 2004. At the end of the appendix III you will find the proposed changes to federal rules of evidence 404, 408, 606 and 609. Absent congressional action these rules are law as of December 1, 2006.

A. *Table of Contents.*

Rule 201. Judicial notice of adjudicative facts:
    (a) Scope of rule
    (b) Kinds of facts
    (c) When discretionary
    (d) When mandatory
    (e) Opportunity to be heard
    (f) Time of taking notice
    (g) Instructing jury

Article III. Presumptions in Civil Actions and Proceedings:

Rule 301. Presumptions in general in civil actions and proceedings

Rule 302. Applicability of State law in civil actions and proceedings

Article IV. Relevancy and Its Limits:

Rule 401. Definition of ''relevant evidence''

Rule 402. Relevant evidence generally admissible; irrelevant evidence inadmissible

Rule 403. Exclusion of relevant evidence on grounds of prejudice, confusion, or waste of time

Rule 404. Character evidence not admissible to prove conduct; exceptions; other crimes:
    (a) Character evidence generally:
        (1) Character of accused
        (2) Character of alleged victim
        (3) Character of witness
    (b) Other crimes, wrongs, or acts

Rule 405. Methods of proving character:
    (a) Reputation or opinion
    (b) Specific instances of conduct

Rule 406. Habit; routine practice

Rule 407. Subsequent remedial measures

Rule 408. Compromise and offers to compromise

Article IV. Relevancy and Its Limits—Continued Page

Rule 801. Definitions:
  (a) Statement
  (b) Declarant
  (c) Hearsay
  (d) Statements which are not hearsay:
    (1) Prior statement by witness
    (2) Admission by party-opponent

Rule 802. Hearsay rule

Rule 803. Hearsay exceptions; availability of declarant immaterial: Page
    (1) Present sense impression
    (2) Excited utterance
    (3) Then existing mental, emotional, or physical condition
    (4) Statements for purposes of medical diagnosis or treatment
    (5) Recorded recollection
    (6) Records of regularly conducted activity
    (7) Absence of entry in records kept in accordance with the provisions
        of paragraph (6)
    (8) Public records and reports
    (9) Records of vital statistics
    (10) Absence of public record or entry
    (11) Records of religious organizations
    (12) Marriage, baptismal, and similar certificates
    (13) Family records
    (14) Records of documents affecting an interest in property
    (15) Statements in documents affecting an interest in property
    (16) Statements in ancient documents
    (17) Market reports, commercial publications
    (18) Learned treatises
    (19) Reputation concerning personal or family history
    (20) Reputation concerning boundaries or general history
    (21) Reputation as to character
    (22) Judgment of previous conviction
    (23) Judgment as to personal, family, or general history, or boundaries
    (24) Other exceptions (Transferred).

Rule 804. Hearsay exceptions; declarant unavailable:
  (a) Definition of unavailability
  (b) Hearsay exceptions:
    (1) Former testimony
    (2) Statement under belief of impending death
    (3) Statement against interest
    (4) Statement of personal or family history
    (5) Other exceptions (Transferred).

B. Federal Rules of Evidence as of December 31, 2004.

FEDERAL RULES OF EVIDENCE
DECEMBER 31, 2004

ARTICLE I. GENERAL PROVISIONS

Rule 101. Scope
These rules govern proceedings in the courts of the United States and before the United States bankruptcy judges and United States magistrate judges, to the extent and with the exceptions stated in rule 1101.

Rule 102. Purpose and Construction
These rules shall be construed to secure fairness in administration, elimination of unjustifiable expense and delay, and promotion of growth and development of the law of evidence to the end that the truth may be ascertained and proceedings justly determined.

Rule 103. Rulings on Evidence
(a) Effect of erroneous ruling.—Error may not be predicated upon a ruling which admits or excludes evidence unless a substantial right of the party is affected, and

(1) Objection.—In case the ruling is one admitting evidence, a timely objection or motion to strike appears of record, stating the specific ground of objection, if the specific ground was not apparent from the context; or

(2) Offer of proof.—In case the ruling is one excluding evidence, the substance of the evidence was made known to the court by offer or was apparent from the context within which questions were asked. Once the court makes a definitive ruling on the record admitting or excluding evidence, either at or before trial, a party need not renew an objection or offer of proof to preserve a claim of error for appeal.

(b) Record of offer and ruling.—The court may add any other or further statement which shows the character of the evidence, the form in which it was offered, the objection made, and the ruling thereon. It may direct the making of an offer in question and answer form.

(c) Hearing of jury.—In jury cases, proceedings shall be conducted, to the extent practicable, so as to prevent inadmissible evidence from being suggested to the jury by any means, such as making statements or offers of proof or asking questions in the hearing of the jury.

(d) Plain error.—Nothing in this rule precludes taking notice of plain errors affecting substantial rights although they were not brought to the attention of the court.

Rule 104. Preliminary Questions

(a) Questions of admissibility generally.—Preliminary questions concerning the qualification of a person to be a witness, the existence of a privilege, or the admissibility of evidence shall be determined by the court, subject to the provisions of subdivision (b). In making its determination it is not bound by the rules of evidence except those with respect to privileges.

(b) Relevancy conditioned on fact.—When the relevancy of evidence depends upon the fulfillment of a condition of fact, the court shall admit it upon, or subject to, the introduction of evidence sufficient to support a finding of the fulfillment of the condition.

(c) Hearing of jury.—Hearings on the admissibility of confessions shall in all cases be conducted out of the hearing of the jury. Hearings on other preliminary matters shall be so conducted when the interests of justice require, or when an accused is a witness and so requests.

(d) Testimony by accused.—The accused does not, by testifying upon a preliminary matter, become subject to cross-examination as to other issues in the case.

(e) Weight and credibility.—This rule does not limit the right of a party to introduce before the jury evidence relevant to weight or credibility.

Rule 105. Limited Admissibility

When evidence which is admissible as to one party or for one purpose but not admissible as to another party or for another purpose is admitted, the court, upon request, shall restrict the evidence to its proper scope and instruct the jury accordingly.

Rule 106. Remainder of or Related Writings or Recorded Statements

When a writing or recorded statement or part thereof is introduced by a party, an adverse party may require the introduction at that time of any other part or any other writing or recorded statement which ought in fairness to be considered contemporaneously with it.

ARTICLE II. JUDICIAL NOTICE

Rule 201. Judicial Notice of Adjudicative Facts

(a) Scope of rule.—This rule governs only judicial notice of adjudicative facts.

(b) Kinds of facts.—A judicially noticed fact must be one not subject to reasonable dispute in that it is either (1) generally known within the territorial jurisdiction of the trial court or (2) capable of accurate and ready determination by resort to sources whose accuracy cannot reasonably be questioned.

(c) When discretionary.—A court may take judicial notice, whether requested or not.

(d) When mandatory.—A court shall take judicial notice if requested by a party and supplied with the necessary information.

(e) Opportunity to be heard.—A party is entitled upon timely request to an opportunity to be heard as to the propriety of taking judicial notice and the tenor of the matter noticed. In the absence of prior notification, the request may be made after judicial notice has been taken.

(f) Time of taking notice.—Judicial notice may be taken at any stage of the proceeding.

(g) Instructing jury.—In a civil action or proceeding, the court shall instruct the jury to accept as conclusive any fact judicially noticed. In a criminal case, the court shall instruct the jury that it may, but is not required to, accept as conclusive any fact judicially noticed.

ARTICLE III. PRESUMPTIONS IN CIVIL ACTIONS AND PROCEEDINGS

Rule 301. Presumptions in General in Civil Actions and Proceedings
In all civil actions and proceedings not otherwise provided for by Act of Congress or by these rules, a presumption imposes on the party against whom it is directed the burden of going forward with evidence to rebut or meet the presumption, but does not shift to such party the burden of proof in the sense of the risk of nonpersuasion, which remains throughout the trial upon the party on whom it was originally cast.

Rule 302. Applicability of State Law in Civil Actions and Proceedings
In civil actions and proceedings, the effect of a presumption respecting a fact which is an element of a claim or defense as to which State law supplies the rule of decision is determined in accordance with State law.

ARTICLE IV. RELEVANCY AND ITS LIMITS

Rule 401. Definition of ''Relevant Evidence''
''Relevant evidence'' means evidence having any tendency to make the existence of any fact that is of consequence to the determination of the action more probable or less probable than it would be without the evidence.

Rule 402. Relevant Evidence Generally Admissible; Irrelevant Evidence Inadmissible

All relevant evidence is admissible, except as otherwise provided by the Constitution of the United States, by Act of Congress, by these rules, or by other rules prescribed by the Supreme Court pursuant to statutory authority. Evidence which is not relevant is not admissible.

Rule 403. Exclusion of Relevant Evidence on Grounds of Prejudice, Confusion, or Waste of Time

Although relevant, evidence may be excluded if its probative value is substantially outweighed by the danger of unfair prejudice, confusion of the issues, or misleading the jury, or by considerations of undue delay, waste of time, or needless presentation of cumulative evidence.

Rule 404. Character Evidence Not Admissible To Prove Conduct; Exceptions; Other Crimes

(a) Character evidence generally.—Evidence of a person's character or a trait of character is not admissible for the purpose of proving action in conformity therewith on a particular occasion, except:

(1) Character of accused.—Evidence of a pertinent trait of character offered by an accused, or by the prosecution to rebut the same, or if evidence of a trait of character of the alleged victim of the crime is offered by an accused and admitted under Rule 404(a)(2), evidence of the same trait of character of the accused offered by the prosecution;

(2) Character of alleged victim.—Evidence of a pertinent trait of character of the alleged victim of the crime offered by an accused, or by the prosecution to rebut the same, or evidence of a character trait of peacefulness of the alleged victim offered by the prosecution in a homicide case to rebut evidence that the alleged victim was the first aggressor;

(3) Character of witness.—Evidence of the character of a witness, as provided in rules 607, 608, and 609.

(b) Other crimes, wrongs, or acts.—Evidence of other crimes, wrongs, or acts is not admissible to prove the character of a person in order to show action in conformity therewith. It may, however, be admissible for other purposes, such as proof of motive, opportunity, intent, preparation, plan, knowledge, identity, or absence of mistake or accident, provided that upon request by the accused, the prosecution in a criminal case shall provide reasonable notice in advance of trial, or during trial if the court excuses pretrial notice on good cause shown, of the general nature of any such evidence it intends to introduce at trial.

Rule 405. Methods of Proving Character

(a) Reputation or opinion.—In all cases in which evidence of character or a trait of character of a person is admissible, proof may be made by testimony as to reputation or by testimony in the form of an opinion. On cross-examination, inquiry is allowable into relevant specific instances of conduct.

(b) Specific instances of conduct.—In cases in which character or a trait of character of a person is an essential element of a charge, claim, or defense, proof may also be made of specific instances of that person's conduct.

Rule 406. Habit; Routine Practice

Evidence of the habit of a person or of the routine practice of an organization, whether corroborated or not and regardless of the presence of eyewitnesses, is relevant to prove that the conduct of the person or organization on a particular occasion was in conformity with the habit or routine practice.

Rule 407. Subsequent Remedial Measures

When, after an injury or harm allegedly caused by an event, measures are taken that, if taken previously, would have made the injury or harm less likely to occur, evidence of the subsequent measures is not admissible to prove negligence, culpable conduct, a defect in a product, a defect in a product's design, or a need for a warning or instruction. This rule does not require the exclusion of evidence of subsequent measures when offered for another purpose, such as proving ownership, control, or feasibility of precautionary measures, if controverted, or impeachment.

Rule 408. Compromise and Offers to Compromise

Evidence of (1) furnishing or offering or promising to furnish, or (2) accepting or offering or promising to accept, a valuable consideration in compromising or attempting to compromise a claim which was disputed as to either validity or amount, is not admissible to prove liability for or invalidity of the claim or its amount. Evidence of conduct or statements made in compromise negotiations is likewise not admissible. This rule does not require the exclusion of any evidence otherwise discoverable merely because it is presented in the course of compromise negotiations. This rule also does not require exclusion when the evidence is offered for another purpose, such as proving bias or prejudice of a witness, negativing a contention of undue delay, or proving an effort to obstruct a criminal investigation or prosecution.

Rule 409. Payment of Medical and Similar Expenses

Evidence of furnishing or offering or promising to pay medical, hospital, or similar expenses occasioned by an injury is not admissible to prove liability for the injury.

Rule 410. Inadmissibility of Pleas, Plea Discussions, and Related Statements

Except as otherwise provided in this rule, evidence of the following is not, in any civil or criminal proceeding, admissible against the defendant who made the plea or was a participant in the plea discussions:

(1) a plea of guilty which was later withdrawn;

(2) a plea of nolo contendere;

(3) any statement made in the course of any proceedings under Rule 11 of the Federal Rules of Criminal Procedure or comparable state procedure regarding either of the foregoing pleas; or

(4) any statement made in the course of plea discussions with an attorney for the prosecuting authority which do not result in a plea of guilty or which result in a plea of guilty later withdrawn. However, such a statement is admissible (i) in any proceeding wherein another statement made in the course of the same plea or plea discussions has been introduced and the statement ought in fairness be considered contemporaneously with it, or (ii) in a criminal proceeding for perjury or false statement if the statement was made by the defendant under oath, on the record and in the presence of counsel.

Rule 411. Liability Insurance

Evidence that a person was or was not insured against liability is not admissible upon the issue whether the person acted negligently or otherwise wrongfully. This rule does not require the exclusion of evidence of insurance against liability when offered for another purpose, such as proof of agency, ownership, or control, or bias or prejudice of a witness.

Rule 412. Sex Offense Cases; Relevance of Alleged Victim's Past Sexual Behavior or Alleged Sexual Predisposition

(a) Evidence Generally Inadmissible.—The following evidence is not admissible in any civil or criminal proceeding involving alleged sexual misconduct except as provided in subdivisions (b) and (c):

(1) Evidence offered to prove that any alleged victim engaged in other sexual behavior.

(2) Evidence offered to prove any alleged victim's sexual predisposition.

(b) Exceptions.

(1) In a criminal case, the following evidence is admissible, if otherwise admissible under these rules:

(A) evidence of specific instances of sexual behavior by the alleged victim offered to prove that a person other than the accused was the source of semen, injury or other physical evidence;

(B) evidence of specific instances of sexual behavior by the alleged victim with respect to the person accused of the sexual misconduct offered by the accused to prove consent or by the prosecution; and

(C) evidence the exclusion of which would violate the constitutional rights of the defendant.

(2) In a civil case, evidence offered to prove the sexual behavior or sexual predisposition of any alleged victim is admissible if it is otherwise admissible under these rules and its probative value substantially outweighs the danger of harm to any victim and of unfair prejudice to any party. Evidence of an alleged victim's reputation is admissible only if it has been placed in controversy by the alleged victim.

(c) Procedure To Determine Admissibility.

(1) A party intending to offer evidence under subdivision (b) must— (A) file a written motion at least 14 days before trial specifically describing the evidence and stating the purpose for which it is offered unless the court, for good cause requires a different time for filing or permits filing during trial; and
(B) serve the motion on all parties and notify the alleged victim or, when appropriate, the alleged victim's guardian or representative.

(2) Before admitting evidence under this rule the court must conduct a hearing in camera and afford the victim and parties a right to attend and be heard. The motion, related papers, and the record of the hearing must be sealed and remain under seal unless the court orders otherwise.

Rule 413. Evidence of Similar Crimes in Sexual Assault Cases
(a) In a criminal case in which the defendant is accused of an offense of sexual assault, evidence of the defendant's commission of another offense or offenses of sexual assault is admissible, and may be considered for its bearing on any matter to which it is relevant.

(b) In a case in which the Government intends to offer evidence under this rule, the attorney for the Government shall disclose the evidence to the defendant, including statements of witnesses or a summary of the substance of any testimony that is expected to be offered, at least fifteen days before the scheduled date of trial or at such later time as the court may allow for good cause.

(c) This rule shall not be construed to limit the admission or consideration of evidence under any other rule.

(d) For purposes of this rule and Rule 415, ''offense of sexual assault'' means a crime under Federal law or the law of a State (as defined in section 513 of title 18, United States Code) that involved— (1) any conduct proscribed by chapter 109A of title 18, United States Code; (2) contact, without consent, between any part of the defendant's body or an object and the genitals or anus of another person; (3) contact, without consent, between the genitals or anus of the defendant and any part of another person's body; (4) deriving sexual pleasure or gratification from the infliction of death, bodily injury, or physical pain on another person; or (5) an attempt or conspiracy to engage in conduct described in paragraphs (1)–(4).

Rule 414. Evidence of Similar Crimes in Child Molestation Cases

(a) In a criminal case in which the defendant is accused of an offense of child molestation, evidence of the defendant's commission of another offense or offenses of child molestation is admissible, and may be considered for its bearing on any matter to which it is relevant.

(b) In a case in which the Government intends to offer evidence under this rule, the attorney for the Government shall disclose the evidence to the defendant, including statements of witnesses or a summary of the substance of any testimony that is expected to be offered, at least fifteen days before the scheduled date of trial or at such later time as the court may allow for good cause.

(c) This rule shall not be construed to limit the admission or consideration of evidence under any other rule.

(d) For purposes of this rule and Rule 415, ''child'' means a person below the age of fourteen, and ''offense of child molestation'' means a crime under Federal law or the law of a State (as defined in section 513 of title 18, United States Code) that involved—

(1) any conduct proscribed by chapter 109A of title 18, United States Code, that was committed in relation to a child;
(2) any conduct proscribed by chapter 110 of title 18, United States Code;
(3) contact between any part of the defendant's body or an object and the genitals or anus of a child;
(4) contact between the genitals or anus of the defendant and any part of the body of a child;
(5) deriving sexual pleasure or gratification from the infliction of death, bodily injury, or physical pain on a child; or
(6) an attempt or conspiracy to engage in conduct described in paragraphs (1)–(5).

Rule 415. Evidence of Similar Acts in Civil Cases Concerning Sexual Assault or Child Molestation

(a) In a civil case in which a claim for damages or other relief is predicated on a party's alleged commission of conduct constituting an offense of sexual assault or child molestation, evidence of that party's commission of another offense or offenses of sexual assault or child molestation is admissible and may be considered as provided in Rule 413 and Rule 414 of these rules.

(b) A party who intends to offer evidence under this Rule shall disclose the evidence to the party against whom it will be offered, including statements of witnesses or a summary of the substance of any testimony that is expected to be offered, at least fifteen days before the scheduled date of trial or at such later time as the court may allow for good cause.

(c) This rule shall not be construed to limit the admission or consideration of evidence under any other rule.

ARTICLE V. PRIVILEGES

Rule 501. General Rule
Except as otherwise required by the Constitution of the United States or provided by Act of Congress or in rules prescribed by the Supreme Court pursuant to statutory authority, the privilege of a witness, person, government, State, or political subdivision thereof shall be governed by the principles of the common law as they may be interpreted by the courts of the United States in the light of reason and experience. However, in civil actions and proceedings, with respect to an element of a claim or defense as to which State law supplies the rule of decision, the privilege of a witness, person, government, State, or political subdivision thereof shall be determined in accordance with State law.

ARTICLE VI. WITNESSES

Rule 601. General Rule of Competency
Every person is competent to be a witness except as otherwise provided in these rules. However, in civil actions and proceedings, with respect to an element of a claim or defense as to which State law supplies the rule of decision, the competency of a witness shall be determined in accordance with State law.

Rule 602. Lack of Personal Knowledge
A witness may not testify to a matter unless evidence is introduced sufficient to support a finding that the witness has personal knowledge of the matter. Evidence to prove personal knowledge may, but need not, consist of the witness' own testimony. This rule is subject to the provisions of rule 703, relating to opinion testimony by expert witnesses.

Rule 603. Oath or Affirmation
Before testifying, every witness shall be required to declare that the witness will testify truthfully, by oath or affirmation administered in a form calculated to

awaken the witness' conscience and impress the witness' mind with the duty to do so.

Rule 604. Interpreters
An interpreter is subject to the provisions of these rules relating to qualification as an expert and the administration of an oath or affirmation to make a true translation.

Rule 605. Competency of Judge as Witness
The judge presiding at the trial may not testify in that trial as a witness. No objection need be made in order to preserve the point.

Rule 606. Competency of Juror as Witness
(a) At the trial.—A member of the jury may not testify as a witness before that jury in the trial of the case in which the juror is sitting. If the juror is called so to testify, the opposing party shall be afforded an opportunity to object out of the presence of the jury.

(b) Inquiry into validity of verdict or indictment.—Upon an inquiry into the validity of a verdict or indictment, a juror may not testify as to any matter or statement occurring during the course of the jury's deliberations or to the effect of anything upon that or any other juror's mind or emotions as influencing the juror to assent to or dissent from the verdict or indictment or concerning the juror's mental processes in connection therewith, except that a juror may testify on the question whether extraneous prejudicial information was improperly brought to the jury's attention or whether any outside influence was improperly brought to bear upon any juror. Nor may a juror's affidavit or evidence of any statement by the juror concerning a matter about which the juror would be precluded from testifying be received for these purposes.

Rule 607. Who May Impeach
The credibility of a witness may be attacked by any party, including the party calling the witness.

Rule 608. Evidence of Character and Conduct of Witness
(a) Opinion and reputation evidence of character.—The credibility of a witness may be attacked or supported by evidence in the form of opinion or reputation, but subject to these limitations: (1) the evidence may refer only to character for truthfulness or untruthfulness, and (2) evidence of truthful character is admissible only after the character of the witness for truthfulness has been attacked by opinion or reputation evidence or otherwise.

(b) Specific instances of conduct.—Specific instances of the conduct of a witness, for the purpose of attacking or supporting the witness' character for truthfulness, other than conviction of crime as provided in rule 609, may not be proved by extrinsic evidence. They may, however, in the discretion of the court, if probative of truthfulness or untruthfulness, be inquired into on cross-examination of the witness (1) concerning the witness' character for truthfulness or untruthfulness, or (2) concerning the character for truthfulness or untruthfulness of another witness as to which character the witness being cross-examined has testified. The giving of testimony, whether by an accused or by any other witness, does not operate as a waiver of the accused's or the witness' privilege against self-incrimination when examined with respect to matters that relate only to character for truthfulness.

Rule 609. Impeachment by Evidence of Conviction of Crime

(a) General rule.—For the purpose of attacking the credibility of a witness, (1) evidence that a witness other than an accused has been convicted of a crime shall be admitted, subject to Rule 403, if the crime was punishable by death or imprisonment in excess of one year under the law under which the witness was convicted, and evidence that an accused has been convicted of such a crime shall be admitted if the court determines that the probative value of admitting this evidence outweighs its prejudicial effect to the accused; and (2) evidence that any witness has been convicted of a crime shall be admitted if it involved dishonesty or false statement, regardless of the punishment.

(b) Time limit.—Evidence of a conviction under this rule is not admissible if a period of more than ten years has elapsed since the date of the conviction or of the release of the witness from the confinement imposed for that conviction, whichever is the later date, unless the court determines, in the interests of justice, that the probative value of the conviction supported by specific facts and circumstances substantially outweighs its prejudicial effect. However, evidence of a conviction more than 10 years old as calculated herein, is not admissible unless the proponent gives to the adverse party sufficient advance written notice of intent to use such evidence to provide the adverse party with a fair opportunity to contest the use of such evidence.

(c) Effect of pardon, annulment, or certificate of rehabilitation.—Evidence of a conviction is not admissible under this rule if (1) the conviction has been the subject of a pardon, annulment, certificate of rehabilitation, or other equivalent procedure based on a finding of the rehabilitation of the person convicted, and that person has not been convicted of a subsequent crime which was punishable by death or imprisonment in excess of one year, or (2) the conviction has been the subject of a pardon, annulment, or other equivalent procedure based on a finding of innocence.

(d) Juvenile adjudications.—Evidence of juvenile adjudications is generally not admissible under this rule. The court may, however, in a criminal case allow evidence of a juvenile adjudication of a witness other than the accused if conviction of the offense would be admissible to attack the credibility of an adult and the court is satisfied that admission in evidence is necessary for a fair determination of the issue of guilt or innocence.

(e) Pendency of appeal.—The pendency of an appeal therefrom does not render evidence of a conviction inadmissible. Evidence of the pendency of an appeal is admissible.

Rule 610. Religious Beliefs or Opinions
Evidence of the beliefs or opinions of a witness on matters of religion is not admissible for the purpose of showing that by reason of their nature the witness' credibility is impaired or enhanced.

Rule 611. Mode and Order of Interrogation and Presentation
(a) Control by court.—The court shall exercise reasonable control over the mode and order of interrogating witnesses and presenting evidence so as to (1) make the interrogation and presentation effective for the ascertainment of the truth, (2) avoid needless consumption of time, and (3) protect witnesses from harassment or undue embarrassment.

(b) Scope of cross-examination.—Cross-examination should be limited to the subject matter of the direct examination and matters affecting the credibility of the witness. The court may, in the exercise of discretion, permit inquiry into additional matters as if on direct examination.

(c) Leading questions.—Leading questions should not be used on the direct examination of a witness except as may be necessary to develop the witness' testimony. Ordinarily leading questions should be permitted on cross-examination. When a party calls a hostile witness, an adverse party, or a witness identified with an adverse party, interrogation may be by leading questions.

Rule 612. Writing Used To Refresh Memory
Except as otherwise provided in criminal proceedings by section 3500 of title 18, United States Code, if a witness uses a writing to refresh memory for the purpose of testifying, either— (1) while testifying, or (2) before testifying, if the court in its discretion determines it is necessary in the interests of justice, an adverse party is entitled to have the writing produced at the hearing, to inspect it, to cross-examine the witness thereon, and to introduce in evidence those portions which relate to the testimony of the witness. If it is claimed that the writing contains matters not related to the subject matter of the testimony the court shall examine the writing in camera, excise any portions not so related, and order delivery of the remainder to the party entitled thereto. Any portion withheld over objections shall be preserved and made available to the appellate court in the event of an appeal. If a writing is not produced or delivered pursuant to order under this rule, the court shall make any order justice requires, except that in criminal cases when the prosecution elects not to comply, the order shall

be one striking the testimony or, if the court in its discretion determines that the interests of justice so require, declaring a mistrial.

Rule 613. Prior Statements of Witnesses

(a) Examining witness concerning prior statement.—In examining a witness concerning a prior statement made by the witness, whether written or not, the statement need not be shown nor its contents disclosed to the witness at that time, but on request the same shall be shown or disclosed to opposing counsel.

(b) Extrinsic evidence of prior inconsistent statement of witness.—Extrinsic evidence of a prior inconsistent statement by a witness is not admissible unless the witness is afforded an opportunity to explain or deny the same and the opposite party is afforded an opportunity to interrogate the witness thereon, or the interests of justice otherwise require. This provision does not apply to admissions of a party-opponent as defined in rule 801(d)(2).

Rule 614. Calling and Interrogation of Witnesses by Court

(a) Calling by court.—The court may, on its own motion or at the suggestion of a party, call witnesses, and all parties are entitled to cross-examine witnesses thus called.

(b) Interrogation by court.—The court may interrogate witnesses, whether called by itself or by a party.

(c) Objections.—Objections to the calling of witnesses by the court or to interrogation by it may be made at the time or at the next available opportunity when the jury is not present.

Rule 615. Exclusion of Witnesses

At the request of a party the court shall order witnesses excluded so that they cannot hear the testimony of other witnesses, and it may make the order of its own motion. This rule does not authorize exclusion of (1) a party who is a natural person, or (2) an officer or employee of a party which is not a natural person designated as its representative by its attorney, or (3) a person whose presence is shown by a party to be essential to the presentation of the party's cause, or (4) a person authorized by statute to be present.

ARTICLE VII. OPINIONS AND EXPERT TESTIMONY

Rule 701. Opinion Testimony by Lay Witnesses

If the witness is not testifying as an expert, the witness' testimony in the form of opinions or inferences is limited to those opinions or inferences which are (a) rationally based on the perception of the witness, and (b) helpful to a clear understanding of the witness' testimony or the determination of a fact in issue, and (c) not based on scientific, technical, or other specialized knowledge within the scope of Rule 702.

Rule 702. Testimony by Experts

If scientific, technical, or other specialized knowledge will assist the trier of fact to understand the evidence or to determine a fact in issue, a witness qualified as an expert by knowledge, skill, experience, training, or education, may testify thereto in the form of an opinion or otherwise, if (1) the testimony is based upon sufficient facts or data, (2) the testimony is the product of reliable principles and methods, and (3) the witness has applied the principles and methods reliably to the facts of the case.

Rule 703. Bases of Opinion Testimony by Experts

The facts or data in the particular case upon which an expert bases an opinion or inference may be those perceived by or made known to the expert at or before the hearing. If of a type reasonably relied upon by experts in the particular field in forming opinions or inferences upon the subject, the facts or data need not be admissible in evidence in order for the opinion or inference to be admitted. Facts or data that are otherwise inadmissible shall not be disclosed to the jury by the proponent of the opinion or inference unless the court determines that their probative value in assisting the jury to evaluate the expert's opinion substantially outweighs their prejudicial effect.

Rule 704. Opinion on Ultimate Issue

(a) Except as provided in subdivision (b), testimony in the form of an opinion or inference otherwise admissible is not objectionable because it embraces an ultimate issue to be decided by the trier of fact.

(b) No expert witness testifying with respect to the mental state or condition of a defendant in a criminal case may state an opinion or inference as to whether the defendant did or did not have the mental state or condition constituting an element of the crime charged or of a defense thereto. Such ultimate issues are matters for the trier of fact alone.

Rule 705. Disclosure of Facts or Data Underlying Expert Opinion

The expert may testify in terms of opinion or inference and give reasons therefor without first testifying to the underlying facts or data, unless the court requires otherwise. The expert may in any event be required to disclose the underlying facts or data on cross examination.

Rule 706. Court Appointed Experts

(a) Appointment.—The court may on its own motion or on the motion of any party enter an order to show cause why expert witnesses should not be appointed, and may request the parties to submit nominations. The court may appoint any expert witnesses agreed upon by the parties, and may appoint expert witnesses of its own selection. An expert witness shall not be appointed by the court unless the witness consents to act. A witness so appointed shall be informed of the witness' duties by the court in writing, a copy of which shall be filed with the clerk, or at a conference in which the parties shall have opportunity to participate. A witness so appointed shall advise the parties of the witness' findings, if any; the witness' deposition may be taken by any party; and the witness may be called to testify by the court or any party. The witness shall be subject to cross-examination by each party, including a party calling the witness.

(b) Compensation.—Expert witnesses so appointed are entitled to reasonable compensation in whatever sum the court may allow. The compensation thus fixed is payable from funds which may be provided by law in criminal cases and civil actions and proceedings involving just compensation under the fifth amendment. In other civil actions and proceedings the compensation shall be paid by the parties in such proportion and at such time as the court directs, and thereafter charged in like manner as other costs.

(c) Disclosure of appointment.—In the exercise of its discretion, the court may authorize disclosure to the jury of the fact that the court appointed the expert witness.

(d) Parties' experts of own selection.—Nothing in this rule limits the parties in calling expert witnesses of their own selection.

ARTICLE VIII. HEARSAY.

Rule 801. Definitions

The following definitions apply under this article:

(a) Statement.—A ''statement'' is (1) an oral or written assertion or (2) nonverbal conduct of a person, if it is intended by the person as an assertion.

(b) Declarant.—A ''declarant'' is a person who makes a statement.

(c) Hearsay.—''Hearsay'' is a statement, other than one made by the declarant while testifying at the trial or hearing, offered in evidence to prove the truth of the matter asserted.

(d) Statements which are not hearsay.—A statement is not hearsay if—
(1) Prior statement by witness.—The declarant testifies at the trial or hearing and is subject to cross-examination concerning the statement, and the statement is (A) inconsistent with the declarant's testimony, and was given under oath subject to the penalty of perjury at a trial, hearing, or other proceeding, or in a deposition, or (B) consistent with the declarant's testimony and is offered to rebut an express or implied charge against the declarant of recent fabrication or improper influence or motive, or (C) one of identification of a person made after perceiving the person; or (2) Admission by party-opponent.—The statement is offered against a party and is (A) the party's own statement, in either an individual or a representative capacity or (B) a statement of which the party has manifested an adoption or belief in its truth, or (C) a statement by a person authorized by the party to make a statement concerning the subject, or (D) a

statement by the party's agent or servant concerning a matter within the scope of the agency or employment, made during the existence of the relationship, or (E) a statement by a coconspirator of a party during the course and in furtherance of the conspiracy. The contents of the statement shall be considered but are not alone sufficient to establish the declarant's authority under subdivision (C), the agency or employment relationship and scope thereof under subdivision (D), or the existence of the conspiracy and the participation therein of the declarant and the party against whom the statement is offered under subdivision (E).

Rule 802. Hearsay Rule

Hearsay is not admissible except as provided by these rules or by other rules prescribed by the Supreme Court pursuant to statutory authority or by Act of Congress.

Rule 803. Hearsay Exceptions; Availability of Declarant Immaterial

The following are not excluded by the hearsay rule, even though the declarant is available as a witness:

(1) Present sense impression.—A statement describing or explaining an event or condition made while the declarant was perceiving the event or condition, or immediately thereafter.

(2) Excited utterance.—A statement relating to a startling event or condition made while the declarant was under the stress of excitement caused by the event or condition.

(3) Then existing mental, emotional, or physical condition.—A statement of the declarant's then existing state of mind, emotion, sensation, or physical condition (such as intent, plan, motive, design, mental feeling, pain, and bodily health), but not including a statement of memory or belief to prove the fact remembered or believed unless it relates to the execution, revocation, identification, or terms of declarant's will.

(4) Statements for purposes of medical diagnosis or treatment.—Statements made for purposes of medical diagnosis or treatment and describing medical history, or past or present symptoms, pain, or sensations, or the inception or general character of the cause or external source thereof insofar as reasonably pertinent to diagnosis or treatment.

(5) Recorded recollection.—A memorandum or record concerning a matter about which a witness once had knowledge but now has insufficient recollection to enable the witness to testify fully and accurately, shown to have been made or adopted by the witness when the matter was fresh in the witness' memory and to reflect that knowledge correctly. If admitted, the memorandum or record may be read into evidence but may not itself be received as an exhibit unless offered by an adverse party.

(6) Records of regularly conducted activity.—A memorandum, report, record, or data compilation, in any form, of acts, events, conditions, opinions, or diagnoses, made at or near the time by, or from information transmitted by, a

person with knowledge, if kept in the course of a regularly conducted business activity, and if it was the regular practice of that business activity to make the memorandum, report, record or data compilation, all as shown by the testimony of the custodian or other qualified witness, or by certification that complies with Rule 902(11), Rule 902(12), or a statute permitting certification, unless the source of information or the method or circumstances of preparation indicate lack of trustworthiness. The term ''business'' as used in this paragraph includes business, institution, association, profession, occupation, and calling of every kind, whether or not conducted for profit. (7) Absence of entry in records kept in accordance with the provisions of paragraph (6).—Evidence that a matter is not included in the memoranda reports, records, or data compilations, in any form, kept in accordance with the provisions of paragraph (6), to prove the nonoccurrence or nonexistence of the matter, if the matter was of a kind of which a memorandum, report, record, or data compilation was regularly made and preserved, unless the sources of information or other circumstances indicate lack of trustworthiness. (8) Public records and reports.—Records, reports, statements, or data compilations, in any form, of public offices or agencies, setting forth (A) the activities of the office or agency, or (B) matters observed pursuant to duty imposed by law as to which matters there was a duty to report, excluding, however, in criminal cases matters observed by police officers and other law enforcement personnel, or (C) in civil actions and proceedings and against the Government in criminal cases, factual findings resulting from an investigation made pursuant to authority granted by law, unless the sources of information or other circumstances indicate lack of trustworthiness. (9) Records of vital statistics. —Records or data compilations, in any form, of births, fetal deaths, deaths, or marriages, if the report thereof was made to a public office pursuant to requirements of law. (10) Absence of public record or entry.—To prove the absence of a record, report, statement, or data compilation, in any form, or the nonoccurrence or nonexistence of a matter of which a record, report, statement, or data compilation, in any form, was regularly made and preserved by a public office or agency, evidence in the form of a certification in accordance with rule 902, or testimony, that diligent search failed to disclose the record, report, statement, or data compilation, or entry. (11) Records of religious organizations.—Statements of births, marriages, divorces, deaths, legitimacy, ancestry, relationship by blood or marriage, or other similar facts of personal or family history, contained in a regularly kept record of a religious organization. (12) Marriage, baptismal, and similar certificates.—Statements of fact contained in a certificate that the maker performed a marriage or other ceremony or administered a sacrament, made by a clergyman, public official, or other person authorized by the rules or practices of a religious organization or by law to perform the act certified, and purporting to have been issued at the time of the act or within a reasonable time thereafter. (13) Family records.—Statements of fact concerning personal or family history contained in family Bibles, genealogies, charts, engravings on rings, inscriptions on family portraits, engravings on urns, crypts, or tombstones, or the like. (14) Records of documents affecting an interest in property.— The record of a document purporting to establish or affect an interest in property, as proof of the content of the original recorded document and its execution and delivery by each person by whom it purports to have been executed, if the record is a record of a public office and an applicable statute authorizes the recording of documents of that kind in that office. (15) Statements in documents affecting an interest in property.— A statement contained in a document purporting to establish or affect an interest in property if the matter stated was relevant to the purpose of the document, unless dealings with the property since the document was made have been inconsistent with the truth of the statement or the purport of the document. (16) Statements in ancient documents.—Statements in a document in existence twenty years or more the authenticity of which is established. (17) Market reports, commercial publications.—Market quotations, tabulations, lists, directories, or other published compilations, generally used and relied upon by the public or by persons in particular occupations. (18) Learned treatises.—To the extent called to the attention of an expert witness upon cross-examination or relied upon by the expert witness in direct examination, statements contained in published treatises, periodicals, or pamphlets on a subject of history, medicine, or other science or art, established as a reliable authority by the testimony or admission of the witness or by other expert testimony or by judicial notice. If admitted, the statements may be read into evidence but may not be received as exhibits. (19) Reputation concerning personal or family history.—Reputation among members of a person's family by blood, adoption, or marriage, or among a person's associates, or in the community, concerning a person's birth, adoption, marriage, divorce, death, legitimacy, relationship by blood, adoption, or marriage, ancestry, or other similar fact of personal or family history. (20) Reputation concerning boundaries or general history.—Reputation in a community, arising before the controversy, as to boundaries of or customs affecting lands in the community, and reputation as to events of general history important to the community or State or nation in which located. (21) Reputation as to character.—Reputation of a person's character among associates or in the community. (22) Judgment of previous conviction.—Evidence of a final judgment, entered after a trial or upon a plea of guilty (but not upon a plea of nolo contendere), adjudging a person guilty of a crime punishable by death or imprisonment in excess of one year, to prove any fact essential to sustain the judgment, but not including, when offered by the Government in a criminal prosecution for purposes other than impeachment, judgments against persons other than the accused. The pendency of an appeal may be shown but does not affect admissibility. (23) Judgment as to personal, family, or general history, or boundaries.—Judgments as proof of matters of personal, family or general history, or boundaries, essential to the judgment, if the same would be provable by evidence of reputation. (24) [Other exceptions.] [Transferred to Rule 807]

Rule 804. Hearsay Exceptions; Declarant Unavailable

(a) Definition of unavailability.—''Unavailability as a witness'' includes situations in which the declarant—

(1) is exempted by ruling of the court on the ground of privilege from testifying concerning the subject matter of the declarant's statement; or (2) persists in refusing to testify concerning the subject matter of the declarant's statement despite an order of the court to do so; or (3) testifies to a lack of memory of the subject matter of the declarant's statement; or (4) is unable to be present or to testify at the hearing because of death or then existing physical or mental illness or infirmity; or (5) is absent from the hearing and the proponent of a statement has been unable to procure the declarant's attendance (or in the case of a hearsay exception under subdivision (b)(2), (3), or (4), the declarant's attendance or testimony) by process or other reasonable means. A declarant is not unavailable as a witness if exemption, refusal, claim of lack of memory, inability, or absence is due to the procurement or wrongdoing of the proponent of a statement for the purpose of preventing the witness from attending or testifying.

(b) Hearsay exceptions.—The following are not excluded by the hearsay rule if the declarant is unavailable as a witness:

(1) Former testimony.—Testimony given as a witness at another hearing of the same or a different proceeding, or in a deposition taken in compliance with law in the course of the same or another proceeding, if the party against whom the testimony is now offered, or, in a civil action or proceeding, a predecessor in interest, had an opportunity and similar motive to develop the testimony by direct, cross, or redirect examination.

(2) Statement under belief of impending death.—In a prosecution for homicide or in a civil action or proceeding, a statement made by a declarant while believing that the declarant's death was imminent, concerning the cause or circumstances of what the declarant believed to be impending death.

(3) Statement against interest.—A statement which was at the time of its making so far contrary to the declarant's pecuniary or proprietary interest, or so far tended to subject the declarant to civil or criminal liability, or to render invalid a claim by the declarant against another, that a reasonable person in the declarant's position would not have made the statement unless believing it to be true. A statement tending to expose the declarant to criminal liability and offered to exculpate the accused is not admissible unless corroborating circumstances clearly indicate the trustworthiness of the statement.

(4) Statement of personal or family history.—(A) A statement concerning the declarant's own birth, adoption, marriage, divorce, legitimacy, relationship by blood, adoption, or marriage, ancestry, or other similar fact of personal or family history, even though declarant had no means of acquiring personal knowledge of the matter stated; or (B) a statement concerning the foregoing matters, and death also, of another person, if the declarant was related to the other by blood, adoption, or marriage or was so intimately associated with the other's family as to be likely to have accurate information concerning the matter declared. (5) [Other exceptions.] [Transferred to Rule 807] (6) Forfeiture by wrongdoing.—A statement offered against a party that has engaged or acquiesced in wrongdoing

that was intended to, and did, procure the unavailability of the declarant as a witness.

Rule 805. Hearsay Within Hearsay

Hearsay included within hearsay is not excluded under the hearsay rule if each part of the combined statements conforms with an exception to the hearsay rule provided in these rules.

Rule 806. Attacking and Supporting Credibility of Declarant

When a hearsay statement, or a statement defined in Rule 801(d)(2)(C), (D), or (E), has been admitted in evidence, the credibility of the declarant may be attacked, and if attacked may be supported, by any evidence which would be admissible for those purposes if declarant had testified as a witness. Evidence of a statement or conduct by the declarant at any time, inconsistent with the declarant's hearsay statement, is not subject to any requirement that the declarant may have been afforded an opportunity to deny or explain. If the party against whom a hearsay statement has been admitted calls the declarant as a witness, the party is entitled to examine the declarant on the statement as if under cross-examination.

Rule 807. Residual Exception

A statement not specifically covered by Rule 803 or 804 but having equivalent circumstantial guarantees of trustworthiness, is not excluded by the hearsay rule, if the court determines that (A) the statement is offered as evidence of a material fact; (B) the statement is more probative on the point for which it is offered than any other evidence which the proponent can procure through reasonable efforts; and (C) the general purposes of these rules and the interests of justice will best be served by admission of the statement into evidence. However, a statement may not be admitted under this exception unless the proponent of it makes known to the adverse party sufficiently in advance of the trial or hearing to provide the adverse party with a fair opportunity to prepare to meet it, the proponent's intention to offer the statement and the particulars of it, including the name and address of the declarant.

ARTICLE IX. AUTHENTICATION AND IDENTIFICATION

Rule 901. Requirement of Authentication or Identification

(a) General provision.—The requirement of authentication or identification as a condition precedent to admissibility is satisfied by evidence sufficient to support a finding that the matter in question is what its proponent claims.

(b) Illustrations.—By way of illustration only, and not by way of limitation, the following are examples of authentication or identification conforming with the requirements of this rule: (1) Testimony of witness with knowledge.—Testimony that a matter is what it is claimed to be. (2) Nonexpert opinion on handwriting.—Nonexpert opinion as to the genuineness of handwriting, based upon familiarity not acquired for purposes of the litigation. (3) Comparison by trier or expert witness.—Comparison by the trier of fact or by expert witnesses with specimens which have been authenticated. (4) Distinctive characteristics and the like.—Appearance, contents, substance, internal patterns, or other distinctive characteristics, taken in conjunction with circumstances. (5) Voice identification.—Identification of a voice, whether heard firsthand or through mechanical or electronic transmission or recording, by opinion based upon hearing the voice at any time under circumstances connecting it with the alleged speaker. (6) Telephone conversations.—Telephone conversations, by evidence that a call was made to the number assigned at the time by the telephone company to a particular person or business, if (A) in the case of a person, circumstances, including self-identification, show the person answering to be the one called, or (B) in the case of a business, the call was made to a place of business and the conversation related to business reasonably transacted over the telephone. (7) Public records or reports.—Evidence that a writing authorized by law to be recorded or filed and in fact recorded or filed in a public office, or a purported public record, report, statement, or data compilation, in any form, is from the public office where items of this nature are kept. (8) Ancient documents or data compilation.—Evidence that a document or data compilation, in any form, (A) is in such condition as to create no suspicion concerning its authenticity, (B) was in a place where it, if authentic, would likely be, and (C) has been in existence 20 years or more at the time it is offered. (9) Process or system.—Evidence describing a process or system used to produce a result and showing that the process or system produces an accurate result. (10) Methods provided by statute or rule.—Any method of authentication or identification provided by Act of Congress or by other rules prescribed by the Supreme Court pursuant to statutory authority.

Rule 902. Self-authentication

Extrinsic evidence of authenticity as a condition precedent to admissibility is not required with respect to the following: (1) Domestic public documents under seal.—A document bearing a seal purporting to be that of the United States, or of any State, district, Commonwealth, territory, or insular possession thereof, or the Panama Canal Zone, or the Trust Territory of the Pacific Islands, or of a political subdivision, department, officer, or agency thereof, and a signature purporting to be an attestation or execution. (2) Domestic public documents not under seal.—A document purporting to bear the signature in the official capacity of an officer or employee of any entity included in paragraph (1) hereof, having no seal, if a public officer having a seal and having official duties in the district or political subdivision of the officer or employee certifies under seal that the signer has the official capacity and that the signature is genuine. (3) Foreign public documents.—A document purporting to be executed or attested in an official capacity by a person authorized by the laws of a foreign country to make the execution or attestation, and accompanied by a final certification as to the genuineness of the signature and official position (A) of the executing or attesting person, or (B) of any foreign official whose certificate of genuineness of signature and official position relates to the execution or attestation or is in a chain of certificates of genuineness of signature and official position relating to the execution or attestation. A final certification may be made by a secretary of an embassy or legation, consul general, consul, vice consul, or consular agent of the United States, or a diplomatic or consular official of the foreign country assigned or accredited to the United States. If reasonable opportunity has been given to all parties to investigate the authenticity and accuracy of official documents, the court may, for good cause shown, order that they be treated as presumptively authentic without final certification or permit them to be evidenced by an attested summary with or without final certification. (4) Certified copies of public records.—A copy of an official record or report or entry therein, or of a document authorized by law to be recorded or filed and actually recorded or filed in a public office, including data compilations in any form, certified as correct by the custodian or other person authorized to make the certification, by certificate complying with paragraph (1), (2), or (3) of this rule or complying with any Act of Congress or rule prescribed by the Supreme Court pursuant to statutory authority. (5) Official publications.—Books, pamphlets, or other publications purporting to be issued by public authority. (6) Newspapers and periodicals.—Printed materials purporting to be newspapers or periodicals. (7) Trade inscriptions and the like.—Inscriptions, signs, tags, or labels purporting to have been affixed in the course of business and indicating ownership, control, or origin. (8) Acknowledged documents.—Documents accompanied by a certificate of acknowledgment executed in the manner provided by law by a notary public or other officer authorized by law to take acknowledgments. (9) Commercial paper and related documents.—Commercial paper, signatures thereon, and documents relating thereto to the extent provided by general commercial law. (10) Presumptions under Acts of Congress.—Any signature, document, or other matter declared by Act of Congress to be presumptively or prima facie genuine or authentic. (11) Certified domestic records of regularly conducted activity.—The original or a duplicate of a domestic record of regularly conducted activity that would be admissible under Rule 803(6) if accompanied by a written declaration of its custodian or other qualified person, in a manner complying with any Act of Congress or rule prescribed by the Supreme Court pursuant to statutory authority, certifying that the record—(A) was made at or near the time of the occurrence of the matters set forth by, or from information transmitted by, a person with knowledge of those matters; (B) was kept in the course of the regularly conducted activity; and (C) was made by the regularly conducted activity as a regular practice. A party intending to offer a record into evidence under this paragraph must provide written notice of that intention to all adverse parties, and must make the record and declaration available for inspection sufficiently in advance of their offer into evidence to provide an adverse party with a fair opportunity to challenge them. (12) Certified foreign records of regularly conducted activity.—In a civil case, the original or a duplicate of a foreign record of regularly conducted activity that would be admissible under Rule 803(6) if accompanied by a written declaration by its custodian or other qualified person certifying that the record—(A) was made at or near the time of the occurrence of the matters set forth by, or from information transmitted by, a person with knowledge of those matters; (B) was kept in the course of the regularly conducted activity; and (C) was made by the regularly conducted activity as a regular practice. The declaration must be signed in a manner that, if falsely made, would subject the maker to criminal penalty under the laws of the country where the declaration is signed. A party intending to offer a record into evidence under this paragraph must provide written notice of that intention to all adverse parties, and must make the record and declaration available for inspection sufficiently in advance of their offer into evidence to provide an adverse party with a fair opportunity to challenge them.

Rule 903. Subscribing Witness' Testimony Unnecessary
The testimony of a subscribing witness is not necessary to authenticate a writing unless required by the laws of the jurisdiction whose laws govern the validity of the writing.

ARTICLE X. CONTENTS OF WRITINGS, RECORDINGS, AND PHOTOGRAPHS

Rule 1001. Definitions
For purposes of this article the following definitions are applicable: (1) Writings and recordings.—''Writings'' and ''recordings'' consist of letters, words, or numbers, or their equivalent, set down by handwriting, typewriting, printing, photostating, photographing, magnetic impulse, mechanical or electronic recording, or other form of data compilation. (2) Photographs.—''Photographs'' include still photographs, X-ray films, video tapes, and motion pictures. (3) Original.—An ''original'' of a writing or recording is the writing or recording itself or any counterpart intended to have the same effect by a person executing or issuing it. An ''original'' of a photograph includes the negative or any print therefrom. If data are stored in a computer or similar device, any printout or other output readable by sight, shown to reflect the data accurately, is an ''original''. (4) Duplicate.—A ''duplicate'' is a counterpart produced by the same impression as the original, or from the same matrix, or by means of photography, including enlargements and miniatures, or by mechanical or electronic re-recording, or by chemical reproduction, or by other equivalent techniques which accurately reproduces the original.

Rule 1002. Requirement of Original
To prove the content of a writing, recording, or photograph, the original writing, recording, or photograph is required, except as otherwise provided in these rules or by Act of Congress.

Rule 1003. Admissibility of Duplicates

A duplicate is admissible to the same extent as an original unless (1) a genuine question is raised as to the authenticity of the original or (2) in the circumstances it would be unfair to admit the duplicate in lieu of the original.

Rule 1004. Admissibility of Other Evidence of Contents

The original is not required, and other evidence of the contents of a writing, recording, or photograph is admissible if—(1) Originals lost or destroyed.—All originals are lost or have been destroyed, unless the proponent lost or destroyed them in bad faith; or (2) Original not obtainable.—No original can be obtained by any available judicial process or procedure; or (3) Original in possession of opponent.—At a time when an original was under the control of the party against whom offered, that party was put on notice, by the pleadings or otherwise, that the contents would be a subject of proof at the hearing, and that party does not produce the original at the hearing; or (4) Collateral matters.—The writing, recording, or photograph is not closely related to a controlling issue.

Rule 1005. Public Records

The contents of an official record, or of a document authorized to be recorded or filed and actually recorded or filed, including data compilations in any form, if otherwise admissible, may be proved by copy, certified as correct in accordance with rule 902 or testified to be correct by a witness who has compared it with the original. If a copy which complies with the foregoing cannot be obtained by the exercise of reasonable diligence, then other evidence of the contents may be given, provided that reference in any other Federal law or any document to the ''United States Claims Court'' shall be deemed to refer to the ''United States Court of Federal Claims''.

Rule 1006. Summaries

The contents of voluminous writings, recordings, or photographs which cannot conveniently be examined in court may be presented in the form of a chart, summary, or calculation. The originals, or duplicates, shall be made available for examination or copying, or both, by other parties at reasonable time and place. The court may order that they be produced in court.

Rule 1007. Testimony or Written Admission of Party

Contents of writings, recordings, or photographs may be proved by the testimony or deposition of the party against whom offered or by that party's written admission, without accounting for the nonproduction of the original.

Rule 1008. Functions of Court and Jury

When the admissibility of other evidence of contents of writings, recordings, or photographs under these rules depends upon the fulfillment of a condition of fact, the question whether the condition has been fulfilled is ordinarily for the court to determine in accordance with the provisions of rule 104. However, when an issue is raised (a) whether the asserted writing ever existed, or (b) whether another writing, recording, or photograph produced at the trial is the original, or (c) whether other evidence of contents correctly reflects the contents, the issue is for the trier of fact to determine as in the case of other issues of fact.

ARTICLE XI. MISCELLANEOUS RULES

Rule 1101. Applicability of Rules

(a) Courts and judges.—These rules apply to the United States district courts, the District Court of Guam, the District Court of the Virgin Islands, the District Court for the Northern Mariana Islands, the United States courts of appeals, the United States Claims Court, 1 and to United States bankruptcy judges and United States magistrate judges, in the actions, cases, and proceedings and to the extent hereinafter set forth. The terms ''judge'' and ''court'' in these rules include United States bankruptcy judges and United States magistrate judges.

(b) Proceedings generally.—These rules apply generally to civil actions and proceedings, including admiralty and maritime cases, to criminal cases and proceedings, to contempt proceedings except those in which the court may act summarily, and to proceedings and cases under title 11, United States Code.

(c) Rule of privilege.—The rule with respect to privileges applies at all stages of all actions, cases, and proceedings. (d) Rules inapplicable.—The rules (other than with respect to privileges) do not apply in the following situations:

(1) Preliminary questions of fact.—The determination of questions of fact preliminary to admissibility of evidence when the issue is to be determined by the court under rule 104. (2) Grand jury.—Proceedings before grand juries.

(3) Miscellaneous proceedings.—Proceedings for extradition or rendition; preliminary examinations in criminal cases; sentencing, or granting or revoking probation; issuance of warrants for arrest, criminal summonses, and search warrants; and proceedings with respect to release on bail or otherwise. (e) Rules applicable in part.—In the following proceedings these rules apply to the extent that matters of evidence are not provided for in the statutes which govern procedure therein or in other rules prescribed by the Supreme Court pursuant to statutory authority: the trial of misdemeanors and other petty offenses before United States magistrate judges; review of agency actions when the facts are subject to trial de novo under section 706(2)(F) of title 5, United States Code; review of orders of the Secretary of Agriculture under section 2 of the Act entitled ''An Act to authorize association of producers of agricultural products'' approved February 18, 1922 (7 U.S.C. 292), and under sections 6 and 7(c) of the Perishable Agricultural Commodities Act, 1930 (7 U.S.C. 499f, 499g(c)); naturalization and revocation of naturalization under sections 310–318 of the Immigration and Nationality Act (8 U.S.C. 1421–1429); prize proceedings in admiralty under sections 7651–7681 of title 10, United States Code; review of orders of the Secretary of the Interior under section 2 of the Act entitled ''An Act authorizing associations of producers of aquatic products'' approved June 25, 1934 (15 U.S.C. 522); review of orders of petroleum control boards under section 5 of the Act entitled ''An Act to regulate interstate and foreign commerce in petroleum and its products by prohibiting the shipment in such

commerce of petroleum and its products produced in violation of State law, and for other purposes'', approved February 22, 1935 (15 U.S.C. 715d); actions for fines, penalties, or forfeitures under part V of title IV of the Tariff Act of 1930 (19 U.S.C. 1581–1624), or under the Anti-Smuggling Act (19 U.S.C. 1701–1711); criminal libel for condemnation, exclusion of imports, or other proceedings under the Federal Food, Drug, and Cosmetic Act (21 U.S.C. 301–392); disputes between seamen under sections 4079, 4080, and 4081 of the Revised Statutes (22 U.S.C. 256–258); habeas corpus under sections 2241–2254 of title 28, United States Code; motions to vacate, set aside or correct sentence under section 2255 of title 28, United States Code; actions for penalties for refusal to transport destitute seamen under section 4578 of the Revised Statutes (46 U.S.C. 679); 2 actions against the United States under the Act entitled ''An Act authorizing suits against the United States in admiralty for damage caused by and salvage service rendered to public vessels belonging to the United States, and for other purposes'', approved March 3, 1925 (46 U.S.C. 781–790), as implemented by section 7730 of title 10, United States Code.

Rule 1102. Amendments
Amendments to the Federal Rules of Evidence may be made as provided in section 2072 of title 28 of the United States Code.

Rule 1103. Title
These rules may be known and cited as the Federal Rules of Evidence.

C. Pending Changes to Federal Rules of Evidence, Proposed Effective Date December 1, 2006.

PENDING CHANGES TO FEDERAL RULES OF EVIDENCE
TENTATIVE EFFECTIVE DATE DECEMBER 1, 2006

Effective December 1, 2006, absent contrary Congressional action, subdivision (a) of rule 404 is amended to read as follows:

(a) **Character evidence generally.**--Evidence of a person's character or a trait of character is not admissible for the purpose of proving action in conformity therewith on a particular occasion, except:

(1) **Character of accused.**--In a criminal case, evidence of a pertinent trait of character offered by an accused, or by the prosecution to rebut the same, or if evidence of a trait of character of the alleged victim of the crime is offered by an accused and admitted under Rule 404(a)(2), evidence of the same trait of character of the accused offered by the prosecution;

(2) Character of alleged victim.--In a criminal case, and subject to the limitations imposed by Rule 412, evidence of a pertinent trait of character of the alleged victim of the crime offered by an accused, or by the prosecution to rebut the same, or evidence of a character trait of peacefulness of the alleged victim offered by the prosecution in a homicide case to rebut evidence that the alleged victim was the first aggressor;

(3) Character of witness.--Evidence of the character of a witness, as provided in Rules 607, 608, and 609.

Effective December 1, 2006, absent contrary Congressional action, rule 408 is amended to read as follows:

 (a) Prohibited uses.--Evidence of the following is not admissible on behalf of any party, when offered to prove liability for, invalidity of, or amount of a claim that was disputed as to validity or amount, or to impeach through a prior inconsistent statement or contradiction:

(1) furnishing or offering or promising to furnish--or accepting or offering or promising to accept--a valuable consideration in compromising or attempting to compromise the claim; and

(2) conduct or statements made in compromise negotiations regarding the claim, except when offered in a criminal case and the negotiations related to a claim by a public office or agency in the exercise of regulatory, investigative, or enforcement authority.

(b) Permitted uses.--This rule does not require exclusion if the evidence is offered for purposes not prohibited by subdivision (a). Examples of permissible purposes include proving a witness's bias or prejudice; negating a contention of undue delay; and proving an effort to obstruct a criminal investigation or prosecution.

Effective December 1, 2006, absent contrary Congressional action, subdivision (b) of rule 606 is amended to read as follows:

(b) Inquiry into validity of verdict or indictment. Upon an inquiry into the validity of a verdict or indictment, a juror may not testify as to any matter or statement occurring during the course of the jury's deliberations or to the effect of anything upon that or any other juror's mind or emotions as influencing the juror to assent to or dissent from the verdict or indictment or concerning the juror's mental processes in connection therewith. But a juror may testify about (1) whether extraneous prejudicial information was improperly brought to the jury's attention, (2) whether any outside influence was improperly brought to bear upon any juror, or (3) whether there was a mistake in entering the verdict onto the verdict form. A juror's affidavit or evidence of any statement by the juror may not be received on a matter about which the juror would be precluded from testifying.

Effective December 1, 2006, absent contrary Congressional action, subdivision (a) of rule 609 is amended to read as follows:

(a) General rule.--For the purpose of attacking the character for truthfulness of a witness,

(1) evidence that a witness other than an accused has been convicted of a crime shall be admitted, subject to Rule 403, if the crime was punishable by death or imprisonment in excess of one year under the law under which the witness was convicted, and evidence that an accused has been convicted of such a crime shall be admitted if the court determines that the probative value of admitting this evidence outweighs its prejudicial effect to the accused; and

(2) evidence that any witness has been convicted of a crime shall be admitted regardless of the punishment, if it readily can be determined that establishing the elements of the crime required proof or admission of an act of dishonesty or false statement by the witness.

Effective December 1, 2006, absent contrary Congressional action, subdivision (c) of rule 609 is amended to read as follows:

(c) Effect of pardon, annulment, or certificate of rehabilitation.--Evidence of a conviction is not admissible under this rule if (1) the conviction has been the subject of a pardon, annulment, certificate of rehabilitation, or other equivalent procedure based on a finding of the rehabilitation of the person convicted, and that person has not been convicted of a subsequent crime that was punishable by death or imprisonment in excess of one year, or (2) the conviction has been the subject of a pardon, annulment, or other equivalent procedure based on a finding of innocence.

INDEX

Recency, 32 -33, 121, 128, 261, 266

Refreshing Recollections, 231
  Keywords, 232

Rule of Threes, 8, 30, 259

S

Silence, 59

Simplicity, 130

Strong Points, 121 - 122

T

Taglines, 25, 122

Technology, 321

Telling the Witness, 123

Theory,
  Factual, 98, 266
  Legal, 48, 98, 266

Theme, Moral - See Moral Theme

Transitional Introductory Phrases, 19

Trust, 58

U

Ultimate Question, 128

V

Video Based, 325

Vignette, 131

Voice, tone of, 60

Voir Dire, 12, 296
  Exhibits, 162, 163

W

Weak Points, 121 -122

Witnesses,
  Forgetful, 229